The Proper for the

Lesser
Feasts and
Fasts · 2003

together with

The Fixed Holy Days

Conforming to General Convention 2003

CHURCH PUBLISHING
New York

5 4 3 2 1

Church Publishing Incorporated
445 Fifth Avenue
New York, NY 10016

Contents

Preface

Lesser Feasts and Fasts contains Lessons and Psalms for the weekdays of Advent, Christmas until the Baptism of Christ, Lent, and Easter Season. In addition, Collects are provided for the weekdays of Lent and Easter. Collects, Psalms and Lessons are also provided for the fixed Holy Days, and for the Lesser Feasts and Fasts. Descriptions of the fixed Holy Days and biographies of the saints in the calendar are included as well.

Christians have since ancient times honored men and women whose lives represent heroic commitment to Christ and who have borne witness to their faith even at the cost of their lives. Such witnesses, by the grace of God, live in every age. The criteria used in the selection of those to be commemorated in the Episcopal Church are set out below (page 477 ff.) and represent a growing consensus among provinces of the Anglican Communion also engaged in enriching their calendars.

What we celebrate in the lives of the saints is the presence of Christ expressing itself in and through particular lives lived in the midst of specific historical circumstances. In the saints we are not dealing primarily with absolutes of perfection but human lives, in all their diversity, open to the motions of the Holy Spirit. Many a holy life, when carefully examined, will reveal flaws or the bias of a particular moment in history or ecclesial perspective: Attitudes toward those outside the Church, assumptions about gender, understandings of the world may appear to be defective and wrong. And what, in one age, was taken as virtue may at another time seem misguided. It should encourage us to realize that the saints, like us, are first and foremost redeemed sinners in whom the risen Christ's words to St. Paul come to fulfillment, "My grace is sufficient for you, for my power is made perfect in weakness."

The "lesser feasts" provide opportunities for optional observance. They are not intended to replace the fundamental celebration of Sunday and major Holy Days.

As the Standing Liturgical Commission and the General Convention add or delete names from the calendar, successive editions of this volume will be published, each edition bearing in the title the date of the General Convention to which it is a response.

Commemorations presented for trial use will appear in brackets; if approved by General Convention at a second reading, the brackets will be removed.

The Calendar
of the Church Year

The Calendar
of the Church Year

The Church Year consists of two cycles of feasts and holy days: one is dependent upon the movable date of the Sunday of the Resurrection or Easter Day; the other, upon the fixed date of December 25, the Feast of our Lord's Nativity or Christmas Day.

Easter Day is always the first Sunday after the full moon that falls on or after March 21. It cannot occur before March 22 or after April 25.

The sequence of all Sundays of the Church Year depends upon the date of Easter Day. But the Sundays of Advent are always the four Sundays before Christmas Day, whether it occurs on a Sunday or a weekday. The date of Easter also determines the beginning of Lent on Ash Wednesday, and the feast of the Ascension on a Thursday forty days after Easter Day.

1. Principal Feasts

The Principal Feasts observed in this Church are the following:

Easter Day	All Saints' Day, *November 1*
Ascension Day	Christmas Day, *December 25*
The Day of Pentecost	The Epiphany, *January 6*
Trinity Sunday	

These feasts take precedence of any other day or observance. All Saints' Day may always be observed on the Sunday following November 1, in addition to its observance on the fixed date.

2. Sundays

All Sundays of the year are feasts of our Lord Jesus Christ. In addition to the dated days listed above, only the following feasts, appointed on fixed days, take precedence of a Sunday:

The Holy Name
The Presentation
The Transfiguration

The feast of the Dedication of a Church, and the feast of its patron or title, may be observed on, or be transferred to, a Sunday, except in the seasons of Advent, Lent, and Easter.

All other Feasts of our Lord, and all other Major Feasts appointed on fixed days in the Calendar, when they occur on a Sunday, are normally transferred to the first convenient open day within the week. When desired, however, the Collect, Preface, and one or more of the Lessons appointed for the Feast may be substituted for those of the Sunday, but not from the Last Sunday after Pentecost through the First Sunday after the Epiphany, or from the Last Sunday after the Epiphany through Trinity Sunday.

With the express permission of the bishop, and for urgent and sufficient reason, some other special occasion may be observed on a Sunday.

3. Holy Days

The following Holy Days are regularly observed throughout the year. Unless otherwise ordered in the preceding rules concerning Sundays, they have precedence over all other days of commemoration or of special observance:

Other Feasts of our Lord

The Holy Name
The Presentation
The Annunciation
The Visitation

Saint John the Baptist
The Transfiguration
Holy Cross Day

Other Major Feasts

All feasts of Apostles	Saint Mary the Virgin
All feasts of Evangelists	Saint Michael and All Angels
Saint Stephen	Saint James of Jerusalem
The Holy Innocents	Independence Day
Saint Joseph	Thanksgiving Day
Saint Mary Magdalene	

Fasts

Ash Wednesday	Good Friday

Feasts appointed on fixed days in the Calendar are not observed on the days of Holy Week or of Easter Week. Major Feasts falling in these weeks are transferred to the week following the Second Sunday of Easter, in the order of their occurrence.

Feasts appointed on fixed days in the Calendar do not take precedence of Ash Wednesday.

Feasts of our Lord and other Major Feasts appointed on fixed days, which fall upon or are transferred to a weekday, may be observed on any open day within the week. This provision does not apply to Christmas Day, the Epiphany, and All Saints' Day.

4. Days of Special Devotion

The following days are observed by special acts of discipline and self-denial:

Ash Wednesday and the other weekdays of Lent and of Holy Week, except the feast of the Annunciation.

Good Friday and all other Fridays of the year, in commemoration of the Lord's crucifixion, except for Fridays in the Christmas and Easter seasons, and any Feasts of our Lord which occur on a Friday.

5. Days of Optional Observance

Subject to the rules of precedence governing Principal Feasts, Sundays, and Holy Days, the following may be observed with the Collects, Psalms, and Lessons duly authorized by this Church:

Commemorations listed in the Calendar
Other Commemorations, using the Common of Saints
The Ember Days, traditionally observed on the Wednesdays, Fridays, and Saturdays after the First Sunday in Lent, the Day of Pentecost, Holy Cross Day, and December 13
The Rogation Days, traditionally observed on Monday, Tuesday, and Wednesday before Ascension Day
Various Occasions

Provided, that there is no celebration of the Eucharist for any such occasion on Ash Wednesday, Maundy Thursday, Good Friday, and Holy Saturday; and provided further, that none of the Propers appointed for Various Occasions is used as a substitute for, or as an addition to, the Proper appointed for the Principal Feasts.

January

1	A	The Holy Name of Our Lord Jesus Christ
2	b	
3	c	
4	d	
5	e	
6	f	The Epiphany of Our Lord Jesus Christ
7	g	
8	A	
9	b	Julia Chester Emery, 1922
10	c	William Laud, Archbishop of Canterbury, 1645
11	d	
12	e	Aelred, Abbot of Rievaulx, 1167
13	f	Hilary, Bishop of Poitiers, 367
14	g	
15	A	
16	b	
17	c	Antony, Abbot in Egypt, 356
18	d	**The Confession of Saint Peter the Apostle**
19	e	Wulfstan, Bishop of Worcester, 1095
20	f	Fabian, Bishop and Martyr of Rome, 250
21	g	Agnes, Martyr at Rome, 304
22	A	Vincent, Deacon of Saragossa, and Martyr, 304
23	b	Phillips Brooks, Bishop of Massachusetts, 1893
24	c	[Ordination of Florence Li Tim-Oi First Woman Priest in the Anglican Communion, 1944]
25	d	**The Conversion of Saint Paul the Apostle**
26	e	Timothy and Titus, Companions of Saint Paul
27	f	John Chrysostom, Bishop of Constantinople, 407
28	g	Thomas Aquinas, Priest and Friar, 1274
29	A	
30	b	
31	c	

February

1	d	Brigid (Bride), 523
2	e	**The Presentation of Our Lord Jesus Christ in the Temple**
3	f	Anskar, Archbishop of Hamburg, Missionary to Denmark and Sweden, 865
4	g	Cornelius the Centurion
5	A	The Martyrs of Japan, 1597
6	b	
7	c	
8	d	
9	e	
10	f	
11	g	
12	A	
13	b	Absalom Jones, Priest, 1818
14	c	Cyril, Monk, and Methodius, Bishop, Missionaries to the Slavs, 869, 885
15	d	Thomas Bray, Priest and Missionary, 1730
16	e	
17	f	[Janani Luwum Archbishop of Uganda, and Martyr, 1977]
18	g	Martin Luther, 1546
19	A	
20	b	
21	c	
22	d	
23	e	Polycarp, Bishop and Martyr of Smyrna, 156
24	f	**Saint Matthias the Apostle**
25	g	
26	A	
27	b	George Herbert, Priest, 1633
28	c	
29		

March

	1	d	David, Bishop of Menevia, Wales, c. 544
	2	e	Chad, Bishop of Lichfield, 672
	3	f	John and Charles Wesley, Priests, 1791, 1788
	4	g	
	5	A	
	6	b	
	7	c	Perpetua and her Companions, Martyrs at Carthage, 202
	8	d	
	9	e	Gregory, Bishop of Nyssa, c. 394
	10	f	
	11	g	
	12	A	Gregory the Great, Bishop of Rome, 604
	13	b	
	14	c	
	15	d	
	16	e	
	17	f	Patrick, Bishop and Missionary of Ireland, 461
	18	g	Cyril, Bishop of Jerusalem, 386
	19	A	**Saint Joseph**
	20	b	Cuthbert, Bishop of Lindisfarne, 687
	21	c	Thomas Ken, Bishop of Bath and Wells, 1711
14	22	d	James De Koven, Priest, 1879
3	23	e	Gregory the Illuminator, Bishop and Missionary of Armenia, c. 332
	24	f	
11	25	g	**The Annunciation of Our Lord Jesus Christ to the Blessed Virgin Mary**
	26	A	
19	27	b	Charles Henry Brent, Bishop of the Philippines, and of Western New York, 1929
8	28	c	
	29	d	John Keble, Priest, 1866
16	30	e	
5	31	f	John Donne, Priest, 1631

April

	1	g	Frederick Denison Maurice, Priest, 1872
13	2	A	James Lloyd Breck, Priest, 1876
2	3	b	Richard, Bishop of Chichester, 1253
	4	c	Martin Luther King, Jr., Civil Rights Leader, 1968
10	5	d	
	6	e	
18	7	f	
7	8	g	William Augustus Muhlenberg, Priest, 1877
	9	A	Dietrich Bonhoeffer, 1945
15	10	b	William Law, Priest, 1761
4	11	c	George Augustus Selwyn, Bishop of New Zealand, and of Lichfield, 1878
	12	d	
12	13	e	
	14	f	
	15	g	
9	16	A	
17	17	b	
6	18	c	
	19	d	Alphege, Archbishop of Canterbury, and Martyr, 1012
	20	e	
	21	f	Anselm, Archbishop of Canterbury, 1109
	22	g	
	23	A	
	24	b	
	25	c	**Saint Mark the Evangelist**
	26	d	
	27	e	
	28	f	
	29	g	Catherine of Siena, 1380
	30	A	

May

1	b	**Saint Philip and Saint James, Apostles**
2	c	Athanasius, Bishop of Alexandria, 373
3	d	
4	e	Monnica, Mother of Augustine of Hippo, 387
5	f	
6	g	
7	A	
8	b	Dame Julian of Norwich, c. 1417
9	c	Gregory of Nazianzus, Bishop of Constantinople, 389
10	d	
11	e	
12	f	
13	g	
14	A	
15	b	
16	c	
17	d	
18	e	
19	f	Dunstan, Archbishop of Canterbury, 988
20	g	Alcuin, Deacon, and Abbot of Tours, 804
21	A	
22	b	
23	c	
24	d	Jackson Kemper, First Missionary Bishop in the United States, 1870
25	e	Bede, the Venerable, Priest, and Monk of Jarrow, 735
26	f	Augustine, First Archbishop of Canterbury, 605
27	g	
28	A	
29	b	
30	c	
31	d	**The Visitation of the Blessed Virgin Mary**

The First Book of Common Prayer, 1549, is appropriately observed on a weekday following the Day of Pentecost.

June

July

1	g	
2	A	
3	b	
4	c	**Independence Day**
5	d	
6	e	
7	f	
8	g	
9	A	
10	b	
11	c	Benedict of Nursia, Abbot of Monte Cassino, c. 540
12	d	
13	e	
14	f	
15	g	
16	A	
17	b	William White, Bishop of Pennsylvania, 1836
18	c	
19	d	Macrina, Monastic and Teacher, 379
20	e	Elizabeth Cady Stanton, Amelia Bloomer, Sojouner Truth, and Harriett Ross Tubman
21	f	
22	g	**Saint Mary Magdalene**
23	A	
24	b	Thomas a Kempis, Priest, 1471
25	c	**Saint James the Apostle**
26	d	The Parents of the Blessed Virgin Mary
27	e	William Reed Huntington, Priest, 1909
28	f	
29	g	Mary and Martha of Bethany
30	A	William Wilberforce, 1833
31	b	Ignatius of Loyola, 1556

August

1	c	Joseph of Arimathaea
2	d	
3	e	
4	f	
5	g	
6	A	**The Transfiguration of Our Lord Jesus Christ**
7	b	John Mason Neale, Priest, 1866
8	c	Dominic, Priest and Friar, 1221
9	d	
10	e	Laurence, Deacon, and Martyr at Rome, 258
11	f	Clare, Abbess at Assisi, 1253
12	g	Florence Nightingale, Nurse, Social Reformer, 1910
13	A	Jeremy Taylor, Bishop of Down, Connor, and Dromore, 1667
14	b	Jonathan Myrick Daniels, Seminarian and Witness for Civil Rights, 1965
15	c	**Saint Mary the Virgin, Mother of Our Lord Jesus Christ**
16	d	
17	e	
18	f	William Porcher DuBose, Priest, 1918
19	g	
20	A	Bernard, Abbot of Clairvaux, 1153
21	b	
22	c	
23	d	
24	e	**Saint Bartholomew the Apostle**
25	f	Louis, King of France, 1270
26	g	
27	A	Thomas Gallaudet, 1902 with Henry Winter Syle, 1890
28	b	Augustine, Bishop of Hippo, 430
29	c	
30	d	
31	e	Aidan, Bishop of Lindisfarne, 651

September

1	f	David Pendleton Oakerhater, Deacon and Missionary, 1931
2	g	The Martyrs of New Guinea, 1942
3	A	
4	b	Paul Jones, 1941
5	c	
6	d	
7	e	
8	f	
9	g	Constance, Nun, and her Companions, 1878
10	A	Alexander Crummell, 1898
11	b	
12	c	John Henry Hobart, Bishop of New York, 1830
13	d	Cyprian, Bishop and Martyr of Carthage, 258
14	e	**Holy Cross Day**
15	f	
16	g	Ninian, Bishop in Galloway, c. 430
17	A	Hildegard, 1179
18	b	Edward Bouverie Pusey, Priest, 1882
19	c	Theodore of Tarsus, Archbishop of Canterbury, 690
20	d	John Coleridge Patteson, Bishop of Melanesia, and his Companions, Martyrs, 1871
21	e	**Saint Matthew, Apostle and Evangelist**
22	f	[Philander Chase Bishop of Ohio, and of Illinois, 1852]
23	g	
24	A	
25	b	Sergius, Abbot of Holy Trinity, Moscow, 1392
26	c	Lancelot Andrewes, Bishop of Winchester, 1626
27	d	
28	e	
29	f	**Saint Michael and All Angels**
30	g	Jerome, Priest, and Monk of Bethlehem, 420

October

1	A	Remigius, Bishop of Rheims, c. 530
2	b	
3	c	
4	d	Francis of Assisi, Friar, 1226
5	e	
6	f	William Tyndale, Priest, 1536
7	g	
8	A	
9	b	Robert Grosseteste, Bishop of Lincoln, 1253
10	c	
11	d	Philip, Deacon and Evangelist
12	e	
13	f	
14	g	Samuel Isaac Joseph Schereschewsky, Bishop of Shanghai, 1906
15	A	Teresa of Avila, Nun, 1582
16	b	Hugh Latimer and Nicholas Ridley, Bishops, 1555 and Thomas Cranmer, Archbishop of Canterbury, 1556
17	c	Ignatius, Bishop of Antioch, and Martyr, c. 115
18	d	**Saint Luke the Evangelist**
19	e	Henry Martyn, Priest, and Missionary to India and Persia, 1812
20	f	
21	g	
22	A	
23	b	**Saint James of Jerusalem, Brother of Our Lord Jesus Christ, and Martyr, c. 62**
24	c	
25	d	
26	e	Alfred the Great, King of the West Saxons, 899
27	f	
28	g	**Saint Simon and Saint Jude, Apostles**
29	A	James Hannington, Bishop of Eastern Equatorial Africa, and his Companions, Martyrs, 1885
30	b	
31	c	

November

1	d	**All Saints**
2	e	Commemoration of All Faithful Departed
3	f	Richard Hooker, Priest, 1600
4	g	
5	A	
6	b	[William Temple Archbishop of Canterbury, 1944]
7	c	Willibrord, Archbishop of Utrecht, Missionary to Frisia, 739
8	d	
9	e	
10	f	Leo the Great, Bishop of Rome, 461
11	g	Martin, Bishop of Tours, 397
12	A	Charles Simeon, Priest, 1836
13	b	
14	c	Consecration of Samuel Seabury, First American Bishop, 1784
15	d	
16	e	Margaret, Queen of Scotland, 1093
17	f	Hugh, Bishop of Lincoln, 1200
18	g	Hilda, Abbess of Whitby, 680
19	A	Elizabeth, Princess of Hungary, 1231
20	b	Edmund, King of East Anglia, 870
21	c	
22	d	[Clive Staples Lewis Apologist and Spiritual Writer, 1963]
23	e	Clement, Bishop of Rome, c. 100
24	f	
25	g	James Otis Sargent Huntington, Priest and Monk, 1935
26	A	
27	b	
28	c	Kamehameha and Emma, King and Queen of Hawaii, 1864, 1885
29	d	
30	e	**Saint Andrew the Apostle**

December

1	f	Nicholas Ferrar, Deacon, 1637
2	g	Channing Moore Williams, Missionary Bishop in China and Japan, 1910
3	A	
4	b	John of Damascus, Priest, c. 760
5	c	Clement of Alexandria, Priest, c. 210
6	d	Nicholas, Bishop of Myra, c. 342
7	e	Ambrose, Bishop of Milan, 397
8	f	
9	g	
10	A	
11	b	
12	c	
13	d	
14	e	
15	f	
16	g	
17	A	
18	b	
19	c	
20	d	
21	e	**Saint Thomas the Apostle**
22	f	
23	g	
24	A	
25	b	**The Nativity of Our Lord Jesus Christ**
26	c	**Saint Stephen, Deacon and Martyr**
27	d	**Saint John, Apostle and Evangelist**
28	e	**The Holy Innocents**
29	f	Thomas Becket, 1170
30	g	
31	A	

The Weekdays
of Advent
and Christmas
until the Baptism
of Christ

Concerning the Proper

Proper Lessons and Psalms are provided for the Eucharist for the weekdays of Advent and Christmas to the First Sunday after Epiphany. These Propers are also suitable for use at Liturgies of the Word held on those days.

During the weeks of Advent 1 through 3, the first Readings from Isaiah point to the coming of God's reign. In the fourth week of Advent, the first Readings are in thematic harmony with the Gospel lections and reflect on the sacred history of God's people in light of God's coming reign. The Gospel Readings for the first three weeks of Advent point to Jesus' words and acts as fulfilling the expectations of God's coming reign. Lections for the fourth week are taken from the first two chapters of Matthew and Luke and prepare the Church for the Christmas celebration. The first Readings for the weekdays following Christmas Day provide a sequential reading of the First Letter of John, which reflects on the significance of Jesus' life for the Church. The Gospel lections recall the early events of Jesus' life and the beginning of his ministry that revealed his authority and power.

Any of the Readings may be lengthened at discretion, and the selections from the Psalter may be lengthened or shortened.

Where there is not a daily celebration of the Eucharist, the Proper appointed for any weekday may be used on any other weekday in the same week.

On days of optional observance on the Calendar, the Collect, Lessons, Psalm and Preface are ordinarily those of the saint. Where there is a daily celebration, however, the weekday Lessons and Psalm may be substituted.

The Collect of the previous Sunday may be used on ordinary weekdays, except that the third collect for the Nativity of Our Lord: Christmas Day is used for any weekdays between Holy Innocents' Day and the First Sunday after Christmas Day. Any of the sets of Proper Lessons for Christmas Day may serve for any weekdays between Holy Innocents' Day and the First Sunday after Christmas Day.

The First Week of Advent

	Psalms	Lessons
Monday	122	Isaiah 2:1-5 (*or* in Year A, Isaiah 4:2-6) Matthew 8:5-13
Tuesday	72:1-8	Isaiah 11:1-10 Luke 10:21-24
Wednesday	23	Isaiah 25:6-9 Matthew 15:29-39
Thursday	118:19-24	Isaiah 26:1-6 Matthew 7:21-27
Friday	27:1-6,17-18	Isaiah 29:17-24 Matthew 9:27-31
Saturday	147:1-12	Isaiah 30:19-21, 23-26 Matthew 9:35 — 10:1,5-8

The Second Week of Advent

	Psalms	Lessons
Monday	85:8-13	Isaiah 35:1-10 Luke 5:17-26
Tuesday	96 *or* in Year B, 50:7-15	Isaiah 40:1-11 (*or* in Year B, Amos 5:18-24) Matthew 18:12-14
Wednesday	103:1-10	Isaiah 40:25-31 Matthew 11:28-30
Thursday	145:1-4,8-13	Isaiah 41:13-20 Matthew 11:7-15
Friday	1	Isaiah 48:17-19 Matthew 11:16-19
Saturday	80:1-3,14-18	Sirach 48:1-11 Matthew 17:9-13

The Third Week of Advent

	Psalms	Lessons
Monday	25:3-8	Numbers 24:2-7,15-17a Matthew 21:23-27
Tuesday	34:1-8	Zephaniah 3:1-2, 9-13 Matthew 21:28-32
Wednesday	85:8-13	Isaiah 45:5-8(9-17)18-25 Luke 7:19-23
Thursday	30	Isaiah 54:1-10 Luke 7:24-30
Friday	67	Isaiah 56:1-8 John 5:33-36

	Psalms	Lessons
17	72:1-8	Genesis 49:2,8-10 Matthew 1:1-7,17
18	72:11-18	Jeremiah 23:5-8 Matthew 1:18-25
19	71:1-8	Judges 13:2-7,24-25 Luke 1:5-25
20	24	Isaiah 7:10-14 Luke 1:26-38
21	33:1-5,20-22	Zephaniah 3:14-18a (*or* in Year C, Song of Solomon 2:8-14) Luke 1:39-45
22	Canticle 9 *or* 113 *or* 122	1 Samuel 1:19-28 Luke 1:46-56
23	25:1-14	Malachi 3:1-5 Luke 1:57-66
24	89:1-4,19-29	2 Samuel 7:1-16 Luke 1:67-79

December 26 – December 31

	Psalms	Lessons
26		Collect and Proper Lessons for St. Stephen
27		Collect and Proper Lessons for St. John
28		Collect and Proper Lessons for the Holy Innocents
29	96:1-9	1 John 2:7-11 Luke 2:22-35
30	96:7-10	1 John 2:12-17 Luke 2:36-40
31	96:1-2,11-13	1 John 2:18-21 John 1: 1-18

January 2 – January 12

	Psalms	Lessons
2	98:1-5	1 John 2:22-29 John 1:19-28
3	98:1-2,4-7	1 John 3:1-6 John 1:29-34
4	98:1-2,8-10	1 John 3:7-10 John 1:35-42
5	100	1 John 3:11-18 John 1:43-51
7	2	1 John 3:18 — 4:6 Matthew 4:12-17,23-25
8	72:1-8	1 John 4:7-12 Mark 6:30-44
9	72:1-2,10-13	1 John 4:11-19 Mark 6:45-52
10	72:1-2,14-19	1 John 4:19 — 5:4 Luke 4:14-22
11	147:13-21	1 John 5:5-12 Luke 5:12-16
12	149:1-4	1 John 5:13-21 John 3:22-30

The Monday after the Baptism of Christ begins Ordinary Time, the Weeks after Epiphany.

Concerning the Proper

Proper Collects, Lessons, and Psalms are provided for the Eurharist on the weekdays of Lent. These Propers are also suitable for use at Liturgies of the Word (preaching services) held on those days. The First Lesson is invariably from the Old Testament, and is chosen to match the appointed Gospel.

Any of the Readings may be lengthened at discretion. Suggested lengthenings are shown in parentheses. The selections from the Psalter may be lengthened or shortened.

Where there is not a daily celebration of the Eucharist, the Proper appointed for any weekday may be used on any other weekday in the same week.

In keeping with ancient tradition, the observance of Lenten weekdays ordinarily takes precedence over Lesser Feasts occuring during this season. It is appropriate, however, to name the saint whose day it is in the Prayers of the People, and, if desired, to use the Collect of the saint to conclude the Prayers.

The Weekdays
of Lent

Thursday after Ash Wednesday

I   Direct us, O Lord, in all our doings with thy most gracious favor, and further us with thy continual help; that in all our works begun, continued, and ended in thee, we may glorify thy holy Name, and finally, by thy mercy, obtain everlasting life; through Jesus Christ our Lord, who liveth and reigneth with thee and the Holy Spirit, one God, for ever and ever. *Amen.*

II   Direct us, O Lord, in all our doings with your most gracious favor, and further us with your continual help; that in all our works begun continued, and ended in you, we may glorify your holy Name, and finally, by your mercy, obtain everlasting life; through Jesus Christ our Lord, who lives and reigns with you and the Holy Spirit, one God, for ever and ever. *Amen.*

Psalm	Lessons
1	Deuteronomy 30:15-20
	Luke 9:18-25

Preface of Lent

Friday after Ash Wednesday

I Support us, O Lord, with thy gracious favor through the fast
we have begun; that as we observe it by bodily self-denial, so
we may fulfill it with inner sincerity of heart; through Jesus
Christ our Lord, who liveth and reigneth with thee and the
Holy Spirit, one God for ever and ever. *Amen.*

II Support us, O Lord, with your gracious favor through the
fast we have begun; that as we observe it by bodily
self-denial, so we may fulfill it with inner sincerity of heart;
through Jesus Christ our Lord, who lives and reigns with
you and the Holy Spirit, one God, for ever and ever. *Amen.*

Psalm	Lessons
51:1-10	Isaiah 58:1-9a
	Matthew 9:10-17

Preface of Lent

Saturday after Ash Wednesday

I   Almighty and everlasting God, mercifully look upon our infirmities, and in all our dangers and necessities stretch forth thy right hand to help and defend us; through Jesus Christ our Lord, who liveth and reigneth with thee and the Holy Spirit, one God, for ever and ever. *Amen.*

II   Almighty and everlasting God, mercifully look upon our infirmities, and in all our dangers and necessities stretch forth your right hand to help and defend us; through Jesus Christ our Lord, who lives and reigns with you and the Holy Spirit, one God, for ever and ever. *Amen.*

Psalm	Lessons
86:1-11	Isaiah 58:9b-14
	Luke 5:27-32

Preface of Lent

Monday in the First Week of Lent

I Almighty and everlasting God, mercifully increase in us thy gifts of holy discipline, in almsgiving, prayer, and fasting; that our lives may be directed to the fulfilling of thy most gracious will; through Jesus Christ our Lord, who liveth and reigneth with thee and the Holy Spirit, one God, for ever and ever. *Amen.*

II Almighty and everlasting God, mercifully increase in us your gifts of holy discipline, in almsgiving, prayer, and fasting; that our lives may be directed to the fulfilling of your most gracious will; through Jesus Christ our Lord, who lives and reigns with you and the Holy Spirit, one God, for ever and ever. *Amen.*

Psalm	Lessons
19:7-14	Leviticus 19:1-2,11-18
	Matthew 25:31-46

Preface of Lent

Tuesday in the First Week of Lent

I   Grant to thy people, Lord, grace to withstand the temptations of the world, the flesh, and the devil, and with pure hearts and minds to follow thee, the only true God; through Jesus Christ thy Son our Lord, who liveth and reigneth with thee and the Holy Spirit, one God, for ever and. ever. *Amen*

II   Grant to your people, Lord, grace to withstand the temptations of the world, the flesh, and the devil, and with pure hearts and minds to follow you, the only true God; through Jesus Christ your Son our Lord, who lives and reigns with you and the Holy Spirit, one God, for ever and ever. *Amen.*

Psalm	Lessons
34:15-22	Isaiah 55:6-11
	Matthew 6:7-15

Preface of Lent

Wednesday in the First Week of Lent

I   Bless us, O God, in this holy season, in which our hearts seek thy help and healing; and so purify us by thy discipline that we may grow in grace and in the knowledge of our Lord and Savior Jesus Christ; who liveth and reigneth with thee and the Holy Spirit, one God, for ever and ever. *Amen.*

II   Bless us, O God, in this holy season, in which our hearts seek your help and healing; and so purify us by your discipline that we may grow in grace and in the knowledge of our Lord and Savior Jesus Christ; who lives and reigns with you and the Holy Spirit, one God, for ever and ever. *Amen.*

Psalm	Lessons
51:11-18	Jonah 3:1-10
	Luke 11:29-32

Preface of Lent

Thursday in the First Week of Lent

I Strengthen us, O Lord, by thy grace, that in thy might we may overcome all spiritual enemies, and with pure hearts serve thee; through Jesus Christ our Lord, who liveth and reigneth with thee and the Holy Spirit, one God, for ever and ever. *Amen.*

II Strengthen us, O Lord, by your grace, that in your might we may overcome all spiritual enemies, and with pure hearts serve you; through Jesus Christ our Lord, who lives and reigns with you and the Holy Spirit, one God, for ever and ever. *Amen.*

Psalm	Lessons
138	Esther (Apocrypha) 14:1-6,12-14
	Matthew 7:7-12

Preface of Lent

Friday in the First Week of Lent

I   Lord Christ, our eternal Redeemer, grant us such fellowship
in thy sufferings, that, filled with thy Holy Spirit, we may
subdue the flesh to the spirit, and the spirit to thee, and at
the last attain to the glory of thy resurrection; who livest and
reignest with the Father and the Holy Spirit, one God, for
ever and ever. *Amen.*

II Lord Christ, our eternal Redeemer, grant us such
fellowship in your sufferings, that, filled with your Holy
Spirit, we may subdue the flesh to the spirit, and the spirit to
you, and at the last attain to the glory of your resurrection;
who live and reign with the Father and the Holy Spirit, one
God, for ever and ever. *Amen.*

Psalm	Lessons
130	Ezekiel 18:21-28
	Matthew 5:20-26

Preface of Lent

Saturday in the First Week of Lent

I   O God, who by thy Word dost marvelously carry out the work of reconciliation: Grant that in our Lenten fast we may be devoted to thee with all our hearts, and united with one another in prayer and holy love; through Jesus Christ our Lord, who liveth and reigneth with thee and the Holy Spirit, one God, for ever and ever. *Amen.*

II   O God, by your Word you marvelously carry out the work of reconciliation: Grant that in our Lenten fast we may be devoted to you with all our hearts, and united with one another in prayer and holy love; through Jesus Christ our Lord, who lives and reigns with you and the Holy Spirit, one God, for ever and ever. *Amen.*

Psalm	Lessons
119:1-8	Deuteronomy 26:16-19
	Matthew 5:43-48

Preface of Lent

Monday in the Second Week of Lent

I   Let thy Spirit, O Lord, come into the midst of us to wash us
with the pure water of repentance, and prepare us to be
always a living sacrifice unto thee; through Jesus Christ our
Lord, who liveth and reigneth with thee and the Holy Spirit,
one God, for ever and ever. *Amen.*

II Let your Spirit, O Lord, come into the midst of us to wash us
with the pure water of repentance, and prepare us to be
always a living sacrifice to you; through Jesus Christ our
Lord, who lives and reigns with you and the Holy Spirit, one
God, for ever and ever. *Amen.*

Psalm	Lessons
79:1-9	Daniel 9:3-10
	Luke 6:27-38

Preface of Lent

Tuesday in the Second Week of Lent

I   O God, who didst will to redeem us from all iniquity by thy
Son: Deliver us when we are tempted to regard sin without
abhorrence, and let the virtue of his passion come between
us and our mortal enemy; through Jesus Christ our Lord,
who liveth and reigneth with thee and the Holy Spirit, one
God, for ever and ever. *Amen.*

II   O God, you willed to redeem us from all iniquity by your
Son: Deliver us when we are tempted to regard sin without
abhorrence, and let the virtue of his passion come between
us and our mortal enemy; through Jesus Christ our Lord,
who lives and reigns with you and the Holy Spirit, one God,
for ever and ever. *Amen.*

Psalm	Lessons
50:7-15,22-24	Isaiah 1:2-4,16-20
	Matthew 23:1-12

Preface of Lent

Wednesday in the Second Week of Lent

I   O God, who didst so love the world that thou gavest thine only-begotten Son to reconcile earth with heaven: Grant that we, loving thee above all things, may love our friends in thee, and our enemies for thy sake; through Jesus Christ our Lord, who liveth and reigneth with thee and the Holy Spirit, one God, for ever and ever. *Amen.*

II   O God, you so loved the world that you gave your only-begotten Son to reconcile earth with heaven: Grant that we, loving you above all things, may love our friends in you, and our enemies for your sake; through Jesus Christ our Lord, who lives and reigns with you and the Holy Spirit, one God, for ever and ever. *Amen.*

Psalm	Lessons
31:9-16	Jeremiah 18:1-11,18-20
	Matthew 20:17-28

Preface of Lent

Thursday in the Second Week of Lent

I   O Lord, strong and mighty, Lord of hosts and King of glory: Cleanse our hearts from sin, keep our hands pure, and turn our minds from what is passing away; so that at the last we may stand in thy holy place and receive thy blessing; through Jesus Christ our Lord, who liveth and reigneth with thee and the Holy Spirit, one God, for ever and ever. *Amen.*

II   O Lord, strong and mighty, Lord of hosts and King of glory: Cleanse our hearts from sin, keep our hands pure, and turn our minds from what is passing away; so that at the last we may stand in your holy place and receive your blessing; through Jesus Christ our Lord, who lives and reigns with you and the Holy Spirit, one God, for ever and ever. *Amen.*

Psalm	Lessons
1	Jeremiah 17:5-10
	Luke 16:19-31

Preface of Lent

Friday in the Second Week of Lent

I   Grant, O Lord, that as thy Son Jesus Christ prayed for his enemies on the cross, so we may have grace to forgive those who wrongfully or scornfully use us, that we ourselves may be able to receive thy forgiveness; through Jesus Christ our Lord, who liveth and reigneth with thee and the Holy Spirit, one God, for ever and ever. *Amen.*

II   Grant, O Lord, that as your Son Jesus Christ prayed for his enemies on the cross, so we may have grace to forgive those who wrongfully or scornfully use us, that we ourselves may be able to receive your forgiveness; through Jesus Christ our Lord, who lives and reigns with you and the Holy Spirit, one God, for ever and ever. *Amen.*

Psalm	Lessons
105:16-22	Genesis 37:3-4,12-28
	Matthew 21:33-43

Preface of Lent

Saturday in the Second Week of Lent

I   Grant, most merciful Lord, to thy faithful people pardon and peace, that they may be cleansed from all their sins, and serve thee with a quiet mind; through Jesus Christ our Lord, who liveth and reigneth with thee and the Holy Spirit, one God, for ever and ever. *Amen.*

II   Grant, most merciful Lord, to your faithful people pardon and peace, that they may be cleansed from all their sins, and serve you with a quiet mind; through Jesus Christ our Lord, who lives and reigns with you and the Holy Spirit, one God, for ever and ever. *Amen.*

Psalm	Lessons
103:1-4(5-8)9-12	Micah 7:14-15,18-20
	Luke 15:11-32

Preface of Lent

Monday in the Third Week of Lent

I   Look upon the hearty desires of thy humble servants, we beseech thee, Almighty God, and stretch forth the right hand of thy majesty to be our defense against all our enemies; through Jesus Christ our Lord, who liveth and reigneth with thee and the Holy Spirit, one God, for ever and ever. *Amen.*

II   Look upon the heart-felt desires of your humble servants, Almighty God, and stretch forth the right hand of your majesty to be our defense against all our enemies; through Jesus Christ our Lord, who lives and reigns with you and the Holy Spirit, one God, for ever and ever. *Amen.*

Psalm	Lessons
42:1-7	2 Kings 5:1-15b
	Luke 4:23-30

Another Proper

The following Psalm and Lessons may be used on any weekday in this week, especially in Years B and C.

95:6-11	Exodus 17:1-7
	John 4:5-26(27-38)39-42

Preface of Lent

Tuesday in the Third Week of Lent

I   O Lord, we beseech thee mercifully to hear us; and grant that we, to whom thou hast given a hearty desire to pray, may, by thy mighty aid, be defended and comforted in all dangers and adversities; through Jesus Christ our Lord, who liveth and reigneth with thee and the Holy Spirit, one God, for ever and ever. *Amen.*

II   O Lord, we beseech you mercifully to hear us; and grant that we, to whom you have given a fervent desire to pray, may, by your mighty aid, be defended and comforted in all dangers and adversities; through Jesus Christ our Lord, who lives and reigns with you and the Holy Spirit, one God, for ever and ever. *Amen.*

Psalm	Lessons
25:3-10	Song of the Three Young Men 2-4,11-20a*
	Matthew 18:21-35

Preface of Lent

* *In some Bibles, Daniel 3:25-27,34-43*

Wednesday in the Third Week of Lent

I Give ear to our prayers, O Lord, and dispose the way of thy servants in safety under thy protection, that, amidst all the changes of our earthly pilgrimage, we may ever be guarded by thy mighty aid; through Jesus Christ our Lord, who liveth and reigneth with thee and the Holy Spirit, one God; for ever and ever. *Amen.*

II Give ear to our prayers, O Lord, and direct the way of your servants in safety under your protection, that, amid all the changes of our earthly pilgrimage, we may be guarded by your mighty aid; through Jesus Christ our Lord, who lives and reigns with you and the Holy Spirit, one God, for ever and ever. *Amen.*

Psalm	Lessons
78:1-6	Deuteronomy 4:1-2,5-9
	Matthew 5:17-19

Preface of Lent

Thursday in the Third Week of Lent

I   Keep watch over thy Church, O Lord, with thine unfailing love; and, seeing that it is grounded in human weakness and cannot maintain itself without thine aid, protect it from all danger, and keep it in the way of salvation; through Jesus Christ thy Son our Lord, who liveth and reigneth with thee and the Holy Spirit, one God, for ever and ever. *Amen.*

II   Keep watch over your Church, O Lord, with your unfailing love; and, since it is grounded in human weakness and cannot maintain itself without your aid, protect it from all danger, and keep it in the way of salvation; through Jesus Christ your Son our Lord, who lives and reigns with you and the Holy Spirit, one God, for ever and ever. *Amen.*

Psalm	Lessons
95:6-11	Jeremiah 7:23-28
	Luke 11:14-23

Preface of Lent

Friday in the Third Week of Lent

I Grant us, O Lord our Strength, to have a true love of thy holy Name; that, trusting in thy grace, we may fear no earthly evil, nor fix our hearts on earthly goods, but may rejoice in thy full salvation; through Jesus Christ our Lord, who liveth and reigneth with thee and the Holy Spirit, one God, for ever and ever. *Amen.*

II Grant us, O Lord our Strength, a true love of your holy Name; so that, trusting in your grace, we may fear no earthly evil, nor fix our hearts on earthly goods, but may rejoice in your full salvation; through Jesus Christ our Lord, who lives and reigns with you and the Holy Spirit, one God, for ever and ever. *Amen.*

Psalm	Lessons
81:8-14	Hosea 14:1-9
	Mark 12:28-34

Preface of Lent

Saturday in the Third Week of Lent

I   O God, who knowest us to be set in the midst of so many
and great dangers, that by reason of the frailty of our nature
we cannot always stand upright: Grant to us such strength
and protection as may support us in all dangers, and carry us
through all temptations; through Jesus Christ our Lord, who
liveth and reigneth with thee and the Holy Spirit, one God,
for ever and ever. *Amen.*

II   O God, you know us to be set in the midst of so many and
great dangers, that by reason of the frailty of our nature we
cannot always stand upright: Grant us such strength and
protection as may support us in all dangers, and carry us
through all temptations; through Jesus Christ our Lord, who
lives and reigns with you and the Holy Spirit, one God, for
ever and ever. *Amen.*

Psalm	Lessons
51:15-20	Hosea 6:1-6
	Luke 18:9-14

Preface of Lent

Monday in the Fourth Week of Lent

I   O Lord our God, who in thy holy Sacraments hast given us a foretaste of the good things of thy kingdom: Direct us, we beseech thee, in the way that leadeth unto eternal life, that we may come to appear before thee in that place of light where thou dost dwell for ever with thy saints; through Jesus Christ our Lord, who liveth and reigneth with thee and the Holy Spirit, one God, for ever and ever. *Amen.*

II   O Lord our God, in your holy Sacraments you have given us a foretaste of the good things of your kingdom: Direct us, we pray, in the way that leads to eternal life, that we may come to appear before you in that place of light where you dwell for ever with your saints; through Jesus Christ our Lord, who lives and reigns with you and the Holy Spirit, one God, for ever and ever. *Amen.*

Psalm	Lessons
30:1-6,11-13	Isaiah 65:17-25
	John 4:43-54

Another Proper

The following Psalm and Lessons may be used on any weekday in this week, especially in Years B and C.

27:1,10-18	Micah 7:7-9
	John 9:1-13(14-27)28-38

Preface of Lent

Tuesday in the Fourth Week of Lent

I   O God, with whom is the well of life, and in whose light we
see light: Quench our thirst, we pray thee, with living water,
and flood our darkened minds with heavenly light; through
Jesus Christ our Lord, who liveth and reigneth with thee and
the Holy Spirit, one God, for ever and ever. *Amen.*

II   O God, with you is the well of life, and in your light we see
light: Quench our thirst with living water, and flood our
darkened minds with heavenly light; through Jesus Christ
our Lord, who lives and reigns with you and the Holy Spirit,
one God, for ever and ever. *Amen.*

Psalm	Lessons
46:1-8	Ezekiel 47:1-9,12
	John 5:1-18

Preface of Lent

Wednesday in the Fourth Week of Lent

I   O Lord our God, who didst sustain thine ancient people in the wilderness with bread from heaven: Feed now thy pilgrim flock with the food that endureth unto everlasting life; through Jesus Christ thy Son our Lord, who liveth and reigneth with thee and the Holy Spirit, one God, for ever and ever. *Amen.*

II   O Lord our God, you sustained your ancient people in the wilderness with bread from heaven: Feed now your pilgrim flock with the food that endures to everlasting life; through Jesus Christ your Son our Lord, who lives and reigns with you and the Holy Spirit, one God, for ever and ever. *Amen.*

Psalm	Lessons
145:8-19	Isaiah 49:8-15
	John 5:19-29

Preface of Lent

Thursday in the Fourth Week of Lent

I   Almighty and most merciful God, drive from us all weakness of body, mind, and spirit; that, being restored to wholeness, we may with free hearts become what thou dost intend us to be and accomplish what thou willest us to do; through Jesus Christ our Lord, who liveth and reigneth with thee and the Holy Spirit, one God, for ever and ever. *Amen.*

II   Almighty and most merciful God, drive from us all weakness of body, mind, and spirit; that, being restored to wholeness, we may with free hearts become what you intend us to be and accomplish what you want us to do; through Jesus Christ our Lord, who lives and reigns with you and the Holy Spirit, one God, for ever and ever. *Amen.*

Psalm	Lessons
106:6-7,19-23	Exodus 32:7-14
	John 5:30-47

Preface of Lent

Friday in the Fourth Week of Lent

I O God, who hast given us the Good News of thine
abounding love in thy Son Jesus Christ: So fill our hearts
with thankfulness that we may rejoice to tell abroad the
good tidings we have received; through Jesus Christ our
Lord, who liveth and reigneth with thee and the Holy Spirit,
one God, for ever and ever. *Amen.*

II O God, you have given us the Good News of your
abounding love in your Son Jesus Christ: So fill our hearts
with thankfulness that we may rejoice to proclaim the good
tidings we have received; through Jesus Christ our Lord,
who lives and reigns with you and the Holy Spirit, one God,
for ever and ever. *Amen.*

Psalm	Lessons
34:15-22	Wisdom 2:1a,12-24
	John 7:1-2,10,25-30

Preface of Lent

Saturday in the Fourth Week of Lent

I   Mercifully hear our prayers, O Lord, and spare all those who confess their sins unto thee; that they, whose consciences by sin are accused, by thy merciful pardon may be absolved; through Jesus Christ thy Son our Lord, who liveth and reigneth with thee and the Holy Spirit, one God, for ever and ever. *Amen.*

II Mercifully hear our prayers, O Lord, and spare all those who confess their sins to you; that those whose consciences are accused by sin may by your merciful pardon be absolved; through Jesus Christ your Son our Lord, who lives and reigns with you and the Holy Spirit, one God, for ever and ever. *Amen.*

Psalm	Lessons
7:6-11	Jeremiah 11:18-20
	John 7:37-52

Preface of Lent

Monday in the Fifth Week of Lent

I Be gracious to thy people, we beseech thee, O Lord, that they, repenting day by day of the things that displease thee, may be more and more filled with love of thee and of thy commandments; and, being supported by thy grace in this life, may come to the full enjoyment of eternal life in thine everlasting kingdom; through Jesus Christ our Lord, who liveth and reigneth with thee and the Holy Spirit, one God, for ever and ever. *Amen.*

II Be gracious to your people, we entreat you, O Lord, that they, repenting day by day of the things that displease you, may be more and more filled with love of you and of your commandments; and, being supported by your grace in this life, may come to the full enjoyment of eternal life in your everlasting kingdom; through Jesus Christ our Lord, who lives and reigns with you and the Holy Spirit, one God, for ever and ever. *Amen.*

Psalm	Lessons
23	Susanna* 1-9,15-29,34-62
	or verses 41-62
	John 8:1-11
	or John 8:12-20

For another proper, see the next page.

Preface of Lent

* In some Bibles, Daniel 13

Tuesday in the Fifth Week of Lent

I Almighty God, who through the incarnate Word dost make
us to be born anew of an imperishable and eternal seed:
Look with compassion, we beseech thee, upon those who are
being prepared for Holy Baptism, and grant that they may
be built as living stones into a spiritual temple acceptable
unto thee; through Jesus Christ our Lord, who liveth and
reigneth with thee and the Holy Spirit, one God, for ever and
ever. *Amen.*

II Almighty God, through the incarnate Word you have caused
us to be born anew of an imperishable and eternal seed:
Look with compassion upon those who are being prepared
for Holy Baptism, and grant that they may be built as living
stones into a spiritual temple acceptable to you; through
Jesus Christ our Lord, who lives and reigns with you and the
Holy Spirit, one God, for ever and ever. *Amen.*

Psalm	Lessons
102:15-22	Numbers 21:4-9
	John 8:21-30

Another Proper

*The following Psalm and Lessons may be used on any weekday of this
week, especially in Years B and C.*

17:1-8	2 Kings 4:18-21,32-37
	John 11:(1-7)18-44

Preface of Lent

Wednesday in the Fifth Week of Lent

I   Almighty God our heavenly Father, renew in us the gifts of
thy mercy; increase our faith, strengthen our hope, enlighten
our understanding, enlarge our charity, and make us ready
to serve thee; through Jesus Christ our Lord, who liveth and
reigneth with thee and the Holy Spirit, one God, for ever and
ever. *Amen.*

II   Almighty God our heavenly Father, renew in us the gifts of
your mercy; increase our faith, strengthen our hope,
enlighten our understanding, widen our charity, and make us
ready to serve you; through Jesus Christ our Lord, who lives
and reigns with you and the Holy Spirit, one God, for ever
and ever. *Amen.*

Psalm	Lessons
Canticle 2 *or* 13	Daniel 3:14-20,24-28
	John 8:31-42

Preface of Lent

Thursday in the Fifth Week of Lent

I   O God, who hast called us to be thy children, and hast promised that those who suffer with Christ will be heirs with him of thy glory: Arm us with such trust in him that we may ask no rest from his demands and have no fear in his service; through the same Jesus Christ our Lord, who liveth and reigneth with thee and the Holy Spirit, one God, for ever and ever. *Amen.*

II   O God, you have called us to be your children, and have promised that those who suffer with Christ will be heirs with him of your glory: Arm us with such trust in him that we may ask no rest from his demands and have no fear in his service; through Jesus Christ our Lord, who lives and reigns with you and the Holy Spirit, one God, for ever and ever. *Amen.*

Psalm	Lessons
105:4-11	Genesis 17:1-8
	John 8:51-59

Preface of Lent

Friday in the Fifth Week of Lent

I   O Lord, who dost, out of the abundance of thy great riches, relieve our necessity: Grant, we beseech thee, that we may accept with joy the salvation thou dost bestow, and by the quality of our lives show forth the same to all the world; through Jesus Christ our Lord, who liveth and reigneth with thee and the Holy Spirit, one God, for ever and ever. *Amen.*

II   O Lord, you relieve our necessity out of the abundance of your great riches: Grant that we may accept with joy the salvation you bestow, and manifest it to all the world by the quality of our lives; through Jesus Christ our Lord, who lives and reigns with you and the Holy Spirit, one God, now and for ever. *Amen.*

Psalm	Lessons
18:1-7	Jeremiah 20:7-13
	John 10:31-42

Preface of Lent

Saturday in the Fifth Week of Lent

I   O Lord, who in thy goodness dost bestow abundant graces on thine elect: Look with favor, we entreat thee, upon those who in these Lenten days are being prepared for Holy Baptism, and grant them the help of thy protection; through Jesus Christ thy Son our Lord, who liveth and reigneth with thee and the Holy Spirit, one God, for ever and ever. *Amen.*

II   O Lord, in your goodness you bestow abundant graces on your elect: Look with favor, we entreat you, upon those who in these Lenten days are being prepared for Holy Baptism, and grant them the help of your protection; through Jesus Christ your Son our Lord, who lives and reigns with you and the Holy Spirit, one God, for ever and ever. *Amen.*

Psalm	Lessons
85:1-7	Ezekiel 37:21-28
	John 11:45-53

Preface of Lent

The Weekdays
of Easter Season

Concerning the Proper

Proper Lessons and Psalms are provided for the weekdays of Easter Season. The First Lessons consist of a semi-continuous reading of the Acts of the Apostles (which is an ancient tradition in this season), the earlier portions of which are appointed in the Prayer Book Lectionary for the weekdays of Easter Week. The Readings from the Gospel according to John are chosen for their appropriateness to the season, and complement the Readings from this Gospel assigned to the season of Lent.

Any of the Readings may be lengthened at discretion. The selections from the Psalter may be lengthened or shortened.

Where there is not a daily celebration of the Eucharist, the Proper appointed for any weekday may be used on any other weekday in the same week.

Since the triumphs of the saints are a continuation and manifestation of the Paschal victory of Christ, the celebration of saints' days is particularly appropriate during this season. On such days, therefore, the Collect, Lessons, Psalm, and Preface are ordinarily those of the saint. Where there is a daily celebration, however, the weekday Lessons and Psalm may be substituted.

A corpus of Collects is provided for use as the Collect of the Day on weekdays which are not saints' days. These Collects are also appropriate for use at the conclusion of the Prayers of the People during this season, including the Sundays.

Weekdays of Easter Season

The Collects which follow are particularly appropriate for use at the times indicated.

The Lessons and Psalms for this season are on pages 76-81 of this book.

From Monday after 2 Easter until 4 Easter

1

I O God, who hast united divers peoples in the confession of thy Name: Grant, we pray thee, that all who have been born again in the font of Baptism may also be united in faith and love; through Jesus Christ our Lord, who liveth and reigneth with thee and the Holy Spirit, one God, for ever and ever. *Amen.*

II O God, you have united diverse peoples in the confession of your Name: Grant that all who have been born again in the font of Baptism may also be united in faith and love; through Jesus Christ our Lord, who lives and reigns with you and the Holy Spirit, one God, for ever and ever. *Amen.*

2

I O God, who by the waters of Baptism hast renewed those who believe in thee: Come to the help of those who have been reborn in Christ, that they may overcome the wiles of the devil, and continue faithful to the gifts of grace that they have received from thee; through Jesus Christ our Lord, who liveth and reigneth with thee and the Holy Spirit, one God, for ever and ever. *Amen.*

II O God, by the waters of Baptism you have renewed those who believe in you: Come to the help of those who have been reborn in Christ, that they may overcome the wiles of the devil, and continue faithful to the gifts of grace they have received from you; through Jesus Christ our Lord, who lives and reigns with you and the Holy Spirit, one God, for ever and ever. *Amen.*

3

I Grant, O Lord, we beseech thee, that we may so live in the Paschal mystery that the joy of these fifty days may continually strengthen us, and assure us of our salvation; through Jesus Christ thy Son our Lord, who liveth and reigneth with thee and the Holy Spirit, one God, for ever and ever. *Amen.*

II Grant, O Lord, that we may so live in the Paschal mystery that the joy of these fifty days may continually strengthen us, and assure us of our salvation; through Jesus Christ your Son our Lord, who lives and reigns with you and the Holy Spirit, one God, for ever and ever. *Amen.*

4

I O Lord, who hast saved us through the Paschal mystery of Christ: Continue to support thy people with heavenly gifts, that we may attain unto true liberty, and enjoy the happiness of heaven which we have begun to taste on earth; through Jesus Christ our Lord, who liveth and reigneth with thee and the Holy Spirit, one God, for ever and ever. *Amen.*

II O Lord, you have saved us through the Paschal mystery of
Christ: Continue to support your people with heavenly gifts,
that we may attain true liberty, and enjoy the happiness of
heaven which we have begun to taste on earth; through
Jesus Christ our Lord, who lives and reigns with you and the
Holy Spirit, one God, for ever and ever. *Amen.*

5

I O Lord, who art the life of the faithful, the glory of the
saints, and the delight of those who trust in thee: Hear our
supplications, and quench, we pray thee, the thirst of those
who long for thy promises; through Jesus Christ our Lord,
who liveth and reigneth with thee and Holy Spirit, one God,
for ever and ever. *Amen.*

II O Lord, the life of the faithful, the glory of the saints, and
the delight of those who trust in you: Hear our
supplications, and quench, we pray, the thirst of those who
long for your promises; through Jesus Christ our Lord, who
lives and reigns with you and the Holy Spirit, one God, for
ever and ever. *Amen.*

6

I O God, who by the abundance of thy grace dost unfailingly
increase the number of thy children: Look with favor upon
those whom thou hast chosen to be members of thy Church,
that, having been born again in Baptism, they may be
granted a glorious resurrection; through Jesus Christ thy Son
our Lord, who liveth and reigneth with thee and the Holy
Spirit, one God, now and for ever. *Amen.*

II   O God, by the abundance of your grace you unfailingly increase the number of your children: Look with favor upon those whom you have chosen to be members of your Church, that, having been born again in Baptism, they may be granted a glorious resurrection; through Jesus Christ your Son our Lord, who lives and reigns with you and the Holy Spirit, one God, now and for ever. *Amen.*

7

I   Let thy people, O Lord, rejoice for ever that they have been renewed in spirit; and let the joy of our adoption as thy sons and daughters strengthen the hope of our glorious resurrection in Jesus Christ our Lord; who liveth and reigneth with thee and the Holy Spirit, one God, for ever and ever. *Amen.*

II   Let your people, O Lord, rejoice for ever that they have been renewed in spirit; and let the joy of our adoption as your sons and daughters strengthen the hope of our glorious resurrection in Jesus Christ our Lord; who lives and reigns with you and the Holy Spirit, one God, for ever and ever. *Amen.*

From Monday after 4 Easter until Ascension Day

8

I   Almighty and everlasting God, who hast given unto thy Church the great joy of the resurrection of Jesus Christ: Give us also the greater joy of the kingdom of thine elect, when the flock of thy Son will share in the final victory of its Shepherd, Jesus Christ our Lord; who liveth and reigneth with thee and the Holy Spirit, one God, now and for ever. *Amen.*

II Almighty and everlasting God, you have given your Church the great joy of the resurrection of Jesus Christ: Give us also the greater joy of the kingdom of your elect, when the flock of your Son will share in the final victory of its Shepherd, Jesus Christ our Lord; who lives and reigns with you and the Holy Spirit, one God, now and for ever. *Amen.*

9

I Almighty God, who showest to them that are in error the light of thy truth, to the intent that they may return into the way of righteousness: Grant unto all those who are admitted into the fellowship of Christ's religion that they may avoid those things that are contrary to their profession, and follow all such things as are agreeable to the same; through Jesus Christ our Lord, who liveth and reigneth with thee and the Holy Spirit, one God, for ever and ever. *Amen.*

II Almighty God, you show the light of your truth to those who are in error, to the intent that they may return to the way of righteousness: Grant to those who are admitted into the fellowship of Christ's religion that they may avoid those things that are contrary to their profession, and follow all such things as are agreeable to it; through Jesus Christ our Lord, who lives and reigns with you and the Holy Spirit, one God, for ever and ever. *Amen.*

10

I God of infinite mercy, who dost renew the faith of thy people by the yearly celebration of these fifty days: Stir up in us, we beseech thee, the gifts of thy grace, that we may more deeply know that Baptism hath cleansed us, the Spirit hath quickened us, and the Blood of Christ hath redeemed us; through the same Jesus Christ our Lord, who liveth and reigneth with thee and the same Holy Spirit, one God, for ever and ever. *Amen.*

II God of infinite mercy, you renew the faith of your people by the yearly celebration of these fifty days: Stir up in us the gifts of your grace, that we may know more deeply that Baptism has cleansed us, the Spirit has quickened us, and the Blood of Christ has redeemed us; through Jesus Christ our Lord, who lives and reigns with you and the Holy Spirit, one God, for ever and ever. *Amen.*

11

I Lord God Almighty, who for no merit on our part hast brought us out of death into life, out of sorrow into joy: Put no end to thy gifts, fulfill thy marvelous acts in us, and grant unto us who have been justified by faith the strength to persevere in that faith; through Jesus Christ our Lord, who liveth and reigneth with thee and the Holy Spirit, one God, for ever and ever. *Amen.*

II Lord God Almighty, for no merit on our part you have brought us out of death into life, out of sorrow into joy: Put no end to your gifts, fulfill your marvelous acts in us, and grant to us who have been justified by faith the strength to persevere in that faith; through Jesus Christ our Lord, who lives and reigns with you and the Holy Spirit, one God, for ever and ever. *Amen.*

12

I O God, who dost continually increase thy Church by the birth of new sons and daughters in Baptism: Grant that they may be obedient all the days of their life to the rule of faith which they did receive in that Sacrament; through Jesus Christ thy Son our Lord, who liveth and reigneth with thee and the Holy Spirit, one God, now and for ever. *Amen.*

II O God, you continually increase your Church by the birth of new sons and daughters in Baptism: Grant that they may be obedient all the days of their life to the rule of faith which they received in that Sacrament; through Jesus Christ your Son our Lord, who lives and reigns with you and the Holy Spirit, one God, now and for ever. *Amen.*

13

I Grant, Almighty God, we beseech thee, that the commemoration of our Lord's death and resurrection may continually transform our lives and be manifest in our deeds; through Jesus Christ our Lord, who liveth and reigneth with thee and the Holy Spirit, one God, for ever and ever. *Amen.*

II Grant, Almighty God, that the commemoration of our Lord's death and resurrection may continually transform our lives and be manifested in our deeds; through Jesus Christ our Lord, who lives and reigns with you and the Holy Spirit, one God, for ever and ever. *Amen.*

14

I Hear our prayers, O Lord, and, as we confess that Christ, the Savior of the world, doth live with thee in glory, grant that, as he himself hath promised, we may perceive him present among us also, to the end of the ages; who liveth and reigneth with thee and the Holy Spirit, one God, for ever and ever. *Amen.*

II Hear our prayers, O Lord, and, as we confess that Christ, the Savior of the world, lives with you in glory, grant that, as he himself has promised, we may perceive him present among us also, to the end of the ages; who lives and reigns with you and the Holy Spirit, one God, for ever and ever. *Amen.*

15

I O Lord, who hast given unto us the grace to know the resurrection of thy Son: Grant that the Holy Spirit, by his love, may raise us to newness of life; through Jesus Christ our Lord, who liveth and reigneth with thee and the same Spirit, one God, for ever and ever. *Amen.*

II O Lord, you have given us the grace to know the resurrection of your Son: Grant that the Holy Spirit, by his love, may raise us to newness of life; through Jesus Christ our Lord, who lives and reigns with you and the Holy Spirit, one God, for ever and ever. *Amen.*

16

I O Lord, who openest the portals of thy kingdom to those who have been reborn by water and the Spirit: Increase the grace which thou hast given to thy children, that those whom thou hast cleansed from sin may attain to all thy promises; through Jesus Christ our Lord, who liveth and reigneth with thee and the Holy Spirit, one God, now and for ever. *Amen.*

II O Lord, you open the portals of your kingdom to those who have been reborn by water and the Spirit: Increase the grace you have given to your children, that those whom you have cleansed from sin may attain to all your promises; through Jesus Christ our Lord, who lives and reigns with you and the Holy Spirit, one God, now and for ever. *Amen.*

From Friday after Ascension Day until Pentecost

17

I O God, who by the resurrection of thy Son hast given unto us a new birth into eternal life: Lift our hearts, we beseech thee, to our Savior, who sitteth at thy right hand, that, when he shall come again, we who have been reborn in Baptism may be clothed in a glorious immortality; through Jesus Christ our Lord, who liveth and reigneth with thee and the Holy Spirit, one God, for ever and ever. *Amen.*

II O God, by the resurrection of your Son you have given us a new birth into eternal life: Lift our hearts to our Savior, who is seated at your right hand, so that, when he comes again, we who have been reborn in Baptism may be clothed in a glorious immortality; through Jesus Christ our Lord, who lives and reigns with you and the Holy Spirit, one God, for ever and ever. *Amen.*

18

I O God, who by the glorification of Jesus Christ and the coming of the Holy Spirit hast opened for us the gates of thy kingdom: Grant that we, who have received such great gifts, may dedicate ourselves more diligently to thy service, and live more fully the riches of our faith; through Jesus Christ our Lord, who liveth and reigneth with thee and the Holy Spirit, one God, for ever and ever. *Amen.*

II O God, by the glorification of Jesus Christ and the coming of the Holy Spirit you have opened for us the gates of your kingdom: Grant that we, who have received such great gifts, may dedicate ourselves more diligently to your service, and live more fully the riches of our faith; through Jesus Christ our Lord, who lives and reigns with you and the Holy Spirit, one God, for ever and ever. *Amen.*

19

I O Lord, whose Son, after he had ascended into heaven, did send down upon the Apostles the Holy Spirit, as he had promised, that they might comprehend the mysteries of the kingdom: Distribute among us also, we pray thee, the gifts of that selfsame Spirit; through Jesus Christ our Lord, who liveth and reigneth with thee and the same Holy Spirit, one God, for ever and ever. *Amen.*

II O Lord, when your Son ascended into heaven he sent down upon the Apostles the Holy Spirit, as he had promised, that they might comprehend the mysteries of the kingdom:

Distribute among us also, we pray, the gifts of the selfsame Spirit; through Jesus Christ our Lord, who lives and reigns with you and the Holy Spirit, one God, for ever and ever. *Amen.*

20

I O loving Father, grant, we pray thee, that thy Church, being gathered by thy Holy Spirit, may be dedicated more fully to thy service, and live united in love, according to thy will; through Jesus Christ our Lord, who liveth and reigneth with thee and the same Spirit, one God, for ever and ever. *Amen.*

II O loving Father, grant that your Church, being gathered by your Holy Spirit, may be dedicated more fully to your service, and live united in love, according to your will; through Jesus Christ our Lord, who lives and reigns with you and the Holy Spirit, one God, for ever and ever. *Amen.*

The Second Week of Easter

	Psalms	Lessons
Monday	2:1-9* or 146:4-9	Acts 4:23-31 John 3:1-8
Tuesday	93	Acts 4:32-37 John 3:7-15
Wednesday	34:1-8	Acts 5:12-26 John 3:16-21
Thursday	34:15-22	Acts 5:27-33 John 3:31-36
Friday	27:1-9	Acts 5:34-42 John 6:1-15
Saturday	33:1-5,18-22	Acts 6:1-7 John 6:16-21

Preface of Easter

* *Appointed also at Morning Prayer on this Day.*

The Third Week of Easter

	Psalms	Lessons
Monday	27:10-18	Acts 6:8-15 John 6:22-29
Tuesday	31:1-5	Acts 7:51—8:1a John 6:30-35
Wednesday	66:1-8	Acts 8:1b-8 John 6:35-40
Thursday	66:14-18 (Years A & B) 65:1-5 (Year C)	Acts 8:26-40 (Years A & B) Acts 8:9-25 (Year C) John 6:44-51
Friday	117	Acts 9:1-20 (Years A & B) Acts 9:10-20,26-31 (Year C) John 6:52-59
Saturday	116:10-17	Acts 9:31-42 (Years A & B) Acts 10:1-5,25-31, 34-35, 44-48 (Year C) John 6:60-69

Preface of Easter

The Fourth Week of Easter

	Psalms	Lessons
Monday	96:1-9	Acts 11:1-18
		John 10:11-18
		(Year A)
		John 10:1-10
		(Years B & C)
Tuesday	87	Acts 11:19-26
		John 10:22-30
Wednesday	67	Acts 12:24—13:5a
		John 12:44-50
Thursday	89:20-29	Acts 13:13-25
		John 13:16-20
Friday	2:6-13	Acts 13:26-33
		John 14:1-6
Saturday	98:1-6	Acts 13:44-52
	(Years A & B)	(Years A & B)
		Acts 13:32-43
		(Year C)
	16:5-11 (Year C)	John 14:7-14

Preface of Easter

The Fifth Week of Easter

	Psalms	Lessons
Monday	115:1-13	Acts 14:5-18 John 14:21-26
Tuesday	145:9-14	Acts 14:19-28 John 14:27-31a
Wednesday	122	Acts 15:1-6 John 15:1-8
Thursday	96:1-10	Acts 15:7-21 John 15:9-11
Friday	57:6-11	Acts 15:22-31 John 15:12-17
Saturday	100	Acts 16:1-10 John 15:18-21

Preface of Easter

The Sixth Week of Easter

	Psalms	Lessons
Monday	149	Acts 16:11-15
		John 15:26—16:4a
Tuesday	138	Acts 16:16-34
		John 16:5-11
Wednesday	148:1-2,11-14	Acts 17:15,22—18:1
		John 16:12-15

Preface of Easter

Friday	98:1-4	Acts 18:1-8
		John 16:20-23a
Saturday	47*	Acts 18:23-28
	or 93	John 16:23b-28

Preface of the Ascension

* *Appointed as an alternative for the following day.*

The Seventh Week of Easter

	Psalms	Lessons
Monday	68:1-8	Acts 19:1-8 John 16:28-33
Tuesday	68:9-10,17-20	Acts 20:17-27 John 17:1-11a
Wednesday	68:28-36	Acts 20:28-38 John 17:11b-19
Thursday	16:5-11	Acts 22:30; 23:6-11 John 17:20-26
Friday	103:1-2,19-22	Acts 25:13-21 John 21:15-19
Saturday	11:4-8	Acts 28:16-20,30-31 John 21:20-25

Preface of the Ascension

The Lesser Feasts

together with

The Fixed Holy Days

Concerning the Proper
for the Lesser Feasts

Proper Collects, Lessons, and Psalms are provided for each of the Lesser Feasts.

On occasions (such as a patronal festival) when a third Reading is desired, an appropriate selection may be made from the Common of Saints.

Any of the Readings may be lengthened at discretion. The selections from the Psalter may be lengthened or shortened.

Because the Psalm assigned to a given Proper can sometimes occur at Morning or Evening Prayer on the same day, alternative Psalmody is always provided. In every instance, the alternative Psalmody is drawn from a small corpus of selected Psalms, which makes possible the use of a limited yet practical repertory in places where weekday services are sung.

The Preface of the Season (when there is one) may be substituted for the Preface indicated in the Proper for Lesser Feasts.

The Prayer Book provided three Prefaces "Of a Saint" which may be used at discretion on certain of the Lesser Feasts. This book indicates the most appropriate of those Prefaces by the use of numerals in parentheses: (1), (2), or (3).

An appropriate Collect, Psalm, and Lessons from the Common of Saints may always be substituted for those assigned to a Lesser Feast.

Most biographical notes on this Apostle begin "Andrew was Simon Peter's brother," and he is so described in the Gospels. Identifying Andrew as Peter's brother makes it easy to know who he is, but it also makes it easy to overlook the fact of Andrew's special gift to the company of Christ. The Gospel according to John tells how Andrew, a disciple of John the Baptist, was one of two disciples who followed Jesus after John had pointed him out, saying, "Behold the Lamb of God" (John 1:29). Andrew and the other disciple went with Jesus and stayed with him, and Andrew's first act afterward was to find his brother and bring him to Jesus. We might call Andrew the first missionary in the company of disciples.

Though Andrew was not a part of the inner circle of disciples (Peter, James, and John), he is always named in the list of disciples, and appears prominently in several incidents. Andrew and Peter were fishermen, and Matthew's Gospel records Jesus' calling them from their occupation, and their immediate response to his call. Andrew was the disciple who brought the boy with the loaves and fishes to Jesus for the feeding of the multitude.

We hear little of Andrew as a prominent leader, and he seems always to be in the shadow of Peter. Eusebius, the Church historian, records his going to Scythia, but there is no reliable information about the end of his life. Tradition has it that he was fastened to an X-shaped cross and suffered death at the hands of angry pagans.

Andrew is the patron saint of Scotland.

Saint Andrew the Apostle

I   Almighty God, who didst give such grace to thine apostle Andrew that he readily obeyed the call of thy Son Jesus Christ, and brought his brother with him: Give unto us, who are called by thy Word, grace to follow him without delay, and to bring those near to us into his gracious presence; who liveth and reigneth with thee and the Holy Spirit, one God, now and for ever. *Amen.*

II   Almighty God, who gave such grace to your apostle Andrew that he readily obeyed the call of your Son Jesus Christ, and brought his brother with him: Give us, who are called by your Holy Word, grace to follow him without delay, and to bring those near to us into his gracious presence; who lives and reigns with you and the Holy Spirit, one God, now and for ever. *Amen.*

Psalm	Lessons
19	Deuteronomy 30:11-14
or 19:1-6	Romans 10:8b-18
	Matthew 4:18-22

Preface of Apostles

Nicholas Ferrar (1592-1637) was the founder of a religious community at Little Gidding, Huntingdonshire, England, which existed from 1626 to 1646. His family had been prominent in the affairs of the Virginia Company, but when that company was dissolved, he took deacon's orders, and retired to the country.

At Little Gidding, his immediate family and a few friends and servants gave themselves wholly to religious observance. They restored the derelict church near the manor house, became responsible for services there, taught many of the local children, and looked after the health and well-being of the people of the neighborhood. A regular round of prayer according to the Book of Common Prayer was observed, along with the daily recital of the whole of the Psalter. The members of the community became widely known for fasting, private prayer and meditation, and for writing stories and books illustrating themes of Christian faith and morality.

One of the most interesting of the activities of the Little Gidding community was the preparation of "harmonies" of the Gospels, one of which was presented to King Charles the First by the Ferrar family.

The community did not long survive the death of Nicholas Ferrar. However, the memory of the religious life at Little Gidding was kept alive, principally through Izaak Walton's description in his *Life of George Herbert*: "He (Ferrar) and his family . . . did most of them keep Lent and all Ember-weeks strictly, both in fasting and using all those mortifications and prayers that the Church hath appointed . . . and he and they did the like constantly on Fridays, and on the vigils or eves appointed to be fasted before the Saints' days; and this frugality and abstinence turned to the relief of the poor . . . ."

The community became an important symbol for many Anglicans when religious orders began to revive. Its life inspired T.S. Eliot, and he gave the title, "Little Gidding," to the last of his *Four Quartets*, one of the great religious poems of the twentieth century.

Nicholas Ferrar

Deacon, 1637

I Lord God, make us worthy of thy perfect love; that, with thy deacon Nicholas Ferrar and his household, we may rule ourselves according to thy Word, and serve thee with our whole heart; through Jesus Christ our Lord, who liveth and reigneth with thee and the Holy Spirit, one God, for ever and ever. *Amen.*

II Lord God, make us worthy of your perfect love; that, with your deacon Nicholas Ferrar and his household, we may rule ourselves according to your Word, and serve you with our whole heart; through Jesus Christ our Lord, who lives and reigns with you and the Holy Spirit, one God, for ever and ever. *Amen.*

Psalm	Lessons
15	Galatians 6:7-10
or 112:1-9	Matthew 13:47-52

Preface of a Saint (1)

Bishop Williams, a farmer's son, was born in Richmond, Virginia, on July 18, 1829, and brought up in straitened circumstances by his widowed mother. He attended the College of William and Mary and the Virginia Theological Seminary.

Ordained deacon in 1855, he offered himself for work in China, where he was ordained priest in 1857. Two years later, he was sent to Japan and opened work in Nagasaki. His first convert was baptized in 1866, the year he was chosen bishop for both China and Japan.

After 1868, he decided to concentrate all his work in Japan, following the revolution that opened the country to renewed contact with the western world. Relieved of his responsibility for China in 1874, Williams made his base at Yedo (now Tokyo), where he founded a divinity school, later to become St. Paul's University. At a synod in 1887 he helped bring together the English and American missions to form the *Nippon Sei Ko Kai,* the Holy Catholic Church of Japan, when the Church there numbered fewer than a thousand communicants.

Williams translated parts of the Prayer Book into Japanese; and he was a close friend and warm supporter of Bishop Schereschewsky, his successor in China, in the latter's arduous work of translating the Bible into Chinese.

After resigning his jurisdiction in 1889, Bishop Williams stayed in Japan to help his successor there, Bishop John McKim, who was consecrated in 1893. Williams lived in Kyoto and continued to work in the opening of new mission stations until his return to America in 1908. He died in Richmond, Virginia, on December 2, 1910.

Channing Moore Williams

Missionary Bishop in China and Japan, 1910

I   Almighty and everlasting God, we thank thee for thy servant Channing Moore Williams, whom thou didst call to preach the Gospel to the people of China and Japan. Raise up, we beseech thee, in this and every land evangelists and heralds of thy kingdom, that thy Church may proclaim the unsearchable riches of our Savior Jesus Christ; who liveth and reigneth with thee and the Holy Spirit, one God, for ever and ever. *Amen.*

II   Almighty and everlasting God, we thank you for your servant Channing Moore Williams, whom you called to preach the Gospel to the people of China and Japan. Raise up in this and every land evangelists and heralds of your kingdom, that your Church may proclaim the unsearchable riches of our Savior Jesus Christ; who lives and reigns with you and the Holy Spirit, one God, for ever and ever. *Amen.*

Psalm	Lessons
96:1-7	Acts 1:1-9
or 98:1-4	Luke 10:1-9

Preface of Pentecost

John of Damascus was the son of a Christian tax collector for the Mohammedan Caliph of Damascus. At an early age, he succeeded his father in this office. In about 715, he entered the monastery of St. Sabas near Jerusalem. There he devoted himself to an ascetic life and to the study of the Fathers.

In the same year that John was ordained priest, 726, the Byzantine Emperor Leo the Isaurian published his first edict against the Holy Images, which signaled the formal outbreak of the iconoclastic controversy. The edict forbade the veneration of sacred images, or icons, and ordered their destruction. In 729-730, John wrote three "Apologies (or *Treatises*) against the Iconoclasts and in Defense of the Holy Images." He argued that such pictures were not idols, for they represented neither false gods nor even the true God in his divine nature; but only saints, or our Lord as man. He further distinguished between the respect, or veneration (*proskynesis*), that is properly paid to created beings, and the worship (*latreia*), that is properly given only to God.

The iconoclast case rested, in part, upon the Monophysite heresy, which held that Christ had only one nature, and since that nature was divine, it would be improper to represent him by material substances such as wood and paint. The Monophysite heresy was condemned by the Council of Chalcedon in 451.

At issue also was the heresy of Manichaeism, which held that matter itself was essentially evil. In both of these heresies, John maintained, the Lord's incarnation was rejected. The Seventh Ecumenical Council, in 787, decreed that crosses, icons, the book of the Gospels, and other sacred objects were to receive reverence or veneration, expressed by salutations, incense, and lights, because the honor paid to them passed on to that which they represented. True worship (*latreia*), however, was due to God alone.

John also wrote a great synthesis of theology, *The Fount of Knowledge,* of which the last part, "On the Orthodox Faith," is best known.

To Anglicans, John is best known as the author of the Easter hymns, "Thou hallowed chosen morn of praise," "Come, ye faithful, raise the strain," and "The day of resurrection."

John of Damascus
Priest, c. 760

I   Confirm our minds, O Lord, in the mysteries of the true faith, set forth with power by thy servant John of Damascus; that we, with him, confessing Jesus to be true God and true Man, and singing the praises of the risen Lord, may, by the power of the resurrection, attain to eternal joy; through Jesus Christ our Lord, who liveth and reigneth with thee and the Holy Spirit, one God, now and for ever. *Amen.*

II   Confirm our minds, O Lord, in the mysteries of the true faith, set forth with power by your servant John of Damascus; that we, with him, confessing Jesus to be true God and true Man, and singing the praises of the risen Lord, may, by the power of the resurrection, attain to eternal joy; through Jesus Christ our Lord, who lives and reigns with you and the Holy Spirit, one God, now and for ever. *Amen.*

Psalm	Lessons
118:14-21	1 Corinthians 15:12-20
or 16:5-11	John 5:24-27

Preface of Easter

Clement was born in the middle of the second century. He was a cultured Greek philosopher who sought truth in many schools until he met Pantheons, founder of the Christian Catechetical School at Alexandria in Egypt. Clement succeeded Pantheons as head of that school in about 190, and was for many years an apologist for the Christian faith to both pagans and Christians. His learning and allegorical exegesis of the Bible helped to commend Christianity to the intellectual circles of Alexandria. His work prepared the way for his pupil Origen, the most eminent theologian of early Greek Christianity, and his liberal approach to secular knowledge laid the foundations of Christian humanism. During the persecution under the Emperor Severus in 202, he fled Alexandria. The exact time and place of his death are unknown.

Clement lived in the age of "Gnosticism," a comprehensive term for many theories or ways of salvation current in the second and third centuries, all emphasizing "Gnosis" or "knowledge." Salvation, for Gnostics, was to be had through a secret and rather esoteric knowledge accessible only to a few. It was salvation *from* the world, rather than salvation *of* the world. Clement asserted that there was a true Christian Gnosis, to be found in the Scriptures, available to all. Although his understanding of this Christian knowledge — ultimately knowledge of Christ — incorporated several notions of Greek philosophy which the Gnostics also held, Clement dissented from the negative Gnostic view of the world and its denial of the role of free will.

What Rich Man Will Be Saved? was the title of a treatise by Clement on Mark 10:17-31, and the Lord's words, "Go, sell what you have, and give to the poor, and you will have treasure in heaven." His interpretation sanctioned the "right use" of material goods and wealth. It has been contrasted to the interpretation of Athanasius in his *Life of Antony*, which emphasized strict renunciation. Both interpretations can be found in early Christian spirituality: Clement's, called "liberal," and that of Athanasius, "literal."

Among Clement's writings are the hymns, "Sunset to sunrise changes now" and "Master of eager youth."

Clement of Alexandria

Priest, c.210

I   O God of unsearchable wisdom, who didst give thy servant Clement grace to understand and teach the truth as it is in Jesus Christ, the source of all truth: Grant to thy Church the same grace to discern thy Word wherever truth is found; through Jesus Christ our unfailing light, who liveth and reigneth with thee and the Holy Spirit, one God, for ever and ever. *Amen.*

II   O God of unsearchable wisdom, you gave your servant Clement grace to understand and teach the truth as it is in Jesus Christ, the source of all truth: Grant to your Church the same grace to discern your Word wherever truth is found; through Jesus Christ our unfailing light, who lives and reigns with you and the Holy Spirit, one God, for ever and ever. *Amen.*

Psalm	Lessons
34:9-14	Colossians 1:11-20
or 103:1-4, 13-18	John 6:57-63

Preface of Baptism

Very little is known about the life of Nicholas, except that he suffered torture and imprisonment during the persecution under the Emperor Diocletian. It is possible that he was one of the bishops attending the First Ecumenical Council of Nicaea in 325. He was honored as a saint in Constantinople in the sixth century by the Emperor Justinian. His veneration became immensely popular in the West after the supposed removal of his body to Bari, Italy, in the late eleventh century. In England almost 400 churches were dedicated to him.

Nicholas is famed as the traditional patron of seafarers and sailors, and, more especially, of children. As a bearer of gifts to children, his name was brought to America by the Dutch colonists in New York, from whom he is popularly known as Santa Claus.

Nicholas

Bishop of Myra, c. 342

I Almighty God, who in thy love didst give to thy servant Nicholas of Myra a perpetual name for deeds of kindness both on land and sea: Grant, we pray thee, that thy Church may never cease to work for the happiness of children, the safety of sailors, the relief of the poor, and the help of those tossed by tempests of doubt or grief; through Jesus Christ our Lord, who liveth and reigneth with thee and the Holy Spirit, one God, for ever and ever. *Amen.*

II Almighty God, in your love you gave your servant Nicholas of Myra a perpetual name for deeds of kindness both on land and sea: Grant, we pray, that your Church may never cease to work for the happiness of children, the safety of sailors, the relief of the poor, and the help of those tossed by tempests of doubt or grief; through Jesus Christ our Lord, who lives and reigns with you and the Holy Spirit, one God, for ever and ever. *Amen.*

Psalm	Lessons
78:3-7	1 John 4:7-14
or 145:8-13	Mark 10:13-16

Preface of a Saint (1)

Ambrose was the son of a Roman governor in Gaul, and in 373 he himself was governor in Upper Italy. Though brought up in a Christian family, Ambrose had not been baptized. He became involved in the election of a Bishop of Milan only as mediator between the battling factions of Arians and orthodox Christians. The election was important, because the victorious party would control the powerful see of Milan.

Ambrose exhorted the nearly riotous mob to keep the peace and to obey the law. Suddenly both sides raised the cry, "Ambrose shall be our bishop!" He protested, but the people persisted. Hastily baptized, he was ordained bishop on December 7, 373.

Ambrose rapidly won renown as a defender of orthodoxy against Arianism and as a statesman of the Church. He was also a skillful hymnodist. He introduced antiphonal chanting to enrich the liturgy, and wrote straightforward, practical discourses to educate his people in such matters of doctrine as Baptism, the Trinity, the Eucharist, and the Person of Christ. His persuasive preaching was an important factor in the conversion of Augustine of Hippo.

Ambrose did not fear to rebuke emperors, including the hot-headed Theodosius, whom he forced to do public penance for the slaughter of several thousand citizens of Salonika.

About Baptism, Ambrose wrote: "After the font (of baptism), the Holy Spirit is poured on you, 'the spirit of wisdom and understanding, the spirit of counsel and strength, the spirit of knowledge and godliness, and the spirit of holy fear'" (*De Sacramentis* 3.8).

A meditation attributed to him includes these words: "Lord Jesus Christ, you are for me medicine when I am sick; you are my strength when I need help; you are life itself when I fear death; you are the way when I long for heaven; you are light when all is dark; you are my food when I need nourishment."

Among hymns attributed to Ambrose are "The eternal gifts of Christ the King," "O Splendor of God's glory bright," and a series of hymns for the Little Hours.

Ambrose

Bishop of Milan, 397

I   O God, who didst give to thy servant Ambrose grace eloquently to proclaim thy righteousness in the great congregation, and fearlessly to bear reproach for the honor of thy Name: Mercifully grant to all bishops and pastors such excellency in preaching, and fidelity in ministering thy Word, that thy people may be partakers with them of the glory that shall be revealed; through Jesus Christ our Lord, who liveth and reigneth with thee and the Holy Spirit, one God, now and for ever. *Amen.*

II   O God, you gave your servant Ambrose grace eloquently to proclaim your righteousness in the great congregation, and fearlessly to bear reproach for the honor of your Name: Mercifully grant to all bishops and pastors such excellence in preaching and faithfulness in ministering your Word, that your people may be partakers with them of the glory that shall be revealed; through Jesus Christ our Lord, who lives and reigns with you and the Holy Spirit, one God, now and for ever. *Amen.*

Psalm	Lessons
27:5-11	Ecclesiasticus 2:7-11,16-18
or 33:1-5,20-21	Luke 12:35-37,42-44

Preface of a Saint (1)

The Gospel according to John records several incidents in which Thomas appears, and from them we are able to gain some impression of the sort of man he was. When Jesus insisted on going to Judea, to visit his friends at Bethany, Thomas boldly declared, "Let us also go, that we may die with him" (John 11:16). At the Last Supper, he interrupted our Lord's discourse with the question, "Lord, we do not know where you are going; how can we know the way?" (John 14:5). And after Christ's resurrection, Thomas would not accept the account of the other apostles and the women, until Jesus appeared before him, showing him his wounds. This drew from him the first explicit acknowledgment of Christ's Godhead, "My Lord and my God!" (John 20:28).

Thomas appears to have been a thoughtful if rather literal-minded man, inclined to scepticism; but he was a staunch friend when his loyalty was once given. The expression "Doubting Thomas," which has become established in English usage, is not entirely fair to Thomas. He did not refuse belief: he wanted to believe, but did not dare, without further evidence. Because of his goodwill, Jesus gave him a sign, though Jesus had refused a sign to the Pharisees. His Lord's rebuke was well deserved: "Blessed are those who have not seen and yet believe" (John 20:29). The sign did not create faith; it merely released the faith which was in Thomas already.

According to an early tradition mentioned by Eusebius and others, Thomas evangelized the Parthians. Syrian Christians of Malabar, India, who call themselves the Mar Thoma Church, cherish a tradition that Thomas brought the Gospel to India. Several apocryphal writings have been attributed to him, the most prominent and interesting being the "Gospel of Thomas."

Thomas' honest questioning and doubt, and Jesus' assuring response to him, have given many modern Christians courage to persist in faith, even when they are still doubting and questioning.

Saint Thomas the Apostle

I   Everliving God, who didst strengthen thine apostle Thomas
with sure and certain faith in thy Son's resurrection: Grant
us so perfectly and without doubt to believe in Jesus Christ,
our Lord and our God, that our faith may never be found
wanting in thy sight; through him who liveth and reigneth
with thee and the Holy Spirit, one God, now and for ever.
Amen.

II   Everliving God, who strengthened your apostle Thomas
with firm and certain faith in your Son's resurrection: Grant
us so perfectly and without doubt to believe in Jesus Christ,
our Lord and our God, that our faith may never be found
wanting in your sight; through him who lives and reigns
with you and the Holy Spirit, one God, now and for ever.
Amen.

Psalm	Lessons
126	Habakkuk 2:1-4
	Hebrews 10:35 — 11:1
	John 20:24-29

Preface of Apostles

That Jesus was born is a fact both of history and revelation. The precise date of his birth, however, is not recorded in the Gospels, which are, after all, not biographies, and show little concern for those biographical details in which more modern Christians are interested. Such interest began to become prominent in the fourth century, together with the development of liturgical observances of the events of biblical history.

It was in Rome, in 336, that the date, December 25, was settled upon for the celebration of the Nativity. The day, coming as it does at the winter solstice, was already a sacred one, as the festival of the birth of the Unconquerable Sun (*dies natalis Solis Invicti*); but its correspondence with the historical date of Jesus' birth was stoutly maintained by learned, if ingenious, writers. The observance spread rapidly throughout the West; and it is accepted also by most of the Eastern Churches, in which, however, it does not have the prominence it has in the West.

The full title of the feast dates from the 1662 edition of the Book of Common Prayer. Prior to that revision, the day was known only as "Christmas Day." The word "Christmas," which can be traced to the twelfth century, is a contraction of "Christ's Mass."

The Nativity of Our Lord

I   O God, who makest us glad with the yearly remembrance of the birth of thy only Son Jesus Christ: Grant that as we joyfully receive him for our Redeemer, so we may with sure confidence behold him when he shall come to be our Judge; who liveth and reigneth with thee and the Holy Ghost, one God, world without end. *Amen.*

II   O God, you make us glad by the yearly festival of the birth of your only Son Jesus Christ: Grant that we, who joyfully receive him as our Redeemer, may with sure confidence behold him when he comes to be our Judge; who lives and reigns with you and the Holy Spirit, one God, now and for ever. *Amen.*

One of the sets of Psalms and Lessons on page 105 is used.

Preface of the Incarnation

A Second Proper for Christmas Day

I O God, who hast caused this holy night to shine with the illumination of the true Light: Grant us, we beseech thee, that as we have known the mystery of that Light upon earth, so may we also perfectly enjoy him in heaven; where with thee and the Holy Spirit he liveth and reigneth, one God, in glory everlasting. *Amen.*

II O God, you have caused this holy night to shine with the brightness of the true Light: Grant that we, who have known the mystery of that Light on earth, may also enjoy him perfectly in heaven; where with you and the Holy Spirit he lives and reigns, one God, in glory everlasting. *Amen.*

One of the sets of Psalms and Lessons on the following page is used.

Preface of the Incarnation

A Third Proper for Christmas Day

I Almighty God, who hast given us thy only-begotten Son to take our nature upon him and as at this time to be born of a pure virgin: Grant that we, being regenerate and made thy children by adoption and grace, may daily be renewed by thy Holy Spirit; through the same our Lord Jesus Christ, who liveth and reigneth with thee and the same Spirit ever, one God, world without end. *Amen.*

II Almighty God, you have given your only-begotten Son to take our nature upon him, and to be born [this day] of a pure virgin: Grant that we, who have been born again and made your children by adoption and grace, may daily be renewed by your Holy Spirit; through our Lord Jesus Christ, to whom with you and the same Spirit be honor and glory, now and for ever. *Amen.*

	Psalm		Lessons
I	96		Isaiah 9:2-4, 6-7
	or	96:1-4, 11-12	Titus 2:11-14
			Luke 2:1-14(15-20)
II	97		Isaiah 62:6-7, 10-12
	or	97:1-4, 11-12	Titus 3:4-7
			Luke 2:(1-14)15-20
III	98		Isaiah 52:7-10
	or	98:1-6	Hebrews 1:1-12
			John 1:1-14

Preface of the Incarnation

Very probably a Hellenistic Jew, Stephen was one of the "seven men of good repute, full of the Spirit and of wisdom" (Acts 6:3), who were chosen by the apostles to relieve them of the administrative burden of "serving tables and caring for the widows." By this appointment to assist the apostles, Stephen, the first named of those the New Testament calls "The Seven," became the first to do what the Church traditionally considers to be the work and ministry of a deacon.

It is apparent that Stephen's activities involved more than simply "serving tables," for the Acts of the Apostles speaks of his preaching and performing many miracles. These activities led him into conflict with some of the Jews, who accused him of blasphemy, and brought him before the Sanhedrin. His powerful sermon before the Council is recorded in the seventh chapter of Acts. His denunciations of the Sanhedrin so enraged its members that, without a trial, they dragged him out of the city and stoned him to death.

Saul, later called Paul, stood by, consenting to Stephen's death, but Stephen's example of steadfast faith in Jesus, and of intercession for his persecutors, was to find fruit in the mission and witness of Paul after his conversion. The Christian community in Jerusalem, taking fright at the hostility of the Judean authorities, was scattered; so that for the first time the Gospel of Christ began to spread beyond Jerusalem.

Saint Stephen, Deacon and Martyr

I   We give thee thanks, O Lord of glory, for the example of the first martyr Stephen, who looked up to heaven and prayed for his persecutors to thy Son Jesus Christ, who standeth at thy right hand; where he liveth and reigneth with thee and the Holy Spirit, one God, in glory everlasting. *Amen.*

II   We give you thanks, O Lord of glory, for the example of the first martyr Stephen, who looked up to heaven and prayed for his persecutors to your Son Jesus Christ, who stands at your right hand; where he lives and reigns with you and the Holy Spirit, one God, in glory everlasting. *Amen.*

Psalm	Lessons
31	Jeremiah 26:1-9,12-15
or 31:1-5	Acts 6:8—7:2a,51c-60
	Matthew 23:34-39

Preface of the Incarnation

John, the son of Zebedee, with his brother James, was called from being a fisherman to be a disciple and "fisher of men." With Peter and James, he became one of the inner group of three disciples whom Jesus chose to be with him at the raising of Jairus' daughter, at the Transfiguration, and in the garden of Gethsemane.

John and his brother James are recorded in the Gospel as being so hotheaded and impetuous that Jesus nicknamed them "Boanerges," which means, "sons of thunder." They also appear ambitious, in that they sought seats of honor at Jesus' right and left when he should come into his kingdom; yet they were faithful companions, willing, without knowing the cost, to share the cup Jesus was to drink. When the other disciples responded in anger to the audacity of the brothers in asking for this honor, Jesus explained that in his kingdom leadership and rule takes the form of being a servant to all.

If, as is commonly held, John is to be identified with the "disciple whom Jesus loved," then he clearly enjoyed a very special relationship with his Master, reclining close to Jesus at the Last Supper, receiving the care of his mother at the cross, and being the first to understand the truth of the empty tomb.

The Acts of the Apostles records John's presence with Peter on several occasions: the healing of the lame man at the Beautiful Gate of the Temple, before the Sanhedrin, in prison, and on the mission to Samaria to lay hands upon the new converts that they might receive the Holy Spirit.

According to tradition, John later went to Asia Minor and settled at Ephesus. Under the Emperor Domitian, he was exiled to the island of Patmos, where he experienced the visions recounted in the Book of Revelation. Irenaeus, at the end of the second century, liked to recall how Polycarp, in his old age, had talked about the apostle whom he had known while growing up at Ephesus. It is probable that John died there. He alone of the Twelve is said to have lived to extreme old age and to have been spared a martyr's death.

Saint John, Apostle and Evangelist

I Shed upon thy Church, we beseech thee, O Lord, the brightness of thy light; that we, being illumined by the teaching of thine apostle and evangelist John, may so walk in the light of thy truth, that we may at length attain to the fullness of life everlasting; through Jesus Christ our Lord, who liveth and reigneth with thee and the Holy Spirit, one God, for ever and ever. *Amen.*

II Shed upon your Church, O Lord, the brightness of your light, that we, being illumined by the teaching of your apostle and evangelist John, may so walk in the light of your truth, that at length we may attain to the fullness of eternal life; through Jesus Christ our Lord, who lives and reigns with you and the Holy Spirit, one God, for ever and ever. *Amen.*

Psalm	Lessons
92	Exodus 33:18-23
or 92:1-4,11-14	1 John 1:1-9
	John 21:19b-24

Preface of the Incarnation

Herod the Great, ruler of the Jews, appointed by the Romans in 40 B.C., kept the peace in Palestine for 37 years. His ruthless control, coupled with genuine ability, has been recorded by the Jewish historian Josephus, who describes him as "a man of great barbarity towards everyone." An Idumaean, married to the daughter of Hyrcanus, the last legal Hasmonean ruler, Herod was continually in fear of losing his throne. It is not surprising that the Wise Men's report of the birth of an infant King of the Jews (Matthew 2) caused him fear and anger. Although the event is not recorded in secular history, the story of the massacre of the Innocents is totally in keeping with what is known of Herod's character.

To protect himself against being supplanted by an infant king, Herod ordered the slaughter of all male children under two years of age in Bethlehem and the surrounding region. No one knows how many were killed, but the Church has always honored these innocent children as martyrs. Augustine of Hippo called them "buds, killed by the frost of persecution the moment they showed themselves."

The Holy Innocents

I   We remember this day, O God, the slaughter of the holy innocents of Bethlehem by the order of King Herod. Receive, we beseech thee, into the arms of thy mercy all innocent victims; and by thy great might frustrate the designs of evil tyrants and establish thy rule of justice, love, and peace; through Jesus Christ our Lord, who liveth and reigneth with thee, in the unity of the Holy Spirit, one God, for ever and ever. *Amen.*

II   We remember today, O God, the slaughter of the holy innocents of Bethlehem by King Herod. Receive, we pray, into the arms of your mercy all innocent victims; and by your great might frustrate the designs of evil tyrants and establish your rule of justice, love, and peace; through Jesus Christ our Lord, who lives and reigns with you, in the unity of the Holy Spirit, one God, for ever and ever. *Amen.*

Psalm	Lessons
124	Jeremiah 31:15-17
	Revelation 21:1-7
	Matthew 2:13-18

Preface of the Incarnation

The life and death of Thomas Becket have intrigued scholars and church people for centuries. Was he a politician or a saint? or perhaps both?

He was born in London in 1118 of a wealthy Norman family and educated in England and in France. He then became an administrator for Theobald, Archbishop of Canterbury. Later he was sent to study law in Italy and France and, after being ordained deacon, he was appointed Archdeacon of Canterbury. His administrative skills eventually brought him to the notice of King Henry II, who to Thomas's surprise, appointed him Chancellor of England. He and the King became intimate friends, and because of Becket's unquestioning loyalty and support of the King's interests in both Church and State, Henry secured Thomas's election as Archbishop of Canterbury in 1162. Becket, foreseeing a break with his Royal Master, was reluctant to accept. As Archbishop he changed, as he tells us, "from a patron of play actors and a follower of hounds, to being a shepherd of souls." He also defended the interests of the Church against those of his former friend and patron, the King. The struggle between the two became so bitter that Thomas sought exile at an abbey in France.

When he returned to England six years later, the fragile reconciliation between Henry and the Archbishop broke down. In a fit of rage the King is alleged to have asked his courtiers, "Who will rid me of this turbulent priest?" Four barons, taking Henry's words as an order, made their way to Canterbury, and upon finding the Archbishop in the cathedral, struck him down with their swords. Later, when the monks of Canterbury undressed Thomas's body to wash it and prepare it for burial, they discovered that under his episcopal robes their worldly and determined Archbishop was wearing a hair shirt. While such a garment hardly proves that a person is a saint, it clearly indicates that Thomas was motivated in the exercise of his office by far more than political considerations. His final words to the four barons before receiving the fatal blow were, "Willingly I die for the name of Jesus and in the defense of the Church."

Thomas Becket

Archbishop of Canterbury, 1170

I   O God, our strength and our salvation, who didst call thy servant Thomas Becket to be a shepherd of thy people and a defender of thy Church: Keep thy household from all evil and raise up among us faithful pastors and leaders who are wise in the ways of the Gospel; through Jesus Christ the shepherd of our souls, who liveth and reigneth with thee and the Holy Spirit, one God, for ever and ever. *Amen.*

II   O God, our strength and our salvation, you called your servant Thomas Becket to be a shepherd of your people and a defender of your Church: Keep your household from all evil and raise up among us faithful pastors and leaders who are wise in the ways of the Gospel; through Jesus Christ the shepherd of our souls, who lives and reigns with you and the Holy Spirit, one God, for ever and ever. *Amen.*

Psalm	Lessons
126	2 Esdras 2:42-48
	Matthew 10:16-22

Preface of a Saint (3)

The designation of this day as the Feast of the Holy Name is new to the 1979 revision of the Prayer Book. Previous Anglican Prayer Books called it the Feast of the Circumcision. January first is, of course, the eighth day after Christmas Day, and the Gospel according to Luke records that eight days after his birth the child was circumcised and given the name Jesus.

The Law of Moses required that every male child be circumcised on the eighth day from his birth (Leviticus 12:3); and it had long been the custom to make of it a festive occasion, when family and friends came together to witness the naming of the child.

The liturgical commemoration of the Circumcision is of Gallican origin, and a Council in Tours in 567 enacted that the day was to be kept as a fast day to counteract pagan festivities connected with the beginning of the new year. In the Roman tradition, January first was observed as the octave day of Christmas, and it was specially devoted to the Virgin Mother.

The early preachers of the Gospel lay stress on the name as showing that Jesus was a man of flesh and blood, though also the Son of God, who died a human death, and whom God raised from death to be the Savior (Acts 2:32; 4:12). The name was given to Jesus, as the angel explained to Joseph, because he would "save his people from their sins" (Matthew 1:21). (The word means "Savior" or "Deliverer" in Hebrew.)

Then as now, people longed to be freed from evils: political, social, and spiritual. The name of Jesus calls to mind the true freedom which is ours through Jesus the Christ.

The Holy Name of Our Lord

I Eternal Father, who didst give to thine incarnate Son the holy name of Jesus to be the sign of our salvation: Plant in every heart, we beseech thee, the love of him who is the Savior of the world, even our Lord Jesus Christ; who liveth and reigneth with thee and the Holy Spirit, one God, in glory everlasting. *Amen.*

II Eternal Father, you gave to your incarnate Son the holy name of Jesus to be the sign of our salvation: Plant in every heart, we pray, the love of him who is the Savior of the world, our Lord Jesus Christ; who lives and reigns with you and the Holy Spirit, one God, in glory everlasting. *Amen.*

Psalm	Lessons
8	Exodus 34:1-8
	Romans 1:1-7
	or, in year A only, Philippians 2:9-13
	Luke 2:15-21

Preface of the Incarnation

The name "Epiphany" is derived from a Greek word meaning "manifestation" or "appearing." Anglican Prayer Books interpret the word with an alternative title, "The Manifestation of Christ to the Gentiles." The last phrase, of course, is a reference to the story of the Wise Men from the East.

A Christian observance on January 6 is found as early as the end of the second century in Egypt. The feast combined commemorations of the visit of the Magi, led by the star of Bethlehem; the Baptism of Jesus in the waters of the River Jordan; and Jesus' first recorded miracle, the changing of water into wine at the marriage of Cana of Galilee — all thought of as manifestations of the incarnate Lord.

The Epiphany is still the primary Feast of the Incarnation in Eastern Churches, and the three-fold emphasis is still prominent. In the West, however, including Anglican Churches, the story of the Wise Men has tended to overshadow the other two events. Modern lectionary reform, reflected in the 1979 Prayer Book, has recovered the primitive trilogy, by setting the event of the Baptism as the theme of the First Sunday after the Epiphany in all three years, and by providing the story of the Miracle at Cana as the Gospel for the Second Sunday after the Epiphany in Year C.

The Epiphany of Our Lord

I O God, who by the leading of a star didst manifest thy
only-begotten Son to the peoples of the earth: Lead us, who
know thee now by faith, to thy presence, where we may
behold thy glory face to face; through the same Jesus Christ
our Lord, who liveth and reigneth with thee and the Holy
Spirit, one God, now and for ever. *Amen.*

II O God, by the leading of a star you manifested your only
Son to the peoples of the earth: Lead us, who know you now
by faith, to your presence, where we may see your glory face
to face; through Jesus Christ our Lord, who lives and reigns
with you and the Holy Spirit, one God, now and for ever.
Amen.

Psalm	Lessons
72	Isaiah 60:1-6,9
or 72:1-2, 10-17	Ephesians 3:1-12
	Matthew 2:1-12

Preface of the Epiphany

Julia Chester Emery was born in Dorchester, Massachusetts, in 1852. In 1876 she succeeded her sister, Mary, as Secretary of the Woman's Auxiliary of the Board of Missions which had been established by the General Convention in 1871.

During the forty years she served as Secretary, Julia helped the Church to recognize its call to proclaim the Gospel both at home and overseas. Her faith, her courage, her spirit of adventure and her ability to inspire others combined to make her a leader respected and valued by the whole Church.

She visited every diocese and missionary district within the United States, encouraging and expanding the work of the Woman's Auxiliary; and in 1908 she served as a delegate to the Pan-Anglican Congress in London. From there she traveled around the world, visiting missions in remote areas of China, in Japan, Hong Kong, the Philippines, Hawaii, and then all the dioceses on the Pacific Coast before returning to New York. In spite of the fact that travel was not easy, she wrote that she went forth "with hope for enlargement of vision, opening up new occasions for service, acceptance of new tasks."

Through her leadership a network of branches of the Woman's Auxiliary was established which shared a vision of and a commitment to the Church's mission. An emphasis on educational programs, a growing recognition of social issues, development of leadership among women, and the creation of the United Thank Offering are a further part of the legacy Julia left to the Church when she retired in 1916.

In 1921, the year before she died, the following appeared in the *Spirit of Missions*: "In all these enterprises of the Church no single agency has done so much in the last half-century to further the Church's Mission as the Woman's Auxiliary." Much of that accomplishment was due to the creative spirit of its Secretary of forty of those fifty years, Julia Chester Emery.

Julia Chester Emery

Missionary, 1922

I God of all creation, thou callest us in Christ to make
disciples of all nations and to proclaim thy mercy and
love: Grant that we, after the example of thy servant
Julia Chester Emery, may have vision and courage
in proclaiming the Gospel to the ends of the earth;
through Jesus Christ our light and our salvation, who
liveth and reigneth with thee and the Holy Spirit, one
God, for ever and ever. *Amen.*

II God of all creation, you call us in Christ to make
disciples of all nations and to proclaim your mercy and
love: Grant that we, after the example of your servant
Julia Chester Emery, may have vision and courage
in proclaiming the Gospel to the ends of the earth;
through Jesus Christ our light and our salvation, who
lives and reigns with you and the Holy Spirit, one God,
for ever and ever. *Amen.*

Psalm	Lessons
67	Romans 12:6-13
or 96:1-7	Mark 10:42-45

Preface of a Saint (2)

William Laud, born in 1573, became Archbishop of Canterbury in 1633, having been Charles the First's principal ecclesiastical adviser for several years before. He was the most prominent of a new generation of Churchmen who disliked many of the ritual practices which had developed during the reign of Elizabeth the First, and who were bitterly opposed by the "Puritans."

Laud believed the Church of England to be in direct continuity with the medieval Church, and he stressed the unity of Church and State, exalting the role of the king as the supreme governor. He emphasized the priesthood and the Sacraments, particularly the Eucharist, and caused consternation by insisting on the reverencing of the Altar, returning it to its pre-Reformation position against the east wall of the church, and hedging it about with rails.

As head of the courts of High Commission and Star Chamber, Laud was abhorred for the harsh sentencing of prominent Puritans. His identification with the unpopular policies of King Charles, his support of the war against Scotland in 1640, and his efforts to make the Church independent of Parliament, made him widely disliked. He was impeached for treason by the Long Parliament in 1640, and finally beheaded on January 10, 1645.

Laud's reputation has remained controversial to this day. Honored as a martyr and condemned as an intolerant bigot, he was compassionate in his defense of the rights of the common people against the landowners. He was honest, devout, loyal to the king and to the rights and privileges of the Church of England. He tried to reform and protect the Church in accordance with his sincere convictions. But in many ways he was out of step with the views of the majority of his countrymen, especially about the "Divine Right of Kings."

He made a noble end, praying on the scaffold: "The Lord receive my soul, and have mercy upon me, and bless this kingdom with peace and charity, that there may not be this effusion of Christian blood amongst them."

William Laud

Archbishop of Canterbury, 1645

I Keep us, O Lord, constant in faith and zealous in witness, that, like thy servant William Laud, we may live in thy fear, die in thy favor, and rest in thy peace; for the sake of Jesus Christ thy Son our Lord, who liveth and reigneth with thee and the Holy Spirit, one God, for ever and ever. *Amen.*

II Keep us, O Lord, constant in faith and zealous in witness, that, like your servant William Laud, we may live in your fear, die in your favor, and rest in your peace; for the sake of Jesus Christ your Son our Lord, who lives and reigns with you and the Holy Spirit, one God, for ever and ever. *Amen.*

Psalm	Lessons
73:24-29	Hebrews 12:5-7, 11-14
or 16:5-11	Matthew 10:32-39

Preface of a Saint (2)

Aelred was born in 1109, of a family which had long been treasurers of the shrine of Cuthbert of Lindisfarne at Durham Cathedral. While still a youth, he was sent for education in upper-class life to the court of King David of Scotland, son of Queen Margaret. The King's stepsons Simon and Waldef were his models and intimate friends. After intense disillusion and inner struggle, Aelred went to Yorkshire, where he became a Cistercian monk at the abbey of Rievaulx in 1133.

Aelred soon became a major figure in English church life. Sent to Rome on diocesan affairs of Archbishop William of York, he returned by way of Clairvaux. Here he made a deep impression on Bernard, who encouraged the young monk to write his first work, *Mirror of Charity*, on Christian perfection. In 1143, Aelred led the founding of a new Cistercian house at Revesby. Four years later he was appointed abbot of Rievaulx. By the time of his death from a painful kidney disease in 1167, the abbey had over 600 monks, including Aelred's biographer and friend, Walter Daniel. During this period, Aelred wrote his best known work, *Spiritual Friendship*.

Friendship, Aelred teaches, is both a gift from God and a creation of human effort. While love is universal, freely given to all, friendship is a particular love between individuals, of which the example is Jesus and John the Beloved Disciple. As abbot, Aelred allowed his monks to hold hands and give other expressions of friendship. In the spirit of Anselm of Canterbury and Bernard of Clairvaux, Aelred writes:

> There are four qualities which characterize a friend: loyalty, right intention, discretion, and patience. Right intention seeks for nothing other than God and natural good. Discretion brings understanding of what is done on a friend's behalf, and ability to know when to correct faults. Patience enables one to be justly rebuked, or to bear adversity on another's behalf. Loyalty guards and protects friendship, in good or bitter times.

Aelred

Abbot of Rievaulx, 1167

I   Pour thou into our hearts, we beseech thee, O God, the Holy Spirit's gift of love, that we, clasping each the other's hand, may share the joy of friendship, human and divine, and with thy servant Aelred draw many into thy community of love; through Jesus Christ the Righteous, who liveth and reigneth with thee in the unity of the Holy Spirit, one God, now and forever. *Amen.*

II   Pour into our hearts, O God, the Holy Spirit's gift of love, that we, clasping each the other's hand, may share the joy of friendship, human and divine, and with your servant Aelred draw many to your community of love; through Jesus Christ the Righteous, who lives and reigns with you, in the unity of the Holy Spirit, one God, now and forever. *Amen.*

Psalm	Lessons
36:5-10	Philippians 2:1-4
or 145:8-13	John 15:9-17
	or Mark 12:28-34a

Preface of a Saint (2)

Hilary, Bishop of Poitiers, was a prolific writer on Scripture and doctrine, an orator, and a poet to whom some of the earliest Latin hymns have been attributed. Augustine called him "the illustrious doctor of the Churches." Jerome considered him "the trumpet of the Latins against the Arians."

Hilary was born in Poitiers in Gaul, about 315, into a pagan family of wealth and power. In his writings, he describes the stages of the spiritual journey that led him to the Christian faith. He was baptized when he was about thirty.

In 350, Hilary was made Bishop of Poitiers. Although he demurred, he was finally persuaded by the people's acclamations. He proved to be a bishop of skill and courage. His Orthodoxy was shown when, in 355, the Emperor Constantius ordered all bishops to sign a condemnation of Athanasius, under pain of exile. Hilary wrote to Constantius, pleading for peace and unity. His plea accomplished nothing, and, when he dissociated himself from three Arian bishops in the West, Constantius ordered Julian (later surnamed the Apostate) to exile him to Phrygia. There he remained for three years, without complaining, writing scriptural commentaries and his principal work, *On the Trinity.*

Hilary was then invited by a party of "semi-Arians," who hoped for his support, to a Council at Seleucia in Asia, largely attended by Arians; but with remarkable courage, in the midst of a hostile gathering, Hilary defended the Council of Nicaea and the Trinity, giving no aid to the "semi-Arians." He wrote again to Constantius, offering to debate Saturninus, the Western bishop largely responsible for his exile. The Arians feared the results of such an encounter and persuaded Constantius to return Hilary to Poitiers.

In 360, Hilary was welcomed back to his see with great demonstrations of joy and affection. He continued his battle against Arianism, but he never neglected the needs of his people. Angry in controversy with heretical bishops, he was always a loving and compassionate pastor to his diocese. Among his disciples was Martin, later Bishop of Tours, whom Hilary encouraged in his endeavors to promote the monastic life.

Hilary

Bishop of Poitiers, 367

I   O Lord our God, who didst raise up thy servant Hilary to be
a champion of the catholic faith: Keep us steadfast in that
true faith which we professed at our baptism, that we may
rejoice in having thee for our Father, and may abide in thy
Son, in the fellowship of the Holy Spirit; thou who livest and
reignest for ever and ever. *Amen.*

II   O Lord our God, you raised up your servant Hilary to be
a champion of the catholic faith: Keep us steadfast in that true
faith which we professed at our baptism, that we may rejoice
in having you for our Father, and may abide in your Son, in
the fellowship of the Holy Spirit; who live and reign for ever
and ever. *Amen.*

Psalm	Lessons
37:3-6,32-33	1 John 2:18-25
or 119:97-104	Luke 12:8-12

Preface of Trinity Sunday

In the third century, many young men turned away from the corrupt and decadent society of the time, and went to live in deserts or mountains, in solitude, fasting, and prayer. Antony of Egypt was an outstanding example of this movement, but he was not merely a recluse. He was a founder of monasticism, and wrote a rule for anchorites.

Antony's parents were Christians, and he grew up to be quiet, devout, and meditative. When his parents died, he and his younger sister were left to care for a sizable estate. Six months later, in church, he heard the reading about the rich young ruler whom Christ advised to sell all he had and give to the poor. Antony at once gave his land to the villagers, and sold most of his goods, giving the proceeds to the poor. Later, after meditating on Christ's bidding, "Do not be anxious about tomorrow," he sold what remained of his possessions, placed his sister in a "house of maidens," and became an anchorite (solitary ascetic).

Athanasius, who knew Antony personally, writes that he spent his days praying, reading, and doing manual labor. For a time, he was tormented by demons in various guises. He resisted, and the demons fled. Moving to the mountains across the Nile from his village, Antony dwelt alone for twenty years. In 305, he left his cave and founded a "monastery," a series of cells inhabited by ascetics living under his rule. Athanasius writes of such colonies: "Their cells like tents were filled with singing, fasting, praying, and working that they might give alms, and having love and peace with one another."

Antony visited Alexandria, first in 321, to encourage those suffering martyrdom under the Emperor Maximinus; later, in 355, to combat the Arians by preaching, conversions, and the working of miracles. Most of his days were spent on the mountain with his disciple Macarius.

He willed a goat-skin tunic and a cloak to Athanasius, who said of him: "He was like a physician given by God to Egypt. For who met him grieving and did not go away rejoicing? Who came full of anger and was not turned to kindness? . . . What monk who had grown slack was not strengthened by coming to him? Who came troubled by doubts and failed to gain peace of mind?"

Antony
Abbot in Egypt, 356

I   O God, who by thy Holy Spirit didst enable thy servant
Antony to withstand the temptations of the world, the flesh,
and the devil: Give us grace, with pure hearts and minds, to
follow thee, the only God; through Jesus Christ our Lord,
who liveth and reigneth with thee and the same Spirit, one
God, for ever and ever. *Amen.*

II   O God, by your Holy Spirit you enabled your servant
Antony to withstand the temptations of the world, the flesh,
and the devil: Give us grace, with pure hearts and minds, to
follow you, the only God; through Jesus Christ our Lord,
who lives and reigns with you and the Holy Spirit, one God,
for ever and ever. *Amen.*

Psalm	Lessons
91:9-16	1 Peter 5:6-10
or 1	Mark 10:17-21

Preface of a Saint (2)

When Simon Bar-Jona confessed, "You are the Christ," Jesus responded, "You are Peter, and on this rock I will build my Church." This rough fisherman and his brother Andrew were the first disciples called by Jesus. Peter figures prominently in the Gospels, often stumbling, impetuous, intense, and uncouth.

It was Peter who attempted to walk on the sea, and began to sink; it was Peter who impulsively wished to build three tabernacles on the mountain of the Transfiguration; it was Peter who, just before the crucifixion, three times denied knowing his Lord.

But it was also Peter who, after Pentecost, risked his life to do the Lord's work, speaking boldly of his belief in Jesus. It was also Peter, the Rock, whose strength and courage helped the young Church in its questioning about the mission beyond the Jewish community. Opposed at first to the baptism of Gentiles, he had the humility to admit a change of heart, and to baptize the Roman centurion Cornelius and his household. Even after this, Peter had a continuing struggle with his Jewish conservatism; for Paul, writing to the Galatians, rebukes him for giving way to the demands of Jewish Christians to dissociate himself from table-fellowship with Gentiles.

Though the New Testament makes no mention of it, the tradition connecting Peter with Rome is early and virtually certain. According to a legend based on that tradition, Peter fled from Rome during the persecution under Nero. On the Appian Way, he met Christ, and asked him, "Domine, quo vadis?" ("Lord, where are you going?"). The Lord answered, "I am coming to be crucified again." Peter thereupon retraced his steps, and was shortly thereafter crucified, head downwards. "I am not worthy to be crucified as my Lord was," he is supposed to have said.

As we watch Peter struggle with himself, often stumble, love his Lord and deny him, speak rashly and act impetuously, his life reminds us that our Lord did not come to save the godly and strong but to save the weak and the sinful. Simon, an ordinary human being, was transformed by the Holy Spirit into the "Rock," and became the leader of the Church.

Confession of Saint Peter the Apostle

I Almighty Father, who didst inspire Simon Peter, first among
the apostles, to confess Jesus as Messiah and Son of the
living God: Keep thy Church steadfast upon the rock of this
faith, that in unity and peace we may proclaim the one truth
and follow the one Lord, our Savior Jesus Christ; who liveth
and reigneth with thee and the Holy Spirit, one God, now
and for ever. *Amen.*

II Almighty Father, who inspired Simon Peter, first among the
apostles, to confess Jesus as Messiah and Son of the living
God: Keep your Church steadfast upon the rock of this
faith, so that in unity and peace we may proclaim the one
truth and follow the one Lord, our Savior Jesus Christ; who
lives and reigns with you and the Holy Spirit, one God, now
and for ever. *Amen.*

Psalm	Lessons
23	Acts 4: 8-13
	1 Peter 5:1-4
	Matthew 16:13-19

Preface of Apostles

Wulfstan was one of the few Anglo-Saxon bishops to retain his see after the Norman Conquest of England in 1066. Beloved by all classes of society for his humility, charity, and courage, he was born in Warwickshire about 1008, and educated in the Benedictine abbeys of Evesham and Peterborough. He spent most of his life in the cathedral monastery of Worcester as monk, prior, and then as bishop of the see from 1062 until his death on January 18, 1095. He accepted the episcopate with extreme reluctance, but having resigned himself to it, he administered the diocese with great effectiveness. Since the see of Worcester was claimed by the province of York before its affiliation as a suffragan see of Canterbury in 1070, Wulfstan was consecrated at York. As bishop, he rapidly became famous for his continued monastic asceticism and personal sanctity.

Even though Wulfstan had been sympathetic to King Harold of Wessex, he was among those who submitted to William the Conqueror at Berkhamstead in 1066. He therefore was allowed to retain his see. At first, the Normans tended to disparage him for his lack of learning and his inability to speak French, but he became one of William's most trusted advisers and administrators, and remained loyal in support of William the First and William the Second in their work of reform and orderly government. He assisted in the compilation of the Domesday Book, and supported William the First against the rebellious barons in 1075. William came to respect a loyalty based on principle and not on self-seeking. Archbishop Lanfranc also recognized the strength of Wulfstan's character, and the two men worked together to end the practice at Bristol of kidnaping Englishmen and selling them as slaves in Ireland.

Because he was the most respected prelate of the Anglo-Saxon Church, Wulfstan's profession of canonical obedience to William the Conqueror's Archbishop of Canterbury, Lanfranc, proved to be a key factor in the transition from Anglo-Saxon to Anglo-Norman Christianity. William's policy, however, was to appoint his own fellow-Normans to the English episcopate, and by the time of William's death, in 1087, Wulfstan was the only English-born bishop still living.

Wulfstan

Bishop of Worcester, 1095

I   Almighty God, whose only-begotten Son hath led captivity captive and given gifts to thy people: Multiply among us faithful pastors, who, like thy holy bishop Wulfstan, will give courage to those who are oppressed and held in bondage; and bring us all, we pray, into the true freedom of thy kingdom; through Jesus Christ our Lord, who liveth and reigneth with thee and the Holy Spirit, one God, for ever and ever. *Amen.*

II   Almighty God, your only-begotten Son led captivity captive and gave gifts to your people: Multiply among us faithful pastors, who, like your holy bishop Wulfstan, will give courage to those who are oppressed and held in bondage; and bring us all, we pray, into the true freedom of your kingdom; through Jesus Christ our Lord, who lives and reigns with you and the Holy Spirit, one God, for ever and ever. *Amen.*

Psalm	Lessons
146:4-9	Exodus 3:1-12
or 84:7-12	John 15:5-8, 14-16

Preface of Baptism

In 236, an assembly was held at Rome to elect a pope as successor to Antherus. In the throng was Fabian, a layman from another part of Italy. Suddenly, according to the historian Eusebius, a dove flew over the crowd and lighted on Fabian's head. In spite of the fact that he was both a total stranger and not even a candidate for election, the people unanimously chose Fabian to be pope, shouting, "He is worthy! He is worthy!" Fabian was ordained to the episcopate without opposition.

During his fourteen years as pontiff, Fabian made numerous administrative reforms. He developed the parochial structure of the Church in Rome, and established the custom of venerating martyrs at their shrines in the catacombs. He appointed seven deacons and seven sub-deacons to write the lives of the martyrs, so that their deeds should not be forgotten in times to come.

When Privatus, in Africa, stirred up a new heresy, Fabian vigorously opposed and condemned his actions. He also brought back to Rome, for proper burial, the remains of Pontian, a pope whom the emperor had exiled in 235 to a certain and rapid death in the mines of Sardinia.

The Emperor Decius ordered a general persecution of the Church in 239 and 240, probably the first persecution to be carried out in all parts of the empire. Fabian was one of the earliest of those martyred, setting a courageous example for his followers, many of whom died in great torment.

Cyprian of Carthage, in a letter to Cornelius, Fabian's successor, wrote that Fabian was an incomparable man. "The glory of his death," Cyprian commented, "befitted the purity and holiness of his life."

Fabian's tombstone, the slab which covered his gravesite, still exists. It is in fragments, but the words "Fabian. . .bishop. . .martyr" are still dimly visible.

Fabian

Bishop and Martyr of Rome, 250

I   O God, who in thy providence didst single out the holy
martyr Fabian as worthy to be chief pastor of thy people,
and didst guide him so to strengthen thy Church that it
stood fast in the day of persecution: Grant that those whom
thou dost call to any ministry in the Church may be obedient
to thy call in all humility, and be enabled to carry out their
tasks with diligence and faithfulness; through Jesus Christ
our Lord, who liveth and reigneth with thee and the Holy
Spirit, one God, now and for ever. *Amen.*

II   O God, in your providence you singled out the holy martyr
Fabian as worthy to be chief pastor of your people, and
guided him so to strengthen your Church that it stood fast in
the day of persecution: Grant that those whom you call to
any ministry in the Church may be obedient to your call in
all humility, and be enabled to carry out their tasks with
diligence and faithfulness; through Jesus Christ our Lord,
who lives and reigns with you and the Holy Spirit, one God,
now and for ever. *Amen.*

Psalm	Lessons
110:1-4	2 Esdras 2:42-48
or 126	Matthew 10:16-22

Preface of a Saint (3)

As a child of twelve years, Agnes suffered for her faith, in Rome, during the cruel persecution of the Emperor Diocletian. After rejecting blandishments and withstanding threats and tortures by her executioner, she remained firm in refusal to offer worship to the heathen gods, and was burned at the stake — or, according to another early tradition, was beheaded with the sword. The early Fathers of the Church praised her courage and chastity, and remarked upon her name, which means "pure" in Greek and "lamb" in Latin.

Pilgrims still visit Agnes' tomb and the catacomb surrounding it, beneath the basilica of her name on the Via Nomentana in Rome that Pope Honorius the First (625-638) built in her honor to replace an older shrine erected by the Emperor Constantine. On her feast day at the basilica, two lambs are blessed, whose wool is woven into a scarf called the pallium, with which the Pope invests archbishops. Pope Gregory the Great sent such a pallium in 601 to Augustine, the first Archbishop of Canterbury. A representation of the pall appears on the coat of arms of Archbishops of Canterbury to this day.

Agnes

Martyr at Rome, 304

I   Almighty and everlasting God, who dost choose those whom the world deemeth powerless to put the powerful to shame: Grant us so to cherish the memory of thy youthful martyr Agnes, that we may share her pure and steadfast faith in thee; through Jesus Christ our Lord, who liveth and reigneth with thee and the Holy Spirit, one God, for ever and ever. *Amen.*

II   Almighty and everlasting God, you choose those whom the world deems powerless to put the powerful to shame: Grant us so to cherish the memory of your youthful martyr Agnes, that we may share her pure and steadfast faith in you; through Jesus Christ our Lord, who lives and reigns with you and the Holy Spirit, one God, for ever and ever. *Amen.*

Psalm	Lessons
45:11-16	Song of Solomon 2:10-13
or 116:1-8	Matthew 18:1-6

Preface of a Saint (3)

Vincent has been called the protomartyr of Spain. Little is known about the actual events surrounding his life, other than his name, his order of ministry, and the place and time of his martyrdom. He was a native of Huesca, in northeastern Spain, and was ordained deacon by Valerius, Bishop of Saragossa. In the early years of the fourth century, the fervent Christian community in Spain fell victim to a persecution ordered by the Roman emperors Diocletian and Maximian. Dacian, governor of Spain, arrested Valerius and his deacon Vincent, and had them imprisoned at Valencia.

According to one legend, Valerius had a speech impediment, and Vincent was often called upon to preach for him. When the two prisoners were challenged to renounce their faith, amid threats of torture and death, Vincent said to his bishop, "Father, if you order me, I will speak." Valerius is said to have replied, "Son, as I committed you to dispense the word of God, so I now charge you to answer in vindication of the faith which we defend." The young deacon then told the governor that he and his bishop had no intention of betraying the true God. The vehemence and enthusiasm of Vincent's defense showed no caution in his defiance of the judges, and Dacian's fury was increased by this exuberance in Christian witness. Valerius was exiled, but the angry Dacian ordered that Vincent be tortured.

Although the accounts of his martyrdom have been heavily embellished by early Christian poets, Augustine of Hippo writes that Vincent's unshakeable faith enabled him to endure grotesque punishments and, finally, death.

Records of the transfer and present whereabouts of Vincent's relics are of questionable authenticity. We are certain, however, that his cult spread rapidly throughout early Christendom and that he was venerated as a bold and outspoken witness to the truth of the living Christ.

Vincent

Deacon of Saragossa, and Martyr, 304

I   Almighty God, whose deacon Vincent, upheld by thee, was not terrified by threats nor overcome by torments: Strengthen us, we beseech thee, to endure all adversity with invincible and steadfast faith; through Jesus Christ our Lord, who liveth and reigneth with thee and the Holy Spirit, one God, for ever and ever. *Amen.*

II   Almighty God, your deacon Vincent, upheld by you, was not terrified by threats nor overcome by torments: Strengthen us to endure all adversity with invincible and steadfast faith; through Jesus Christ our Lord, who lives and reigns with you and the Holy Spirit, one God, for ever and ever. *Amen.*

Psalm	Lessons
31:1-5	Revelation 7:13-17
or 116:10-17	Luke 12:4-12

Preface of a Saint (3)

Writing about Phillips Brooks in 1930, William Lawrence, who as a young man had known him, began, "Phillips Brooks was a leader of youth. . . . His was the spirit of adventure, in thought, life, and faith." To many who know him only as the author of "O little town of Bethlehem," this part of Brooks' life and influence is little known.

Born in Boston in 1835, Phillips Brooks began his ministry in Philadelphia. His impressive personality and his eloquence immediately attracted attention. After ten years in Philadelphia, he returned to Boston as rector of Trinity Church, which was destroyed in the Boston fire three years later. It is a tribute to Brooks' preaching, character, and leadership that in four years of worshiping in temporary and bare surroundings, the congregation grew and flourished. The new Trinity Church was a daring architectural enterprise for its day, with its altar placed in the center of the chancel, "a symbol of unity; God and man and all God's creation," and was a symbol of Brooks' vision — a fitting setting for the greatest preacher of the century.

This reputation has never been challenged. His sermons have passages that still grasp the reader, though they do not convey the warmth and vitality which so impressed his hearers. James Bryce wrote, "There was no sign of art about his preaching, no touch of self-consciousness. He spoke to his audience as a man might speak to his friend, pouring forth with swift, yet quiet and seldom impassioned earnestness, the thoughts of his singularly pure and lofty spirit."

Brooks ministered with tenderness, understanding. and warm friendliness. He inspired men to enter the ministry, and taught many of them the art of preaching. He was conservative and orthodox in his theology; but his generosity of heart led him to be regarded as the leader of the liberal circles of the Church.

In 1891, he was elected Bishop of Massachusetts. The force of his personality and preaching, together with his deep devotion and loyalty, provided the spiritual leadership needed for the time. His constant concern was to turn his hearers' thoughts to the revelations of God. "Whatever happens," he wrote, "always remember the mysterious richness of human nature and the nearness of God to each one of us."

Phillips Brooks

Bishop of Massachusetts, 1893

I   O everlasting God, who didst reveal truth to thy servant Phillips Brooks, and didst so form and mold his mind and heart that he was able to mediate that truth with grace and power: Grant, we pray, that all whom thou dost call to preach the Gospel may steep themselves in thy Word, and conform their lives to thy will; through Jesus Christ our Lord, who liveth and reigneth with thee and the Holy Spirit, one God, for ever and ever. *Amen.*

II   O everlasting God, you revealed truth to your servant Phillips Brooks, and so formed and molded his mind and heart that he was able to mediate that truth with grace and power: Grant, we pray, that all whom you call to preach the Gospel may steep themselves in your Word, and conform their lives to your will; through Jesus Christ our Lord, who lives and reigns with you and the Holy Spirit, one God, for ever and ever. *Amen.*

Psalm	Lessons
84:7-12	Ephesians 3:14-21
or 33:1-5, 20-21	Matthew 24:24-27

Preface of a Saint (1)

Named by her father "much beloved daughter," Li Tim-Oi was born in Hong Kong in 1907. When she was baptized as a student, she chose the name of Florence in honor of Florence Nightingale. Florence studied at Union Theological College in Guangzhou (Canton). In 1938, upon graduation, she served in a lay capacity, first in Kowloon and then in nearby Macao.

In May 1941 Florence was ordained deaconess. Some months later Hong Kong fell to Japanese invaders, and priests could not travel to Macao to celebrate the Eucharist. Despite this setback, Florence continued her ministry. Her work came to the attention of Bishop Ronald Hall of Hong Kong, who decided that "God's work would reap better results if she had the proper title" of priest.

On January 25, 1944, the Feast of the Conversion of St. Paul, Bishop Hall ordained her priest, the first woman so ordained in the Anglican Communion.

When World War II came to an end, Florence Li Tim-Oi's ordination was the subject of much controversy. She made the personal decision not to exercise her priesthood until it was acknowledged by the wider Anglican Communion. Undeterred, she continued to minister with great faithfulness, and in 1947 was appointed rector of St. Barnabas Church in Hepu where, on Bishop Hall's instructions, she was still to be called priest.

When the Communists came to power in China in 1949, Florence undertook theological studies in Beijing to further understand the implications of the Three-Self Movement (self-rule, self-support, and self-propagation) which now determined the life of the churches. She then moved to Guangzhou to teach and to serve at the Cathedral of Our Savior. However, for sixteen years, from 1958 onwards, during the Cultural Revolution, all churches were closed. Florence was forced to work first on a farm and then in a factory. Accused of counter-revolutionary activity, she was required to undergo political re-education. Finally, in 1974, she was allowed to retire from her work in the factory.

In 1979 the churches reopened, and Florence resumed her public ministry. Then, two years later, she was allowed to visit family members living in Canada. While there, to her great joy, she was licensed as a priest in the Diocese of Montreal and later in the Diocese of Toronto, where she finally settled, until her death on February 26, 1992.

[Ordination of Florence Li Tim-Oi]

First Woman Priest in the Anglican Communion, 1944

I   Gracious God, we thank thee for calling Florence Li Tim-Oi, much-beloved daughter, to be the first woman to exercise the office of a priest in our Communion: By the grace of thy Spirit inspire us to follow her example, serving thy people with patience and happiness all our days, and witnessing in every circumstance to our Savior Jesus Christ, who liveth and reigneth with thee and the same Spirit, one God, for ever and ever. *Amen.*

II   Gracious God, we thank you for calling Florence Li Tim-Oi, much-beloved daughter, to be the first woman to exercise the office of a priest in our Communion: By the grace of your Spirit inspire us to follow her example, serving your people with patience and happiness all our days, and witnessing in every circumstance to our Savior Jesus Christ, who lives and reigns with you and the same Spirit, one God, for ever and ever. *Amen.*

Psalm	Lessons
116:1-12	Galatians 3:23-28
	Luke 10:1-9

Preface of a Saint (2)

Paul, or Saul as he was known until he became a Christian, was a Roman citizen, born at Tarsus, in present-day Turkey. He was brought up as an orthodox Jew, studying in Jerusalem for a time under Gamaliel, the most famous rabbi of the day. Describing himself, he said, "I am an Israelite, a descendant of Abraham, a member of the tribe of Benjamin" (Romans 11:1).

A few years after the death of Jesus, Saul came in contact with the new Christian movement, and became one of the most fanatical of those who were determined to stamp out this "dangerous heresy." Saul witnessed the stoning of Stephen. He was on the way to Damascus to lead in further persecution of the Christians when his dramatic conversion took place.

From that day, Paul devoted his life totally to Christ, and especially to the conversion of Gentiles. The Acts of the Apostles describes the courage and determination with which he planted Christian congregations over a large area of the land bordering the eastern Mediterranean.

His letters, the earliest of Christian writings, reveal him as the greatest of the interpreters of Christ's mind, and as the founder of Christian theology. He writes, "I have been crucified with Christ; it is no longer I who live, but Christ who lives in me; and the life I now live in the flesh I live by faith in the Son of God, who loved me and gave himself for me" (Galatians 2:20).

Paul describes himself as small and insignificant in appearance: "His letters are weighty and strong," it was said of him, "but his bodily presence is weak, and his speech of no account" (2 Corinthians 10:10). He writes of having a disability which he had prayed God to remove from him, and quotes the Lord's reply, "My grace is sufficient for you, for my power is made perfect in weakness." Therefore, Paul went on to say, "I will all the more gladly boast of my weaknesses, that the power of Christ may rest upon me" (2 Corinthians 12:9).

Paul is believed to have been martyred at Rome in the year 64 under Nero.

Conversion of Saint Paul the Apostle

I O God, who, by the preaching of thine apostle Paul, hast caused the light of the Gospel to shine throughout the world: Grant, we beseech thee, that we, having his wonderful conversion in remembrance, may show forth our thankfulness unto thee for the same by following the holy doctrine which he taught; through Jesus Christ our Lord, who liveth and reigneth with thee, in the unity of the Holy Spirit, one God, now and for ever. *Amen.*

II O God, by the preaching of your apostle Paul you have caused the light of the Gospel to shine throughout the world: Grant, we pray, that we, having his wonderful conversion in remembrance, may show ourselves thankful to you by following his holy teaching; through Jesus Christ our Lord, who lives and reigns with you, in the unity of the Holy Spirit, one God, now and for ever. *Amen.*

Psalm	Lessons
67	Acts 26:9-21
	Galatians 1:11-24
	Matthew 10:16-22

Preface of Apostles

Timothy was a native of Lystra in Asia Minor, the son of a Greek father and a Jewish mother who was a believer. We learn from the Acts of the Apostles that "He was well spoken of by the brethren at Lystra and Iconium. Paul wanted Timothy to accompany him; and he took him and circumcised him because of the Jews who were in those places, for they all knew that his father was a Greek" (Acts 16:1-3). In addition to being a devoted companion of Paul, Timothy was entrusted with missions to the Thessalonians, to encourage them under persecution, and to the Corinthians, to strengthen the converts in the faith. Timothy became Paul's representative at Ephesus, and, according to Eusebius, the first bishop of that city.

Titus was, like Timothy, a companion of Paul, who calls him "my true child in the common faith" (Titus 1:4). Titus, a Greek, accompanied Paul and Barnabas from Antioch to Jerusalem at the time of the apostolic council. During Paul's third missionary journey, Titus was sent on urgent missions to Corinth. Paul writes, "And besides our own comfort we rejoice still more at the joy of Titus because his mind has been set at rest by you all. . . . And his heart goes out all the more to you, as he remembers the obedience of you all and the fear and trembling with which you received him" (2 Corinthians 7:13, 15).

Later, Titus was entrusted with the organization of the Church in Crete, where Eusebius reports he was the first bishop. Paul writes, "This is why I left you in Crete, that you might amend what was defective and appoint presbyters in every town as I directed you" (Titus 1:5).

As companions of Paul, Timothy and Titus are commemorated together close to the feast of Paul's conversion. Paul several times mentions their youth, while entrusting them with great responsibilities in administration and in the proclaiming of the Gospel, a reminder that not age but faithfulness, care, and the love of Christ are the important qualities for Christian witness to the Lord.

Timothy and Titus

Companions of Saint Paul

I   Almighty God, who didst call Timothy and Titus to do the
work of evangelists and teachers, and didst make them
strong to endure hardship: Strengthen us to stand fast in
adversity, and to live godly and righteous lives in this present
time, that with sure confidence we may look for our blessed
hope, the glorious appearing of our great God and Savior
Jesus Christ; who liveth and reigneth with thee and the Holy
Spirit, one God, now and for ever. *Amen.*

II   Almighty God, you called Timothy and Titus to be
evangelists and teachers, and made them strong to endure
hardship: Strengthen us to stand fast in adversity, and to live
godly and righteous lives in this present time, that with sure
confidence we may look for our blessed hope, the glorious
appearing of our great God and Savior Jesus Christ; who
lives and reigns with you and the Holy Spirit, one God, now
and for ever. *Amen.*

Psalm	Lessons
112:1-9	2 Timothy 1:1-8
or 23	*or* Titus 1:1-5
	John 10:1-10

Preface of Pentecost

John Chrysostom, Patriarch of Constantinople, is one of the great saints of the Eastern Church. He was born about 354 in Antioch, Syria. As a young man, he responded to the call of desert monasticism until his health was impaired. He returned to Antioch after six years, and was ordained a presbyter. In 397, he became Patriarch of Constantinople. His episcopate was short and tumultuous. Many criticized his ascetical life in the episcopal residence, and he incurred the wrath of the Empress Eudoxia, who believed that he had called her a "Jezebel." He was twice exiled, and he died during the second period of banishment, on September 14, 407. Thirty-one years later, his remains were brought back to Constantinople, and buried on January 27.

John, called "Chrysostom," which means "the golden-mouthed," was one of the greatest preachers in the history of the Church. People flocked to hear him. His eloquence was accompanied by an acute sensitivity to the needs of people. He saw preaching as an integral part of pastoral care, and as a medium of teaching. He warned that if a priest had no talent for preaching the Word, the souls of those in his charge "will fare no better than ships tossed in the storm."

His sermons provide insights into the liturgy of the Church, and especially into eucharistic practices. He describes the liturgy as a glorious experience, in which all of heaven and earth join. His sermons emphasize the importance of lay participation in the Eucharist. "Why do you marvel," he wrote, "that the people anywhere utter anything with the priest at the altar, when in fact they join with the Cherubim themselves, and the heavenly, powers, in offering up sacred hymns?"

His treatise, *Six Books on the Priesthood*, is a classic manual on the priestly office and its awesome demands. The priest, he wrote, must be "dignified, but not haughty; awe-inspiring, but kind; affable in his authority; impartial, but courteous; humble, but not servile, strong but gentle. . . ."

John Chrysostom

Bishop of Constantinople, 407

I   O God, who didst give to thy servant John Chrysostom grace eloquently to proclaim thy righteousness in the great congregation, and fearlessly to bear reproach for the honor of thy Name: Mercifully grant to all bishops and pastors such excellency in preaching, and fidelity in ministering thy Word, that thy people may be partakers with them of the glory that shall be revealed; through Jesus Christ our Lord, who liveth and reigneth with thee and the Holy Spirit, one God, for ever and ever. *Amen.*

II   O God, you gave your servant John Chrysostom grace eloquently to proclaim your righteousness in the great congregation, and fearlessly to bear reproach for the honor of your Name: Mercifully grant to all bishops and pastors such excellence in preaching, and faithfulness in ministering your Word, that your people may be partakers with them of the glory that shall be revealed; through Jesus Christ our Lord, who lives and reigns with you and the Holy Spirit, one God, for ever and ever. *Amen.*

Psalm	Lessons
49:1-8	Jeremiah 1:4-10
or 34:15-22	Luke 21:12-15

Preface of a Saint (2)

Thomas Aquinas is the greatest theologian of the high Middle Ages, and, next to Augustine, perhaps the greatest theologian in the history of Western Christianity. Born into a noble Italian family, probably in 1225, he entered the new Dominican Order of Preachers, and soon became an outstanding teacher in an age of intellectual ferment.

Perceiving the challenges that the recent rediscovery of Aristotle's works might entail for traditional catholic doctrine, especially in its emphasis upon empirical knowledge derived from reason and sense perception, independent of faith and revelation, Thomas asserted that reason and revelation are in basic harmony. "Grace" (revelation), he said, "is not the denial of nature" (reason), "but the perfection of it." This synthesis Thomas accomplished in his greatest works, the *Summa Theologica* and the *Summa Contra Gentiles*, which even today continue to exercise profound influence on Christian thought and philosophy. He was considered a bold thinker, even a "radical," and certain aspects of his thought were condemned by the ecclesiastical authorities. His canonization on July 18, 1323, vindicated him.

Thomas understood God's disclosure of his Name, in Exodus 3:14, "I Am Who I Am," to mean that God is Being, the Ultimate Reality from which everything else derives its being. The difference between God and the world is that God's essence is to exist, whereas all other beings derive their being from him by the act of creation. Although, for Thomas, God and the world are distinct, there is, nevertheless, an analogy of being between God and the world, since the Creator is reflected in his creation. It is possible, therefore, to have a limited knowledge of God, by analogy from the created world. On this basis, human reason can demonstrate that God exists; that he created the world; and that he contains in himself, as their cause, all the perfections which exist in his creation. The distinctive truths of Christian faith, however, such as the Trinity and the Incarnation, are known only by revelation.

Thomas died in 1274, just under fifty years of age. In 1369, on January 28, his remains were transferred to Toulouse. In addition to his many theological writings, he composed several eucharistic hymns. They include "O saving Victim" and "Now my tongue, the mystery telling."

Thomas Aquinas
Priest and Friar, 1274

I Almighty God, who hast enriched thy Church with the
singular learning and holiness of thy servant Thomas
Aquinas: Enlighten us more and more, we pray thee, by the
disciplined thinking and teaching of Christian scholars, and
deepen our devotion by the example of saintly lives; through
Jesus Christ our Lord, who liveth and reigneth with thee and
the Holy Spirit, one God, for ever and ever. *Amen.*

II Almighty God, you have enriched your Church with the
singular learning and holiness of your servant Thomas
Aquinas: Enlighten us more and more, we pray, by the
disciplined thinking and teaching of Christian scholars, and
deepen our devotion by the example of saintly lives; through
Jesus Christ our Lord, who lives and reigns with you and the
Holy Spirit, one God, for ever and ever. *Amen.*

Psalm	Lessons
37:3-6,32-33	Wisdom 7:7-14
or 119:97-104	Matthew 13:47-52

Preface of Trinity Sunday

Next to Patrick, Brigid is the most beloved of Irish saints. Born at Fauchart about the middle of the fifth century, she may have met Patrick as a young girl. She was said to be the daughter of Dubhthach, poet laureate of King Loeghaire, and was reared in a Druid household. She decided early in life to dedicate her life to God alone as a Christian. She received a nun's veil from Bishop Macaile of Westmeath.

Gathering around her a group of women, Brigid, in 470, founded a nunnery at Kildare, a place whose name meant "Church of the Oak." Here had flourished the cult of a pagan goddess, from which it was said to have derived the sacred fire, which she and her successors maintained. To secure the sacraments, Brigid persuaded the anchorite Conlaed to receive episcopal ordination and to bring his community of monks to Kildare, thus establishing the only known Irish double monastery of men and women. Brigid actively participated in policy-making decisions in Church conventions. One story has it that she received episcopal orders, which may reflect only the fact that she exercised the jurisdictional authority that was customarily wielded by medieval abbesses.

Many stories are told of Brigid's concern for the poor and needy. When a leper woman asked for milk she was healed also of her infirmity. Two blind men were given their sight. Best known is the tale that tells of Brigid's taming of a wolf at the request of a local chieftain whose pet dog had been killed accidentally by a peasant. The Gaelic name given to the oyster-catching bird, *galle-brigade*, attests to her affinity for birds. Her feast day itself, February 1, was long held sacred as Imbolg, the Celtic festival of Spring.

Brigid died about 523 at Kildare, outside whose small cathedral the foundations of her fire-house are still shown to tourists. Her remains are said to have been re-interred, at the time of the Danish invasions of the ninth century, with those of Patrick, at Downpatrick.

Brigid, also known as Bride, was very popular both in Scotland and England, where many churches have been dedicated to her. The best known of them is that church which was designed by Christopher Wren on Fleet Street in London. In Wales, Brigid achieved fame under her Gaelic name Ffraid.

Brigid (Bride)

I   Everliving God, we rejoice today in the fellowship of thy blessed servant Brigid, and we give thee thanks for her life of devoted service. Inspire us with life and light, and give us perseverance to serve thee all our days; through Jesus Christ our Lord, who with thee and the Holy Spirit liveth and reigneth, one God, for ever and ever. *Amen.*

II   Everliving God, we rejoice today in the fellowship of your blessed servant Brigid, and we give you thanks for her life of devoted service. Inspire us with life and light, and give us perseverance to serve you all our days; through Jesus Christ our Lord, who with you and the Holy Spirit lives and reigns, one God, for ever and ever. *Amen.*

Psalm	Lessons
138	1 Corinthians 1:26-31
or 1	Matthew 6:25-33

Preface of a Saint (2)

Today's Feast is sometimes known as the Purification of Saint Mary the Virgin, sometimes as Candlemas. In the Eastern Church it has been called the Meeting of Christ with Simeon. Such a variety of names is sufficient testimony to the wealth of spiritual meaning that generations of Christians have discovered in this small incident.

The title, "The Presentation," reminds us of the Jewish law (Exodus 13:2; 22:29) that every firstborn son had to be dedicated to God in memory of the Israelites' deliverance from Egypt, when the firstborn sons of the Egyptians died and those of Israel were spared.

When Mary placed her small son into the arms of Simeon, it was the meeting of the Old and New Dispensations. The old sacrifices, the burnt offerings and oblations, were done away; a new and perfect offering had come into the temple. God had provided himself a lamb for the burnt-offering (Genesis 22:8), his only Son. The offering was to be made once for all on the cross. At every Eucharist those who are in Christ recall that sinless offering and unite "themselves, their souls and bodies" with the self-oblation of their Lord and Savior.

The Presentation of Our Lord

I Almighty and everliving God, we humbly beseech thee that, as thy only-begotten Son was this day presented in the temple, so we may be presented unto thee with pure and clean hearts by the same thy Son Jesus Christ our Lord; who liveth and reigneth with thee and the Holy Spirit, one God, now and for ever. *Amen.*

II Almighty and everliving God, we humbly pray that, as your only-begotten Son was this day presented in the temple, so we may be presented to you with pure and clean hearts by Jesus Christ our Lord; who lives and reigns with you and the Holy Spirit, one God, now and for ever. *Amen.*

Psalm	Lesson
84	Malachi 3:1-4
or 84:1-6	Hebrews 2:14-18
	Luke 2:22-40

Preface of the Epiphany

Anskar (Latinized as Ansgarius) was one of those valiant Christians of whom it might be said, "These shall plant the seed, but others shall reap the harvest." As Archbishop of Hamburg, he was papal legate for missionary work among the Scandinavians. The immediate result of his devoted and perilous labors was slight: two churches established on the border of Denmark and one priest settled in Sweden. He also participated in the consecration of Gotbert, first bishop in Sweden.

Anskar was born in Corbie, France, in 801, and educated in the outstanding monastic school there. His teaching skill led him to be chosen master of a new monastery school, sent out by Corbie, in Saxon Germany. His strongest call, however, was to be a missionary.

He was stirred, his biographer Rimbert says, by a prolonged vision, in which a voice said, "Go and return to me crowned with martyrdom." When King Harald of Denmark sought missionaries for that country in 826, Anskar was one of those selected. Rimbert notes that Anskar's missionary purpose caused astonishment. Why should he wish to leave his brothers to deal with "unknown and barbarous folk?" Some of the brethren tried to deter him; others considered him a freak.

Steadfast in his resolve, Anskar established a school and mission in Denmark, working conscientiously but unsuccessfully to convert and evangelize. He was not totally discouraged. Another vision appeared, with a voice saying, "Go and declare the work of God to the nations." Shortly afterward (about 829), he was called to Sweden and eagerly accepted. Meager aid both from the monastery and the emperor frustrated his efforts.

While still a young man, Anskar was consecrated Archbishop of Hamburg in 831, and continued his work among the Scandinavians until 848, when he retired to the See of Bremen. The seeds of his efforts were not to bear fruit until over one hundred years later, when Viking devastation, weakness in the Frankish Church, and the lowest ebb of missionary enthusiasm, came to an end. The rich harvest of conversion was three generations away. Nevertheless, Anskar is looked upon by Scandinavians as their apostle.

Anskar

Archbishop of Hamburg, Missionary to Denmark and Sweden, 865

I   Almighty and everlasting God, who didst send thy servant Anskar as an apostle to the people of Scandinavia, and didst enable him to lay a firm foundation for their conversion, though he did not see the results of his labors: Keep thy Church from discouragement in the day of small things, knowing that when thou hast begun a good work thou wilt bring it to a fruitful conclusion; through Jesus Christ our Lord, who liveth and reigneth with thee and the Holy Spirit, one God, for ever and ever. *Amen.*

II   Almighty and everlasting God, you sent your servant Anskar as an apostle to the people of Scandinavia, and enabled him to lay a firm foundation for their conversion, though he did not see the results of his labors: Keep your Church from discouragement in the day of small things, knowing that when you have begun a good work you will bring it to a fruitful conclusion; through Jesus Christ our Lord, who lives and reigns with you and the Holy Spirit, one God, for ever and ever. *Amen.*

Psalm	Lessons
96:1-7	Acts 1:1-9
or 98:1-4	Mark 6:7-13

Preface of Apostles

All that we know about Cornelius is contained in the Acts of the Apostles (chapters 10-11). He was the first Gentile converted to the Christian faith, along with his household. A centurion was commander of a company of one hundred men in the Roman army, responsible for their discipline, both on the field of battle and in camp. A centurion was a Roman citizen, a military career man, well-paid, and generally noted for courage and competence. Some centurions, such as Cornelius, and those whom we know about from the Gospel narratives, were men of deep religious piety.

The author of Acts considered Cornelius' conversion very momentous for the future of Christianity. He records that it occurred as the result of divine intervention and revelation, and as a response to the preaching of Peter the chief apostle. The experience of Cornelius' household was regarded as comparable to a new Pentecost, and it was a primary precedent for the momentous decision of the apostolic council, held in Jerusalem a few years later, to admit Gentiles to full and equal partnership with Jewish converts in the household of faith.

According to tradition, Cornelius was the second Bishop of Caesarea, the metropolitan see of Palestine. Undoubtedly, Cornelius and his household formed the nucleus of the first Church in this important city, a Church that was gathered by Philip the Evangelist (Acts 8:40 and 21:8).

Cornelius the Centurion

I   O God, who by thy Spirit didst call Cornelius the Centurion to be the first Christian among the Gentiles: Grant to thy Church, we beseech thee, such a ready will to go where thou dost send and to do what thou dost command, that under thy guidance it may welcome all who turn to thee in love and faith, and proclaim the Gospel to all nations; through Jesus Christ our Lord, who liveth and reigneth with thee and the Holy Spirit, one God, for ever and ever. *Amen.*

II   O God, by your Spirit you called Cornelius the Centurion to be the first Christian among the Gentiles: Grant to your Church such a ready will to go where you send and to do what you command, that under your guidance it may welcome all who turn to you in love and faith, and proclaim the Gospel to all nations; through Jesus Christ our Lord, who lives and reigns with you and the Holy Spirit, one God, for ever and ever. *Amen.*

Psalm	Lessons
67	Acts 11:1-18
or 33:1-5,20-21	Luke 13:22-29

Preface of Pentecost

The introduction of Christianity into Japan in the sixteenth century, first by the Jesuits under Francis Xavier, and then by the Franciscans, has left exciting records of heroism and self-sacrifice in the annals of Christian missionary endeavor. It has been estimated that by the end of that century there were about 300,000 baptized believers in Japan.

Unfortunately, these initial successes were compromised by rivalries among the religious orders; and the interplay of colonial politics, both within Japan and between Japan and the Spanish and Portuguese, aroused suspicion about western intentions of conquest. After a half century of ambiguous support by some of the powerful Tokugawa *shoguns*, the Christian enterprise suffered cruel persecution and suppression.

The first victims were six Franciscan friars and twenty of their converts who were crucified at Nagasaki, February 5, 1597. By 1630, what was left of Christianity in Japan was driven underground. Yet it is remarkable that two hundred and fifty years later there were found many men and women, without priests, who had preserved through the generations a vestige of Christian faith.

The Martyrs of Japan
1597

I   O God our Father, who art the source of strength to all thy saints, and who didst bring the holy martyrs of Japan through the suffering of the cross to the joys of life eternal: Grant that we, being encouraged by their example, may hold fast the faith that we profess, even unto death; through Jesus Christ our Lord, who liveth and reigneth with thee and the Holy Spirit, one God, now and for ever. *Amen.*

II   O God our Father, source of strength to all your saints, you brought the holy martyrs of Japan through the suffering of the cross to the joys of eternal life: Grant that we, encouraged by their example, may hold fast the faith we profess, even to death itself; through Jesus Christ our Lord, who lives and reigns with you and the Holy Spirit, one God, now and for ever. *Amen.*

Psalm	Lessons
116:1-8	Galatians 2:19-20
or 16:5-11	Mark 8:34-38

Preface of Holy Week

Absalom Jones was born a house slave in 1746 in Delaware. He taught himself to read out of the New Testament, among other books. When sixteen, he was sold to a store owner in Philadelphia. There he attended a night school for Blacks, operated by Quakers. At twenty, he married another slave, and purchased her freedom with his earnings.

Jones bought his own freedom in 1784. At St. George's Methodist Episcopal Church, he served as lay minister for its Black membership. The active evangelism of Jones and that of his friend, Richard Allen, greatly increased Black membership at St. George's. The alarmed vestry decided to segregate Blacks into an upstairs gallery, without notifying them. During a Sunday service when ushers attempted to remove them, the Blacks indignantly walked out in a body.

In 1787, Black Christians organized the Free African Society, the first organized Afro-American society, and Absalom Jones and Richard Allen were elected overseers. Members of the Society paid monthly dues for the benefit of those in need. The Society established communication with similar Black groups in other cities. In 1792, the Society began to build a church, which was dedicated on July 17, 1794.

The African Church applied for membership in the Episcopal Diocese of Pennsylvania on the following conditions: 1, that they be received as an organized body; 2, that they have control over their local affairs; 3, that Absalom Jones be licensed as layreader, and, if qualified, be ordained as minister. In October 1794 it was admitted as St. Thomas African Episcopal Church. Bishop White ordained Jones as deacon in 1795 and as priest on September 21, 1802.

Jones was an earnest preacher. He denounced slavery, and warned the oppressors to "clean their hands of slaves." To him, God was the Father, who always acted on "behalf of the oppressed and distressed." But it was his constant visiting and mild manner that made him beloved by his own flock and by the community. St. Thomas Church grew to over 500 members during its first year. Known as "the Black Bishop of the Episcopal Church," Jones was an example of persistent faith in God and in the Church as God's instrument.

Absalom Jones

Priest, 1818

I   Set us free, O heavenly Father, from every bond of prejudice
and fear; that, honoring the steadfast courage of thy servant
Absalom Jones, we may show forth in our lives the
reconciling love and true freedom of the children of God,
which thou hast given us in thy Son our Savior Jesus Christ;
who liveth and reigneth with thee and the Holy Spirit, one
God, now and for ever. *Amen.*

II   Set us free, heavenly Father, from every bond of prejudice
and fear; that, honoring the steadfast courage of your
servant Absalom Jones, we may show forth in our lives the
reconciling love and true freedom of the children of God,
which you have given us in your Son our Savior Jesus Christ;
who lives and reigns with you and the Holy Spirit, one God,
now and for ever. *Amen.*

Psalm	Lessons
137:1-6	Isaiah 61:1-4*
or 126	*or* Isaiah 42:5-9
	John 15:12-15

Preface of a Saint (1)

* *In some years this passage will occur at the Daily Office on this day.*

Cyril and Methodius, brothers born in Thessalonika, are honored as apostles to the southern Slavs and as the founders of Slavic literary culture. Cyril was a student of philosophy and a deacon, who eventually became a missionary monastic. Methodius was first the governor of a Slavic colony, then turned to the monastic life, and was later elected abbot of a monastery in Constantinople.

In 862, the King of Moravia asked for missionaries who would teach his people in their native language. Since both Cyril and Methodius knew Slavonic, and both were learned men—Cyril was known as "the Philosopher"—the Patriarch chose them to lead the mission.

As part of his task among the Moravians, Cyril invented an alphabet to transcribe the native tongue, probably the "glagolithic," in which Slavo-Roman liturgical books in Russian and Serbian are still written. The so-called "cyrillic" alphabet is thought to have been originated by Cyril's followers.

Pressures by the German clergy, who opposed the brothers' teaching, preaching, and writing in Slavonic, and the lack of a bishop to ordain new priests for their people, caused the two brothers to seek foreign help. They found a warm welcome at Rome from Pope Adrian the Second, who determined to ordain both men bishops and approved the Slavonic liturgy. Cyril died in Rome and was buried there. Methodius, now a bishop, returned to Moravia as Metropolitan of Sirmium.

Methodius, still harassed by German bishops, was imprisoned at their behest. Eventually, he was released by Pope John the Eighth, on the condition that Slavonic, "a barbarous language," be used only for preaching. Later, the enmity of the Moravian prince caused Methodius to be recalled to Rome on charges of heresy. Papal support again allowed him to return to Moravia and to use Slavonic in the liturgy.

Methodius completed a Slavonic translation of the Bible and of Byzantine ecclesiastical law, while continuing his missionary activities. At his funeral, celebrated in Greek, Latin, and Slavonic, "the people came together in huge numbers . . . for Methodius had been all things to all people that he might lead them all to heaven."

Cyril and Methodius

Monk and Bishop, Missionaries to the Slavs, 869, 885

I   Almighty and everlasting God, who by the power of the Holy Spirit didst move thy servant Cyril and his brother Methodius to bring the light of the Gospel to a hostile and divided people: Overcome, we pray thee, by the love of Christ, all bitterness and contention among us, and make us one united family under the banner of the Prince of Peace; who liveth and reigneth with thee and the Holy Spirit, one God, now and for ever. *Amen.*

II   Almighty and everlasting God, by the power of the Holy Spirit you moved your servant Cyril and his brother Methodius to bring the light of the Gospel to a hostile and divided people: Overcome all bitterness and strife among us by the love of Christ, and make us one united family under the banner of the Prince of Peace; who lives and reigns with you and the Holy Spirit, one God, now and for ever. *Amen.*

Psalm	Lessons
96:1-7	Ephesians 3:1-7
or 98:1-4	Mark 16:15-20

Preface of Apostles

In 1696, Thomas Bray, an English country parson, was invited by the Bishop of London to be responsible for the oversight of Church work in the colony of Maryland. Three years later, as the Bishop's Commissary, he sailed to America for his first, and only, visitation. Though he spent only two and a half months in Maryland, Bray was deeply concerned about the neglected state of the American churches, and the great need for the education of clergymen, lay people, and children. At a general visitation of the clergy at Annapolis, before his return to England, he emphasized the need for the instruction of children, and insisted that no clergyman be given a charge unless he had a good report from the ship he came over in, "whether . . . he gave no matter of scandal, and whether he did constantly read prayers twice a day and catechize and preach on Sundays, which, notwithstanding the common excuses, I know can be done by a minister of any zeal for religion." His understanding of, and concern for, Native Americans and Blacks were far ahead of his time. He founded thirty-nine lending libraries in America, as well as numerous schools. He raised money for missionary work and influenced young English priests to go to America.

Bray tried hard to have a bishop consecrated for America, but failed. His greatest contributions were the founding of the Society for Promoting Christian Knowledge and the Society for the Propagation of the Gospel, both of which are still effectively in operation after two and a half centuries of work all over the world.

From 1706 to 1730, Bray was the rector of St. Botolph Without, Aldgate, London, where, until his death at the age of 72, he served with energy and devotion, while continuing his efforts on behalf of Black slaves in America, and in the founding of parochial libraries.

When the deplorable condition of English prisons was brought to Bray's attention, he set to work to influence public opinion and to raise funds to alleviate the misery of the inmates. He organized Sunday "Beef and Beer" dinners in prisons, and advanced proposals for prison reform. It was Thomas Bray who first suggested to General Oglethorpe the idea of founding a humanitarian colony for the relief of honest debtors, but he died before the Georgia colony became a reality.

Thomas Bray

Priest and Missionary, 1730

I   O God of compassion, who didst open the eyes of thy
servant Thomas Bray to see the needs of the Church in the
New World, and didst lead him to found societies to meet
those needs: Make the Church in this land diligent at all
times to propagate the Gospel among those who have not
received it, and to promote the spread of Christian
knowledge; through Jesus Christ our Lord, who liveth and
reigneth with thee and the Holy Spirit, one God, for ever and
ever. *Amen.*

II   O God of compassion, you opened the eyes of your servant
Thomas Bray to see the needs of the Church in the New
World, and led him to found societies to meet those needs:
Make the Church in this land diligent at all times to
propagate the Gospel among those who have not received it,
and to promote the spread of Christian knowledge; through
Jesus Christ our Lord, who lives and reigns with you and the
Holy Spirit, one God, for ever and ever. *Amen.*

Psalm	Lessons
102:15-22	Isaiah 52:7-10
or 85:8-13	Luke 10:1-9

Preface of Pentecost

Janani Luwum was born in 1922 at Acholi in Uganda, near the Sudanese border. After his early years as a teacher and lay reader in Gulu, he was sent to St. Augustine's College, Canterbury. He was ordained priest in 1956 and returned to Uganda to assume responsibility for twenty-four congregations. After several years of service that included work at a local theological college, Luwum returned to England on scholarship for further study at the London College of Divinity.

In 1969 Luwum became Bishop of Northern Uganda, where he was a faithful visitor to his parishes as well as a growing influence at international gatherings of the Anglican Communion. In 1974 he was elected Archbishop of the Church of Uganda, Rwanda, Burundi, and Boga-Zaire.

Luwum's new position brought him into direct contact and eventual confrontation with the Ugandan military dictator, Idi Amin, as the Archbishop sought to protect his people from the brutality of Amin's regime. In August of 1976 Makerere University was sacked by government troops. With Archbishop Luwum as their chair, the Christian leaders of the country drafted a strong memorandum of protest against officially sanctioned rape and murder.

In early February 1977 the Archbishop's residence was searched for arms by government security forces. On February 16 President Amin summoned Luwum to his palace. He went there, accompanied by the other Anglican bishops and by the Roman Catholic cardinal archbishop and a senior leader of the Muslim community. After being accused of complicity in a plot to murder the President, most of the clerics were allowed to leave. However, Archbishop Luwum was ordered to remain behind. As his companions departed, Luwum said, "They are going to kill me. I am not afraid." He was never seen alive again. The following day the government announced that he had been killed in an automobile accident while resisting arrest. Only after some weeks had passed was his bullet-riddled body released to his family for burial.

Early in his confrontation with the Ugandan government, Archbishop Luwum answered one of his critics by saying, "I do not know how long I shall occupy this chair. I live as though there will be no tomorrow. . . . While the opportunity is there, I preach the Gospel with all my might, and my conscience is clear before God."

[Janani Luwum]
Archbishop of Uganda, and Martyr, 1977

I   O God, whose Son the Good Shepherd laid down his life for
the sheep: We give thee thanks for thy faithful shepherd Janani
Luwum, who after his Savior's example, gave up his life for the
people of Uganda. Grant us to be so inspired by his witness that
we make no peace with oppression, but live as those who are
sealed with the cross of Christ, who died and rose again, and now
liveth and reigneth with thee and the Holy Spirit, one God, for
ever and ever. *Amen.*

II   O God, whose Son the Good Shepherd laid down his life for
the sheep: We give you thanks for your faithful shepherd Janani
Luwum, who after his Savior's example, gave up his life for the
people of Uganda. Grant us to be so inspired by his witness that
we make no peace with oppression, but live as those who are
sealed with the cross of Christ, who died and rose again, and now
lives and reigns with you and the Holy Spirit, one God, for ever
and ever. *Amen.*

Psalm

119:41-48
John 12: 24-32

Lessons

Ecclesiasticus 4:20-28

Preface of Holy Week

Martin Luther was born November 10, 1483. His intellectual abilities were evident early, and his father planned a career for him in law. Luther's real interest lay elsewhere, however, and in 1505 he entered the local Augustinian monastery. He was ordained a priest April 3, 1507.

In October 1512 Luther received his doctorate in theology, and shortly afterward he was installed as a professor of biblical studies at the University of Wittenberg. His lectures on the Bible were popular, and within a few years he made the university a center for biblical humanism. As a result of his theological and biblical studies he called into question the practice of selling indulgences. On the eve of All Saints' Day, October 31, 1517, he posted on the door of the castle church in Wittenberg the notice of an academic debate on indulgences, listing 95 theses for discussion. As the effects of the theses became evident, the Pope called upon the Augustinian order to discipline their member. After a series of meetings, political maneuvers, and attempts at reconciliation, Luther, at a meeting with the papal legate in 1518, refused to recant.

Luther was excommunicated on January 3, 1521. The Emperor Charles V summoned him to the meeting of the Imperial Diet at Worms. There Luther resisted all efforts to make him recant, insisting that he had to be proved in error on the basis of Scripture. The Diet passed an edict calling for the arrest of Luther. Luther's own prince, the Elector Frederick of Saxony, however, had him spirited away and placed for safekeeping in his castle, the Wartburg.

Here Luther translated the New Testament into German and began the translation of the Old Testament. He then turned his attention to the organization of worship and education. He introduced congregational singing of hymns, composing many himself, and issued model orders of services. He published his large and small catechisms for instruction in the faith. During the years from 1522 to his death, Luther wrote a prodigious quantity of books, letters, sermons and tracts. Luther died on February 18, 1546.

Martin Luther
Reformer, 1546

I   O God, our refuge and our strength: Thou didst raise up thy servant Martin Luther to reform and renew thy Church in the light of thy word. Defend and purify the Church in our own day and grant that, through faith, we may boldly proclaim the riches of thy grace which thou hast made known in Jesus Christ our Savior, who with thee and the Holy Spirit, liveth and reigneth, one God, now and for ever. *Amen.*

II   O God, our refuge and our strength: You raised up your servant Martin Luther to reform and renew your Church in the light of your word. Defend and purify the Church in our own day and grant that, through faith, we may boldly proclaim the riches of your grace which you have made known in Jesus Christ our Savior, who with you and the Holy Spirit, lives and reigns, one God, now and for ever. *Amen.*

Psalm	Lessons
46	Isaiah 55:6-11
	John 15:1-11

Preface of Trinity Sunday

Polycarp was one of the leaders of the Church who carried on the tradition of the apostles through the troubled period of Gnostic heresies in the second century. According to Irenaeus, who had known him in his early youth, Polycarp was a pupil of John, "the disciple of the Lord," and had been appointed a bishop by "apostles in Asia."

We possess a letter from Polycarp to the Church in Philippi. It reveals his firm adherence to the faith, and his pastoral concern for fellow Christians in trouble.

An authentic account of the martyrdom of Polycarp on February 23 is also preserved. It probably occurred in the year 156. The account tells of Polycarp's courageous witness in the amphitheater at Smyrna. When the proconsul asked him to curse Christ, Polycarp said, "Eighty-six years I have served him, and he never did me any wrong. How can I blaspheme my King who saved me?" The account reports that the magistrate was reluctant to kill the gentle and harmless old man, but his hand was forced by the mob, who clamored that he be thrown to wild beasts, as was the fate of other Christians on that dreadful day.

Polycarp was burned at the stake. Before his ordeal, he is reported to have looked up to heaven, and to have prayed: "Lord God Almighty, Father of your beloved and blessed child Jesus Christ, through whom we have received knowledge of you, God of angels and hosts and all creation, and of the whole race of the upright who live in your presence, I bless you that you have thought me worthy of this day and hour, to be numbered among the martyrs and share in the cup of Christ, for resurrection to eternal life, for soul and body in the incorruptibility of the Holy Spirit. Among them may I be accepted before you today, as a rich and acceptable sacrifice just as you, the faithful and true God, have prepared and foreshown and brought about. For this reason and for all things I praise you, I bless you, I glorify you, through the eternal heavenly high priest Jesus Christ, your beloved child, through whom be glory to you, with him and the Holy Spirit, now and for the ages to come. Amen."

Polycarp
Bishop and Martyr of Smyrna, 156

I   O God, the maker of heaven and earth, who didst give to thy
venerable servant, the holy and gentle Polycarp, boldness to
confess Jesus Christ as King and Savior, and steadfastness to
die for his faith: Give us grace, after his example, to share
the cup of Christ and rise to eternal life; through Jesus Christ
our Lord, who liveth and reigneth with thee and the Holy
Spirit, one God, now and for ever. *Amen.*

II   O God, the maker of heaven and earth, you gave your
venerable servant, the holy and gentle Polycarp, boldness to
confess Jesus Christ as King and Savior, and steadfastness to
die for his faith: Give us grace, following his example, to
share the cup of Christ and rise to eternal life; through Jesus
Christ our Lord, who lives and reigns with you and the Holy
Spirit, one God, now and for ever. *Amen.*

Psalm	Lessons
116:10-17*	Revelation 2:8-11
34:1-8 †	Matthew 20:20-23
or 121	

Preface of a Saint (3)

* *When the feast falls before Ash Wednesday.*
† *When the feast falls after Ash Wednesday.*

In the nine days of waiting between Jesus' Ascension and the Day of Pentecost, the disciples remained together in prayer. During this time, Peter reminded them that the defection and death of Judas had left the fellowship of the Twelve with a vacancy. The Acts of the Apostles records Peter's proposal that "one of the men who have accompanied us during all the time that the Lord Jesus went in and out among us, beginning from the baptism of John until the day when he was taken up from us — one of these men must become with us a witness to his resurrection" (Acts 1:21-22). Two men were nominated, Joseph called Barsabbas who was surnamed Justus, and Matthias. After prayer, the disciples cast lots, and the lot fell to Matthias, who was then enrolled with the eleven.

Nothing further is told of Matthias after his selection. According to tradition he was an exemplary Apostle, but we know nothing more. Matthias seems an appropriate example to Christians of one whose faithful companionship with Jesus qualifies him to be a suitable witness to the resurrection, and whose service is unheralded and unsung.

Saint Matthias the Apostle

I   O Almighty God, who into the place of Judas didst choose
thy faithful servant Matthias to be of the number of the
Twelve: Grant that thy Church, being delivered from false
apostles, may always be ordered and guided by faithful and
true pastors; through Jesus Christ our Lord, who liveth and
reigneth with thee, in the unity of the Holy Spirit, one God,
now and for ever. *Amen.*

II   Almighty God, who in the place of Judas chose your faithful
servant Matthias to be numbered among the Twelve: Grant
that your Church, being delivered from false apostles, may
always be guided and governed by faithful and true pastors;
through Jesus Christ our Lord, who lives and reigns with
you, in the unity of the Holy Spirit, one God, now and for
ever. *Amen.*

Psalm

15

Lessons

Acts 1:15-26
Philippians 3:13-21
John 15:1,6-16

Preface of Apostles

George Herbert is famous for his poems and his prose work, *A Priest in the Temple: or The Country Parson.* He is portrayed by his biographer Izaak Walton as a model of the saintly parish priest. Herbert described his poems as "a picture of the many spiritual conflicts that have passed betwixt God and my soul, before I could submit mine to the will of Jesus my Master; in whose service I have found perfect freedom."

Herbert was born in 1593, a member of an ancient family, a cousin of the Earl of Pembroke, and acquainted with King James the First and Prince (later King) Charles. Through his official position as Public Orator of Cambridge, he was brought into contact with the Court. Whatever hopes he may have had as a courtier were dimmed, however, because of his associations with persons who were out of favor with King Charles the First — principally John Williams, Bishop of Lincoln.

Herbert had begun studying divinity in his early twenties, and in 1626 he took Holy Orders. King Charles provided him with a living as rector of the parishes of Fugglestone and Bemerton in 1630.

His collection of poems, *The Temple*, was given to his friend, Nicholas Ferrar, and published posthumously. Two of his poems are well known hymns: "Teach me, my God and King," and "Let all the world in every corner sing." Their grace, strength, and metaphysical imagery influenced later poets, including Henry Vaughan and Samuel Taylor Coleridge.

Lines from his poem on prayer have moved many readers:
> Prayer, the Church's banquet, Angel's age,
> God's breath in man returning to his birth,
> The soul in paraphrase, the heart in pilgrimage,
> The Christian plummet sounding heav'n and earth.

Herbert was unselfish in his devotion and service to others. Izaak Walton writes that many of the parishioners "let their plow rest when Mr. Herbert's saints-bell rung to prayers, that they might also offer their devotion to God with him." His words, "Nothing is little in God's service," have reminded Christians again and again that everything in daily life, small or great, may be a means of serving and worshiping God.

George Herbert

Priest, 1633

I   Our God and King, who didst call thy servant George Herbert from the pursuit of worldly honors to be a pastor of souls, a poet, and a priest in thy temple: Give unto us the grace, we beseech thee, joyfully to perform the tasks thou givest us to do, knowing that nothing is menial or common that is done for thy sake; through Jesus Christ our Lord, who liveth and reigneth with thee and the Holy Spirit, one God, for ever and ever. *Amen.*

II   Our God and King, you called your servant George Herbert from the pursuit of worldly honors to be a pastor of souls, a poet, and a priest in your temple: Give us grace, we pray, joyfully to perform the tasks you give us to do, knowing that nothing is menial or common that is done for your sake; through Jesus Christ our Lord, who lives and reigns with you and the Holy Spirit, one God, for ever and ever. *Amen.*

Psalm	Lessons
23	1 Peter 5:1-4
or 1	Matthew 5:1-10

Preface of a Saint (1)

Despite the overwhelming victory of the pagan Angles, Saxons, and Jutes in the fifth century, one part of Britain continued in the ways of Christianity — Wales, the land west of the Wye River. In this last stronghold of the old Britons, the faith sprung from Glastonbury continued to flourish.

To the family of one Sanctus in Menevia there was born a son David ("the beloved"). Little is known of his early, life, but while fairly young he founded a monastery, near Menevia and became its abbot. He was later elected bishop. His strongest desire was to study and meditate in the quiet of his monastery, but he was virtually dragged to an assembly of bishops called to combat the heresy of Pelagianism. Once there, David proved to be so eloquent and learned that Archbishop Dubricius chose him as his own successor as Primate of Wales. In time, David founded eleven other monasteries in Wales, and made a pilgrimage to Jerusalem.

He is said to have been strict in the governing of his own monastery at Menevia, yet loving in his treatment and correction of wrongdoers. One of his nicknames, "the Waterman," may indicate that he allowed the monks in his care to drink only water at meals instead of the customary wine or mead.

A scholar, a competent administrator, and a man of moderation, David filled the offices he held with distinction. He became a leader and guardian of the Christian faith in Wales. Eventually he moved the center of episcopal government to Menevia, which is still an episcopal city, now called Ty-Dewi (House of David).

Some facts of his life can be historically established. Among them is that toward the end of his life he had several Irish saints as his pupils at the monastery. In legend — and many legends surround his life — David is clearly the foremost saint of Wales. He is revered and loved to this day as patron of Wales, foremost Christian priest, and courageous leader.

David

Bishop of Menevia, Wales, c. 544

I Almighty God, who didst call thy servant David to be a
faithful and wise steward of thy mysteries for the people of
Wales: Mercifully grant that, following his purity of life and
zeal for the Gospel of Christ, we may with him receive our
heavenly reward; through Jesus Christ our Lord, who liveth
and reigneth with thee and the Holy Spirit, one God, for ever
and ever. *Amen.*

II Almighty God, you called your servant David to be a faithful
and wise steward of your mysteries for the people of Wales:
Mercifully grant that, following his purity of life and zeal for
the Gospel of Christ, we may with him receive our heavenly
reward; through Jesus Christ our Lord, who lives and reigns
with you and the Holy Spirit, one God, for ever and ever.
Amen.

Psalm	Lessons
16:5-11	1 Thessalonians 2:2b-12
or 96:1-7	Mark 4:26-29

Preface of Apostles

One of four brothers dedicated to service in the Church, Chad was trained by Aidan of Lindisfarne as a follower of the Celtic tradition in ritual. His elder brother Cedd, a godly and upright man, had built a monastery at Lastingham, where he governed as abbot. At his death, Cedd left the abbacy to Chad. According to the Venerable Bede, Chad was "a holy man, modest in his ways, learned in the Scriptures, and zealous in carrying out their teaching."

Impressed by Chad's qualities, the King appointed him Bishop of York. Chad was ordained by "bishops of the British race who had not been canonically ordained," Bede tells us. Chad was, Bede also notes, "a man who kept the Church in truth and purity, humility, and temperance." Following apostolic example. he traveled about his diocese on foot.

The new Archbishop of Canterbury, Theodore, arrived in England four years after Chad's ordination as bishop. Theodore made it clear that Chad's ordination had been irregular, that is, not according to Roman custom; and Chad most humbly offered to resign from office. "Indeed, I never believed myself worthy of it," he said.

Theodore, impressed by such humility, reordained him, and appointed him Bishop of Mercia and Northumbria. Chad continued his custom of traveling on foot, until Theodore ordered him to ride, at least on longer journeys. When Chad hesitated, the Archbishop is said to have lifted him bodily onto the horse, "determined to compel him to ride when the need arose."

Chad administered his new diocese with devout concern. He built a monastery, and established monastic rule at Barrow. In his see city of Lichfield, where he had an official dwelling, he preferred to read and meditate in a small house he had built nearby.

Two and one-half years after his reordination, plague broke out, killing many residents of the diocese including Chad himself, whose death Bede describes thus: "He joyfully beheld . . . the day of the Lord, whose coming he had always anxiously awaited. He was mindful to his end of all that the Lord did." He was buried at the Cathedral Church of St. Peter in Lichfield.

Chad

Bishop of Lichfield, 672

I   Almighty God, whose servant Chad, for the peace of the Church, relinquished cheerfully the honors that had been thrust upon him, only to be rewarded with equal responsibility: Keep us, we pray thee, from thinking of ourselves more highly than we ought to think, and ready at all times to step aside for others, that the cause of Christ may be advanced; through the same Jesus Christ our Lord, who liveth and reigneth with thee and the Holy Spirit, one God, now and for ever. *Amen.*

II   Almighty God, for the peace of the Church your servant Chad relinquished cheerfully the honors that had been thrust upon him, only to be rewarded with equal responsibility: Keep us, we pray, from thinking of ourselves more highly than we ought to think, and ready at all times to step aside for others, that the cause of Christ may be advanced; through him who lives and reigns with you and the Holy Spirit, one God, now and for ever. *Amen.*

Psalm	Lessons
84:7-12	Philippians 4:10-13
or 23	Luke 14:1,7-14

Preface of a Saint (2)

John was the fifteenth, and Charles the eighteenth, child of Samuel Wesley, Rector of Epworth, Lincolnshire. John was born June 17, 1703, and Charles, December 18, 1707.

The lives and fortunes of the brothers were closely intertwined. As founders and leaders of the "Methodist" or evangelical revival in eighteenth-century England, their continuing influence redounds throughout the world and is felt in many Churches.

Although their theological writings and sermons are still widely appreciated, it is through their hymns—especially those of Charles, who wrote over six thousand of them—that their religious experience, and their Christian faith and life, continue to affect the hearts of many. Both brothers were profoundly attached to the doctrine and worship of the Church of England; and no amount of abuse and opposition to their cause and methods ever shook their confidence in, and love of it.

Both Wesleys were educated at Christ Church, Oxford. It was there that they gathered a few friends to join in strict adherence to the worship and discipline of the Prayer Book, and were thus given the name "Methodists." John was ordained in 1728 and Charles in 1735.

The two brothers went together to Georgia in 1735, John as a missionary of the Society for the Propagation of the Gospel, and Charles as secretary to James Oglethorpe, the Governor.

Shortly after their return to England, they both experienced an inner conversion, Charles on May 21, 1738, and John on May 24, at a meeting in Aldersgate Street with a group of Moravians, during a reading of Luther's Preface to the Epistle to the Romans. John recorded, "I felt my heart strangely warmed. I felt I did trust in Christ, Christ alone, for salvation; and an assurance was given me that he had taken away my sins, even mine, and saved me from the law of sin and death." So the revival was born.

The later schism of the Methodists from the Church of England occurred after the death of the two brothers—Charles on March 29, 1788, and John on March 2, 1791—but John's uncanonical ordinations of "elders" for America (bitterly opposed by Charles) doubtless set the basis for it.

John and Charles Wesley

Priests, 1791, 1788

I   Lord God, who didst inspire thy servants John and Charles Wesley with burning zeal for the sanctification of souls, and didst endow them with eloquence in speech and song: Kindle in thy Church, we beseech thee, such fervor, that those whose faith has cooled may be warmed, and that those who have not known thy Christ may turn to him and be saved; who liveth and reigneth with thee and the Holy Spirit, one God, now and for ever. *Amen.*

II   Lord God, you inspired your servants John and Charles Wesley with burning zeal for the sanctification of souls, and endowed them with eloquence in speech and song: Kindle in your Church, we entreat you, such fervor, that those whose faith has cooled may be warmed, and those who have not known Christ may turn to him and be saved; who lives and reigns with you and the Holy Spirit, one God, now and for ever. *Amen.*

Psalm

98:1-4 (5-10)
or   103:1-4,13-18

Lessons

Isaiah 49:5-6
Luke 9:2-6

Preface of Pentecost

Vibia Perpetua was a young widow, mother of an infant and owner of several slaves, including Felicitas and Revocatus. With two other young Carthaginians, Secundulus and Saturninus, they were catechumens preparing for baptism.

Early in the third century, Emperor Septimius Severus decreed that all persons should sacrifice to the divinity of the emperor. There was no way that a Christian, confessing faith in the one Lord Jesus Christ, could do this. Perpetua and her companions were arrested and held in prison under miserable conditions.

In a document attributed to Perpetua, we learn of visions she had in prison. One was of a ladder to heaven, which she climbed to reach a large garden; another was of her brother who had died when young of a dreadful disease, but was now well and drinking the water of life; the last was of herself as a warrior battling the Devil and defeating him to win entrance to the gate of life. "And I awoke, understanding that I should fight, not with beasts, but with the Devil. . . . So much about me up to the day before the games; let him who will write of what happened then."

At the public hearing before the Proconsul, she refused even the entreaties of her aged father, saying, "I am a Christian."

On March 7, Perpetua and her companions, encouraging one another to bear bravely whatever pain they might suffer, were sent to the arena to be mangled by a leopard, a boar, a bear, and a savage cow. Perpetua and Felicitas, tossed by the cow, were bruised and disheveled, but Perpetua, "lost in spirit and ecstasy," hardly knew that anything had happened. To her companions she cried, "Stand fast in the faith and love one another. And do not let what we suffer be a stumbling block to you."

Eventually, all were put to death by a stroke of a sword through the throat. The soldier who struck Perpetua was inept. His first blow merely pierced her throat between the bones. She shrieked with pain, then aided the man to guide the sword properly. The report of her death concludes, "Perhaps so great a woman, feared by the unclean spirit, could not have been killed unless she so willed it."

Perpetua and her Companions

Martyrs at Carthage, 202

I   O God the King of saints, who didst strengthen thy servants Perpetua and Felicitas and their companions to make a good confession, staunchly resisting, for the cause of Christ, the claims of human affection, and encouraging one another in their time of trial: Grant that we who cherish their blessed memory may share their pure and steadfast faith, and win with them the palm of victory; through the same Jesus Christ our Lord, who liveth and reigneth with thee and the Holy Spirit, one God, for ever and ever. *Amen.*

II O God the King of saints, you strengthened your servants Perpetua and Felicitas and their companions to make a good confession, staunchly resisting, for the cause of Christ, the claims of human affection, and encouraging one another in their time of trial: Grant that we who cherish their blessed memory may share their pure and steadfast faith, and win with them the palm of victory; through Jesus Christ our Lord, who lives and reigns with you and the Holy Spirit, one God, for ever and ever. *Amen.*

Psalm	Lessons
34: 1-8	Hebrews 10:32-39
or 124	Matthew 24:9-14

Preface of a Saint (3)

Gregory was a man enchanted with Christ and dazzled by the meaning of his Passion. He was born in Caesarea about 334, the younger brother of Basil the Great, and, in his youth, was but a reluctant Christian.

When he was twenty, the transfer of the relics of the Forty Martyrs of Sebaste to the family chapel at Annesi quickened Gregory's faith, and he became a practicing Christian and a lector. He abandoned this ministry, however, to become a rhetorician like his father.

His brother Basil, in his struggle against the Emperor Valens, compelled Gregory to become Bishop of Nyssa, a town ten miles from Caesarea. Knowing himself to be unfit for the charge, Gregory described his ordination as the most miserable day of his life. He lacked the important episcopal skills of tact and understanding, and had no sense of the value of money. Falsely-accused of embezzling Church funds, Gregory went into hiding for two years, not returning to his diocese until Valens died.

Although he resented his brother's dominance, Gregory was shocked by Basil's death in 379. Several months later, he received another shock: his beloved sister Macrina was dying. Gregory hastened to Annesi and conversed with her for two days about death, and the soul, and the meaning of the resurrection. Choking with asthma, Macrina died in her brother's arms.

The two deaths, while stunning Gregory, also freed him to develop as a deeper and richer philosopher and theologian. He reveals his delight in the created order in his treatise, *On the Making of Man*. He exposes the depth of his contemplative and mystical nature in his *Life of Moses* and again in his *Commentary on the Song of Songs*. His *Great Catechism* is still considered second only to Origen's treatise, *On First Principles*.

In 381, Gregory attended the Second Ecumenical Council at Constantinople, where he was honored as the "pillar of the Church." In the fight for the Nicene faith, he was one of the three great Eastern theologians, known with Basil the Great and Gregory of Nazianzus, as the Cappadocian Fathers.

Gregory

Bishop of Nyssa, c. 394

I Almighty God, who hast revealed to thy Church thine eternal Being of glorious majesty and perfect love as one God in Trinity of Persons: Give us grace that, like thy bishop Gregory of Nyssa, we may continue steadfast in the confession of this faith, and constant in our worship of thee, Father, Son, and Holy Spirit; who livest and reignest now and for ever. *Amen.*

II Almighty God, you have revealed to your Church your eternal Being of glorious majesty and perfect love as one God in Trinity of Persons: Give us grace that, like your bishop Gregory of Nyssa, we may continue steadfast in the confession of this faith, and constant in our worship of you, Father, Son, and Holy Spirit; for you live and reign for ever and ever. *Amen.*

Psalm	Lessons
19:7-11 (12-14)	Wisdom 7:24-28
or 119:97-104	John 5:19-24*
	or John 14:23-26

Preface of Trinity Sunday

* *In some years this passage will occur at the Daily Office on this day.*

Only two Popes, Leo the First and Gregory the First, have been given the popular title of "the Great." Both served in the difficult times of the barbarian invasions of Italy. Gregory also knew the horrors of "plague, pestilence, and famine." He was born of a patrician family about 540, and became Prefect of Rome in 573. Shortly thereafter he retired to a monastic life in a community which he founded in his ancestral home on the Coelian Hill. Pope Pelagius the Second made him Ambassador to Constantinople in 579, where he learned much about the larger affairs of the Church. Not long after his return home, Pope Pelagius died of the plague, and in 590 Gregory was elected as his successor.

Gregory's pontificate was one of strenuous activity. He organized the defense of Rome against the attacks of the Lombards, and fed its populace from papal granaries in Sicily. In this as in other matters, he administered "the patrimony of St. Peter" with energy and efficiency. His ordering of the Church's liturgy and chant has molded the spirituality of the Western Church until the present day. Though unoriginal in theology, his writings provided succeeding generations with basic texts, especially the *Pastoral Care,* a classic on the work of the ministry.

In the midst of all his cares and duties, Gregory prepared and fostered the evangelizing mission to the Anglo-Saxons under Augustine and other monks from his own monastery. The Venerable Bede justly called Gregory the Apostle of the English.

Gregory died on March 12, 604, and was buried in St. Peter's basilica. His life was a true witness to the title he assumed for his office: "Servant of the servants of God."

Gregory the Great

Bishop of Rome, 604

I   Almighty and merciful God, who didst raise up Gregory of Rome to be a servant of the servants of God, and didst inspire him to send missionaries to preach the Gospel to the English people: Preserve in thy Church the catholic and apostolic faith they taught, that thy people, being fruitful in every good work, may receive the crown of glory that fadeth not away; through Jesus Christ our Lord, who liveth and reigneth with thee and the Holy Spirit, one God, for ever and ever. *Amen.*

II   Almighty and merciful God, you raised up Gregory of Rome to be a servant of the servants of God, and inspired him to send missionaries to preach the Gospel to the English people: Preserve in your Church the catholic and apostolic faith they taught, that your people, being fruitful in every good work, may receive the crown of glory that never fades away; through Jesus Christ our Lord, who lives and reigns with you and the Holy Spirit, one God, for ever and ever. *Amen.*

Psalm	Lessons
57:6-11	1 Chronicles 25:1a,6-8
or 33:1-5,20-21	Mark 10:42-45

Preface of Apostles

Patrick was born into a Christian family somewhere on the northwest coast of Britain in about 390. His grandfather had been a Christian priest and his father, Calpornius, a deacon. Calpornius was an important official in the late Roman imperial government of Britain. It was not unusual in this post-Constantinian period for such state officials to be in holy orders. When Patrick was about sixteen, he was captured by a band of Irish slave-raiders. He was carried off to Ireland and forced to serve as a shepherd. When he was about twenty-one, he escaped and returned to Britain, where he was educated as a Christian. He tells us that he took holy orders as both presbyter and bishop, although no particular see is known as his at this time. A vision then called him to return to Ireland. This he did about the year 431.

Tradition holds that Patrick landed not far from the place of his earlier captivity, near what is now known as Downpatrick (a "down" or "dun" is a fortified hill, the stronghold of a local Irish king). He then began a remarkable process of missionary conversion throughout the country that continued until his death, probably in 461. He made his appeal to the local kings and through them to their tribes. Christianizing the old pagan religion as he went, Patrick erected Christian churches over sites already regarded as sacred, had crosses carved on old druidic pillars, and put sacred wells and springs under the protection of Christian saints.

Many legends of Patrick's Irish missionary travels possess substrata of truth, especially those telling of his conversion of the three major Irish High Kings. At Armagh, he is said to have established his principal church. To this day, Armagh is regarded as the primatial see of all Ireland.

Two works are attributed to Patrick: an autobiographical *Confession*, in which he tells us, among other things, that he was criticized by his contemporaries for lack of learning, and a *Letter to Coroticus*, a British chieftain. *The Lorica* or *St. Patrick's Breastplate* ("I bind unto myself today") is probably not his, but it expresses his faith and zeal.

Patrick
Bishop and Missionary of Ireland, 461

I   Almighty God, who in thy providence didst choose thy servant Patrick to be the apostle of the Irish people, to bring those who were wandering in darkness and error to the true light and knowledge of thee: Grant us so to walk in that light that we may come at last to the light of everlasting life; through Jesus Christ our Lord, who liveth and reigneth with thee and the Holy Spirit, one God, for ever and ever. *Amen.*

II   Almighty God, in your providence you chose your servant Patrick to be the apostle of the Irish people, to bring those who were wandering in darkness and error to the true light and knowledge of you: Grant us so to walk in that light that we may come at last to the light of everlasting life; through Jesus Christ our Lord, who lives and reigns with you and the Holy Spirit, one God, for ever and ever. *Amen.*

Psalm	Lessons
97:1-2,7-12	1 Thessalonians 2:2b-12
or 96:1-7	Matthew 28:16-20

Preface of Apostles

Cyril is the one we have most to thank for the development of catechetical instruction and liturgical observances during Lent and Holy Week. Born in Jerusalem about 315, Cyril became bishop of that city probably in 349. In the course of political and ecclesiastical disputes, he was banished and restored three times. His *Catechetical Lectures* on the Christian faith, given before Easter to candidates for Baptism, were probably written by him sometime between 348 and 350.

The work consists of an introductory lecture, or *Procatechesis*, and eighteen *Catecheses* based upon the articles of the creed of the Church at Jerusalem, All these lectures (the earliest catechetical materials surviving today) may have been used many times over by Cyril and his successors, and considerably revised in the process. They were probably part of the pre-baptismal instruction that Egeria, a pilgrim nun from western Europe, witnessed at Jerusalem in the fourth century and described with great enthusiasm in the account of her pilgrimage. Many of the faithful would also attend these instructions.

Cyril's five *Mystagogical Catecheses* on the Sacraments, intended for the newly baptized after Easter, are now thought to have been composed, or at least revised, by John, Cyril's successor as Bishop of Jerusalem from 386 to 417.

It is likely that it was Cyril who instituted the observances of Palm Sunday and Holy Week during the latter years of his episcopate in Jerusalem. In doing so, he was taking practical steps to organize devotions for countless pilgrims and local inhabitants around the sacred sites. In time, as pilgrims returned to their homes from Palestine, these services were to influence the development of Holy Week observances throughout the entire Church. Cyril attended the Second Ecumenical Council at Constantinople, in 381, and died at Jerusalem on March 18, 386.

Cyril's thought has greatly enriched the observance of Holy Week in the 1979 Book of Common Prayer.

Cyril
Bishop of Jerusalem, 386

I Strengthen, O Lord, we beseech thee, the bishops of thy
Church in their special calling to be teachers and ministers of
the Sacraments, that they, like thy servant Cyril of
Jerusalem, may effectively instruct thy people in Christian
faith and practice; and that we, taught by them, may enter
more fully into the celebration of the Paschal mystery;
through Jesus Christ our Lord, who liveth and reigneth with
thee and the Holy Spirit, one God, now and for ever. *Amen.*

II Strengthen, O Lord, the bishops of your Church in their
special calling to be teachers and ministers of the
Sacraments, so that they, like your servant Cyril of
Jerusalem, may effectively instruct your people in Christian
faith and practice; and that we, taught by them, may enter
more fully into the celebration of the Paschal mystery;
through Jesus Christ our Lord, who lives and reigns with
you and the Holy Spirit, one God, now and for ever. *Amen.*

Psalm	Lessons
122	Ecclesiasticus 47:8-10
or 34:1-8	Luke 24:44-48

Preface of the Dedication of a Church

In the face of circumstances that distressed even a man of such tenderness and obedience to God as Joseph, he accepted the vocation of protecting Mary and being a father to Jesus. He is honored in Christian tradition for the nurturing care and protection he provided for the infant Jesus and his mother in taking them to Egypt to escape Herod's slaughter of the innocents, and in rearing him as a faithful Jew at Nazareth. The Gospel according to Matthew pictures Joseph as a man of deep devotion, open to mystical experiences, and as a man of compassion, who accepted his God-given responsibility with gentleness and humility.

Joseph was a pious Jew, a descendant of David, and a carpenter by trade. As Joseph the Carpenter, he is considered the patron saint of the working man, one who not only worked with his hands, but taught his trade to Jesus. The little that is told of him is a testimony to the trust in God which values simple everyday duties, and gives an example of a loving husband and father.

Saint Joseph

I O God, who from the family of thy servant David didst raise up Joseph to be the guardian of thy incarnate Son and the spouse of his virgin mother: Give us grace to imitate his uprightness of life and his obedience to thy commands; through the same thy Son Jesus Christ our Lord, who liveth and reigneth with thee and the Holy Spirit, one God, for ever and ever. *Amen.*

II O God, who from the family of your servant David raised up Joseph to be the guardian of your incarnate Son and the spouse of his virgin mother: Give us grace to imitate his uprightness of life and his obedience to your commands; through Jesus Christ our Lord, who lives and reigns with you and the Holy Spirit, one God, for ever and ever. *Amen.*

Psalm	Lessons
89:1-29	2 Samuel 7:4,8-16
or 89:1-4, 26-29	Romans 4:13-18
	Luke 2:41-52

Preface of the Epiphany

Cuthbert was the most popular saint of the pre-Conquest Anglo-Saxon Church. He was born about 625.

The Venerable Bede, who wrote a life of Cuthbert, tells us that in his youth, while tending sheep one night and praying, "as was his wont," he saw a stream of light break through the darkness, and in its midst, "a company of the heavenly host descended to the earth, and having received among them a spirit of surpassing brightness, returned without delay to their heavenly home." Learning the next day that Aidan of Lindisfarne had died at that very time, Cuthbert "determined forthwith to enter a monastery."

Trained in the austere traditions of Celtic monasticism, Cuthbert was Prior of Melrose Abbey from 651 to 664, and then of Lindisfarne for twelve years. Bede says that he was accustomed to make visitations even to remote villages to preach to simple folk who, "neglecting the sacrament of their creed, had recourse to idolatrous remedies; as if by charms or amulets, or any other mysteries of the magical art, they were able to avert a stroke inflicted upon them by the Lord. . . ." Bede says that Cuthbert "often remained a week, sometimes two or three, nay, even a whole month, without returning home; but dwelling among the mountains, taught the poor people, both by words of his preaching, and also by his own holy conduct."

Archbishop Theodore recognized Cuthbert's greatness of character and made him Bishop of Hexham in 684, but Cuthbert continued to make his see at Lindisfarne. He returned two years later to his hermitage on the neighboring island of Farne, where he died on March 20, 687.

Cuthbert accepted the decisions of the synod of Whitby in 663 that brought the usages of' the English Church into line with Roman practice. He was thus a "healer of the breach" that threatened to divide the Church into Celtic and Roman factions.

At the time of the Viking invasions, the monks of Lindisfarne carefully protected his relics during their wanderings, until, finally, they brought them to Durham, where one may see today the remnants of his shrine and visit his tomb.

Cuthbert
Bishop of Lindisfarne, 687

I   Almighty God, who didst call Cuthbert from following the flock to be a shepherd of thy people: Mercifully grant that, as he sought in dangerous and remote places those who had erred and strayed from thy ways, so we may seek the indifferent and the lost, and lead them back to thee; through Jesus Christ our Lord, who liveth and reigneth with thee and the Holy Spirit, one God, for ever and ever. *Amen.*

II   Almighty God, you called Cuthbert from following the flock to be a shepherd of your people: Mercifully grant that, as he sought in dangerous and remote places those who had erred and strayed from your ways, so we may seek the indifferent and the lost, and lead them back to you; through Jesus Christ our Lord, who lives and reigns with you and the Holy Spirit, one God, for ever and ever. *Amen.*

Psalm	Lessons
23	2 Corinthians 6:1-10
or 1	Matthew 6:24-33

Preface of a Saint (2)

Thomas Ken was born in 1637. Throughout his life he was both rewarded and punished for his integrity. His close relationship with the royal family began when he became chaplain to Princess Mary of Orange at The Hague. Ken was appalled at the Prince of Orange's treatment of his wife, and rebuked him publicly.

In 1683, Ken returned to England and became chaplain to Charles the Second. His integrity stirred him to rebuke Charles for lax behavior. When Ken was notified that the King's mistress, the actress Nell Gwyn, was to be lodged at his house, he refused, saying, "a woman of ill-repute ought not to be endured in the house of a clergyman, and especially the King's chaplain." The King took no offense, but in the next year made Ken the Bishop of Bath and Wells, declaring that none should have the position except "the little black fellow that refused his lodging to poor Nelly."

In 1688, when Charles' successor, James the Second, tried to undermine the authority of the Church of England, Ken was one of seven bishops who refused to read the King's Declaration of Indulgence, which offered toleration to Protestant non-conformists and to Roman Catholics. The seven bishops were sent to the Tower, but were acquitted in the courts, and became popular heroes. After the resolution of 1688, however, Ken's conscience did not permit him to swear allegiance to William of Orange, who became King William the Third. As a Non-Juror, Ken was deprived of his see.

Ken's conscience would not let him rest and his disagreement with others of the "Non-Juring" party over various matters troubled him for the rest of his life. He deplored the Non-Juror schism, and after the accession of Queen Anne, he made his peace with the Church of England.

A man of deep piety, Ken was the author of several religious works which were immensely popular in the eighteenth century. He is best known as a writer of hymns, particularly the well-known evening hymn, "All praise to thee, my God, this night," which concludes with his doxology, "Praise God from whom all blessings flow."

Thomas Ken

Bishop of Bath and Wells, 1711

I   Almighty God, who didst give to thy servant Thomas Ken grace and courage to bear witness to the truth before rulers and kings: Give us also thy strength that, following his example, we may constantly defend what is right, boldly reprove what is evil, and patiently suffer for the truth's sake; through Jesus Christ our Lord, who liveth and reigneth with thee and the Holy Spirit, one God, for ever and ever. *Amen.*

II   Almighty God, you gave your servant Thomas Ken grace and courage to bear witness to the truth before rulers and kings: Give us strength also that, following his example, we may constantly defend what is right, boldly reprove what is evil, and patiently suffer for the truth's sake; through Jesus Christ our Lord, who lives and reigns with you and the Holy Spirit, one God, for ever and ever. *Amen.*

Psalm	Lessons
34:1-8	Philippians 4:4-9
or 145:8-13	Luke 6:17-23

Preface of a Saint (2)

James De Koven was born in Middletown, Connecticut, in 1831, ordained by Bishop Kemper in 1855, and appointed professor of ecclesiastical history at Nashotah House. In addition, he administered a preparatory school, and assisted at the Church of St. John Chrysostom in Delafield, Wisconsin.

Nashotah House was associated, from the time of its foundation, with many of the principles of the Oxford Movement, above all in its emphasis on the sacramental life of the Church and the expression of devotion to the Eucharist — including such practices as bowing to the Altar, at the name of Jesus, and before receiving Communion. In 1859, De Koven became Warden of the Church college at Racine, Wisconsin, where he emphasized the life of worship. He died there in 1879.

De Koven came to national attention at the General Conventions of 1871 and 1874, when the controversy over "ritualism" was at its height. In 1871, he asserted that the use of candles on the Altar, incense, and genuflections were lawful, because they symbolized "the real, spiritual presence of Christ" which the Episcopal Church upheld, along with the Orthodox and the Lutherans. He cited a recent decision of an ecclesiastical court of the Church of England, which affirmed as the teaching of the Church of England that "the spiritual presence of the Body and Blood of our Lord in the Holy Communion is objective and real."

Because of his advocacy of the "ritualist" cause, consents were not given to his consecration as Bishop of Wisconsin in 1874, and of Illinois in 1875.

To the General Convention of 1874, De Koven expressed the religious conviction that underlay his Churchmanship: "You may take away from us, if you will, every external ceremony; you may take away altars, and super-altars, lights and incense and vestments; . . . and we will submit to you. But, gentlemen . . . to adore Christ's Person in his Sacrament — that is the inalienable privilege of every Christian and Catholic heart. How we do it, the way we do it, the ceremonies with which we do it, are utterly, utterly, indifferent. The *thing itself* is what we plead for."

James De Koven

Priest, 1879

I   Almighty and everlasting God, the source and perfection of all virtues, who didst inspire thy servant James De Koven to do what is right and to preach what is true: Grant that all ministers and stewards of thy mysteries may afford to thy faithful people, by word and example, the knowledge of thy grace; through Jesus Christ our Lord, who liveth and reigneth with thee and the Holy Spirit, one God, for ever and ever. *Amen.*

II   Almighty and everlasting God, the source and perfection of all virtues, you inspired your servant James De Koven to do what is right and to preach what is true: Grant that all ministers and stewards of your mysteries may impart to your faithful people, by word and example, the knowledge of your grace; through Jesus Christ our Lord, who lives and reigns with you and the Holy Spirit, one God, for ever and ever. *Amen.*

Psalm	Lessons
103:1-4,13-18	2 Timothy 2:10-15,19
or 84:7-12	Matthew 13:47-52

Preface of a Saint (1)

Armenia was the first nation-state to become officially Christian, and this set a precedent for the adoption of Christianity by the Emperor Constantine. As a buffer state between the more powerful empires of Rome and Persia, Armenia endured many shifts of policy, as first one and then the other empire took it "under protection."

The accounts of Gregory, known as the Illuminator and as Apostle of the Armenians, are a mixture of legend and fact. He was born about 257. After his father assassinated the Persian King Chosroes the First, the infant boy was rescued and taken to Caesarea in Cappadocia, where he was brought up as a Christian. He married a woman named Mary, who bore him two sons. About 280, he returned to Armenia, and succeeded, after experiencing various fortunes of honor and imprisonment, in converting King Tiridates to his faith. With the help of the King the country was Christianized, and paganism was rooted out. About 300, Gregory was ordained a bishop at Caesarea. He established his cathedral at Valarshapat, with his center of work nearby at Echmiadzin, now in Armenia, and still the spiritual center of Armenian Christianity.

There is no record that Gregory attended the First Ecumenical Council at Nicaea in 325, but a tradition records that he sent in his stead his younger son Aristages, whom he ordained as his successor. His last years were spent in solitude, and he died about 332.

Gregory the Illuminator

Bishop and Missionary of Armenia, c. 332

I Almighty God, who willest to be glorified in thy saints, and
didst raise up thy servant Gregory the Illuminator to be a
light in the world, and to preach the Gospel to the people of
Armenia: Shine, we pray thee, in our hearts, that we also in
our generation may show forth thy praise, who hast called
us out of darkness into thy marvelous light; through Jesus
Christ our Lord, who liveth and reigneth with thee and the
Holy Spirit, one God, now and for ever. *Amen.*

II Almighty God, whose will it is to be glorified in your saints,
and who raised up your servant Gregory the Illuminator to
be a light in the world, and to preach the Gospel to the
people of Armenia: Shine, we pray, in our hearts, that we
also in our generation may show forth your praise, who
called us out of darkness into your marvelous light; through
Jesus Christ our Lord, who lives and reigns with you and the
Holy Spirit, one God, now and for ever. *Amen.*

Psalm	Lessons
33:6-11	Acts 17:22-31
or 98:1-4	Matthew 5:11-16

Preface of Apostles

Today's feast commemorates how God made known to a young Jewish woman that she was to be the mother of his Son, and how Mary accepted her vocation with perfect conformity of will. It has been said, "God made us without us, and redeemed us without us, but cannot save us without us." Mary's assent to Gabriel's message opened the way for God to accomplish the salvation of the world. It is for this reason that all generations are to call her "blessed."

The Annunciation has been a major theme in Christian art, in both East and West. Innumerable sermons and poems have been composed about it. The term coined by Cyril of Jerusalem for the Blessed Virgin, *Theotokos* ("the God-bearer"), was affirmed by the General Council of Ephesus in 451.

Mary's self-offering in response to God's call has been compared to that of Abraham, the father of believers. Just as Abraham was called to be the father of the chosen people, and accepted his call, so Mary was called to be the mother of the faithful, the new Israel. She is God's human agent in the mystery of the Incarnation. Her response to the angel, "Let it be to me according to your word," is identical with the faith expressed in the prayer that Jesus taught, "Your will be done on earth as in heaven."

Gerard Manley Hopkins, comparing Mary to the air we breathe, writes:

> Wild air, world-mothering air . . .
> Of her flesh he took flesh:
> He does take fresh and fresh,
> Though much the mystery how,
> Not flesh but spirit now,
> And makes, O marvellous!
> New Nazareths in us,
> Where she shall yet conceive
> Him, morning, noon, and eve,
> New Bethlems, and he born
> There, evening, noon, and morn —

The Annunciation of Our Lord

I We beseech thee, O Lord, pour thy grace into our hearts, that we who have known the incarnation of thy Son Jesus Christ, announced by an angel to the Virgin Mary, may by his cross and passion be brought unto the glory of his resurrection; who liveth and reigneth with thee, in the unity of the Holy Spirit, one God, now and for ever. *Amen.*

II Pour your grace into our hearts, O Lord, that we who have known the incarnation of your Son Jesus Christ, announced by an angel to the Virgin Mary, may by his cross and passion be brought to the glory of his resurrection; who lives and reigns with you, in the unity of the Holy Spirit, one God, now and for ever. *Amen.*

Psalm	Lessons
40:1-11	Isaiah 7:10-14
or 40:5-10	Hebrews 10:5-10
or Canticle 3 *or* 15	Luke 1:26-38

Preface of the Epiphany

Charles Henry Brent was born in Canada in 1862 and was educated at Trinity College, University of Toronto. Ordained in Canada, he came to the United States where, in 1901, he was elected by the House of Bishops as Missionary Bishop of the Philippines. In the Philippines, he began a crusade against the opium traffic, a campaign he later expanded to the continent of Asia. He became President of the Opium Conference in Shanghai in 1909, and represented the United States on the League of Nations Narcotics Committee. He also established cordial relations with the Philippine Independent Church, which led, ultimately, to intercommunion with that Church.

Bishop Brent served as Senior Chaplain of the American Expeditionary Forces in World War I, and in 1918 he accepted election as Bishop of Western New York, having declined three previous elections in order to remain at his post in the Philippines.

Brent was the outstanding figure of the Episcopal Church on the world scene for two decades. The central focus of his life and ministry was the cause of Christian unity. After attending the World Missionary Conference in Edinburgh in 1910, he led the Episcopal Church in the movement that culminated in the first World Conference on Faith and Order, which was held in Lausanne, Switzerland, in 1927, and over which he presided. He died in 1929.

James Thayer Addison, the historian, described Brent as "a saint of disciplined mental vigor, one whom soldiers were proud to salute and whom children were happy to play with, who could dominate a parliament and minister to an invalid, a priest and bishop who gloried in the heritage of his Church, yet who stood among all Christian brothers as one who served. . . . He was everywhere an ambassador of Christ."

Brent was also a man of prayer. One of his prayers for the mission of the Church has been included in the Book of Common Prayer: "Lord Jesus Christ, you stretched out your arms of love on the hard wood of the cross that everyone might come within the reach of your saving embrace: So clothe us with your Spirit that we, reaching forth our hands in love, may bring those who do not know you to the knowledge and love of you; for the honor of your Name."

Charles Henry Brent

Bishop of the Philippines, and of Western New York, 1929

I   Heavenly Father, whose Son did pray that we all might be one: Deliver us, we beseech thee, from arrogance and prejudice, and give us wisdom and forbearance, that, following thy servant Charles Henry Brent, we may be united in one family with all who confess the Name of thy Son Jesus Christ; who liveth and reigneth with thee and the Holy Spirit, one God, now and for ever. *Amen.*

II   Heavenly Father, whose Son prayed that we all might be one: Deliver us from arrogance and prejudice, and give us wisdom and forbearance, that, following your servant Charles Henry Brent, we may be united in one family with all who confess the Name of your Son Jesus Christ; who lives and reigns with you and the Holy Spirit, one God, now and for ever. *Amen.*

Psalm	Lessons
122	Ephesians 4:1-7,11-13
or 133	Matthew 9:35-38

Preface of Pentecost

New ev'ry morning is the love
Our wakening and uprising prove:
Through sleep and darkness safely brought,
Restored to life and power and thought.

These familiar words of John Keble are from his cycle of poems
entitled *The Christian Year* (1827), which he wrote to restore among
Anglicans a deep feeling for the Church Year. The work went through
ninety-five editions, but this was not the fame he sought: his consuming
desire was to be a faithful pastor, who finds his fulfillment in daily
services, confirmation classes, visits to village schools, and a voluminous
correspondence with those seeking spiritual counsel.

Keble, born in 1792, received his early education in his father's vicarage.
At fourteen, he won a scholarship to Oxford and graduated in 1811 with
highest honors. He served the University in several capacities, including
ten years as Professor of Poetry. After ordination in 1816 he had a series
of rural curacies, and finally settled in 1836 into a thirty-year pastorate
at the village of Hursley, near Winchester.

England was going through a turbulent change from a rural to an
industrial and urban society. Among the reforms of the 1830's,
Parliament acted to abolish ten Anglican bishoprics in Ireland. Keble
vigorously attacked this action as undermining the independence of the
Church.

His Assize Sermon of 1833 was the spark that ignited the Oxford
Movement. Those drawn to the Movement began to publish a series of
"Tracts for the Times" (hence the popular name "Tractarians") — which
sought to recall the Church to its ancient sacramental heritage. John
Henry Newman was the intellectual leader of the Movement, Edward
Bouverie Pusey was the prophet of its devotional life, and John Keble
was its pastoral inspiration.

Though bitterly attacked, his loyalty to his Church was unwavering.
Within three years of his death at age 74, a college bearing his name was
established at Oxford "to give an education in strict fidelity to the
Church of England." For Keble, this would have meant dedication to
learning in order "to live more nearly as we pray."

John Keble

Priest, 1866

I   Grant, O God, that in all time of our testing we may know thy presence and obey thy will; that, following the example of thy servant John Keble, we may accomplish with integrity and courage that which thou givest us to do, and endure that which thou givest us to bear; through Jesus Christ our Lord, who liveth and reigneth with thee and the Holy Spirit, one God, for ever and ever. *Amen.*

II   Grant, O God, that in all time of our testing we may know your presence and obey your will; that, following the example of your servant John Keble, we may accomplish with integrity and courage what you give us to do, and endure what you give us to bear; through Jesus Christ our Lord, who lives and reigns with you and the Holy Spirit, one God, for ever and ever. *Amen.*

Psalm	Lessons
26:1-8	Romans 12:9-21
or 15	Matthew 5:1-12

Preface of a Saint (1)

"Any man's death diminishes me, because I am involved in mankind. And therefore never send to know for whom the bell tolls: It tolls for thee."

These words are familiar to many; their author, John Donne, though less well known, is one of the greatest of English poets. In his own time, he was the best-known preacher in the Church of England. He came to that eminence by a tortuous path. Born into a wealthy and pious Roman Catholic family in 1573, he was educated at both Oxford and Cambridge, and studied law at Lincoln's Inn. Some time later he conformed to the Established Church and embarked upon a promising political career of service to the State. The revelation of his secret marriage in 1601 to the niece of his employer, the Lord Keeper of the Great Seal, brought his public career to an end. In 1615, he was persuaded by King James the First and others to receive ordination.

Following several brief cures, Donne rose rapidly in popularity as Dean of St. Paul's Cathedral, London, from 1622 until his death. He drew great throngs to the Cathedral and to Paul's Cross, a nearby open-air pulpit. His sermons reflect the wide learning of the scholar, the passionate intensity of the poet, and the profound devotion of one struggling in his own life to relate the freedom and demands of the Gospel to the concerns of a common humanity, on every level, and in all its complexities.

In one of his poems, he wrote:

> We thinke that *Paradise* and *Calvarie*,
> *Christs Crosse*, and *Adams* tree, stood in one place;
> Looke, Lord, and finde both *Adams* met in me;
> As the first *Adams* sweat surrounds my face
> May the last *Adams* blood my soule embrace.
>
> So, in his purple wrapp'd receive mee Lord,
> By these his thornes give me his other Crowne;
> And as to others soules I preach'd thy word,
> Be this my Text, my Sermon to my owne.
> Therefore that he may raise the Lord throws down.

John Donne

Priest, 1631

I   Almighty God, the root and fountain of all being: Open our eyes to see, with thy servant John Donne, that whatsoever hath any being is a mirror in which we may behold thee; through Jesus Christ our Lord, who liveth and reigneth with thee and the Holy Spirit, one God, for ever and ever. *Amen.*

II   Almighty God, the root and fountain of all being: Open our eyes to see, with your servant John Donne, that whatever has any being is a mirror in which we may behold you; through Jesus Christ our Lord, who lives and reigns with you and the Holy Spirit, one God, for ever and ever. *Amen.*

Psalm	Lessons
27:5-11	Wisdom 7:24—8:1
or 16:5-11	John 5:19-24

Preface of the Epiphany

In the same year that Karl Marx declared religion to be the "opiate of the people," Frederick Denison Maurice wrote, "We have been dosing our people with religion when what they want is not this but the living God." Like Marx, Maurice wanted to solve the questions of our complex society; unlike Marx, he called for a radical, but non-violent, reform, by the renewal of "faith in a God who has redeemed mankind, in whom I may vindicate my rights as a man." Maurice was a founder of the Christian Socialist Movement, which, he wrote, "will commit us at once to the conflict we must engage in sooner or later with the unsocial Christians and unchristian Socialists."

Maurice was born in 1805 into the family of a Unitarian minister whose life was marked by intense religious controversy. Maurice studied civil law at Cambridge, but refused the degree in 1827, because, as a Dissenter, he could not subscribe to the Thirty-nine Articles of Religion. After several personal crises, however, he became an Anglican and was ordained in 1814. Soon afterwards he was appointed Professor of English Literature and History at King's College, London, and, in 1846, to the chair of Theology.

In his book, *The Kingdom of Christ*, published in 1838, Maurice investigates the causes and cures of Christian divisions. The book has become a source of Anglican ecumenism. Maurice was dismissed from his professorships because of his leadership in the Christian Socialist Movement, and because of the supposed unorthodoxy of his *Theological Essays* (1859).

Maurice saw worship as the meeting point of time and eternity, and as the fountain of energies for the Church's mission. He wrote, "I do not think we are to praise the liturgy but to use it. When we do not want it for our life, we may begin to talk of it as a beautiful composition."

After the death of the Christian Socialist Movement in 1814, Maurice founded the Working Men's College, and resumed teaching at Queen's College, London. Maurice awakened Anglicanism to the need for concern with the problems of society. In later years, he was honored even by former opponents. He was rector of two parishes, and was professor of Moral Theology at Cambridge from 1866 until his death.

Frederick Denison Maurice

Priest, 1872

I   Almighty God, who hast restored our human nature to
heavenly glory through the perfect obedience of our Savior
Jesus Christ: Keep alive in thy Church, we beseech thee, a
passion for justice and truth; that we, like thy servant
Frederick Denison Maurice, may work and pray for the
triumph of the kingdom of thy Christ; who liveth and
reigneth with thee and the Holy Spirit, one God, now and
for ever. *Amen.*

II   Almighty God, you restored our human nature to heavenly
glory through the perfect obedience of our Savior Jesus
Christ: Keep alive in your Church, we pray, a passion for
justice and truth; that, like your servant Frederick Denison
Maurice, we may work and pray for the triumph of the
kingdom of your Christ; who lives and reigns with you and
the Holy Spirit, one God, now and for ever. *Amen.*

Psalm	Lessons
72:11-17	Ephesians 3:14-19
or 145:8-13	John 18:33-37

Preface of Baptism

James Lloyd Breck was one of the most important missionaries of the Episcopal Church in the nineteenth century. He was called "The Apostle of the Wilderness."

Breck was born in Philadelphia in 1818, and like many important Churchmen of his time, was greatly influenced by the pastoral devotion, liturgical concern, and sacramental emphasis of William Augustus Muhlenberg. Breck attended Muhlenberg's school in Flushing, New York, before entering the University of Pennsylvania. Muhlenberg inspired him, when he was sixteen years old, to dedicate himself to a missionary life. The dedication was crystallized when Breck, with three other classmates from the General Theological Seminary, founded a religious community at Nashotah, Wisconsin, which in 1844 was on the frontier.

Nashotah became a center of liturgical observance, of pastoral care, and of education. Isolated families were visited, mission stations established, and, probably for the first time since the Revolution, Episcopal missionaries were the first to reach the settlers.

Though Nashotah House flourished, and became one of the seminaries of the Episcopal Church, the "religious house" ideal did not. Breck moved on to St. Paul, Minnesota, where he began the work of the Episcopal Church. At Gull Lake, he organized St. Columba's Mission for the Chippewa. It laid the foundation for work among the Indians by their own native priests, although the mission itself did not survive.

In 1855, Breck married, and in 1858 settled in Faribault, Minnesota, where his mission was associated with one of the first cathedrals established in the Episcopal Church in the United States. He also founded Seabury Divinity School, which later merged with Western Theological Seminary, to become Seabury-Western. In 1867, Breck went on to California, inspired principally by the opportunity of founding a new, theological school. His schools at Benicia, California, did not survive, but the five parishes which he founded did, and the Church in California was strengthened immensely through his work. He died prematurely, at the age of 55, in 1876.

James Lloyd Breck

Priest, 1876

I   Teach thy Church, O Lord, we beseech thee, to value and support pioneering and courageous missionaries, whom thou callest, as thou didst call thy servant James Lloyd Breck, to preach, and teach, and plant thy Church on new frontiers; through Jesus Christ our Lord, who liveth and reigneth with thee and the Holy Spirit, one God, for ever and ever. *Amen.*

II Teach your Church, O Lord, we pray, to value and support pioneering and courageous missionaries, whom you call, as you called your servant James Lloyd Breck, to preach, and teach, and plant your Church on new frontiers; through Jesus Christ our Lord, who lives and reigns with you and the Holy Spirit, one God, for ever and ever. *Amen.*

Psalm	Lessons
145:1-7	1 Corinthians 3:4-11
or 98:1-4	Mark 4:26-32

Preface of Pentecost

Richard and his older brother Robert were quite young when their parents died, leaving a rich estate with a guardian to manage it. The guardian allowed the estate to dwindle, and Richard worked long hours to restore it.

Pressure was put on Richard to marry, but he, who from earliest years had preferred books to almost anything else, turned the estate over to his brother and went to Oxford. Often hungry, cold, and not always sure of his next day's keep, Richard managed to succeed in his studies under such teachers as Robert Grosseteste.

He continued to study law at Paris and Bologna, earned a doctorate, and returned to Oxford to become University Chancellor. Shortly afterward, the Archbishop of Canterbury, Edmund Rich, appointed him to be his own chancellor. The friendship between the primate and his young assistant was close: Richard also became his biographer. Conflict with King Henry the Third eventually forced Archbishop Rich into exile in France, where Richard nursed him in his final illness. After the Archbishop's death, Richard moved to the Dominican house at Orleans for further study and teaching. He was ordained priest in 1243.

He then returned to England, and was elected Bishop of Chichester in 1244. King Henry opposed the election, confiscated all the revenues of the diocese, and even locked Richard out of the episcopal dwelling. Richard was given lodging by a priest, Simon of Tarring. During these years he functioned as a missionary bishop, traveling about the diocese on foot, visiting fishermen and farmers, holding synods with great difficulty, and endeavoring to establish order. Threatened by the Pope, Henry finally acknowledged Richard as Bishop in 1246.

For eight years, he served his diocese as preacher, confessor, teacher, and counselor. While campaigning in 1253, for a new crusade against the Saracens, he contracted a fatal fever. Nine years after his death, he was canonized. His best remembered words are:

> Dear Lord, of thee three things I pray:
> To see thee more clearly,
> Love thee more dearly,
> Follow thee more nearly.

Richard
Bishop of Chichester, 1253

I   We thank thee, Lord God, for all the benefits thou hast given us in thy Son Jesus Christ, our most merciful Redeemer, Friend, and Brother, and for all the pains and insults he hath borne for us; and we pray that, following the example of thy saintly bishop Richard of Chichester, we may see Christ more clearly, love him more dearly, and follow him more nearly; who liveth and reigneth with thee and the Holy Spirit, one God, now and for ever. *Amen.*

II   We thank you, Lord God, for all the benefits you have given us in your Son Jesus Christ, our most merciful Redeemer, Friend, and Brother, and for all the pains and insults he has borne for us; and we pray that, following the example of your saintly bishop Richard of Chichester, we may see Christ more clearly, love him more dearly, and follow him more nearly; who lives and reigns with you and the Holy Spirit, one God, now and for ever. *Amen.*

Psalm	Lessons
84:7-12	Philippians 4:10-13
or 23	Matthew 25:31-40

Preface of a Saint (2)

Martin Luther King, Jr. was born on January 15, 1929, in Atlanta. As the son and grandson of Baptist preachers, he was steeped in the Black Church tradition. To this heritage he added a thorough academic preparation, earning the degrees of B.A., B.D., and Ph.D. in Systematic Theology from Boston University.

In 1954, King became pastor of a church in Montgomery, Alabama. There, Black indignation at inhumane treatment on segregated buses culminated in December, 1955, in the arrest of Rosa Parks for refusing to give up her seat to a white man. King was catapulted into national prominence as the leader of the Montgomery bus boycott. He became increasingly the articulate prophet, who could not only rally the Black masses, but could also move the consciences of Whites.

King founded the Southern Christian Leadership Conference to spearhead non-violent mass demonstrations against racism. Many confrontations followed, most notably in Birmingham and Selma, Alabama, and in Chicago. King's campaigns were instrumental to the passage of the Civil Rights acts of 1964, 1965 and 1968. King then turned his attention to economic empowerment of the poor and opposition to the Vietnam War, contending that racism, poverty and militarism were interrelated.

King lived in constant danger: his home was dynamited, he was almost fatally stabbed, and he was harassed by death threats. He was even jailed 30 times; but through it all he was sustained by his deep faith. In 1957, he received, late at night, a vicious telephone threat. Alone in his kitchen he wept and prayed. He relates that he heard the Lord speaking to him and saying, "Martin Luther, stand up for righteousness, stand up for justice," and promising never to leave him alone—"No, never alone." King refers to his vision as his "Mountain-top Experience."

After preaching at Washington Cathedral on March 31, 1968, King went to Memphis in support of sanitation workers in their struggle for better wages. There, he proclaimed that he had been "to the mountain-top" and had seen "the Promised Land," and that he knew that one day he and his people would be "free at last." On the following day, April 4, he was cut down by an assassin's bullet.

Martin Luther King, Jr.

Civil Rights Leader, 1968

I Almighty God, who by the hand of Moses thy servant didst lead thy people out of slavery, and didst make them free at last: Grant that thy Church, following the example of thy prophet Martin Luther King, may resist oppression in the name of thy love, and may strive to secure for all thy children the blessed liberty of the Gospel of Jesus Christ; who liveth and reigneth with thee and the Holy Spirit, one God, now and forever. *Amen.*

II Almighty God, by the hand of Moses your servant you led your people out of slavery, and made them free at last: Grant that your Church, following the example of your prophet Martin Luther King, may resist oppression in the name of your love, and may secure for all your children the blessed liberty of the Gospel of Jesus Christ; who lives and reigns with you and the Holy Spirit, one God, now and for ever. *Amen.*

Psalm	Lessons
77:11-20	Exodus 3:7-12
or 98:1-4	Luke 6:27-36

Preface of Baptism

William Augustus Muhlenberg was born on Philadelphia in 1796, into a prominent German Lutheran family, and was drawn to the Episcopal Church by its use of English. He deliberately chose to remain unmarried to free himself for a variety of ministries. As a young clergyman, he was deeply involved in the Sunday School movement, and was concerned that the Church should minister to all social groups. Aware of the limitations of the hymnody of his time, he wrote hymns and compiled hymnals, thus widening the range of music in Episcopal churches.

For twenty years he was head of a boys' school in Flushing, New York, where many influential Churchmen were educated. The use of music, flowers, and color, and the emphasis on the Church Year in the worship there became a potent influence. In 1846, he founded the Church of the Holy Communion in New York City. Again, he was bold and innovative: free pews for everyone, a parish school, a parish unemployment fund, and trips to the country for poor city children. His conception of beauty in worship, vivid and symbolic, had at its heart the Holy Communion itself, celebrated every Sunday. It was there that Anne Ayres founded the Sisterhood of the Holy Communion. In 1857, the two of them founded St. Luke's Hospital, where Muhlenberg was the pastor-superintendent and she the matron.

Muhlenberg's concern for sacramental worship and evangelism led him and several associates to memorialize the General Convention of 1853, calling for flexibility in worship and polity to enable the Church better to fulfill its mission. The insistence of the "Memorial" on traditional Catholic elements — the Creeds, the Eucharist, and Episcopal ordination — together with the Reformation doctrine of grace, appealed to people of varying views. Although the Church was not ready to adopt the specific suggestions of the Memorial, its influence was great, notably in preparing the ground for liturgical reform and ecumenical action.

Muhlenberg's last great project was an experiment in Christian social living, St. Johnland on Long Island. Although his dream of a Christian city was not realized, several of its philanthropic institutions survive.

William Augustus Muhlenberg

Priest, 1877

I   Do not let thy Church close its eyes, O Lord, to the plight of
the poor and neglected, the homeless and destitute, the old
and the sick, the lonely and those who have none to care for
them. Give us the vision and compassion with which thou
didst so richly endow thy servant William Augustus
Muhlenberg, that we may labor tirelessly to heal those who
are broken in body or spirit, and to turn their sorrow into
joy; through Jesus Christ our Lord, who liveth and reigneth
with thee and the Holy Spirit, one God, for ever and ever.
Amen.

II   Do not let your Church close its eyes, O Lord, to the plight
of the poor and neglected, the homeless and destitute, the
old and the sick, the lonely and those who have none to care
for them. Give us the vision and compassion with which
you so richly endowed your servant William Augustus
Muhlenberg, that we may labor tirelessly to heal those who
are broken in body or spirit, and to turn their sorrow into
joy; through Jesus Christ our Lord, who lives and reigns
with you and the Holy Spirit, one God, for ever and ever.
Amen.

Psalm	Lessons
84:1-6	Ephesians 4:11-16
or 133	Matthew 21:12-16

Preface of a Saint (1)

Dietrich Bonhoeffer was born February 4, 1906. He studied at the universities of Berlin and Tuebingen. His doctoral thesis was published in 1930 as *Commuunio Sanctorum*.

From the first days of the Nazi accession to power in 1933, Bonhoeffer was involved in protests against the regime. From 1933 to 1935 he was the pastor of two small congregations in London, but nonetheless was a leading spokesman for the Confessing Church, the center of Protestant resistance to the Nazis. In 1935 Bonhoeffer was appointed to organize and head a new seminary for the Confessing Church at Finkenwald. He described the community in *Life Together* and later wrote *The Cost of Discipleship*.

Bonhoeffer became increasingly involved in the political struggle after 1939, when he was introduced to the group seeking Hitler's overthrow. Bonhoeffer considered refuge in the United States, but he returned to Germany where he was able to continue his resistance. In May 1942 he flew to Sweden to meet Bishop Bell and convey through him to the British government proposals for a negotiated peace. The offer was rejected by the Allies who insisted upon unconditional surrender.

Bonhoeffer was arrested April 5, 1943, and imprisoned in Berlin. After an attempt on Hitler's life failed April 9, 1944, documents were discovered linking Bonhoeffer to the conspiracy. He was taken to Buchenwald concentration camp, then to Schoenberg Prison. On Sunday, April 8, 1945, just as he concluded a service in a school building in Schoenberg, two men came in with the chilling summons, "Prisoner Bonhoeffer . . . come with us." He said to another prisoner, "This is the end. For me, the beginning of life." Bonhoeffer was hanged the next day, April 9, at Flossenburg Prison.

There is in Bonhoeffer's life a remarkable unity of faith, prayer, writing and action. The pacifist theologian came to accept the guilt of plotting the death of Hitler because he was convinced that not to do so would be a greater evil. Discipleship was to be had only at great cost.

Dietrich Bonhoeffer

Pastor and Theologian, 1945

I Gracious God, the Beyond in the midst of our life, thou
gavest grace to thy servant Dietrich Bonhoeffer to
know and to teach the truth as it is in Jesus Christ, and
to bear the cost of following him: Grant that we,
strengthened by his teaching and example, may receive
thy word and embrace its call with an undivided heart;
through Jesus Christ our Savior, who liveth and
reigneth with thee and the Holy Spirit, one God, for
ever and ever. *Amen.*

II Gracious God, the Beyond in the midst of our life, you
gave grace to your servant Dietrich Bonhoeffer to
know and to teach the truth as it is in Jesus Christ, and
to bear the cost of following him: Grant that we,
strengthened by his teaching and example, may receive
your word and embrace its call with an undivided
heart; through Jesus Christ our Savior, who lives and
reigns with you and the Holy Spirit, one God, for ever
and ever. *Amen.*

Psalm	Lessons
119:89-96	Proverbs 3:1-7
	Matthew 13:47-52

Preface of a Saint (2)

"If we are to follow Christ, it must be in our common way of spending every day. If we are to live unto God at any time or in any place, we are to live unto him in all times and in all places. If we are to use anything as the gift of God, we are to use everything as his gift." So wrote William Law in 1728 in *A Serious Call to a Devout and Holy Life*.

This quiet schoolmaster of Putney, England, could hardly be considered a revolutionary, yet his book had near-revolutionary repercussions. His challenge to take Christian living very seriously received more enthusiastic response than he could ever have imagined, especially in the lives of Henry Venn, George Whitefield, and John Wesley, all of whom he strongly influenced. More than any other man, William Law laid the foundation for the religious revival of the eighteenth century, the Evangelical Movement in England, and the Great Awakening in America.

Law came to typify the devout parson in the eyes of many. His life was characterized by simplicity, devotion, and works of charity. Because he was a Non-juror, who refused to swear allegiance to the House of Hanover, he was deprived of the usual means of making a living as a clergyman in the Church of England. He therefore worked as a tutor to the father of Edward Gibbon, the historian, from 1727 to 1737. He organized schools and homes for the poor. He stoutly defended the Sacraments and Scriptures against attacks of the Deists. He spoke out eloquently against the warfare of his day. His richly inspired sermons and writings have gained him a permanent place in Christian literature.

William Law

Priest, 1761

I   O God, by whose grace thy servant William Law, enkindled with the fire of thy love, became a burning and shining light in thy Church: Grant that we also may be aflame with the spirit of love and discipline, and may ever walk before thee as children of light; through Jesus Christ our Lord, who with thee, in the unity of the Holy Spirit, liveth and reigneth, one God, now and for ever. *Amen.*

II   O God, by whose grace your servant William Law, kindled with the flame of your love, became a burning and shining light in your Church: Grant that we also may be aflame with the spirit of love and discipline, and walk before you as children of light; through Jesus Christ our Lord, who lives and reigns with you, in the unity of the Holy Spirit, one God, now and for ever. *Amen.*

Psalm	Lessons
1	Philippians 3:7-14
or 103:1-4,13-18	Matthew 6:1-6,16-21

Preface of a Saint (2)

George Augustus Selwyn was born on April 5, 1809, at Hampstead, London. He was prepared at Eton, and in 1831 was graduated from St. John's College, Cambridge, of which he became a Fellow.

Ordained in 1833, Selwyn served as a curate at Windsor until his selection as first Bishop of New Zealand in 1841. On the voyage to his new field, he mastered the Maori language and was able to preach in it upon his arrival. In the tragic ten-year war between the English and the Maoris, Selwyn was able to minister to both sides, and to keep the affection and admiration of both natives and colonists. He began missionary work in the Pacific islands in 1847.

Selwyn's first general synod in 1859 laid down a constitution, influenced by that of the American Church, which was important for all English colonial Churches.

After the first Lambeth Conference in 1867, Selwyn was reluctantly persuaded to accept the See of Lichfield in England. He died on April 11, 1878, and his grave in the cathedral close has been a place of pilgrimage for the Maoris to whom he first brought the light of the Gospel.

Bishop Selwyn twice visited the Church in America, and was the preacher at the 1874 General Convention.

George Augustus Selwyn

Bishop of New Zealand, and of Lichfield, 1878

I Almighty and everlasting God, we thank thee for thy servant George Augustus Selwyn, whom thou didst call to preach the Gospel to the people of New Zealand and Melanesia, and to lay a firm foundation for the growth of thy Church in many nations. Raise up, we beseech thee, in this and every land evangelists and heralds of thy kingdom, that thy Church may proclaim the unsearchable riches of our Savior Jesus Christ; who liveth and reigneth with thee and the Holy Spirit, one God, now and for ever. *Amen.*

II Almighty and everlasting God, we thank you for your servant George Augustus Selwyn, whom you called to preach the Gospel to the people of New Zealand and Melanesia, and to lay a firm foundation for the growth of your Church in many nations. Raise up in this and every land evangelists and heralds of your kingdom, that your Church may proclaim the unsearchable riches of our Savior Jesus Christ; who lives and reigns with you and the Holy Spirit, one God, now and for ever. *Amen.*

Psalm	Lessons
96: 1-7	Ephesians 2:11-18
or 98:1-4	Matthew 10:7-16

Preface of Apostles

Born in 954, Alphege (or Aelfheah) gave his witness in the troubled time of the second wave of Scandinavian invasion and settlement in England. After serving as a monk at Deerhurst, and then as Abbot of Bath, he became in 984, through Archbishop Dunstan's influence, Bishop of Winchester. He was instrumental in bringing the Norse King Olaf Tryggvason, only recently baptized, to King Aetheired in 994 to make his peace and to be confirmed at Andover.

Transferred to Canterbury in 1005, Alphege was captured by the Danes in 1011. He refused to allow a personal ransom to be collected from his already over-burdened people. Seven months later he was brutally murdered, despite the Viking commander Thorkell's effort to save him by offering all his possessions except his ship for the Archbishop's life.

The Anglo-Saxon Chronicle relates that the Danes were "much stirred against the Bishop, because he would not promise them any fee, and forbade that any man should give anything for him. They were also much drunken . . . and took the Bishop, and led him to their hustings, on the eve of the Saturday after Easter . . . and then they shamefully killed him. They overwhelmed him with bones and horns of oxen; and one of them smote him with an axe-iron on the head; so that he sunk downwards with the blow. And his holy blood fell on the earth, whilst his sacred soul was sent to the realm of God."

Alphege

Archbishop of Canterbury, and Martyr, 1012

I   O loving God, whose martyr bishop Alphege of Canterbury suffered violent death because he refused to permit a ransom to be extorted from his people: Grant, we pray thee, that all pastors of thy flock may pattern themselves on the Good Shepherd, who laid down his life for the sheep; through him who with thee and the Holy Spirit liveth and reigneth, one God, for ever and ever. *Amen.*

II   O loving God, your martyr bishop Alphege of Canterbury suffered violent death when he refused to permit a ransom to be extorted from his people: Grant that all pastors of your flock may pattern themselves on the Good Shepherd, who laid down his life for the sheep; and who with you and the Holy Spirit lives and reigns, one God, for ever and ever. *Amen.*

Psalm	Lessons
34:1-8	Revelation 7:13-17
or 31:1-5	Luke 12:4-12

Preface of a Saint (3)

Anselm was born in Italy about 1033, and took monastic vows in 1060 at the Abbey of Bec in Normandy. He succeeded his teacher Lanfranc as Prior of Bec in 1063, and as Archbishop of Canterbury in 1093. His episcopate was stormy, in continual conflict with the crown over the rights and freedom of the Church. His greatest talent lay in theology and spiritual direction.

As a pioneer in the scholastic method, Anselm remains the great exponent of the so-called "ontological argument" for the existence of God: God is "that than which nothing greater can be thought." Even the fool, who (in Psalm 14) says in his heart "There is no God," must have an idea of God in his mind, the concept of an unconditional being (*ontos*) than which nothing greater can be conceived; otherwise he would not be able to speak of "God" at all. And so this something, "God," must exist outside the mind as well; because, if he did not, he would not in fact be that than which nothing greater can be thought. Since the greatest thing that can be thought must have existence as one of its properties, Anselm asserts, "God" can be said to exist in reality as well as in the intellect, but is not dependent upon the material world for verification. To some, this "ontological argument" has seemed mere deductive rationalism; to others it has the merit of showing that faith in God need not be contrary to human reason.

Anselm is also the most famous exponent of the "satisfaction theory" of the atonement. Anselm explains the work of Christ in terms of the feudal society of his day. If a vassal breaks his bond, he has to atone for this to his lord; likewise, sin violates a person's bond with God, the supreme Lord, and atonement or satisfaction must be made. Of ourselves, we are unable to make such atonement, because God is perfect and we are not. Therefore, God himself has saved us, becoming perfect man in Christ, so that a perfect life could be offered in satisfaction for sin.

Undergirding Anselm's theology is a profound piety. His spirituality is best summarized in the phrase, "faith seeking understanding." He writes, "I do not seek to understand that I may believe, but I believe in order that I may understand. For this, too, I believe, that unless I first believe, I shall not understand."

Anselm

Archbishop of Canterbury, 1109

I Almighty God, who didst raise up thy servant Anselm to teach the Church of his day to understand its faith in thine eternal Being, perfect justice, and saving mercy: Provide thy Church in every age with devout and learned scholars and teachers, that we may be able to give a reason for the hope that is in us; through Jesus Christ our Lord, who liveth and reigneth with thee and the Holy Spirit, one God, for ever and ever. *Amen.*

II Almighty God, you raised up your servant Anselm to teach the Church of his day to understand its faith in your eternal Being, perfect justice, and saving mercy: Provide your Church in every age with devout and learned scholars and teachers, that we may be able to give a reason for the hope that is in us; through Jesus Christ our Lord, who lives and reigns with you and the Holy Spirit, one God, for ever and ever. *Amen.*

Psalm	Lessons
139:1-9	Romans 5:1-11
or 37:3-6, 32-33	Matthew 11:25-30

Preface of the Epiphany

A disciple of Jesus, named Mark, appears in several places in the New Testament. If all references to Mark can be accepted as referring to the same person, we learn that he was the son of a woman who owned a house in Jerusalem, perhaps the same house in which Jesus ate the Last Supper with his disciples. Mark may have been the young man who fled naked when Jesus was arrested in the Garden of Gethsemane. In his letter to the Colossians, Paul refers to "Mark the cousin of Barnabas," who was with him in his imprisonment. Mark set out with Paul and Barnabas on their first missionary journey, but he turned back for reasons which failed to satisfy Paul (Acts 15:36-40). When another journey was planned, Paul refused to have Mark with him. Instead, Mark went with Barnabas to Cyprus. The breach between Paul and Mark was later healed, and Mark became one of Paul's companions in Rome, as well as a close friend of Peter's.

An early tradition recorded by Papias, Bishop of Hieropolis in Asia Minor at the beginning of the second century, names Mark as the author of the Gospel bearing his name. This tradition, which holds that Mark drew his information from the teaching of Peter, is generally accepted. In his First Letter, Peter refers to "my son Mark," which shows a close relationship between the two men (1 Peter 5:13).

The Church of Alexandria in Egypt claimed Mark as its first bishop and most illustrious martyr, and the great Church of St. Mark in Venice commemorates the disciple who progressed from turning back while on a missionary journey with Paul and Barnabas to proclaiming in his Gospel Jesus of Nazareth as Son of God, and bearing witness to that faith in his later life as friend and companion to the apostles Peter and Paul.

Saint Mark the Evangelist

I   Almighty God, who by the hand of Mark the evangelist hast given to thy Church the Gospel of Jesus Christ the Son of God: We thank thee for this witness, and pray that we may be firmly grounded in its truth; through the same Jesus Christ our Lord, who liveth and reigneth with thee and the Holy Spirit, one God, for ever and ever. *Amen.*

II Almighty God, by the hand of Mark the evangelist you have given to your Church the Gospel of Jesus Christ the Son of God: We thank you for this witness, and pray that we may be firmly grounded in its truth; through Jesus Christ our Lord, who lives and reigns with you and the Holy Spirit, one God, for ever and ever. *Amen.*

Psalm	Lessons
2	Isaiah 52:7-10
or 2:7-10	Ephesians 4:7-8, 11-16
	Mark 1:1-15
	or Mark 16:15-20

Preface of All Saints

Catherine Benincasa was the youngest of twenty-five children of a wealthy dyer of Siena. At six years of age, she had a remarkable vision that probably decided her life's vocation. Walking home from a visit, she stopped on the road and gazed upward, oblivious to everything around her. "I beheld our Lord seated in glory with St. Peter, St. Paul, and St. John." She went on to say, later, that the Savior smiled on her and blessed her.

From then on, Catherine spent most of her time in prayer and meditation, despite her mother's attempts to force her to be like other girls. To settle matters, Catherine cut off her hair, her chief beauty. The family harassed her continually; but in the end, convinced that she was deaf to all opposition, her father let her do as she would: close herself away in a darkened room, fast, and sleep on boards. Eventually, she was accepted as a Dominican postulant.

Catherine had numerous visions, and was also tried most severely by loathsome temptations and degrading images. Frequently, she felt totally abandoned by the Lord. At last, in 1366, the Savior appeared with Mary and the Heavenly Host, and espoused her to himself, so ending her years of lonely prayer and struggle. She became a nurse, as Dominicans regularly did, caring for patients with leprosy and cancer whom other nurses disliked to treat.

Opinion in Siena was sharply divided about whether she was a saint or a fanatic, but when the Bishop of Capua was appointed her confessor, he helped her to win full support from the Dominican Mother House. Catherine was a courageous worker in time of severe plague; she visited prisoners condemned to death; she constantly was called upon to arbitrate feuds and to prepare troubled sinners for confession.

During the great schism of the papacy, with rival popes in Rome and Avignon, Catherine wrote tirelessly to princes, kings, and popes, urging them to restore the unity of the Church. She even went to Rome to press further for the cause.

Besides her many letters to all manner of people, Catherine wrote a *Dialogue,* a mystical work dictated in ecstasy. Exhausted and paralyzed, she died at the age of thirty-three.

Catherine of Siena

1380

I   Everlasting God, who didst so kindle the flame of holy love in the heart of blessed Catherine of Siena, as she meditated on the passion of thy Son our Savior, that she devoted her life to the poor and the sick, and to the peace and unity of the Church: Grant that we also may share in the mystery of Christ's death, and rejoice in the revelation of his glory; who liveth and reigneth with thee and the Holy Spirit, one God, now and for ever. *Amen.*

II   Everlasting God, you so kindled the flame of holy love in the heart of blessed Catherine of Siena, as she meditated on the passion of your Son our Savior, that she devoted her life to the poor and the sick, and to the peace and unity of the Church: Grant that we also may share in the mystery of Christ's death, and rejoice in the revelation of his glory; who lives and reigns with you and the Holy Spirit, one God, now and for ever. *Amen.*

Psalm	Lessons
36:5-10	1 John 1:5—2:2
or 16:5-11	Luke 12:22-24,29-31

Preface of a Saint (2)

The two apostles commemorated on this day are among those about whom little is known, except for their mention in the Gospels. James the Less is so called to distinguish him from James the son of Zebedee and from James "the brother of the Lord," or perhaps to indicate youth or lack of stature. He is known to us from the list of the Twelve, where he is called James the son of Alpheus. He may also be the person referred to in Mark's Gospel as James the younger, who, with his mother Mary and the other women, watched the crucifixion from a distance.

Philip figures in several important incidents in Jesus' ministry as reported in John's Gospel. There we read that Jesus called Philip soon after calling Andrew and Peter. Philip, in turn, found his friend Nathanael, and convinced him to come and see Jesus, the Messiah. Later, when Jesus saw the hungry crowd, he asked Philip, "How are we to buy bread, so that these people may eat?" (John 6:5). Philip's practical response, "Two hundred denarii would not buy enough bread for each of them to get a little" (John 6:7), was the prelude to the feeding of the multitude with the loaves and fishes. In a later incident in John's Gospel, some Greeks came to Philip asking to see Jesus. At the Last Supper, Philip's request, "Lord, show us the Father, and we shall be satisfied," evokes the response, "Have I been with you so long, and yet you do not know me, Philip? He who has seen me has seen the Father" (John 14:8, 9).

Saint Philip and Saint James, Apostles

I Almighty God, who didst give to thine apostles Philip and James grace and strength to bear witness to the truth: Grant that we, being mindful of their victory of faith, may glorify in life and death the Name of our Lord Jesus Christ; who liveth and reigneth with thee and the Holy Spirit, one God, now and for ever. *Amen.*

II Almighty God, who gave to your apostles Philip and James grace and strength to bear witness to the truth: Grant that we, being mindful of their victory of faith, may glorify in life and death the Name of our Lord Jesus Christ; who lives and reigns with you and the Holy Spirit, one God, now and for ever. *Amen.*

Psalm	Lessons
119:33-40	Isaiah 30:18-21
	2 Corinthians 4:1-6
	John 14:6-14

Preface of Apostles

Rarely in the history of the Church has the course of its development been more significantly determined by one person than it was by Athanasius in the fourth century. Gregory of Nazianzus called him "the pillar of the Church," and Basil the Great said he was "the God-given physician of her wounds."

Athanasius was born about 295 in Alexandria, and was ordained deacon in 319. He quickly attracted attention by his opposition to the presbyter Arius, whose denial of the full divinity of the Second Person of the Trinity was gaining widespread acceptance. Alexander, the Bishop of Alexandria, took Athanasius as his secretary and adviser to the first Ecumenical Council, at Nicaea in 325, which dealt with the Arian conflict. Athanasius was successful in winning approval for the phrase in the Nicene Creed which has ever since been recognized as expressing unequivocally the full godhead of the Son: "of one Being with the Father" *(homoousios)*.

When Alexander died in 328, Athanasius became bishop. He fearlessly defended the Nicene Christology against emperors, magistrates, bishops, and theologians. Five times he was sent into exile. He often seemed to stand alone for the orthodox faith. *"Athanasius contra mundum* (against the world)"* became a by-word. Yet, by the time of his last exile, his popularity among the citizens of Alexandria was so great that the Emperor had to recall him to avoid insurrection in the city.

Athanasius wrote voluminously: biblical interpretation, theological exposition, sermons, and letters. His treatise, *On the Incarnation of the Word of God*, is a still widely read classic.

In it, he writes, "The Savior of us all, the Word of God, in his great love took to himself a body and moved as Man among men, meeting their senses, so to speak, half way. He became himself an object for the senses, so that those who were seeking God in sensible things might apprehend the Father through the works which he, the Word of God, did in the body. Human and human-minded as men were, therefore, to whichever side they looked in the sensible world, they found themselves taught the truth."

Athanasius

Bishop of Alexandria, 373

I Uphold thy Church, O God of truth, as thou didst uphold thy servant Athanasius, to maintain and proclaim boldly the catholic faith against all opposition, trusting solely in the grace of thine eternal Word, who took upon himself our humanity that we might share his divinity; who liveth and reigneth with thee and the Holy Spirit, one God, now and for ever. *Amen.*

II Uphold your Church, O God of truth, as you upheld your servant Athanasius, to maintain and proclaim boldly the catholic faith against all opposition, trusting solely in the grace of your eternal Word, who took upon himself our humanity that we might share his divinity; who lives and reigns with you and the Holy Spirit, one God, now and for ever. *Amen.*

Psalm	Lessons
71:1-8	1 John 5:1-5
or 112:1-9	Matthew 10:22-32

Preface of the Epiphany

Monnica's life story is enshrined in the spiritual autobiography of her eldest son, in *The Confessions of Saint Augustine*. Born in North Africa about 331, of Berber parents, Monnica was married to a Latinized provincial of Tagaste named Patricius, whom she won to the Christian faith before his death. In her earlier years she was not without worldly ambitions and tastes. She grew in Christian maturity and spiritual insight through an ever-deepening life of prayer.

Her ambition for her gifted son was transformed into a passionate desire for his conversion to Christ. After his baptism in Milan in 387, by Bishop Ambrose, Augustine and his mother, together with a younger brother, planned to return home to Africa. While awaiting ship at Ostia, the port of Rome, Monnica fell ill.

Augustine writes, "One day during her illness she had a fainting spell and lost consciousness for a short time. We hurried to her bedside, but she soon regained consciousness and looked up at my brother and me as we stood beside her. With a puzzled look, she asked, 'Where was I?' Then, watching us closely as we stood there speechless with grief, she said, 'You will bury your mother here.' "

Augustine's brother expressed sorrow, for her sake, that she would die so far from her own country. She said to the two brothers, "It does not matter where you bury my body. Do not let that worry you. All I ask of you is that, wherever you may be, you should remember me at the altar of the Lord." To the question, whether she was not afraid at the thought of leaving her body in an alien land, she replied, "Nothing is far from God, and I need have no fear that he will not know where to find me, when he comes to raise me to life at the end of the world."

Recent excavations at Ostia have uncovered her original tomb. Her mortal remains, however, were transferred in 1430 to the Church of St. Augustine in Rome.

Monnica

Mother of Augustine of Hippo, 387

I   O Lord, who through spiritual discipline didst strengthen they servant Monnica to persevere in offering her love and prayers and tears for the conversion of her husband and of Augustine their son: Deepen our devotion, we beseech thee, and use us in accordance with thy will to bring others, even our own kindred, to acknowledge Jesus Christ as Savior and Lord; who with thee and the Holy Spirit liveth and reigneth, one God, for ever and ever. *Amen.*

II   O Lord, through spiritual discipline you strengthened your servant Monnica to persevere in offering her love and prayers and tears for the conversion of her husband and of Augustine their son: Deepen our devotion, we pray, and use us in accordance with your will to bring others, even our own kindred, to acknowledge Jesus Christ as Savior and Lord; who with you and the Holy Spirit lives and reigns, one God, for ever and ever. *Amen.*

Psalm	Lessons
115:12-18	1 Samuel 1:10-11, 20
or 116:10-17	Luke 7:11-17*
	or John 16:20-24*

Preface of Baptism

* *In some years this passage will occur at the Daily Office on this day.*

Of Dame Julian's early life we know little, only the probable date of her birth (1342). Her own writings in the *Revelations of Divine Love* are concerned only with her visions, or "showings," that she experienced when she was thirty years old.

She had been gravely ill and was given the last rites; suddenly, on the seventh day, all pain left her, and she had fifteen visions of the Passion. These brought her great peace and joy. "From that time I desired oftentimes to learn what was our Lord's meaning," she wrote, "and fifteen years after I was answered in ghostly understanding: 'Wouldst thou learn the Lord's meaning in this thing? Learn it well. Love was his meaning. Who showed it thee? Love. What showed he thee? Love. Wherefore showed it he? For Love. Hold thee therein and thou shalt learn and know more in the same.' Thus it was I learned that Love was our Lord's meaning."

Julian had long desired three gifts from God: "the mind of his passion, bodily sickness in youth, and three wounds — of contrition, of compassion, of will-full longing toward God." Her illness brought her the first two wounds, which then passed from her mind. The third, "will-full longing" (divinely inspired longing), never left her.

She became a recluse, an anchoress, at Norwich soon after her recovery from illness, living in a small dwelling attached to the Church of St. Julian. Even in her lifetime, she was famed as a mystic and spiritual counselor and was frequently visited by clergymen and lay persons, including the famous mystic Margery Kempe. Kempe says of Julian: "This anchoress was expert in knowledge of our Lord and could give good counsel. I spent much time with her talking of the love of our Lord Jesus Christ."

The Lady Julian's book is a tender and beautiful exposition of God's eternal and all-embracing love, showing how his charity toward the human race is exhibited in the Passion. Again and again she referred to Christ as "our courteous Lord." Many have found strength in the words the Lord had given her: "I can make all things well; I will make all things well; I shall make all things well; and thou canst see for thyself that all manner of things shall be well."

Dame Julian of Norwich

c. 1417

I   Lord God, who in thy compassion didst grant to the Lady Julian many revelations of thy nurturing and sustaining love: Move our hearts, like hers, to seek thee above all things, for in giving us thyself thou givest us all; through Jesus Christ our Lord, who liveth and reigneth with thee and the Holy Spirit, one God, for ever and ever. *Amen.*

II   Lord God, in your compassion you granted to the Lady Julian many revelations of your nurturing and sustaining love: Move our hearts, like hers, to seek you above all things, for in giving us yourself you give us all; through Jesus Christ our Lord, who lives and reigns with you and the Holy Spirit, one God, for ever and ever. *Amen.*

Psalm	Lessons
27:5-11	Hebrews 10:19-24
or 103:1-4,13-18	John 4:23-26

Preface of the Epiphany

Gregory of Nazianzus, one of the Cappadocian Fathers, loved God, the art of letters, and the human race — in that order. He was born about 330 in Nazianzus in Cappadocia (now Turkey), the son of a local bishop. He studied rhetoric in Athens with his friend Basil of Caesarea, and Julian, later to be the apostate emperor.

Gregory, together with Basil, compiled an anthology of Origen's works, *The Philokalia*. Two years later, he returned to his home, a town then rent by heresies and schism. His defense of his father's orthodoxy in the face of a violent mob brought peace to the town and prominence to Gregory.

In 361, against his will, Gregory was ordained presbyter, and settled down to live an austere, priestly life. He was not to have peace for long. Basil, in his fight against the Arian Emperor Valens, compelled Gregory to become Bishop of Sasima. According to Gregory, it was "a detestable little place without water or grass or any mark of civilization." He felt, he said, like "a bone flung to the dogs." His friendship with Basil suffered a severe break.

Deaths in his family, and that of his estranged friend Basil, brought Gregory himself to the point of death. He withdrew for healing.

In 379, Gregory moved to Constantinople, a new man and no longer in despair. He appeared as one afire with the love of God. His fame as a theologian rests on five sermons he delivered during this period on the doctrine of the Trinity. They are marked by clarity, strength, and a charming gaiety.

The next year, the new Emperor Theodosius entered Constantinople, and expelled its Arian bishop and clergy. Then, on a rainy day, the crowds in the Great Church of Hagia Sophia acclaimed Gregory bishop, after a ray of sunlight suddenly shone on him.

Power and position meant nothing to Gregory. After the Ecumenical Council of 381, he retired to Nazianzus where he died in 389. Among the Fathers of the Church, he alone is known as "The Divine," "The Theologian."

Gregory of Nazianzus

Bishop of Constantinople, 389

I   Almighty God, who hast revealed to thy Church thine eternal Being of glorious majesty and perfect love as one God in Trinity of Persons: Give us grace that, like thy bishop Gregory of Nazianzus, we may continue steadfast in the confession of this faith, and constant in our worship of thee, Father, Son, and Holy Spirit; who livest and reignest for ever and ever. *Amen.*

II   Almighty God, you have revealed to your Church your eternal Being of glorious majesty and perfect love as one God in Trinity of Persons: Give us grace that, like your bishop Gregory of Nazianzus, we may continue steadfast in the confession of this faith, and constant in our worship of you, Father, Son, and Holy Spirit; for you live and reign for ever and ever. *Amen.*

Psalm	Lessons
19:7-11 (12-14)	Wisdom 7:7-14
or 37:3-6,32-33	John 8:25-32

Preface of Trinity Sunday

In the ninth century, under King Alfred the Great, England had achieved considerable military, political, cultural, and even some ecclesiastical recovery from the Viking invasions. It was not until the following century that there was a revival of monasticism. In that, the leading figure was Dunstan.

Dunstan was born about 909 into a family with royal connections. He became a monk and in 943 was made Abbot of Glastonbury. During a year-long political exile in Flanders, he encountered the vigorous currents of the Benedictine monastic revival. King Edgar recalled Dunstan to England in 957, appointed him Bishop of Worcester, then of London; and, in 960, named him Archbishop of Canterbury. Together with his former pupils, Bishops Aethelwold of Winchester and Oswald of Worcester (later of York), Dunstan was a leader of the English Church. All three have been described as "contemplatives in action" — bringing the fruits of their monastic prayer-life to the immediate concerns of Church and State. They sought better education and discipline among the clergy, the end of landed family interest in the Church, the restoration of former monasteries and the establishment of new ones, a revival of monastic life for women, and a more elaborate and carefully ordered liturgical worship.

This reform movement was set forth in the "Monastic Agreement," a common code for English monasteries drawn up by Aethelwold about 970, primarily under the inspiration of Dunstan. It called for continual intercession for the royal house, and emphasized the close tie between the monasteries and the crown. This close alliance of Church and State, sacramentalized in the anointing of the King, was expressed liturgically in the earliest English coronation ceremony of which a full text survives, compiled for King Edgar by Dunstan and his associates.

The long-term effects of this tenth-century reform resulted in the development of two peculiarly English institutions: the "monastic cathedral," and "monk-bishops."

Dunstan is reputed to have been an expert craftsman. His name is especially associated with the working of metals and the casting of bells, and he was regarded as the patron saint of those crafts.

Dunstan

Archbishop of Canterbury, 988

I O God of truth and beauty, who didst richly endow thy bishop Dunstan with skill in music and the working of metals, and with gifts of administration and reforming zeal: Teach us, we beseech thee, to see in thee the source of all our talents, and move us to offer them for the adornment of worship and the advancement of true religion; through Jesus Christ our Lord, who liveth and reigneth with thee and the Holy Spirit, one God, now and for ever. *Amen.*

II O God of truth and beauty, you richly endowed your bishop Dunstan with skill in music and the working of metals, and with gifts of administration and reforming zeal: Teach us, we pray, to see in you the source of all our talents, and move us to offer them for the adornment of worship and the advancement of true religion; through Jesus Christ our Lord, who lives and reigns with you and the Holy Spirit, one God, now and for ever. *Amen.*

Psalm	Lessons
57:6-11	Ecclesiasticus 44:1-7
or 33:1-5, 20-21	Matthew 24:42-47

Preface of the Dedication of a Church

Alcuin was born about 730 near York into a noble family related to Willibrord, the first missionary to the Netherlands. He was educated at the cathedral school in York under Archbishop Egbert, a pupil of Bede. He thus inherited the best traditions of learning and zeal of the early English Church. After ordination as a deacon in 770, he became head of the York school. Following a meeting in 781 with the Emperor Charlemagne in Pavia (Italy), he was persuaded to become the Emperor's "prime minister," with special responsibility for the revival of education and learning in the Frankish dominions.

Alcuin was named Abbot of Tours in 796, where he died on May 19, 804, and was buried in the church of St. Martin.

Alcuin was a man of vast learning, personal charm, and integrity of character. In his direction of Charlemagne's Palace School at Aachen, he was chiefly responsible for the preservation of the classical heritage of western civilization. Schools were revived in cathedrals and monasteries, and manuscripts of both pagan and Christian writings of antiquity were collated and copied.

Under the authority of Charlemagne, the liturgy was reformed, and service books gathered from Rome were edited and adapted. To this work we owe the preservation of many of the Collects that have come down to us, including the Collect for Purity at the beginning of the Holy Eucharist.

Alcuin

Deacon, and Abbot of Tours, 804

I   Almighty God, who in a rude and barbarous age didst raise up thy deacon Alcuin to rekindle the light of learning: Illumine our minds, we pray thee, that amid the uncertainties and confusions of our own time we may show forth thine eternal truth; through Jesus Christ our Lord, who liveth and reigneth with thee and the Holy Spirit, one God, for ever and ever. *Amen.*

II   Almighty God, in a rude and barbarous age you raised up your deacon Alcuin to rekindle the light of learning: Illumine our minds, we pray, that amid the uncertainties and confusions of our own time we may show forth your eternal truth; through Jesus Christ our Lord, who lives and reigns with you and the Holy Spirit, one God, for ever and ever. *Amen.*

Psalm	Lessons
37:3-6,32-33	Ecclesiasticus 39:1-9
or 112:1-9	Matthew 13:47-52

Preface of a Saint (1)

When the General Convention of 1835 made all the members of the Episcopal Church members also of the Domestic and Foreign Missionary Society, it provided at the same time for missionary bishops to serve in the wilderness and in foreign countries. Jackson Kemper was the first such bishop. Although he was assigned to Missouri and Indiana, he laid foundations also in Iowa, Wisconsin, Minnesota, Nebraska, and Kansas, and made extensive missionary tours in the South and Southwest.

Kemper was born in Pleasant Valley, New York, on December 24, 1789. He graduated from Columbia College in 1809, and was ordained deacon in 1811, and priest in 1814.

He served Bishop White as Assistant at Christ Church, Philadelphia. At his urging, Bishop White made his first and only visitation in western Pennsylvania. In 1835, Kemper was ordained bishop, and immediately set out on his travels.

Because Episcopal clergymen, mostly from well-to-do Eastern homes, found it hard to adjust to the harsh life of the frontier — scorching heat, drenching rains, and winter blizzards — Kemper established Kemper College in St. Louis, Missouri, the first of many similar attempts to train clergymen, and in more recent times lay persons as well, for specialized tasks in the Church. The College failed in 1845 from the usual malady of such projects in the church — inadequate funding. Nashotah House, in Wisconsin, which he founded in 1842, with the help of James Lloyd Breck and his companions, was more successful. So was Racine College, founded in 1852. Both these institutions reflected Kemper's devotion to beauty in ritual and worship.

Kemper pleaded for more attention to the Indians, and encouraged the translation of services into native languages. He described a service among Oneida Indians which was marked by "courtesy, reverence, worship — and obedience to that Great Spirit in whose hands are the issues of life."

From 1859 until his death, Kemper was diocesan Bishop of Wisconsin. He is more justly honored by his unofficial title, "The Bishop of the Whole Northwest."

Jackson Kemper

First Missionary Bishop in the United States, 1870

I   Lord God, in whose providence Jackson Kemper was chosen first missionary bishop in this land, that by his arduous labor and travel congregations might be established in scattered settlements of the West: Grant that the Church may always be faithful to its mission, and have the vision, courage, and perseverance to make known to all people the Good News of Jesus Christ; who with thee and the Holy Spirit liveth and reigneth, one God, for ever and ever. *Amen.*

II   Lord God, in your providence Jackson Kemper was chosen first missionary bishop in this land, and by his arduous labor and travel congregations were established in scattered settlements of the West: Grant that the Church may always be faithful to its mission, and have the vision, courage, and perseverance to make known to all people the Good News of Jesus Christ; who with you and the Holy Spirit lives and reigns, one God, for ever and ever. *Amen.*

Psalm	Lessons
67	1 Corinthians 3:8-11
or 96:1-7	Matthew 28:16-20

Preface of Pentecost

At the age of seven, Bede's parents brought him to the nearby monastery at Jarrow (near Durham in northeast England) for his education. There, as he later wrote, "spending all the remaining time of my life. . . I wholly applied myself to the study of Scripture, and amidst the observance of regular discipline, and the daily care of singing in the church, I always took delight in learning, teaching, and writing."

Bede was ordained deacon at nineteen, and presbyter at thirty. He died on the eve of the Ascension while dictating a vernacular translation of the Gospel according to John. About 1020 his body was removed to Durham, and placed in the Galilee, the Lady Chapel at the west end of the Cathedral nave.

Bede was the greatest scholar of his time in the Western Church. He wrote commentaries on the Scriptures based on patristic interpretations. His treatise on chronology was standard for a long time. He also wrote on orthography, poetic meter, and especially on history. His most famous work, *The Ecclesiastical History of England,* written in Latin, remains the primary source for the period 597 to 731, when Anglo-Saxon culture developed and Christianity triumphed. In this work, Bede was clearly ahead of his time. He consulted many documents, carefully evaluated their reliability, and cited his sources. His interpretations were balanced and judicious. He also wrote the *History of the Abbots* (of Wearmouth and Jarrow), and a notable biography of Cuthbert, both in prose and verse.

His character shines through his work — an exemplary monk, an ardent Christian, devoted scholar, and a man of pure and winsome manners. He received the unusual title of *Venerable* more than a century after his death. According to one legend, the monk writing the inscription for his tomb was at a loss for a word to fill out the couplet:

> *Hac sunt in fossa*
> *Bedae* — blank — *ossa*

> (This grave contains
> the — *blank* — Bede's remains)

That night an angel filled in the blank: *Venerabilis.*

Bede the Venerable
Priest, and Monk of Jarrow, 735

I   Heavenly Father, who didst call thy servant Bede, while still a child, to devote his life to thy service in the disciplines of religion and scholarship; Grant that as he labored in the Spirit to bring the riches of thy truth to his generation, so we, in our various vocations, may strive to make thee known in all the world; through Jesus Christ our Lord, who liveth and reigneth with thee and the Holy Spirit, one God, for ever and ever. *Amen.*

II   Heavenly Father, you called your servant Bede, while still a child, to devote his life to your service in the disciplines of religion and scholarship: Grant that as he labored in the Spirit to bring the riches of your truth to his generation, so we, in our various vocations, may strive to make you known in all the world; through Jesus Christ our Lord, who lives and reigns with you and the Holy Spirit, one God, for ever and ever. *Amen.*

Psalm	Lessons
78:1-4	Wisdom 7:15-22
or 19:7-11 (12-14)	Matthew 13:47-52

Preface of a Saint (1)

Although Christianity had existed in Britain before the invasions of Angles and Saxons in the fifth century, Pope Gregory the Great decided tn 596 to send a mission to the pagan Anglo-Saxons. He selected, from his own monastery on the Coelian hill in Rome, a group of monks, led by their prior, Augustine. They arrived in Kent in 597, carrying a silver cross and an image of Jesus Christ painted on a board, which thus became, so far as we know, "Canterbury's first icon." King Ethelbert tolerated their presence and allowed them the use of an old church built on the east side of Canterbury, dating from the Roman occupation of Britain. Here, says the Venerable Bede, they assembled "to sing the psalms, to pray, to say Mass, to preach, and to baptize." This church of St. Martin is the earliest place of Christian worship in England still in use.

Probably in 601, Ethelbert was converted, thus becoming the first Christian king in England. About the same time, Augustine was ordained bishop somewhere in France and named "Archbishop of the English Nation." Thus, the see of Canterbury and its Cathedral Church of Christ owe their establishment to Augustine's mission, as does the nearby Abbey of SS. Peter and Paul, later re-named for Augustine. The "chair of St. Augustine" in Canterbury Cathedral, however, dates from the thirteenth century.

Some correspondence between Augustine and Gregory survives. One of the Pope's most famous counsels to the first Archbishop of Canterbury has to do with diversity in the young English Church. Gregory writes, "If you have found customs, whether in the Roman, Gallican, or any other Churches that may be more acceptable to God, I wish you to make a careful selection of them, and teach the Church of the English, which is still young in the faith, whatever you can profitably learn from the various Churches. For things should not be loved for the sake of places, but places for the sake of good things."

This counsel bears on the search for Christian "unity in diversity" of the ecumenical movement of today.

Augustine died on May 26, probably in 605.

Augustine

First Archbishop of Canterbury, 605

I   O Lord our God, who by thy Son Jesus Christ didst call thine apostles and send them forth to preach the Gospel to the nations: We bless thy holy Name for thy servant Augustine, first Archbishop of Canterbury, whose labors in propagating thy Church among the English people we commemorate today; and we pray that all whom thou dost call and send may do thy will, and bide thy time, and see thy glory; through Jesus Christ our Lord, who liveth and reigneth with thee and the Holy Spirit, one God, for ever and ever. *Amen.*

II O Lord our God, by your Son Jesus Christ you called your apostles and sent them forth to preach the Gospel to the nations: We bless your holy Name for your servant Augustine, first Archbishop of Canterbury, whose labors in propagating your Church among the English people we commemorate today; and we pray that all whom you call and send may do your will, and bide your time, and see your glory; through Jesus Christ our Lord, who lives and reigns with you and the Holy Spirit, one God, for ever and ever. *Amen.*

Psalm	Lessons
66:1-8	2 Corinthians 5:17-20a
or 103:1-4,13-18	Luke 5:1-11

Preface of Apostles

This Feast commemorates the visit of the Blessed Virgin to her cousin Elizabeth, recorded in the Gospel according to Luke (1:39-56).

Elizabeth, who was then carrying John the Baptist, greeted Mary with the words, "Blessed are you among women, and blessed is the fruit of your womb." Mary broke into the song of praise and thanksgiving which we call the Magnificat, "My soul proclaims the greatness of the Lord."

In this scene, the unborn John the Baptist, the prophet who was to prepare the way of the Lord, rejoices in the presence of him whose coming he is later to herald publicly to all Israel, for the Gospel records that when Mary's greeting came to her kinswoman's ears, the babe in Elizabeth's womb leaped for joy.

Visitation of the Blessed Virgin Mary

I   Father in heaven, by whose grace the virgin mother of thy incarnate Son was blessed in bearing him, but still more blessed in keeping thy word: Grant us who honor the exaltation of her lowliness to follow the example of her devotion to thy will; through the same Jesus Christ our Lord, who liveth and reigneth with thee and the Holy Spirit, one God, for ever and ever. *Amen.*

II   Father in heaven, buy your grace the virgin mother of your incarnate Son was blessed in bearing him, but still more blessed in keeping your word: Grant us who honor the exaltation of her lowliness to follow the example of her devotion to your will; through Jesus Christ our Lord, who lives and reigns with you and the Holy Spirit, one God, for ever and ever. *Amen.*

Psalm

113
or   Canticle 9

Preface of the Epiphany

Lessons

Zephaniah 3:14-18a
Colossians 3:12-17
Luke 1:39-49

The first Book of Common Prayer came into use on the Day of Pentecost, June 9, 1549, in the second year of the reign of King Edward the Sixth. From it have descended all subsequent editions and revisions of the Book in the Churches of the Anglican Communion.

Though prepared by a commission of learned bishops and priests, the format, substance, and style of the Prayer Book were primarily the work of Thomas Cranmer, Archbishop of Canterbury, 1533-1556. The principal sources employed in its compilation were the medieval Latin service books of the Use of Sarum (Salisbury), with enrichments from the Greek liturgies, certain ancient Gallican rites, the vernacular German forms prepared by Luther, and a revised Latin liturgy of the reforming Archbishop Hermann of Cologne. The Psalter and other biblical passages were drawn from the English "Great Bible" authorized by King Henry the Eighth in 1539, and the Litany was taken from the English form issued as early as 1544.

The originality of the Prayer Book, apart from the felicitous translations and paraphrases of the old Latin forms, lay in its simplification of the complicated liturgical usages of the medieval Church, so that it was suitable for use by the laity as well as by the clergy. The Book thus became both a manual of common worship for Anglicans and a primary resource for their personal spirituality.

The First Book of Common Prayer

This feast is appropriately observed on a weekday following the Day of Pentecost.

I   Almighty and everliving God, whose servant Thomas Cranmer, with others, did restore the language of the people in the prayers of thy Church: Make us always thankful for this heritage; and help us so to pray in the Spirit and with the understanding, that we may worthily magnify thy holy Name; through Jesus Christ our Lord, who liveth and reigneth with thee and the Holy Spirit, one God, for ever and ever. *Amen.*

II   Almighty and everliving God, whose servant Thomas Cranmer, with others, restored the language of the people in the prayers of your Church: Make us always thankful for this heritage; and help us so to pray in the Spirit and with the understanding, that we may worthily magnify your holy Name; through Jesus Christ our Lord, who lives and reigns with you and the Holy Spirit, one God, for ever and ever. *Amen.*

Psalm	Lessons
96:1-9	Acts 2:38-42
or 33:1-5,20-21	John 4:21-24

Preface of Pentecost

Toward the middle of the second century, there came into the young Christian community a seeker for the truth, whose wide interests, noble spirit, and able mind, greatly enriched it.

Justin was born into a Greek-speaking pagan family about the year 110 in Samaria, near Shechem. He was educated in Greek philosophy. Like Augustine after him, he was left restless by all this knowledge. During a walk along the beach at Ephesus, he fell in with a stranger, who told him about Christ. "Straightway a flame was kindled in my soul," he writes, "and a love of the prophets and those who are friends of Christ possessed me." He became a Christian as a result of this encounter, and thereafter regarded Christianity as the only "safe and profitable philosophy."

About a 150, Justin moved to Rome. As philosophers did in those days, he started a school — in this case, a school of Christian philosophy — and accepted students. He also wrote. Three of his works are known to us: a dialogue in Platonic style with a Jew named Trypho, and two "apologies." (An apology in this sense, of course, is not an excuse, but a spirited defense.) Justin's *First* and *Second Apologies* defend Christianity against the Greek charge of irrationality and the Roman charge of disloyalty to the empire. These two works provide us with important insights into developing theological ideas and liturgical practices of early Christianity. In the *Dialogue with Trypho*, Justin defends the Church against the Jewish charge of distorting the Old Testament. He interprets the Old Testament as the foreshadowing of the New.

While teaching in Rome, he engaged in a public debate with a philosopher of the Cynic school named Crescens, accusing him of ignorance and immorality. Angered, Crescens preferred legal charges against him. Justin and six of his students were arrested and brought before the prefect Rusticus. As the custom was, Rusticus gave them an opportunity to renounce their faith. All steadfastly refused to do so. Justin and his companions were put to death about the year 167.

Justin

Martyr at Rome, c. 167

I   Almighty and everlasting God, who didst find thy martyr Justin wandering from teacher to teacher, seeking the true God, and didst reveal to him the sublime wisdom of thine eternal Word: Grant that all who seek thee, or a deeper knowledge of thee, may find and be found by thee; through Jesus Christ our Lord, who liveth and reigneth with thee and the Holy Spirit, one God, for ever and ever. *Amen.*

II   Almighty and everlasting God, you found your martyr Justin wandering from teacher to teacher, seeking the true God, and you revealed to him the sublime wisdom of your eternal Word: Grant that all who seek you, or a deeper knowledge of you, may find and be found by you; through Jesus Christ our Lord, who lives and reigns with you and the Holy Spirit, one God, for ever and ever. *Amen.*

Psalm	Lessons
16:5-11	1 Corinthians 1:18-25
or 116:1-8	John 12:44-50

Preface of a Saint (3)

In the second century, after a brief respite, Christians in many parts of the Roman empire were once again subjected to persecution. At Lyons and Vienne, in Gaul, there were missionary centers which had drawn many Christians from Asia and Greece. They were living a devout life under the guidance of Pothinus, elderly Bishop of Lyons, when persecution began in 177.

At first, the Christians were socially excluded from Roman homes, the public baths, and the market place; insults, stones, and blows were rained on them by pagan mobs, and Christian homes were vandalized. Soon after, the imperial officials forced Christians to come to the market place for harsh questioning, followed by imprisonment.

Some slaves from Christian households were tortured to extract public accusations that Christians practiced cannibalism, incest, and other perversions. These false accusations roused the mob to such a pitch of wrath that any leniency toward the imprisoned Christians was impossible. Even friendly pagans now turned against them.

The fury of the mob fell most heavily on Sanctus, a deacon; Attalus; Maturus, a recent convert; and Blandina, a slave. According to Eusebius, Blandina was so filled with power to withstand torments that her torturers gave up. "I am a Christian," she said, "and nothing vile is done among us." Sanctus was tormented with red-hot irons. The aged Pothinus, badly beaten, died soon after. Finally, the governor decided to set aside several days for a public spectacle in the amphitheater.

On the final day of the spectacle, writes Eusebius, "Blandina, last of all, like a noble mother who had encouraged her children and sent them ahead victorious to the King, hastened to join them." Beaten, torn, burned with irons, she was wrapped in a net and tossed about by a wild bull. The spectators were amazed at her endurance.

Eusebius concludes: "They offered up to the Father a single wreath, but it was woven of diverse colors and flowers of all kinds. It was fitting that the noble athletes should endure a varied conflict, and win a great victory, that they might be entitled in the end to receive the crown supreme of life everlasting."

The Martyrs of Lyons

177

I   Grant, O Lord, we beseech thee, that we who keep the feast of the holy martyrs Blandina and her companions may be rooted and grounded in love of thee, and may endure the sufferings of this life for the glory that shall be revealed in us; through Jesus Christ our Lord, who liveth and reigneth with thee and the Holy Spirit, one God, now and for ever. *Amen.*

II   Grant, O Lord, that we who keep the feast of the holy martyrs Blandina and her companions may be rooted and grounded in love of you, and may endure the sufferings of this life for the glory that shall be revealed in us; through Jesus Christ our Lord, who lives and reigns with you and the Holy Spirit, one God, now and for ever. *Amen.*

Psalm	Lessons
126	1 Peter 1:3-9
or 34:1-8	Mark 8:34-38

Preface of a Saint (3)

On June 3, 1886, thirty-two young men, pages of the court of King Mwanga of Buganda, were burned to death at Namugongo for their refusal to renounce Christianity. In the following months many other Christians throughout the country died by fire or spear for their faith.

These martyrdoms totally changed the dynamic of Christian growth in Uganda. Introduced by a handful of Anglican and Roman Catholic missionaries after 1877, the Christian faith had been preached only to the immediate members of the court, by order of King Mutesa. His successor, Mwanga, became increasingly angry as he realized that the first converts put loyalty to Christ above the traditional loyalty to the king. Martyrdoms began in 1885 (including Bishop Hannington and his Companions: see October 29th). Mwanga first forbade anyone to go near a Christian mission on pain of death, but finding himself unable to cool the ardor of the converts, resolved to wipe out Christianity.

The Namugongo martyrdoms produced a result entirely opposite to Mwanga's intentions. The example of these martyrs, who walked to their death singing hymns and praying for their enemies, so inspired many of the bystanders that they began to seek instruction from the remaining Christians. Within a few years the original handful of converts had multiplied many times and spread far beyond the court. The martyrs had left the indelible impression that Christianity was truly African, not simply a white man's religion. Most of the missionary work was carried out by Africans rather than by white missionaries, and Christianity spread steadily. Uganda is now the most Christian nation in Africa.

Renewed persecution of Christians by a Muslim military dictatorship in the 1970's proved the vitality of the example of the Namugongo martyrs. Among the thousands of new martyrs, both Anglican and Roman Catholic, was Janani Luwum, Archbishop of the (Anglican) Church of Uganda, whose courageous ministry and death inspired not only his countrymen but also Christians throughout the world.

The Martyrs of Uganda

1886

I   O God, by whose providence the blood of the martyrs is the
seed of the Church: Grant that we who remember before
thee the blessed martyrs of Uganda, may, like them, be
steadfast in our faith in Jesus Christ, to whom they gave
obedience even unto death, and by their sacrifice brought
forth a plentiful harvest; through Jesus Christ our Lord, who
liveth and reigneth with thee and the Holy Spirit, one God,
for ever and ever. *Amen.*

II   O God, by your providence the blood of the martyrs is the
seed of the Church: Grant that we who remember before
you the blessed martyrs of Uganda, may, like them, be
steadfast in our faith in Jesus Christ, to whom they gave
obedience, even to death, and by their sacrifice brought forth
a plentiful harvest; through Jesus Christ our Lord, who lives
and reigns with you and the Holy Spirit, one God, for ever
and ever. *Amen.*

Psalm	Lessons
138	Hebrews 10:32-39
or 116:10-17	Matthew 24:9-14

Preface of Holy Week

Boniface is justly called one of the "Makers of Europe." He was born at Crediton in Devonshire, England, about 675, and received the English name of Winfred. He was educated at Exeter, and later at Nursling, near Winchester, where he was professed a monk and ordained to the presbyterate.

Inspired by the examples of Willibrord and others, Winfred decided to become a missionary, and made his first Journey to Frisia (Netherlands) in 716 — a venture with little success. In 719 he started out again; but this time he first went to Rome to seek papal approval. Pope Gregory the Second commissioned him to work in Germany, and gave him the name of Boniface.

For the rest of his days, Boniface devoted himself to reforming, planting, and organizing churches, monasteries, and dioceses in Hesse, Thuringia, and Bavaria. Many helpers and supplies came to him from friends in England. In 722 the Pope ordained him a bishop, ten years later made him an archbishop, and in 743 gave him a fixed see at Mainz.

The Frankish rulers also supported his work. At their invitation, he presided over reforming councils of the Frankish Church; and in 752, with the consent of Pope Zacharias, he anointed Pepin (Pippin) as King of the Franks. Thus, the way was prepared for Charlemagne, son of Pepin, and the revival of a unified Christian dominion in western Europe.

In 753 Boniface resigned his see, to spend his last years again as a missionary in Frisia. On June 5, 754, while awaiting a group of converts for confirmation, he and his companions were murdered by a band of pagans, near Dokkum. His body was buried at Fulda, a monastery he had founded in 744, near Mainz.

Boniface

Archbishop of Mainz, Missionary to Germany, and Martyr, 754

I   Almighty God, who didst call thy faithful servant Boniface
to be a witness and martyr in Germany, and by his labor and
suffering didst raise up a people for thine own possession:
Pour forth thy Holy Spirit upon thy Church in every land,
that by the service and sacrifice of many thy holy Name may
be glorified and thy kingdom enlarged; through Jesus Christ
our Lord, who liveth and reigneth with thee and the same
Spirit, one God, for ever and ever. *Amen.*

II   Almighty God, you called your faithful servant Boniface to
be a witness and martyr in Germany, and by his labor and
suffering you raised up a people for your own possession:
Pour out your Holy Spirit upon your Church in every land,
that by the service and sacrifice of many your holy Name
may be glorified and your kingdom enlarged; through Jesus
Christ our Lord, who lives and reigns with you and the Holy
Spirit, one God, for ever and ever. *Amen.*

Psalm	Lessons
115:1-8	Acts 20:17-28
or 31:1-5	Luke 24:44-53

Preface of Apostles

Many legends have gathered about Columba, but there are also some historical data concerning his many works in the writings of Bede and Adamnan. According to one story, Patrick of Ireland foretold Columba's birth in a prophecy:

> He will be a saint and will be devout,
> He will be an abbot, the king of royal graces,
> He will be lasting and for ever good;
> The eternal kingdom be mine by his protection.

Columba was born in Ireland in 521, and early in life showed scholarly and clerical ability. He entered the monastic life, and almost immediately set forth on missionary travels. Even before ordination to the presbyterate in 551, he had founded monasteries at Derry and Durrow.

Twelve years after his ordination, Columba and a dozen companions set out for northern Britain, where the Picts were still generally ignorant of Christianity. Columba was kindly received, allowed to preach, convert, and baptize. He was also given possession of the island of Iona, where, according to legend, his tiny boat had washed ashore. Here he founded the celebrated monastery which became the center for the conversion of the Picts. From Iona, also, his disciples went out to found other monasteries, which, in turn, became centers of missionary activity.

Columba made long journeys through the Highlands, as far as Aberdeen. He often returned to Ireland to attend synods, and thus established Iona as a link between Irish and Pictish Christians. For thirty years, he evangelized, studied, wrote, and governed his monastery at Iona. He supervised his monks in their work in the fields and workrooms, in their daily worship and Sunday Eucharist, and in their study and teaching. He died peacefully while working on a copy of the Psalter. He had put down his pen, rested a few hours, and at Matins was found dead before the Altar, a smile on his face. He is quoted by his biographer Adamnan as having said, "This day is called in the sacred Scriptures a day of rest, and truly to me it will be such, for it is the last of my life and I shall enter into rest after the fatigues of my labors."

Columba

Abbot of Iona, 597

I   O God, who by the preaching of thy blessed servant
Columba didst cause the light of the Gospel to shine in
Scotland: Grant, we beseech thee, that, having his life and
labors in remembrance, we may show forth our thankfulness
to thee by following the example of his zeal and patience;
through Jesus Christ our Lord, who liveth and reigneth with
thee and the Holy Spirit, one God, for ever and ever. *Amen.*

II   O God, by the preaching of your blessed servant Columba
you caused the light of the Gospel to shine in Scotland:
Grant, we pray, that, having his life and labors in
remembrance, we may show our thankfulness to you by
following the example of his zeal and patience; through
Jesus Christ our Lord, who lives and reigns with you and the
Holy Spirit, one God, for ever and ever. *Amen.*

Psalm	Lessons
97:1-2, 7-12	1 Corinthians 3:11-23
or 98:1-4	Luke 10:17-20

Preface of Apostles

Ephrem of Edessa was a teacher, poet, orator, and defender of the faith — a voice of Aramaic Christianity, speaking the language Jesus spoke, using the imagery Jesus used. Edessa, a Syrian city, was a center for the spread of Christianity in the East long before the conversion of the western Roman empire.

The Syrians called Ephrem "The harp of the Holy Spirit," and his hymns still enrich the liturgies of the Syrian Church. Ephrem was one whose writings were influential in the development of Church doctrine. Jerome writes: "I have read in Greek a volume of his on the Holy Spirit; though it was only a translation, I recognized therein the sublime genius of the man."

Ephrem was born at Nisibis in Mesopotamia. At eighteen, he was baptized by James, Bishop of Nisibis. It is believed that Ephrem accompanied James to the famous Council of Nicaea in 325. He lived at Nisibis until 363, when the Persians captured the city and drove out the Christians.

Ephrem retired to a cave in the hills above the city of Edessa. There he wrote most of his spiritual works. He lived on barley bread and dried herbs, sometimes varied by greens. He drank only water. His clothing was a mass of patches. But he was not a recluse, and frequently went to Edessa to preach. Discovering that hymns could be of great value in support of the true faith, he opposed Gnostic hymns with his own, sung by a choir of women.

During a famine in 372-373, he distributed food and money to the poor and organized a sort of ambulance service for the sick. He died of exhaustion, brought on by his long hours of relief work.

Of his writings, there remain 72 hymns, commentaries on the Old and New Testaments, and numerous homilies. In his commentary on the Passion, he wrote: "No one has seen or shall see the things which you have seen. The Lord himself has become the altar, priest, and bread, and the chalice of salvation. He alone suffices for all, yet none suffices for him. He is Altar and Lamb, victim and sacrifice, priest as well as food."

Ephrem of Edessa

Deacon, 373

I   Pour out upon us, O Lord, that same Spirit by which thy deacon Ephrem rejoiced to proclaim in sacred song the mysteries of faith; and so gladden our hearts that we, like him, may be devoted to thee alone; through Jesus Christ our Lord, who liveth and reigneth with thee and the Holy Spirit, one God, now and for ever. *Amen.*

II   Pour out on us, O Lord, that same Spirit by which your deacon Ephrem rejoiced to proclaim in sacred song the mysteries of faith; and so gladden our hearts that we, like him, may be devoted to you alone; through Jesus Christ our Lord, who lives and reigns with you and the Holy Spirit, one God, now and for ever. *Amen.*

Psalm	Lessons
98:5-10	Proverbs 3:1-7
or 33:1-5,20-21	Matthew 13:47-52

Preface of a Saint (I)

"Joseph, a Levite born in Cyprus, whom the apostles called Barnabas (which means son of encouragement) sold a field he owned, brought the money, and turned it over to the apostles" (Acts 4:36-37). This first reference in the New Testament to Barnabas introduces one whose missionary efforts would cause him to be called, like the Twelve, an apostle. As a Jew of the Dispersion, he had much in common with Paul. When Paul came to Jerusalem after his conversion, the disciples were afraid to receive him. It was Barnabas who brought Paul to the apostles, and declared to them how, on the road to Damascus, Paul had seen the Lord, and had preached boldly in the name of Jesus (Acts 9:27). Later, Barnabas, having settled in Antioch, sent for Paul to join him in leading the Christian Church in that city.

Barnabas and Paul were sent by the disciples in Antioch to carry famine relief to the Church in Jerusalem. Upon their return, the Church in Antioch sent them on their first missionary journey beginning at Cyprus. At Lystra in Asia Minor, the superstitious people took them to be gods, supposing the eloquent Paul to be Mercury, the messenger of the gods, and Barnabas to be Jupiter, the chief of the gods, a testimony, to the commanding presence of Barnabas. The association of Barnabas and Paul was broken, after their journey, by a disagreement about Mark, who had left the mission to return to Jerusalem. After attending the Council of Jerusalem with Barnabas, Paul made a return visit to the Churches he and Barnabas had founded in Asia Minor. Barnabas and Mark went to Cyprus, where Barnabas is traditionally honored as the founder of the Church.

It seems that Barnabas continued his journeys for the Gospel, because Paul mentions him several times in his letters to the Galatians, the Corinthians, and the Colossians. Tradition has it that he was martyred at Salamis in Cyprus.

Saint Barnabas the Apostle

I   Grant, O God, that we may follow the example of thy faithful servant Barnabas, who, seeking not his own renown but the well-being of thy Church, gave generously of his life and substance for the relief of the poor and the spread of the Gospel; through Jesus Christ our Lord, who liveth and reigneth with thee and the Holy Spirit, one God, for ever and ever. *Amen.*

II   Grant, O God, that we may follow the example of your faithful servant Barnabas, who, seeking not his own renown but the well-being of your Church, gave generously of his life and substance for the relief of the poor and the spread of the Gospel; through Jesus Christ our Lord, who lives and reigns with you and the Holy Spirit, one God, for ever and ever. *Amen.*

Psalm

112

Lessons

Isaiah 42:5-12
Acts 11:19-30;13:1-3
Matthew 10:7-16

Preface of Apostles

John Johnson Enmegahbowh, an Odawa (Ottawa) Indian from Canada, was raised in the Midewiwin traditional healing way of his grandfather and the Christian religion of his mother. He came into the United States as a Methodist missionary in 1832. At one point Enmegahbowh attempted to abandon missionary work and return to Canada, but the boat was turned back by storms on Lake Superior, providing him a vision: "Here Mr. Jonah came before me and said, 'Ah, my friend Enmegahbowh, I know you. You are a fugitive. You have sinned and disobeyed God. Instead of going to the city of Nineveh, where God sent you to spread his word to the people, you started to go, and then turned aside. You are now on your way to the city of Tarsish....'"

Enmegahbowh invited James Lloyd Breck to Gull Lake, where together they founded St. Columba's Mission in 1852. The mission was later moved to White Earth, where Enmegahbowh served until his death in 1902. Unwelcome for a time among some Ojibway groups because he warned the community at Fort Ripley about the 1862 uprising, Enmegahbowh was consistent as a man of peace, inspiring the Waubanaquot (Chief White Cloud) mission, which obtained a lasting peace between the Ojibway and the Dakota peoples.

Enmegahbowh ("The One who Stands Before his People") is the first recognized Native American priest in the Episcopal Church. He was ordained deacon by Bishop Kemper in 1859 and priest by Bishop Whipple in the cathedral at Faribault in 1867. Enmegahbowh helped train many others to serve as deacons throughout northern Minnesota. The powerful tradition of Ojibway hymn singing is a living testimony to their ministry. His understanding of Native tradition enabled him to enculturate Christianity in the language and traditions of the Ojibway. He tirelessly traveled throughout Minnesota and beyond, actively participating in the development of mission strategy and policy for the Episcopal Church.

Enmegahbowh

Priest and Missionary, 1902

I   Almighty God, thou didst lead thy pilgrim people of old with fire and cloud: Grant that the ministers of thy Church, following the example of blessed Enmegahbowh, may stand before thy holy people, leading them with fiery zeal and gentle humility. This we ask through Jesus, the Christ, who liveth and reigneth with thee in the unity of the Holy Spirit, one God now and for ever. *Amen.*

II   Almighty God, you led your pilgrim people of old with fire and cloud: Grant that the ministers of your Church, following the example of blessed Enmegahbowh, may stand before your holy people, leading them with fiery zeal and gentle humility. This we ask through Jesus, the Christ, who lives and reigns with you in the unity of the Holy Spirit, one God now and for ever. *Amen.*

Psalm	Lessons
129	Isaiah 52:7-10 *or* 1 Peter 5:1-4
	Luke 6:17-23

Preface of a Saint (1)

Basil was born about 329, in Caesarea of Cappadocia, into a Christian family of wealth and distinction. Educated in classical Hellenism, Basil might have continued in academic life, had it not been for the death of a beloved younger brother and the faith of his sister, Macrina. He was baptized at the age of twenty-eight, and ordained a deacon soon after.

Macrina had founded the first monastic order for women at Annesi. Fired by her example, Basil made a journey to study the life of anchorites in Egypt and elsewhere. In 358 he returned to Cappadocia and founded the first monastery for men at Ibora. Assisted by Gregory Nazianzus, he compiled *The Longer and Shorter Rules*, which transformed the solitary anchorites into a disciplined community of prayer and work. The *Rules* became the foundation for all Eastern monastic discipline. The monasteries also provided schools to train leaders for Church and State.

Basil was ordained presbyter in 364. In the conflict between the Arians (supported by an Arian Emperor) and orthodox Christians, Basil became convinced that he should be made Bishop of Caesarea. By a narrow margin, he was elected Bishop of Caesarea, Metropolitan of Cappadocia, and Exarch of Pontus. He was relentless in his efforts to restore the faith and discipline of the clergy, and in defense of the Nicene faith. When the Emperor Valens sought to undercut Basil's power by dividing the See of Cappadocia, Basil forced his brother Gregory to become Bishop of Nyssa.

In his treatise, *On the Holy Spirit*, Basil maintained that both the language of Scripture and the faith of the Church require that the same honor, glory, and worship is to be paid to the Spirit as to the Father and the Son. It was entirely proper, he asserted, to adore God in liturgical prayer, not only with the traditional words, "Glory to the Father *through* the Son *in* the Holy Spirit;" but also with the formula, "Glory to the Father *with* the Son *together with* the Holy Spirit."

Basil was also concerned about the poor, and when he died, he willed to Caesarea a complete new town, built on his estate, with housing, a hospital and staff, a church for the poor, and a hospice for travelers.

He died at the age of fifty, in 379, just two years before the Second Ecumenical Council, which affirmed the Nicene faith.

Basil the Great

Bishop of Caesarea, 379

I Almighty God, who hast revealed to thy Church thine eternal Being of glorious majesty and perfect love as one God in Trinity of Persons: Give us grace that, like thy bishop Basil of Caesarea, we may continue steadfast in the confession of this faith, and constant in our worship of thee, Father, Son, and Holy Spirit; who livest and reignest for ever and ever. *Amen.*

II Almighty God, you have revealed to your Church your eternal Being of glorious majesty and perfect love as one God in Trinity of Persons: Give us grace that, like your bishop Basil of Caesarea, we may continue steadfast in the confession of this faith, and constant in our worship of you, Father, Son, and Holy Spirit; for you live and reign for ever and ever. *Amen.*

Psalm	Lessons
139:1-9	1 Corinthians 2:6-13
or 34:1-8	Luke 10:21-24

Preface of Trinity Sunday

The only child of a prominent barrister and his wife, Evelyn Underhill was born in Wolverhampton England, and grew up in London. She was educated there and in a girls' school in Folkestone, where she was confirmed in the Church of England. She had little other formal religious training, but her spiritual curiosity was naturally lively, and she read widely, developing quite early a deep appreciation for mysticism. At sixteen, she began a life-long devotion to writing.

Evelyn had few childhood companions, but one of them, Hubert Stuart Moore, she eventually married. Other friends, made later, included such famous persons as Laurence Housman, Maurice Hewlett, and Sarah Bernhardt. Closest of all were Ethel Ross Barker, a devout Roman Catholic, and Baron Friedrich von Hügel, with whom she formed a strong spiritual bond. He became her director in matters mystical.

In the 1890's, Evelyn began annual visits to the Continent, and especially to Italy. There she became influenced by the paintings of the Italian masters and by the Roman Catholic Church. She spent nearly fifteen years wrestling painfully with the idea of converting to Roman Catholicism, but decided in the end that it was not for her.

In 1921, Evelyn Underhill became reconciled to her Anglican roots, while remaining what she called a "Catholic Christian." She continued with her life of reading, writing, meditation, and prayer. She had already published her first great spiritual work, *Mysticism*. This was followed by many other books, culminating in her most widely read and studied book, *Worship* (1937).

Evelyn Underhill's most valuable contribution to spiritual literature must surely be her conviction that the mystical life is not only open to a saintly few, but to anyone who cares to nurture it and weave it into everyday experience, and also (at the time, a startling idea) that modern psychological theories and discoveries, far from hindering or negating spirituality, can actually enhance and transform it.

Evelyn Underhill's writings proved appealing to many, resulting in a large international circle of friends and disciples, making her much in demand as a lecturer and retreat director. She died, at age 65, in 1941.

Evelyn Underhill

I   O God, Origin, Sustainer, and End of all creatures: Grant
that thy Church, taught by thy servant Evelyn Underhill,
guarded evermore by thy power, and guided by thy Spirit
into the light of truth, may continually offer to thee all glory
and thanksgiving, and attain with thy saints to the blessed
hope of everlasting life, which thou hast promised us by our
Savior Jesus Christ; who with thee and the same Holy Spirit
liveth and reigneth, one God, now and for ever. *Amen.*

II   O God, Origin, Sustainer, and End of all your creatures:
Grant that your Church, taught by your servant Evelyn
Underhill, guarded evermore by your power, and guided by
your Spirit into the light of truth, may continually offer to
you all glory and thanksgiving and attain with your saints to
the blessed hope of everlasting life, which you have promised
by our Savior Jesus Christ; who with you and the Holy
Spirit, lives and reigns, one God, now and for ever. *Amen.*

Psalm	Lessons
96:7-13	Wisdom 7:24—8:1
or 37:3-6,32-33	John 4:19-24

Preface of the Dedication of a Church

Joseph Butler, once called "the greatest of all the thinkers of the English Church," was born at Wantage, Berkshire, May 18, 1692, into a Presbyterian family. He was educated at dissenting academies; but in his early twenties he decided to become an Anglican. He entered Oriel College, Oxford, in 1715, and was ordained in 1718.

As a preacher at the Rolls Chapel for eight years, he made his mark, especially for his sermons on human nature. He served as rector of Houghton-le-Skerne (1712-25) and of Stanhope (1715-40), and as prebendary of Rochester (1736-38), before his appointment as Bishop of Bristol. He declined the primacy of Canterbury, but accepted the bishopric of Durham in 1750. He died at Bath, June 16, 1752, and was buried in Bristol Cathedral.

Butler's fame rests chiefly on his acute apology for orthodox Christianity against the Deistic thought prevalent in England in his time, *The Analogy of Religion, Natural and Revealed, to the Constitution and Course of Nature*, published in 1736. By careful argument, Butler maintained the "reasonable probability" of Christianity, with action upon that probability as a basis for faith. His rationalism was grounded in a deep personal piety, although he had little sympathy for the enthusiasm of the Wesleyan revival movement. Yet, in their different ways, Bishop Butler and John Wesley contributed to the renewal of the Church in eighteenth century England.

Joseph Butler

Bishop of Durham, 1752

I   O God, who by thy Holy Spirit dost give to some the word
of wisdom, to others the word of knowledge, and to others
the word of faith: We praise thy Name for the gifts of grace
manifested in thy servant Joseph Butler, and we pray that
thy Church may never be destitute of such gifts; through
Jesus Christ our Lord, who with thee and the same Spirit
liveth and reigneth, one God, for ever and ever. *Amen.*

II   O God, by your Holy Spirit you give to some the word of
wisdom, to others the word of knowledge, and to others the
word of faith: We praise your Name for the gifts of grace
manifested in your servant Joseph Butler, and we pray that
your Church may never be destitute of such gifts; through
Jesus Christ our Lord, who with you and the Holy Spirit
lives and reigns, one God, for ever and ever. *Amen.*

Psalm	Lessons
119:89-96	Wisdom 7:7-14
or 1	Luke 10:25-28

Preface of a Saint (1)

Bernard Mizeki was born about the year 1861 in Portuguese East Africa (Mozambique). In his early teens he escaped from his native land and arrived in Capetown, South Africa, where he was befriended and converted by Anglican missionaries. He was baptized on March 9, 1886.

In 1891 Bernard Mizeki volunteered as a catechist for the pioneer mission in Mashonaland, and was stationed at Nhowe. In June, 1896, during an uprising of the native people against the Europeans and their African friends, Bernard was marked out especially. Though warned to flee, he would not desert his converts at the mission station. He was stabbed to death, but his body was never found, and the exact site of his burial is unknown.

A shrine near Bernard's place of martyrdom attracts many pilgrims today, and the Anglican Churches of Central and of South Africa honor him as their primary native martyr and witness.

Bernard Mizeki

Catechist and Martyr in Rhodesia, 1896

I   Almighty and everlasting God, who didst enkindle the flame of thy love in the heart of thy holy martyr Bernard Mizeki: Grant to us, thy humble servants, a like faith and power of love, that we who rejoice in his triumph may profit by his example; through Jesus Christ our Lord, who liveth and reigneth with thee and the Holy Spirit, one God, for ever and ever. *Amen.*

II   Almighty and everlasting God, who kindled the flame of your love in the heart of your holy martyr Bernard Mizeki: Grant to us, your humble servants, a like faith and power of love, that we who rejoice in his triumph may profit by his example; through Jesus Christ our Lord, who lives and reigns with you and the Holy Spirit, one God, for ever and ever. *Amen.*

Psalm	Lessons
116:1-8	Revelation 7:13-17
or 124	Luke 12:2-12

Preface of Holy Week

Alban is the earliest Christian in Britain who is known by name and, according to tradition, the first British martyr. He was a soldier in the Roman army stationed at Verulamium, a city about twenty miles northeast of London, now called St. Alban's. He gave shelter to a Christian priest who was fleeing from persecution, and was converted by him. When officers came to Alban's house, he dressed himself in the garments of the priest and gave himself up. Alban was tortured and martyred in place of the priest, on the hilltop where the Cathedral of St. Alban's now stands. The traditional date of his martyrdom is 303 or 304, but recent studies suggest that the year was actually 209, during the persecution under the Emperor Septimius Severus.

The site of Alban's martyrdom soon became a shrine. King Offa of Mercia established a monastery, there about the year 793, and in the high Middle Ages St. Alban's ranked as the premier Abbey in England. The great Norman abbey church, begun in 1077, now serves as the cathedral of the diocese of St. Alban's, established in 1877. It is the second longest church in England (Winchester Cathedral is the longest, by six feet), and it is built on higher ground than any other English cathedral. In a chapel east of the choir and high Altar, there are remains of the fourteenth century marble shrine of St. Alban.

The Venerable Bede gives this account of Alban's trial: "When Alban was brought in, the judge happened to be standing before an altar, offering sacrifice to devils . . . 'What is your family and race?' demanded the judge. 'How does my family concern you?' replied Alban; 'If you wish to know the truth about my religion, know that I am a Christian and am ready to do a Christian's duty.' 'I demand to know your name,' insisted the judge. 'Tell me at once.' 'My parents named me Alban,' he answered, 'and I worship and adore the living and true God, who created all things.' "

Alban

First Martyr of Britain, c. 304

I Almighty God, by whose grace and power thy holy martyr
   Alban triumphed over suffering and was faithful even unto
   death: Grant to us, who now remember him with
   thanksgiving, to be so faithful in our witness to thee in this
   world, that we may receive with him the crown of life;
   through Jesus Christ our Lord, who liveth and reigneth with
   thee and the Holy Spirit, one God, for ever and ever. *Amen.*

II Almighty God, by whose grace and power your holy martyr
   Alban triumphed over suffering and was faithful even to
   death: Grant us, who now remember him in thanksgiving, to
   be so faithful in our witness to you in this world, that we
   may receive with him the crown of life; through Jesus Christ
   our Lord, who lives and reigns with you and the Holy Spirit,
   one God, for ever and ever. *Amen.*

Psalm	Lessons
34:1-8	1 John 3:13-16
or 31:1-5	Matthew 10:34-42

Preface of a Saint (3)

John the Baptist, the prophet, and forerunner of Jesus, was the son of elderly parents, Elizabeth and Zechariah, and was related to Jesus on his mother's side. His birth is celebrated six months before Christmas Day, since, according to Luke, Elizabeth became pregnant six months before the Angel Gabriel appeared to Mary.

John figures prominently in all four Gospels, but the account of his birth is given only in the Gospel according to Luke. His father, Zechariah, a priest of the Temple at Jerusalem, was struck speechless because he doubted a vision foretelling John's birth. When his speech was restored, Zechariah uttered a canticle of praise, the Benedictus, which is one of the canticles in the Daily Office.

John lived ascetically in the desert. He was clothed with camel's hair, with a leather belt, and ate locusts and wild honey. He preached repentance, and called upon people to prepare for the coming of the Kingdom and of the Messiah, baptizing his followers to signify their repentance and new life. Jesus himself was baptized by John in the Jordan.

John had many followers, some of whom became Jesus' disciples. Because of his denunciation of the sins of Herod, especially Herod's incestuous marriage, John incurred the enmity of Herodias, Herod's wife, and was put in prison. Through Herodias' plotting with Salome, her daughter, Herod was led to promise a gift to Salome, who demanded John's head. John was thereupon executed.

John is remembered during Advent as a prophet, and at Epiphany as the baptizer of Jesus. The Gospel according to John quotes the Baptist as saying to his followers that Jesus is the Lamb of God, and prophesying, "He must increase, but I must decrease" (John 3:30).

The Nativity of Saint John the Baptist

I   Almighty God, by whose providence thy servant John the Baptist was wonderfully born, and sent to prepare the way of thy Son our Savior by preaching repentance: Make us so to follow his doctrine and holy life, that we may truly repent according to his preaching; and after his example constantly speak the truth, boldly rebuke vice, and patiently suffer for the truth's sake; through the same thy Son Jesus Christ our Lord, who liveth and reigneth with thee and the Holy Spirit one God, for ever and ever. *Amen.*

II   Almighty God, by whose providence your servant John the Baptist was wonderfully born, and sent to prepare the way of your Son our Savior by preaching repentance: Make us so to follow his teaching and holy life, that we may truly repent according to his preaching; and, following his example, constantly speak the truth, boldly rebuke vice, and patiently suffer for the truth's sake; through Jesus Christ your Son our Lord, who lives and reigns with you and the Holy Spirit, one God, for ever and ever. *Amen.*

Psalm	Lessons
85	Isaiah 40:1-11
or 85:7-13	Acts 13:14b-26
	Luke 1:57-80

Preface of Advent

If theology is "thinking about faith" and arranging those thoughts in some systematic order, then Irenaeus has been rightly recognized by Catholics and Protestants alike as the first great systematic theologian.

There is considerable doubt about the year of Irenaeus' birth; estimates vary from 97 to 160. It is certain that he learned the Christian faith in Ephesus at the feet of the venerable Polycarp, who in turn had known John the Evangelist. Some years before 177, probably while Irenaeus was still in his teens, he carried the tradition of Christianity to Lyons in southern France.

His name means "the peaceable one" — and suitably so. The year 177 brought hardship to the mission in Gaul. Persecution broke out, and a mounting tide of heresy threatened to engulf the Church. Irenaeus, by now a presbyter, was sent to Rome to mediate the dispute regarding Montanism, which the Bishop of Rome, Eleutherus, seemed to embrace. While Irenaeus was on this mission, the aged Bishop of Lyons, Pothinus, died in prison during a local persecution. When Irenaeus returned to Lyons, he was elected bishop to succeed Pothinus.

Irenaeus' enduring fame rests mainly on a large treatise, entitled *The Refutation and Overthrow of Gnosis, Falsely So-Called*, usually shortened to *Against Heresies*. In it, lrenaeus describes the major Gnostic systems, thoroughly, clearly, and often with biting humor. It is one of our chief sources of knowledge about Gnosticism. He also makes a case for Christianity which has become a classic, resting heavily on Scripture, and on the continuity between the teaching of the Apostles and the teaching of bishops, generation after generation, especially in the great see cities. Against the Gnostics, who despised the flesh and exalted the spirit, he stressed two doctrines: that of the creation as good, and that of the resurrection of the body.

A late and uncertain tradition claims that he suffered martyrdom, about 202.

Irenaeus

Bishop of Lyons, c. 202

I Almighty God, who didst uphold thy servant Irenaeus with strength to maintain the truth against every blast of vain doctrine: Keep us, we beseech thee, steadfast in thy true religion, that in constancy and peace we may walk in the way that leadeth to eternal life; through Jesus Christ our Lord, who liveth and reigneth with thee and the Holy Spirit, one God, now and for ever. *Amen.*

II Almighty God, you upheld your servant Irenaeus with strength to maintain the truth against every blast of vain doctrine: Keep us, we pray, steadfast in your true religion, that in constancy and peace we may walk in the way that leads to eternal life; through Jesus Christ our Lord, who lives and reigns with you and the Holy Spirit, one God, now and for ever. *Amen.*

Psalm	Lessons
85:8-13	2 Timothy 2:22b-26
or 145:8-13	Luke 11:33-36

Preface of the Epiphany

Peter and Paul, the two greatest leaders of the early Church, are commemorated separately, Peter on January 18, for his confession of Jesus as the Messiah, and Paul on January 25, for his conversion, but they are commemorated together on June 29 in observance of the tradition of the Church that they both died as martyrs in Rome during the persecution under Nero, in 64.

Paul, the well-educated and cosmopolitan Jew of the Dispersion, and Peter, the uneducated fisherman from Galilee, had differences of opinion in the early years of the Church concerning the mission to the Gentiles. More than once, Paul speaks of rebuking Peter for his continued insistence on Jewish exclusiveness; yet their common commitment to Christ and the proclamation of the Gospel proved stronger than their differences; and both eventually carried that mission to Rome, where they were martyred. According to tradition, Paul was granted the right of a Roman citizen to be beheaded by a sword, but Peter suffered the fate of his Lord, crucifixion, though with head downward.

A generation after their martyrdom, Clement of Rome, writing to the Church in Corinth, probably in 96 A.D., says: "Let us come to those who have most recently proved champions; let us take up the noble examples of our own generation. Because of jealousy and envy the greatest and most upright pillars of the Church were persecuted and competed unto death. Let us bring before our eyes the good apostles — Peter, who because of unrighteous jealousy endured not one or two, but numerous trials, and so bore a martyr's witness and went to the glorious place that he deserved. Because of jealousy and strife Paul pointed the way to the reward of endurance; seven times he was imprisoned, he was exiled, he was stoned, he was a preacher in both east and west, and won renown for his faith, teaching uprightness to the whole world, and reaching the farthest limit of the west, and bearing a martyr's witness before the rulers, he passed out of the world and was taken up into the holy place, having proved a very great example of endurance."

Saint Peter and Saint Paul, Apostles

I   Almighty God, whose blessed apostles Peter and Paul
glorified thee by their martyrdom: Grant that thy Church,
instructed by their teaching and example, and knit together
in unity by thy Spirit, may ever stand firm upon the one
foundation, which is Jesus Christ our Lord; who liveth and
reigneth with thee, in the unity of the same Spirit, one God,
for ever and ever. *Amen.*

II   Almighty God, whose blessed apostles Peter and Paul
glorified you by their martyrdom: Grant that your Church,
instructed by their teaching and example, and knit together
in unity by your Spirit, may ever stand firm upon the one
foundation, which is Jesus Christ our Lord; who lives and
reigns with you, in the unity of the Holy Spirit, one God,
now and for ever. *Amen.*

Psalm	Lessons
87	Ezekiel 34:11-16
	2 Timothy 4:1-8
	John 21:15-19

Preface of Apostles

Proper Psalms, Lessons, and Prayers were first appointed for this national observance in the Proposed Prayer Book of 1786. They were deleted, however, by the General Convention of 1789, primarily as a result of the intervention of Bishop William White. Though himself a supporter of the American Revolution, he felt that the required observance was inappropriate, since the majority of the Church's clergy had, in fact, been loyal to the British crown.

Writing about the Convention which had called for the observance of the day throughout "this Church, on the fourth of July, for ever," White said, "The members of the convention seem to have thought themselves so established in their station of ecclesiastical legislators, that they might expect of the many clergy who had been averse to the American revolution the adoption of this service; although, by the use of it, they must make an implied acknowledgment of their error, in an address to Almighty God. . . . The greater stress is laid on this matter because of the notorious fact, that the majority of the clergy could not have used the service, without subjecting themselves to ridicule and censure. For the author's part, having no hindrance of this sort, he contented himself with having opposed the measure, and kept the day from respect to the requisition of the convention; but could never hear of its being kept, in above two or three places beside Philadelphia."

It was not until the revision of 1928 that provision was again made for the liturgical observance of the day.

Independence Day

I Lord God Almighty, in whose Name the founders of this country won liberty for themselves and for us, and lit the torch of freedom for nations then unborn: Grant, we beseech thee, that we and all the people of this land may have grace to maintain these liberties in righteousness and peace; through Jesus Christ our Lord, who liveth and reigneth with thee and the Holy Spirit, one God, for ever and ever. *Amen.*

II Lord God Almighty, in whose Name the founders of this country won liberty for themselves and for us, and lit the torch of freedom for nations then unborn: Grant that we and all the people of this land may have grace to maintain our liberties in righteousness and peace; through Jesus Christ our Lord, who lives and reigns with you and the Holy Spirit, one God, for ever and ever. *Amen.*

Psalm	Lessons
145	Deuteronomy 10:17-21
or 145:1-9	Hebrews 11:8-16
	Matthew 5:43-48

Preface of Trinity Sunday

Benedict is generally accounted the father of western monasticism. He was born about 480, at Nursia in central Italy, and was educated at Rome. The style of life he found there disgusted him. Rome at this time was overrun by various barbarian tribes; the period was one of considerable political instability, a breakdown of western society, and the beginnings of barbarian kingdoms. Benedict's disapproval of the manners and morals of Rome led him to a vocation of monastic seclusion. He withdrew to a hillside cave above Lake Subiaco, about forty miles west of Rome, where there was already at least one other monk. Gradually, a community grew up around Benedict. Sometime between 525 and 530, he moved south with some of his disciples to Monte Cassino, midway between Rome and Naples, where he established another community, and, about 540, composed his monastic *Rule*. He does not appear to have been ordained or to have contemplated the founding of an "order." He died sometime between 540 and 550 and was buried in the same grave as his sister, Scholastica.

No personality or text in the history of monasticism, it has been said, has occasioned more studies than Benedict and his rule. The major problem for historians is the question of how much of the rule is original. This is closely related to the question of the date of another, very similar but anonymous, rule for monks, known as the "Rule of the Master," which may antedate Benedict's *Rule* by ten years. This does not detract from the fact that Benedict's firm but reasonable rule has been the basic source document from which most later monastic rules were derived. Its average day provides for a little over four hours to be spent in liturgical prayer, a little over five hours in spiritual reading, about six hours of work, one hour for eating, and about eight hours of sleep. The entire Psalter is to be recited in the Divine Office once every week.

At profession, the new monk takes vows of "stability, amendment of life, and obedience." Pope Gregory the Great wrote Benedict's "Life" in the second book of his *Dialogues*. He adopted Benedict's monasticism as an instrument of evangelization when in 596 he sent Augustine and his companions to convert the Anglo-Saxon people. In the Anglican Communion today, the rules of many religious orders are influenced by Benedict's rule.

Benedict of Nursia

Abbot of Monte Cassino, c. 540

I   Almighty and everlasting God, whose precepts are the wisdom of a loving Father: Give us grace, following the teaching and example of thy servant Benedict, to walk with loving and willing hearts in the school of the Lord's service; let thine ears be open unto our prayers; and prosper with thy blessing the work of our hands; through Jesus Christ our Lord, who liveth and reigneth with thee and the Holy Spirit, one God, for ever and ever. *Amen.*

II   Almighty and everlasting God, your precepts are the wisdom of a loving Father: Give us grace, following the teaching and example of your servant Benedict, to walk with loving and willing hearts in the school of the Lord's service; let your ears be open to our prayers; and prosper with your blessing the work of our hands; through Jesus Christ our Lord, who lives and reigns with you and the Holy Spirit, one God, for ever and ever. *Amen.*

Psalm	Lessons
1	Proverbs 2:1-9
or 34:1-8	Luke 14:27-33

Preface of a Saint (2)

William White was born in Philadelphia, March 24, 1747, and was educated at the college of that city, graduating in 1765. In 1770 he went to England, was ordained deacon on December 23, and priest on April 25, 1772. On his return home, he became assistant minister of Christ and St. Peter's, 1772-1779, and rector from that year until his death, July 17, 1836. He also served as chaplain of the Continental Congress from 1777 to 1789, and then of the United States Senate until 1800. Chosen unanimously as first Bishop of Pennsylvania, September 14, 1786, he went to England again, with Samuel Provoost, Bishop-elect of New York; and the two men were consecrated in Lambeth Chapel on Septuagesima Sunday, February 4, 1787, by the Archbishops of Canterbury and York and the Bishops of Bath and Wells and of Peterborough.

Bishop White was the chief architect of the Constitution of the American Episcopal Church and the wise overseer of its life during the first generation of its history. He was the Presiding Bishop at its organizing General Convention in 1789 and again from 1795 until his death. He was a theologian of no mean ability, and among his proteges, in whose formation he had a large hand, were such leaders of a new generation as John Henry Hobart, Jackson Kemper, and William Augustus Muhlenberg. White's gifts of statesmanship and reconciling moderation steered the American Church through the first decades of its independent life. His influence in his native city made it its "first citizen." To few men has the epithet "venerable" been more aptly applied.

William White

Bishop of Pennsylvania, 1836

I O Lord, who in a time of turmoil and confusion didst raise up thy servant William White, and didst endow him with wisdom, patience, and a reconciling temper, that he might lead thy Church into ways of stability and peace: Hear our prayer, we beseech thee, and give us wise and faithful leaders, that through their ministry thy people may be blessed and thy will be done; through Jesus Christ our Lord, who liveth and reigneth with thee and the Holy Spirit, one God, for ever and ever. *Amen.*

II O Lord, in a time of turmoil and confusion you raised up your servant William White, and endowed him with wisdom, patience, and a reconciling temper, that he might lead your Church into ways of stability and peace: Hear our prayer, and give us wise and faithful leaders, that through their ministry your people may be blessed and your will be done; through Jesus Christ our Lord, who lives and reigns with you and the Holy Spirit, one God, for ever and ever. *Amen.*

Psalm	Lessons
92:1-4,11-14	Jeremiah 1:4-10
or 84:7-12	John 21:15-17

Preface of a Saint (1)

Macrina (340-379) was a monastic, theologian and teacher. She founded one of the earliest Christian communities in the Cappadocian city of Pontus. Macrina left no writings; we know of her through the works of her brother St. Gregory of Nyssa (page 181). In his *Life of St. Macrina*, Gregory describes her as both beautiful and brilliant, an authoritative spiritual teacher.

Macrina persuaded her mother Emmelia to renounce their wealthy lifestyle and to help her establish a monastery on the family's estate. Macrina's ideal of community emphasized caring for the poor and ministering to the wider community. She literally picked up young women who lay in the road starving. Many joined her order.

Gregory credits Macrina as the spiritual and theological intelligence behind her siblings' notable careers in the Church. Gregory, and their brothers St. Basil (page 269), St. Peter of Sebaste, and Naucratios went to her often for theological counsel. Macrina frequently challenged her celebrated brothers. She told Gregory his fame was not due to his own merit, but to the prayers of his parents. She took Basil in hand when he returned from Athens "monstrously conceited about his skill in rhetoric." Under her influence, Basil and Peter renounced material possessions and turned away from secular academia to become monks and theologians. Basil and Peter wrote a Rule for community life, ensuring that Macrina's ideas for Christian community would have lasting authority. Basil, Gregory and Peter all became bishops, in no small measure because of Macrina's influence, and became leading defenders of the Nicene faith.

Gregory visited Macrina as she lay dying on two planks on the floor. He relates Macrina's last words as a classical Greek farewell oration imbued with Holy Scripture. In both his *Life of St. Macrina* and in his later treatise of *The Soul and Resurrection*, Gregory presents Macrina admiringly as a Christian Socrates, delivering beautiful deathbed prayers and teachings about the resurrection.

Macrina

Monastic and Teacher, 379

I   Merciful God, thou didst call thy servant Macrina to reveal in her life and her teaching the riches of thy grace and truth: May we, following her example, seek after thy wisdom and live according to her way; through Jesus Christ our Savior, who liveth and reigneth with thee and the Holy Spirit, one God, for ever and ever. *Amen.*

II   Merciful God, you called your servant Macrina to reveal in her life and her teaching the riches of your grace and truth: May we, following her example, seek after your wisdom and live according to her way; through Jesus Christ our Savior, who lives and reigns with you and the Holy Spirit, one God, for ever and ever. *Amen.*

Psalm	Lessons
119:97-104	Ecclesiasticus 51:13-22
	Matthew 11:27-30

Preface of a Saint (2)

Elizabeth Cady Stanton 1815-1902

Born into an affluent, strict Calvinist family in upstate New York, Elizabeth, as a young woman, took seriously the Presbyterian doctrines of predestination and human depravity. She became very depressed, but resolved her mental crises through action. She dedicated her life to righting the wrongs perpetrated upon women by the Church and society.

She and four other women organized the first Women's Rights Convention at Seneca Falls, New York, July 19-20, 1848. The event set her political and religious agenda for the next 50 years. She held the Church accountable for oppressing women by using Scripture to enforce subordination of women in marriage and to prohibit them from ordained ministry. She held society accountable for denying women equal access to professional jobs, property ownership, the vote, and for granting less pay for the same work.

In 1881, the Revised Version of the Bible was published by a committee which included no women scholars. Elizabeth founded her own committee of women to write a commentary on Scripture, and applying the Greek she learned as a child from her minister, focused on passages used to oppress and discriminate against women.

Although Elizabeth blamed male clergy for women's oppression, she attended Trinity Episcopal Church in Seneca Falls, with her friend Amelia Bloomer. As a dissenting prophet, Elizabeth preached hundreds of homilies and political speeches in pulpits throughout the nation. Wherever she visited, she was experienced as a holy presence and a liberator. She never lost her sense of humor despite years of contending with opposition, even from friends. In a note to Susan B. Anthony, she said: "Do not feel depressed, my dear friend, what is good in us is immortal, and if the sore trials we have endured are sifting out pride and selfishness, we shall not have suffered in vain." Shortly before she died, she said: "My only regret is that I have not been braver and bolder and truer in the honest conviction of my soul."

Amelia Jenks Bloomer 1818-1894

Amelia Jenks, the youngest of six children, born in New York to a pious Presbyterian family, early on demonstrated a kindness of heart and strict regard for truth and right. As a young woman, she joined in the temperance, anti-slavery and women's rights movements.

Amelia Jenks Bloomer never intended to make dress reform a major platform in women's struggle for justice. But, women's fashion of the day prescribed waist-cinching corsets, even for pregnant women, resulting in severe health problems. Faith and fashion collided explosively when she published in her newspaper, The Lily, a picture of herself in loose-fitting Turkish trousers, and began wearing them publicly. Clergy, from their pulpits, attacked women who wore them, citing Moses: "Women should not dress like men." Amelia fired back: "It matters not what Moses had to say to the men and women of his time about what they should wear. If clergy really cared about what Moses said about clothes, they would all put fringes and blue ribbons on their garments." Her popularity soared as she engaged clergy in public debate.

She insisted that "certain passages in the Scriptures relating to women had been given a strained and unnatural meaning." And, of St. Paul she said: "Could he have looked into the future and foreseen all the sorrow and strife the cruel exactions and oppression on the one hand and the blind submission and cringing fear on the other, that his words have sanctioned and caused, he would never have uttered them." And of women's right to freedom, "The same Power that brought the slave out of bondage will, in His own good time and way, bring about the emancipation of woman, and make her the equal in power and dominion that she was in the beginning."

Later in life, in Council Bluffs, Iowa, a frontier town, she worked to establish churches, libraries, and school houses. She provided hospitality for traveling clergy of all denominations, and for temperance lecturers and reformers. Trinity Episcopal Church, Seneca Falls, New York, where she was baptized, records her as a "faithful Christian missionary all her life."

Sojourner Truth, "Miriam of the Later Exodus" 1797-8 to 1883

Isabella (Sojourner Truth) was the next-to-youngest child of several born to James and Elizabeth, slaves owned by a wealthy Dutchman in New York. For the first 28 years of her life she was a slave, sold from household to household.

She fled slavery with the help of Quaker friends, first living in Philadelphia, then New York, where she joined the Mother Zion African Methodist Episcopal Church when African-Americans were being denied the right to worship with white members of St. George's Church in Philadelphia. Belle (as Isabella was called) became a street-corner evangelist in poverty-stricken areas of New York City, but quickly realized people needed food, housing and warm clothing. She focused her work on a homeless shelter for women.

When she was about 46, Belle believed she heard God say to her, "Go east." So, she set out east for Long Island and Connecticut. Stopping at a Quaker farm for a drink of water, she was asked her name. "My name is Sojourner," Belle said. "What is your last name?" the woman asked. Belle thought of all her masters' names she had carried through life. Then the thought came: "The only master I have now is God, and His name is Truth."

Sojourner became a traveling preacher, approaching white religious meetings and campgrounds and asking to speak. Fascinated by her charismatic presence, her wit, wisdom, and imposing six-foot height, they found her hard to refuse. She never learned to read or write, but quoted extensive Bible passages from memory in her sermons. She ended by singing a "home-made" hymn and addressing the crowd on the evils of slavery. Her reputation grew and she became part of the abolitionist and women's rights speakers' network.

During a women's rights convention in Ohio, Sojourner gave the speech for which she is best remembered: "Ain't I a Woman." She had listened for hours to clergy attack women's rights and abolition, using the Bible to support their oppressive logic: God had created women to be weak and blacks to be a subservient race.

Harriet Ross Tubman, "Moses of her People" 1820-1913

Slave births were recorded under property, not as persons with names; but we know that Harriet Ross, sometime during 1820 on a Maryland Chesapeake Bay plantation, was the sixth of eleven children born to Ben Ross and Harriet Green. Although her parents were loving and they enjoyed a cheerful family life inside their cabin, they lived in fear of the children being sold off at any time.

Harriet suffered beatings and a severe injury, but grew up strong and defiant, refusing to appear happy and smiling to her owners. To cope with brutality and oppression, she turned to religion. Her favorite Bible story was about Moses who led the Israelites out of slavery. The slaves prayed for a Moses of their own.

When she was about 24, Harriet escaped to Canada, but could not forget her parents and other slaves she left behind. Working with the Quakers, she made at least 19 trips back to Maryland between 1851 and 1861, freeing over 300 people by leading them into Canada. She was so successful, $40,000 was offered for her capture.

Guided by God through omens, dreams, warnings, she claimed her struggle against slavery had been commanded by God. She foresaw the Civil War in a vision. When it began, she quickly joined the Union Army, serving as cook and nurse, caring for both Confederate and Union soldiers. She served as a spy and scout. She led 300 black troops on a raid which freed over 750 slaves, making her the first American woman to lead troops into military action.

In 1858-9, she moved to upstate New York where she opened her home to African-American orphans and to helpless old people. Although she was illiterate, she founded schools for African-American children. She joined the fight for women's rights, working with Elizabeth Cady Stanton and Susan B. Anthony, but supported African-American women in their efforts to found their own organizations to address equality, work and education.

Elizabeth Cady Stanton, Amelia Bloomer, Sojourner Truth, and Harriet Ross Tubman

Liberators and Prophets

I   O God, whose Spirit guideth us into all truth and maketh us free: Strengthen and sustain us as thou didst thy servants Elizabeth, Amelia, Sojourner, and Harriet. Give us vision and courage to stand against oppression and injustice and all that worketh against the glorious liberty to which thou callest all thy children; through Jesus Christ our Savior, who liveth and reigneth with thee and the Holy Spirit, one God, for ever and ever. *Amen.*

II   O God, whose Spirit guides us into all truth and makes us free: Strengthen and sustain us as you did your servants Elizabeth, Amelia, Sojourner, and Harriet. Give us vision and courage to stand against oppression and injustice and all that works against the glorious liberty to which you call all your children; through Jesus Christ our Savior, who lives and reigns with you and the Holy Spirit, one God, for ever and ever. *Amen.*

Psalm	Lessons
146	Wisdom 7:24-28
	Luke 11:5-10

Preface of Baptism

Mary of Magdala near Capernaum was one of several women who followed Jesus and ministered to him in Galilee. The Gospel according to Luke records that Jesus "went on through cities and villages, preaching and bringing the good news of the kingdom of God. And the Twelve were with him, and also some women who had been healed of evil spirits and infirmities: Mary, called Magdalene, from whom seven demons had gone out. . ." (Luke 8:1-2). The Gospels tell us that Mary was healed by Jesus, followed him, and was one of those who stood near his cross at Calvary.

It is clear that Mary Magdalene's life was radically changed by Jesus' healing. Her ministry of service and steadfast companionship, even as a witness to the crucifixion, has, through the centuries, been an example of the faithful ministry of women to Christ. All four Gospels name Mary as one of the women who went to the tomb to mourn and to care for Jesus' body. Her weeping for the loss of her Lord strikes a common chord with the grief of all others over the death of loved ones. Jesus' tender response to her grief — meeting her in the garden, revealing himself to her by calling her name — makes her the first witness to the risen Lord. She is given the command, "Go to my brethren and say to them, I am ascending to my Father and your Father, to my God and your God" (John 20:17). As the first messenger of the resurrection, she tells the disciples, "I have seen the Lord" (John 20:18).

In the tradition of the Eastern Church, Mary is regarded as the equal of an apostle; and she is held in veneration as the patron saint of the great cluster of monasteries on Mount Athos.

Saint Mary Magdalene

I   Almighty God, whose blessed Son restored Mary Magdalene to health of body and mind, and called her to be a witness of his resurrection: Mercifully grant that by thy grace we may be healed of all our infirmities and know thee in the power of his endless life; who with thee and the Holy Spirit liveth and reigneth, one God, now and for ever. *Amen.*

II   Almighty God, whose blessed Son restored Mary Magdalene to health of body and of mind, and called her to be a witness of his resurrection: Mercifully grant that by your grace we may be healed from all our infirmities and know you in the power of his unending life; who with you and the Holy Spirit lives and reigns, one God, now and for ever. *Amen.*

Psalm	Lessons
42:1-7	Judith 9:1,11-14
	2 Corinthians 5:14-18
	John 20:11-18

Preface of All Saints

The name of Thomas a Kempis is perhaps more widely known than that of any other medieval Christian writer. *The Imitation of Christ*, which he composed or compiled, has been translated into more languages than any other book except the Holy Scriptures. Millions of Christians have found in this manual a treasured and constant source of edification.

His name was Thomas Hammerken, and he was born at Kempen in the Duchy of Cleves about 1380. He was educated at Deventer by the Brethren of the Common Life, and joined their order in 1399 at their house of Mount St. Agnes in Zwolle (in the Low Countries). He took his vows (those of the Augustinian Canons Regular) there in 1407, was ordained a priest in 1415, and was made sub-prior in 1425. He died on July 25, 1471.

The Order of the Brethren of the Common Life was founded by Gerard Groote (1340-1384) at Deventer. It included both clergy and lay members who cultivated a biblical piety of a practical rather than speculative nature, with stress upon the inner life and the practice of virtues. They supported themselves by copying manuscripts and teaching. One of their most famous pupils was the humanist Erasmus. Many have seen in them harbingers of the Reformation; but the Brethren had little interest in the problems of the institutional Church. Their spirituality, known as the "New Devotion" (*Devotio moderna*), has influenced both Catholic and Protestant traditions of prayer and meditation.

Thomas a Kempis

Priest, 1471

I   Holy Father, who hast nourished and strengthened thy Church by the inspired writings of thy servant Thomas a Kempis: Grant that we may learn from him to know what is necessary to be known, to love what is to be loved, to praise what highly pleaseth thee, and always to seek to know and follow thy will; through Jesus Christ our Lord, who liveth and reigneth with thee and the Holy Spirit, one God, for ever and ever. *Amen.*

II   Holy Father, you have nourished and strengthened your Church by the inspired writings of your servant Thomas a Kempis: Grant that we may learn from him to know what is necessary to be known, to love what is to be loved, to praise what highly pleases you, and always to seek to know and follow your will; through Jesus Christ our Lord, who lives and reigns with you and the Holy Spirit, one God, for ever and ever. *Amen.*

Psalm	Lessons
34:1-8	Philippians 4:4-9
or 33:1-5,20-21	Luke 6:17-23

Preface of a Saint (2)

James, the brother of John, is often known as James the Greater, to distinguish him from the other Apostle of the same name, commemorated in the calendar with Philip, and also from James "the brother of our Lord." He was the son of a prosperous Galilean fisherman, Zebedee, and with his brother John left his home and his trade in obedience to the call of Christ. With Peter and John, he seems to have belonged to an especially privileged group, whom Jesus chose to be witnesses of the Transfiguration, the raising of Jairus' daughter, and the agony in the garden.

Apparently, James shared John's hot-headed disposition, and Jesus nicknamed the brothers, "Boanerges" (Sons of Thunder). James' expressed willingness to share the cup of Christ was realized in his being the first of the Apostles to die for him. As the Acts of the Apostles records, "About that time Herod the King laid violent hands upon some who belonged to the Church. He killed James the brother of John with the sword" (Acts 12:1-2).

According to an old tradition, the body of James was taken to Compostela, Spain, which has been a shrine for pilgrims for centuries. Among the Spaniards, James is one of the most popular saints. In the Middle Ages, under the title of Santiago de Compostela, his aid was especially invoked in battle against the Moors.

Saint James the Apostle

I   O gracious God, we remember before thee this day thy
servant and apostle James, first among the Twelve to suffer
martyrdom for the Name of Jesus Christ; and we pray that
thou wilt pour out upon the leaders of thy Church that spirit
of self-denying service by which alone they may have true
authority among thy people; through the same Jesus Christ
our Lord, who liveth and reigneth with thee and the Holy
Spirit, one God, now and for ever. *Amen.*

II   O gracious God, we remember before you today your
servant and apostle James, first among the Twelve to suffer
martyrdom for the Name of Jesus Christ; and we pray that
you will pour out upon the leaders of your Church that spirit
of self-denying service by which alone they may have true
authority among your people; through Jesus Christ our
Lord, who lives and reigns with you and the Holy Spirit, one
God, now and for ever. *Amen.*

Psalm	Lessons
7:1-10	Jeremiah 45:1-5
	Acts 11:27-12:3
	Matthew 20:20-28

Preface of Apostles

The Gospels tell us little about the home of our Lord's mother. She is thought to have been of Davidic descent and to have been brought up in a devout Jewish family that cherished the hope of Israel for the coming kingdom of God, in remembrance of the promise to Abraham and the forefathers.

In the second century, a devout Christian sought to supply a fuller account of Mary's birth and family, to satisfy the interest and curiosity of believers. An apocryphal gospel, known as the *Protevangelium of James* or *The Nativity of Mary*, appeared. It included legendary stories of Mary's parents Joachim and Anne. These stories were built out of Old Testament narratives of the births of Isaac and of Samuel (whose mother's name, Hannah, is the original form of Anne), and from traditions of the birth of John the Baptist. In these stories, Joachim and Anne — the childless, elderly couple who grieved that they would have no posterity — were rewarded with the birth of a girl whom they dedicated in infancy to the service of God under the tutelage of the temple priests.

In 550 the Emperor Justinian the First erected in Constantinople the first church to Saint Anne. The Eastern Churches observe her festival on July 25. Not until the twelfth century did her feast become known in the West. Pope Urban the Sixth fixed her day, in 1378, to follow the feast of Saint James. Joachim has had several dates assigned to his memory; but the new Roman Calendar of 1969 joins his festival to that of Anne on this day.

Parents of the Blessed Virgin Mary

I   Almighty God, heavenly Father, we remember in thanksgiving this day the parents of the Blessed Virgin Mary; and we pray that we all may be made one in the heavenly family of thy Son Jesus Christ our Lord; who with thee and the Holy Spirit liveth and reigneth, one God, for ever and ever. *Amen.*

II   Almighty God, heavenly Father, we remember in thanksgiving this day the parents of the Blessed Virgin Mary; and we pray that we all may be made one in the heavenly family of your Son Jesus Christ our Lord; who with you and the Holy Spirit lives and reigns, one God, for ever and ever. *Amen.*

Psalm	Lessons
132:11-19	Genesis 17:1-8
or 85:8-13	Luke 1:26-33

Preface of the Incarnation

"First presbyter of the Church," was the well-deserved, if unofficial, title of the sixth rector of Grace Church, New York City. Huntington provided a leadership characterized by breadth, generosity, scholarship, and boldness. He was the acknowledged leader in the House of Deputies of the Episcopal Church's General Convention during a period of intense stress and conflict within the Church. His reconciling spirit helped preserve the unity of the Episcopal Church in the painful days after the beginning of the schism, led by the Assistant Bishop of Kentucky, which resulted in the formation of the Reformed Episcopal Church.

In the House of Deputies, of which he was a member from 1871 until 1907, Huntington showed active and pioneering vision in making daring proposals. As early as 1871, his motion to revive the primitive order of "deaconesses" began a long struggle which culminated in 1889 in canonical authorization for that order. Huntington's parish immediately provided facilities for this new ministry, and Huntington House became a training center for deaconesses and other women workers in the Church.

Christian unity was Huntington's great passion throughout his ministry. In his book, *The Church Idea* (1870), he attempted to articulate the essentials of Christian unity. The grounds he proposed as a basis for unity were presented to, and accepted by, the House of Bishops in Chicago in 1886, and, with some slight modification, were adopted by the Lambeth Conference in 1888. The "Chicago-Lambeth Quadrilateral" has become a historic landmark for the Anglican Communion. It is included on pages 876-878 of the Book of Common Prayer, among the Historical Documents of the Church.

In addition to his roles as ecumenist and statesman, Huntington is significant as a liturgical scholar. It was his bold proposal to revise the Prayer Book that led to the revision of 1892, providing a hitherto unknown flexibility and significant enrichment. His Collect for Monday in Holy Week, now used also for Fridays at Morning Prayer, is itself an example of skillful revision. In it he takes two striking clauses from the exhortation to the sick in the 1662 Prayer Book, and uses them as part of a prayer for grace to follow the Lord in his sufferings.

William Reed Huntington

Priest, 1909

I O Lord our God, we thank thee for instilling in the heart of thy servant William Reed Huntington a fervent love for thy Church and its mission in the world; and we pray that, with unflagging faith in thy promises, we may make known to all people thy blessed gift of eternal life; through Jesus Christ our Lord, who liveth and reigneth with thee and the Holy Spirit, one God, for ever and ever. *Amen.*

II O Lord our God, we thank you for instilling in the heart of your servant William Reed Huntington a fervent love for your Church and its mission in the world; and we pray that, with unflagging faith in your promises, we may make known to all people your blessed gift of eternal life; through Jesus Christ our Lord, who lives and reigns with you and the Holy Spirit, one God, for ever and ever. *Amen.*

Psalm

133
or 145:8-13

Lessons

Ephesians 4:11-16*
or Ephesians 1:3-10
John 17:20-26

Preface of Baptism

* This passage is also appointed for the Sunday closest to this date in Year B.

Mary and Martha of Bethany, with Lazarus their brother, are described in the Gospels according to Luke and John, as close and well-loved friends of Jesus. Luke records the well-known story of their hospitality, which has made Martha a symbol of the active life and Mary of the contemplative, though some commentators would take the words of Jesus to be a defense of that which Mary does best, and a commendation of Martha for what she does best — neither vocation giving grounds for despising the other.

John's Gospel sheds additional light on the characters of Mary and Martha. When Lazarus is dying, Jesus delays his visit to the family and arrives after Lazarus' death. Martha comes to meet him, still trusting in his power to heal and restore. The exchange between them evokes Martha's deep faith and acknowledgment of Jesus as the Messiah (John 11:21-27).

John also records the supper at Bethany at which Mary anointed Jesus' feet with fragrant ointment and wiped them with her hair. This tender gesture of love evoked criticism from the disciples. Jesus interpreted the gift as a preparation for his death and burial.

The devotion and friendship of Mary and Martha have been an example of fidelity and service to the Lord. Their hospitality and kindness, and Jesus' enjoyment of their company, show us the beauty of human friendship and love at its best.

Mary and Martha of Bethany

I   O God, heavenly Father, whose Son Jesus Christ enjoyed
rest and refreshment in the home of Mary and Martha of
Bethany: Give us the will to love thee, open our hearts to
hear thee, and strengthen our hands to serve thee in others
for his sake; who liveth and reigneth with thee and the Holy
Spirit, one God, now and for ever. *Amen.*

II   O God, heavenly Father, your Son Jesus Christ enjoyed rest
and refreshment in the home of Mary and Martha of
Bethany: Give us the will to love you, open our hearts to
hear you, and strengthen our hands to serve you in others
for his sake; who lives and reigns with you and the Holy
Spirit, one God, now and for ever. *Amen.*

Psalm	Lessons
36:5-10	Romans 12:9-13
or 33:1-5,20-21	Luke 10:38-42

Preface of Epiphany

The life of William Wilberforce refutes the popular notion that a politician cannot be a saintly Christian, dedicated to the service of humanity.

Wilberforce was born into an affluent family in Hull, Yorkshire, on August 24, 1759, and was educated at St. John's College, Cambridge. In 1780, he was elected to the House of Commons, and he served in it until 1825. He died in London, July 29, 1833, and was buried in Westminster Abbey.

His conversion to an evangelical Christian life occurred in 1784, several years after he entered Parliament. Fortunately, he was induced by his friends not to abandon his political activities after this inward change in his life, but thereafter he steadfastly refused to accept high office or a peerage.

He gave himself unstintingly to the promotion of overseas missions, popular education, and the reformation of public manners and morals. He also supported parliamentary reform and Catholic emancipation. Above all, his fame rests upon his persistent, uncompromising, and single-minded crusade for the abolition of slavery and the slave-trade. That sordid traffic was abolished in 1807. He died just one month before Parliament put an end to slavery in the British dominions. One of the last letters written by John Wesley was addressed to Wilberforce. In it Wesley gave him his blessing for his noble enterprise.

Wilberforce's eloquence as a speaker, his charm in personal address, an his profound religious spirit, made him a formidable power for good; and his countrymen came to recognize in him a man of heroic greatness.

William Wilberforce

1833

I   Let thy continual mercy, O Lord, enkindle in thy Church the never-failing gift of love, that, following the example of thy servant William Wilberforce, we may have grace to defend the poor, and maintain the cause of those who have no helper; for the sake of him who gave his life for us, thy Son our Savior Jesus Christ, who liveth and reigneth with thee and the Holy Spirit, one God, now and for ever. *Amen.*

II   Let your continual mercy, O Lord, kindle in your Church the never-failing gift of love, that, following the example of your servant William Wilberforce, we may have grace to defend the poor, and maintain the cause of those who have no helper; for the sake of him who gave his life for us, your Son our Savior Jesus Christ, who lives and reigns with you and the Holy Spirit, one God, now and for ever. *Amen.*

Psalm	Lessons
146:4-9	Galatians 3:23-29
or 112:1-9	Matthew 25:31-40

Preface of a Saint (2)

Ignatius was born into a noble Basque family in 1491. In his autobiography he tells us, "Up to his twenty-sixth year, he was a man given over to the vanities of the world and took special delight in the exercise of arms with a great and vain desire of winning glory." An act of reckless heroism at the Battle of Pamplona in 1521 led to his being seriously wounded. During his convalescence at Loyola, Ignatius experienced a profound spiritual awakening. Following his recovery and an arduous period of retreat, a call to be Christ's knight in the service of God's kingdom was deepened and confirmed.

Ignatius began to share the fruits of his experience with others, making use of a notebook which eventually became the text of the *Spiritual Exercises*. Since his time, many have found the *Exercises* to be a way of encountering Christ as intimate companion and responding to Christ's call: "Whoever wishes to come with me must labor with me."

The fact that Ignatius was an unschooled layman made him suspect in the eyes of church authorities and led him, at the age of 37, to study theology at the University of Paris in preparation for the priesthood. While there, Ignatius gave the *Exercises* to several of his fellow students; and in 1534, together with six companions, he took vows to live lives of strict poverty and to serve the needs of the poor. Thus, what later came to be known as the Society of Jesus was born.

In 1540 the Society was formally recognized, and Ignatius become its first Superior General. According to his journals and many of his letters, a profound sense of sharing God's work in union with Christ made the season of intense activity which followed a time of great blessing and consolation.

Ignatius died on July 31, 1556, in the simple room which served both as his bedroom and chapel, having sought to find God in all things and to do all things for God's greater glory. His life and teaching, as Evelyn Underhill and others have acknowledged, represents the best of the Counter-Reformation.

Ignatius of Loyola

Priest, Monastic, and Founder of the Society of Jesus, 1556

I   Almighty God, from whom all good things come: Thou didst call Ignatius of Loyola to the service of thy Divine Majesty and to find thee in all things. Inspired by his example and strengthened by his companionship, may we labor without counting the cost and seek no reward other than knowing that we do thy will; through Jesus Christ our Savior, who liveth and reigneth with thee and the Holy Spirit, one God, now and for ever. *Amen.*

II   Almighty God, from whom all good things come: You called Ignatius of Loyola to the service of your Divine Majesty and to find you in all things. Inspired by his example and strengthened by his companionship, may we labor without counting the cost and seek no reward other than knowing that we do your will; through Jesus Christ our Savior, who lives and reigns with you and the Holy Spirit, now and for ever. *Amen.*

Psalm	Lessons
34:1-8	1 Corinthians 10:31—11:1
	Luke 9:57-62

Preface of a Saint (3)

All that is certainly known of Joseph of Arimathaea comes from the narratives of the burial of Jesus in the Gospels. Though John speaks of Joseph as a secret disciple of our Lord, and associates him with Nicodemus, another member of the Jewish Sanhedrin who was drawn to Jesus, we know nothing of any further activity of these men in the early Christian community. Later, however, legends developed about their leadership in the Church. One of the more attractive is the story of Joseph's coming to the ancient Church of Glastonbury in Britain and bringing with him the Holy Grail (the cup used at the Last Supper). This tradition cannot be dated earlier than the thirteenth century. Although this and other stories obtained wide credence, they are not based on historical facts.

Joseph's claim for remembrance does not depend upon such legends, however beautiful and romantic. When our Lord's intimate disciples were hiding for fear of the authorities, Joseph came forward boldly and courageously to do, not only what was demanded by Jewish piety, but to act generously and humanely by providing his own tomb for the decent and proper burial of our Lord's body, thus saving it from further desecration.

Joseph of Arimathaea

I   Merciful God, whose servant Joseph of Arimathaea with
reverence and godly fear did prepare the body of our Lord
and Savior for burial, and did lay it in his own tomb: Grant,
we beseech thee, to us thy faithful people, grace and courage
to love and serve Jesus with sincere devotion all the days of
our life; through the same Jesus Christ our Lord, who liveth
and reigneth with thee and the Holy Spirit, one God, for ever
and ever. *Amen.*

II   Merciful God, whose servant Joseph of Arimathaea with
reverence and godly fear prepared the body of our Lord and
Savior for burial, and laid it in his own tomb: Grant to us,
your faithful people, grace and courage to love and serve
Jesus with sincere devotion all the days of our life; through
Jesus Christ our Lord, who lives and reigns with you and the
Holy Spirit, one God, for ever and ever. *Amen.*

Psalm	Lessons
16:5-11	Proverbs 4:10-18
or 112:1-9	Luke 23:50-56

Preface of the Commemoration of the Dead

The Transfiguration is not to be understood only as a spiritual experience of Jesus while at prayer, which three chosen disciples, Peter, James, and John, were permitted to witness. It is one of a series of supernatural manifestations, by which God authenticated Jesus as his Son. It is at one with the appearance of the angels at the birth and at his resurrection, and with the descent of the Spirit at Jesus' baptism. Matthew records the voice from heaven saying, "This is my beloved with whom I am well pleased; listen to him" (Matthew 17:5). Briefly the veil is drawn aside, and a chosen few are permitted to see Jesus, not only as the earth-born son of Mary, but as the eternal Son of God. Moses and Elijah witness to Jesus as the fulfillment of the Law and the Prophets. In Luke's account of the event, they speak of the "exodus" which Jesus is to accomplish at Jerusalem. A cloud, a sign of divine presence, envelops the disciples, and a heavenly voice proclaims Jesus to be the Son of God.

Immediately thereafter Jesus announces to Peter, James, and John the imminence of his death. As Paul was later to say of Jesus, "Though he was in the form of God, he did not count equality with God a thing to be grasped, but emptied himself, taking the form of a servant, and was born in human likeness. And, being found in human form, he humbled himself, and became obedient unto death, even death on a cross" (Philippians 2:6-8).

The Feast of the Transfiguration is held in the highest esteem by the Eastern Churches. The figure of the transfigured Christ is regarded as a foreshadowing of the Risen and Ascended Lord. The festival, however, was only accepted into the Roman calendar on the eve of the Reformation, and for that reason was not included in the reformed calendar of the English Church. Since its inclusion in the American revision of 1892, it has been taken into most modern Anglican calendars.

The Transfiguration of Our Lord

I   O God, who on the holy mount didst reveal to chosen witnesses thy well-beloved Son, wonderfully transfigured, in raiment white and glistening: Mercifully grant that we, being delivered from the disquietude of this world, may by faith behold the King in his beauty; who with thee, O Father, and thee, O Holy Ghost, liveth and reigneth, one God, world without end. *Amen.*

II   O God, who on the holy mount revealed to chosen witnesses your well-beloved Son, wonderfully transfigured, in raiment white and glistening: Mercifully grant that we, being delivered from the disquietude of this world, may by faith behold the King in his beauty; who with you, O Father, and you, O Holy Spirit, lives and reigns, one God, for ever and ever. *Amen.*

Psalm	Lessons
99	Exodus 34:29-35
or 99:5-9	2 Peter 1:13-21
	Luke 9:28-36

Preface of the Epiphany

John Mason Neale was a priest of many talents. As a hymnodist, he furnished *The Hymnal 1982* with several original hymns and more than thirty translations of Latin and Greek hymns. As a priest, he gave active support to the Oxford Movement in its revival of medieval liturgical forms. As a humanitarian, he founded the Sisterhood of St. Margaret for the relief of suffering women and girls.

Neale was born in London in 1818, studied at Cambridge, where he also served as tutor and chaplain, and was ordained to the priesthood in 1842. He was both a scholar and a creative poet, whose skills in composing original verse and translating Latin and Greek hymns into effective English speech patterns were devoted to the Church. With such familiar words as "Good Christian men, rejoice," "Come, ye faithful, raise the strain," and "Creator of the stars of night," he has greatly enriched our hymnody.

Gentleness combined with firmness, good humor, modesty, patience, and devotion, with "an unbounded charity," describe Neale's character. Despite poor health, he was a prolific writer and compiler. Among his works are *Medieval Hymns and Sequences, Hymns of the Eastern Church, Liturgiology and Church History*, and a four-volume commentary on the Psalms. In a busy life, he also found time to establish the Camden Society, later called the Ecclesiological Society.

Though he never received preferment in England, his great contributions were recognized both in the United States and in Russia, where the Metropolitan presented him with a rare copy of the Old Believers' Liturgy. He died on the Feast of the Transfiguration at the age of 46, leaving a lasting mark on our worship.

No future hymnal is conceivable without the inclusion of some of Neale's fine devotional poetry. The Prayer Book, for example, cites two of his translations by name as being especially appropriate for Palm Sunday and Good Friday: "All glory, laud, and honor" for the procession with the palms, and "Sing, my tongue, the glorious battle" at the climactic point of the Good Friday service.

John Mason Neale

Priest, 1866

I   Grant unto us, O God, that in all time of our testing we may know thy presence and obey thy will; that, following the example of thy servant John Mason Neale, we may with integrity and courage accomplish what thou givest us to do, and endure what thou givest us to bear; through Jesus Christ our Lord, who liveth and reigneth with thee and the Holy Spirit, one God, for ever and ever. *Amen.*

II   Grant, O God, that in all time of our testing we may know your presence and obey your will; that, following the example of your servant John Mason Neale, we may with integrity and courage accomplish what you give us to do, and endure what you give us to bear; through Jesus Christ our Lord, who lives and reigns with you and the Holy Spirit, one God, for ever and ever. *Amen.*

Psalm	Lessons
106:1-5	2 Chronicles 20:20-21
or 33:1-5,20-21	Matthew 13:44-52

Preface of the Dedication of a Church

Dominic was the founder of the Order of Preachers, commonly known as Dominicans. In England they were called Blackfriars, because of the black mantle they wore over their white habits. Dominic was born about 1170 or shortly thereafter, in Spain.

Influenced by the contemporary search for a life of apostolic poverty, Dominic is said to have sold all his possessions to help the poor during a famine in 1191. Ordained in 1196, he soon became a canon and then sub-prior of the Cathedral of Osma, where a rule of strict discipline was established among the canons.

In 1203 he began a number of preaching tours in Languedoc, a region in Southern France, against the Albigensian heretics, who held Manichaean, dualistic views. He kept himself aloof, however, from the repressive crusade which was instigated against them. In 1214, his plan to found a special preaching order for the conversion of the Albigensians began to take shape, and in the following year he took his followers to Toulouse.

At the Fourth Lateran Council in October, 1215, Dominic sought confirmation of his order from Pope Innocent the Third. This was granted by Innocent's successor, Honorius the Third, in 1216 and 1217.

Over the next few years, Dominic traveled extensively, establishing friaries, organizing the order, and preaching, until his death on August 6, 1221. He is said to have been a man of austere poverty and heroic sanctity, always zealous to win souls by the preaching of pure doctrine.

The Dominican *Constitutions*, first formulated in 1216, and revised and codified by the Master-General of the Order, Raymond of Peñafort, in 1241, place a strong emphasis on learning, preaching, and teaching, and, partly through the influence of Francis of Assisi, on absolute poverty.

The Dominicans explicitly gave priority to intellectual work. They established major houses in most university centers, to which they contributed such notable teachers as Thomas Aquinas. Their *Constitutions* express the priority this way: "In the cells, moreover, they can write, read, pray, sleep, and even stay awake at night, if they desire, on account of study."

Dominic

Priest and Friar, 1221

I   O God of the prophets, who didst open the eyes of thy
servant Dominic to perceive a famine of hearing the word of
the Lord, and didst move him, and those he did draw about
him, to satisfy that hunger with sound preaching and fervent
devotion: Make thy Church, dear Lord, in this and every
age, attentive to the hungers of the world, and quick to
respond in love to those who are perishing; through Jesus
Christ our Lord, who liveth and reigneth with thee and the
Holy Spirit, one God, for ever and ever. *Amen.*

II   O God of the prophets, you opened the eyes of your servant
Dominic to perceive a famine of hearing the word of the
Lord, and moved him, and those he drew about him, to
satisfy that hunger with sound preaching and fervent
devotion: Make your Church, dear Lord, in this and every
age, attentive to the hungers of the world, and quick to
respond in love to those who are perishing; through Jesus
Christ our Lord, who lives and reigns with you and the Holy
Spirit, one God, for ever and ever. *Amen.*

Psalm	Lessons
96:1-7	Romans 10:13-17
or 98:1-4	John 7:16-18

Preface of a Saint (2)

Laurence the Deacon, one of the most popular saints of the Roman Church, was martyred during the persecution initiated in 257 by the Emperor Valerian. That persecution was aimed primarily at the clergy and the laity of the upper classes. All properties used by the Church were confiscated, and assemblies for Christian worship were forbidden. On August 4, 258, Pope Sixtus the Second and his seven deacons were apprehended in the Roman catacombs. They were summarily executed, except for the archdeacon, Laurence, who was martyred on the tenth. Though no authentic "Acts" of Laurence's ordeal have been preserved, the tradition is that the prefect demanded information from him about the Church's treasures. Laurence, in reply, assembled the sick and poor to whom, as archdeacon, he had distributed the Church's relief funds, and presented them to the prefect, saying, "These are the treasures of the Church." Laurence is believed to have been roasted alive on a gridiron.

The Emperor Constantine erected a shrine and basilica over Laurence's tomb, which is in a catacomb on the Via Tiburtina. The present Church of St. Laurence Outside the Walls, a beautiful double basilica (damaged in World War II), includes a choir and sanctuary erected by Pope Pelagius the Second (579-590) and a nave by Pope Honorius the Third (1216-1227).

Laurence is the subject of a small round glass medallion, probably dating from the fourth century, now in the Metropolitan Museum in New York. It bears the simple inscription, "Live with Christ and Laurence."

The Greek word from which we get our English word "martyr" simply means "witness;" but, in the age of the persecutions, before Constantine recognized the Church early in the fourth century, a "martyr" was generally one who had witnessed even to death. For Laurence, as for all the martyrs, to die for Christ was to live with Christ.

Laurence

Deacon, and Martyr at Rome, 258

I   Almighty God, who didst call thy deacon Laurence to serve thee with deeds of love, and didst give him the crown of martyrdom: Grant we beseech thee, that we, following his example, may fulfill thy commandments by defending and supporting the poor, and by loving thee with all our hearts; through Jesus Christ our Lord, who liveth and reigneth with thee and the Holy Spirit, one God, for ever and ever. *Amen.*

II   Almighty God, you called your deacon Laurence to serve you with deeds of love, and gave him the crown of martyrdom: Grant that we, following his example, may fulfill your commandments by defending and supporting the poor, and by loving you with all our hearts; through Jesus Christ our Lord, who lives and reigns with you and the Holy Spirit, one God, for ever and ever. *Amen.*

Psalm	Lessons
112:1-9	2 Corinthians 9:6-10
or 126	John 12:24-26

Preface of a Saint (3)

In the latter part of the twelfth century, the Church had fallen on evil days, and was weak and spiritually impoverished. It was then that Francis of Assisi renounced his wealth and established the mendicant order of Franciscans. At the first gathering of the order in 1212, Francis preached a sermon that was to make a radical change in the life of an eighteen-year-old young woman named Clare.

The daughter of a wealthy family, and a noted beauty, Clare was inspired by Francis' words with the desire to serve God and to give her life to the following of Christ's teaching. She sought out Francis, and begged that she might become a member of his order, placing her jewelry and rich outer garments on the altar as an offering. Francis could not refuse her pleas. He placed her temporarily in a nearby Benedictine convent.

When this action became known, friends and relatives tried to take Clare from her retreat. She was adamant. She would be the bride of Christ alone. She prevailed, and soon after was taken by Francis to a poor dwelling beside the Church of St. Damian at Assisi. Several other women joined her. She became Mother Superior of the order, which was called the "Poor Ladies of St. Damian."

The order's practices were austere. They embraced the Franciscan rule of absolute poverty. Their days were given over to begging and to works of mercy for the poor and the neglected. Clare herself was servant, not only to the poor, but to her nuns.

Clare governed the convent for forty years, caring for the sisters, ready to do whatever Francis directed. She said to him, "I am yours by having given my will to God." Her biographer says that she "radiated a spirit of fervor so strong that it kindled those who but heard her voice."

In 1253 her last illness began. Daily she weakened, and daily she was visited by devoted people, by priests, and even by the Pope. On her last day, as she saw many weeping by her bedside, she exhorted them to love "holy poverty" and to share their possessions. She was heard to say: "Go forth in peace, for you have followed the good road. Go forth without fear, for he that created you has sanctified you, has always protected you, and loves you as a mother. Blessed be God, for having created me."

Clare

Abbess at Assisi, 1253

I O God, whose blessed Son became poor that we through his poverty might be rich: Deliver us, we pray thee, from an inordinate love of this world, that, inspired by the devotion of thy servant Clare, we may serve thee with singleness of heart, and attain to the riches of the age to come; through Jesus Christ our Lord, who liveth and reigneth with thee, in the unity of the Holy Spirit, one God, now and for ever. *Amen.*

II O God, whose blessed Son became poor that we through his poverty might be rich: Deliver us from an inordinate love of this world, that we, inspired by the devotion of your servant Clare, may serve you with singleness of heart, and attain to the riches of the age to come; through Jesus Christ our Lord, who lives and reigns with you and the Holy Spirit, one God, for ever and ever. *Amen.*

Psalm	Lessons
63:1-8	Song of Solomon 2:10-13
or 34:1-8	Luke 12:32-37

Preface of a Saint (2)

Florence Nightingale was born in Florence, Italy, on May 12, 1820. She was trained as a nurse at Kaiserwerth (1851) and Paris and in 1853 became superintendent of a hospital for invalid women in London. In response to God's call and animated by a spirit of service, in 1854 she volunteered for duty during the Crimean War and recruited 38 nurses to join her. With them she organized the first modern nursing service in the British field hospitals of Scutari and Balclava. By imposing strict discipline and high standards of sanitation she radically reduced the drastic death toll and rampant infection then typical in field hospitals. She returned to England in 1856 and a fund of £50,000 was subscribed to enable her to form an institution for the training of nurses at St. Thomas's Hospital and at King's College Hospital. Her school at St. Thomas's Hospital became significant in helping to elevate nursing into a profession. She devoted many years to the question of army sanitary reform, to the improvement of nursing and to public health in India. Her main work, *Notes on Nursing*, 1859, went through many editions.

An Anglican, she remained committed to a personal mystical religion which sustained her through many years of poor health until her death in 1910. Until the end of her life, although her illness prevented her from leaving her home, she continued in frequent spiritual conversation with many prominent church leaders of the day, including the local parish priest who regularly brought Communion to her. By the time of her death on August 13, 1910, her reputation as a healer and holy person had assumed mythical proportions, and she is honored throughout the world as the founder of the modern profession of nursing.

Florence Nightingale
Nurse, Social Reformer, 1910

I   Life-giving God, thou alone hast power over life and death, over health and sickness: Give power, wisdom, and gentleness unto those who follow the lead of Florence Nightingale, that they, bearing with them thy presence, may not only heal but bless, and shine as lanterns of hope in the darkest hours of pain and fear; through Jesus Christ, the healer of body and soul, who liveth and reigneth with thee and the Holy Spirit, one God, now and for ever. *Amen.*

II   Life-giving God, you alone have power over life and death, over health and sickness: Give power, wisdom, and gentleness to those who follow the lead of Florence Nightingale, that they, bearing with them your presence, may not only heal but bless, and shine as lanterns of hope in the darkest hours of pain and fear; through Jesus Christ, the healer of body and soul, who lives and reigns with you and the Holy Spirit, one God, now and for ever. *Amen.*

Psalm	Lessons
73:23-29	Isaiah 58:6-11
	Matthew 25:31-46

Preface of a Saint (1)

Jeremy Taylor, one of the most influential of the "Caroline Divines," was educated at Cambridge and, through the influence of William Laud, became a Fellow of All Souls at Oxford. He was still quite young when he became chaplain to Charles the First and, later, during the Civil War, a chaplain in the Royalist army.

The successes of Cromwell's forces brought about Taylor's imprisonment and, after Cromwell's victory, Taylor spent several years in forced retirement as chaplain to the family of Lord Carberry in Wales. It was during this time that his most influential works were written, especially *Holy Living* and *Holy Dying* (1651).

Among his other works, *Liberty of Prophesying* proved to be a seminal work in encouraging the development of religious toleration in the seventeenth century. The principles set forth in that book rank with those of Milton's *Areopagitica* in its plea for freedom of thought.

Despite Taylor's unquestioned literary genius, he was, unfortunately, not asked to have a part in the Prayer Book revision of 1662. The first American Prayer Book, however, incorporated one of his prayers, part of which has been adapted to serve as the Collect of his commemoration; and another has been added in the present Prayer Book.

Taylor's theology has sometimes been criticized, most bitingly by Samuel Taylor Coleridge, who claims that Taylor seems to "present our own holy life as the grounds of our religious hope, rather than as the fruit of that hope, whose ground is the mercies of Christ." No such complaint, however, was ever made about his prayers, which exemplify the best of Caroline divinity, blended with great literary genius.

In later life, Taylor and his family moved to the northeastern part of Ireland where, after the restoration of the monarchy, he became Bishop of Down and Connor. To this was later added the small adjacent diocese of Dromore. As Bishop, he labored tirelessly to rebuild churches, restore the use of the Prayer Book, and overcome continuing Puritan opposition. As Vice-chancellor of Trinity College, Dublin, he took a leading part in reviving the intellectual life of the Church of Ireland. He remained to the end a man of prayer and a pastor.

Jeremy Taylor
Bishop of Down, Connor, and Dromore, 1667

I   O God, whose days are without end, and whose mercies cannot be numbered: Make us, we beseech thee, like thy servant Jeremy Taylor, deeply sensible of the shortness and uncertainty of human life; and let thy Holy Spirit lead us in holiness and righteousness all our days; through Jesus Christ our Lord, who liveth and reigneth with thee and the Holy Spirit, one God, now and for ever. *Amen.*

II   O God, whose days are without end, and whose mercies cannot be numbered: Make us, like your servant Jeremy Taylor, deeply aware of the shortness and uncertainty of human life; and let your Holy Spirit lead us in holiness and righteousness all our days; through Jesus Christ our Lord, who lives and reigns with you and the Holy Spirit, one God, now and for ever. *Amen.*

Psalm	Lessons
139:1-9	Romans 14:7-9,10b-12
or 16:5-11	Matthew 24:42-47

Preface of a Saint (1)

Jonathan Myrick Daniels was born in Keene, New Hampshire, in 1939. He was shot and killed by an unemployed highway worker in Hayneville, Alabama, August 20, 1965.

From high school in Keene to graduate school at Harvard, Jonathan wrestled with the meaning of life and death and vocation. Attracted to medicine, the ordained ministry, law and writing, he found himself close to a loss of faith when his search was resolved by a profound conversion on Easter Day 1962 at the Church of the Advent in Boston. Jonathan then entered the Episcopal Theological School in Cambridge, Massachusetts. In March 1965, the televised appeal of Martin Luther King, Jr. to come to Selma to secure for all citizens the right to vote drew Jonathan to a time and place where the nation's racism and the Episcopal Church's share in that inheritance were exposed.

He returned to seminary and asked leave to work in Selma where he would be sponsored by the Episcopal Society for Cultural and Racial Unity. Conviction of his calling was deepened at Evening Prayer during the singing of the Magnificat: "'He hath put down the mighty from their seat and hath exalted the humble and meek. He hath filled the hungry with good things.' I knew that I must go to Selma. The Virgin's song was to grow more and more dear to me in the weeks ahead."

Jailed on August 14 for joining a picket line, Jonathan and his companions were unexpectedly released. Aware that they were in danger, four of them walked to a small store. As sixteen-year-old Ruby Sales reached the top step of the entrance, a man with a gun appeared, cursing her. Jonathan pulled her to one side to shield her from the unexpected threats. As a result, he was killed by a blast from the 12-gauge gun.

The letters and papers Jonathan left bear eloquent witness to the profound effect Selma had upon him. He writes, "The doctrine of the creeds, the enacted faith of the sacraments, were the essential preconditions of the experience itself. The faith with which I went to Selma has not changed: it has grown. . . . I began to know in my bones and sinews that I had been truly baptized into the Lord's death and resurrection. . . with them, the black men and white men, with *all* life, in him whose Name is above all the names that the races and nations shout. . . .We are indelibly and unspeakably one."

Jonathan Myrick Daniels

Seminarian and Witness for Civil Rights, 1965

I O God of justice and compassion, who didst put down
the proud and the mighty from their place, and dost lift
up the poor and the afflicted: We give thee thanks for
thy faithful witness Jonathan Myrick Daniels, who, in
the midst of injustice and violence, risked and gave his
life for another; and we pray that we, following his
example, may make no peace with oppression; through
Jesus Christ the just one, who with thee and the Holy
Spirit liveth and reigneth, one God, for ever and ever.
Amen.

II O God of justice and compassion, you put down the
proud and mighty from their place, and lift up the poor
and the afflicted: We give you thanks for your faithful
witness Jonathan Myrick Daniels, who, in the midst of
injustice and violence, risked and gave his life for
another; and we pray that we, following his example,
may make no peace with oppression; through Jesus
Christ the just one, who lives and reigns with you and
the Holy Spirit, one God, for ever and ever. *Amen.*

Psalm

85:7-13

Lessons

Galatians 3:22-28
Luke 1: 46-55

Preface of a Saint (2)

The honor paid to Mary, the Mother of Jesus Christ, goes back to the earliest days of the Church. Two Gospels tell of the manner of Christ's birth, and the familiar Christmas story testifies to the Church's conviction that he was born of a virgin. In Luke's Gospel, we catch a brief glimpse of Jesus' upbringing at Nazareth, when the child was wholly in the care of his mother and his foster-father, Joseph.

During Jesus' ministry in Galilee, we learn that Mary was often with the other women who followed Jesus and ministered to his needs. At Calvary, she was among the little band of disciples who kept watch at the cross. After the resurrection, she was to be found with the Twelve in the upper room, watching and praying until the coming of the Spirit at Pentecost.

Mary was the person closest to Jesus in his most impressionable years, and the words of the Magnificat, as well as her humble acceptance of the divine will, bear more than an accidental resemblance to the Lord's Prayer and the Beatitudes of the Sermon on the Mount.

Later devotion has claimed many things for Mary which cannot be proved from Holy Scripture. What we can believe is that one who stood in so intimate a relationship with the incarnate Son of God on earth must, of all the human race, have the place of highest honor in the eternal life of God. A paraphrase of an ancient Greek hymn expresses this belief in very familiar words: "O higher than the cherubim, more glorious than the seraphim, lead their praises, alleluia."

Saint Mary the Virgin

Mother of Our Lord Jesus Christ

I   O God, who hast taken to thyself the blessed Virgin Mary, mother of thy incarnate Son: Grant that we, who have been redeemed by his blood, may share with her the glory of thine eternal kingdom; through the same thy Son Jesus Christ our Lord, who liveth and reigneth with thee, in the unity of the Holy Spirit, one God, now and for ever. *Amen.*

II   O God, you have taken to yourself the blessed Virgin Mary, mother of your incarnate Son: Grant that we, who have been redeemed by his blood, may share with her the glory of your eternal kingdom; through Jesus Christ our Lord, who lives and reigns with you, in the unity of the Holy Spirit, one God, now and for ever. *Amen.*

Psalm	Lessons
34	Isaiah 61:10-11
or 34:1-9	Galatians 4:4-7
	Luke 1:46-55

Preface of the Incarnation

William Porcher DuBose, probably the most original and creative thinker the American Episcopal Church has ever produced, spent most of his life as a professor at the University of the South, in Sewanee, Tennessee. He was not widely traveled, and not widely known, until, at the age of 56, he published the first of several books on theology that made him respected, not only in his own country, but also in England and France.

DuBose was born in 1836 in South Carolina, into a wealthy and cultured Huguenot family. At the University of Virginia, he acquired a fluent knowledge of Greek and other languages, which helped him lay the foundation for a profound understanding of the New Testament. His theological studies were begun at the Episcopal seminary in Camden, South Carolina. He was ordained in 1861, and became an officer and chaplain in the Confederate Army.

Doctrine and life were always in close relationship for DuBose. In a series of books he probed the inner meaning of the Gospels, the Epistles of Paul, and the Epistle to the Hebrews. He treated life and doctrine as a dramatic dialogue, fusing the best of contemporary thought and criticism with his own strong inner faith. The result was both a personal and scriptural catholic theology. He reflected, as he acknowledged, the great religious movements of the nineteenth century: the tractarianism of Oxford; the liberalism of F.D. Maurice; the scholarship of the Germans; and the evangelical spirit that was so pervasive at the time.

The richness and complexity of DuBose's thought are not easily captured in a few words, but the following passage written, shortly before his death in 1918, is a characteristic sample of his theology: "God has placed forever before our eyes, not the image but the Very Person of the Spiritual Man. We have not to ascend into Heaven to bring Him down, nor to descend into the abyss to bring Him up, for He is with us, and near us, and in us. We have only to confess with our mouths that He is Lord, and believe in our hearts that God has raised Him from the dead — and raised us in Him — and we shall live."

William Porcher DuBose

Priest, 1918

I Almighty God, who didst give to thy servant William
Porcher DuBose special gifts of grace to understand the
Scriptures and to teach the truth as it is in Christ Jesus:
Grant, we beseech thee, that by this teaching we may know
thee, the one true God, and Jesus Christ whom thou hast
sent; who liveth and reigneth with thee and the Holy Spirit,
one God, now and for ever. *Amen.*

II Almighty God, you gave to your servant William Porcher
DuBose special gifts of grace to understand the Scriptures
and to teach the truth as it is in Christ Jesus: Grant that by
this teaching we may know you, the one true God, and Jesus
Christ whom you have sent; who lives and reigns with you
and the Holy Spirit, one God, now and for ever. *Amen.*

Psalm	Lessons
19:7-11(12-14)	2 Timothy 1:11-14
or 37:3-6, 32-33	Luke 24:25-32

Preface of the Epiphany

Bernard, fiery defender of the Church in the twelfth century, was famed for the ardor with which he preached love for God "without measure." He was completely absorbed, even to the neglect of his own health, in support of the purity, doctrine, and prerogatives of the Church. He fulfilled his own definition of a holy man: "seen to be good and charitable, holding back nothing for himself, but using his every gift for the common good."

Bernard was the son of a knight and landowner who lived near Dijon, France. He was born in 1090 and given a secular education, but in 1113 he entered the Benedictine Abbey of Citeaux. His family was not pleased with his choice of a monastic life, but he nevertheless persuaded four of his brothers and about twenty-six of his friends to join him in establishing a monastery at Clairvaux in 1115.

During the following ten years, Bernard denied himself sleep that he might have time to write letters and sermons. He preached so persuasively that sixty new Cistercian abbeys were founded, all affiliated with Clairvaux. By 1140, his writings had made him one of the most influential figures in Christendom. He participated actively in every controversy that threatened the Church. He was an ardent critic of Peter Abelard's attempt to reconcile inconsistencies of doctrine by reason, because he felt that such an approach was a downgrading of the mysteries.

When a former monk of Clairvaux was elected Pope, as Eugenius the Third, Bernard became his troubleshooter. He preached the Crusade against the Albigensians, and the Second Crusade to liberate Jerusalem, winning much support for the latter in France and Germany. When that Crusade ended in disaster, Bernard was roundly attacked for having supported it. He died soon after in 1153. He was canonized in 1174.

Among Bernard's writings are treatises on papal duty, on love, on the veneration of Mary, and a commentary on the Song of Songs. Among well known hymns, he is credited with having written "O sacred head sore wounded," "Jesus, the very thought of thee," and "Jesus, thou joy of loving hearts."

Bernard
Abbot of Clairvaux, 1153

I O God, by whose grace thy servant Bernard of Clairvaux,
enkindled with the fire of thy love, became a burning and a
shining light in thy Church: Grant that we also may be
aflame with the spirit of love and discipline, and may ever
walk before thee as children of light; through Jesus Christ
our Lord, who with thee, in the unity of the Holy Spirit,
liveth and reigneth, one God, now and for ever. *Amen.*

II O God, by whose grace your servant Bernard of Clairvaux,
kindled with the flame of your love, became a burning and a
shining light in your Church: Grant that we also may be
aflame with the spirit of love and discipline, and walk before
you as children of light; through Jesus Christ our Lord, who
lives and reigns with you, in the unity of the Holy Spirit, one
God, now and for ever. *Amen.*

Psalm	Lessons
139:1-9	Ecclesiasticus 39:1-10
or 19:7-11(12-14)	John 15:7-11

Preface of a Saint (1)

Bartholomew is one of the twelve Apostles known to us only by his being listed among them in the Gospels according to Matthew, Mark, and Luke. His name means "Son of Tolmai," and he is sometimes identified with Nathanael, the friend of Philip, the "Israelite without guile" in John's Gospel, to whom Jesus promised the vision of angels ascending and descending on the Son of Man.

Nothing more is heard of him in the four Gospels.

Some sources credit Bartholomew with having written a Gospel, whose existence was known to Jerome and Bede, but which is lost today. There is a tradition that Bartholomew traveled to India, and Eusebius reports that when Pantaenus of Alexandria visited India, between 150 and 200, he found there "the Gospel according to Matthew" in Hebrew, which had been left behind by "Bartholomew, one of the Apostles."

An ancient tradition maintains that Bartholomew was flayed alive at Albanopolis in Armenia.

Saint Bartholomew the Apostle

I   O Almighty and everlasting God, who didst give to thine
apostle Bartholomew grace truly to believe and to preach thy
Word: Grant, we beseech thee, unto thy Church to love what
he believed and to preach what he taught; through Jesus
Christ our Lord, who liveth and reigneth with thee and the
Holy Spirit, one God, for ever and ever. *Amen.*

II   Almighty and everlasting God, who gave to your apostle
Bartholomew grace truly to believe and to preach your
Word: Grant that your Church may love what he believed
and preach what he taught; through Jesus Christ our Lord,
who lives and reigns with you and the Holy Spirit, one God,
for ever and ever. *Amen.*

Psalm	Lessons
91	Deuteronomy 18:15-18
or 91:1-4	1 Corinthians 4:9-15
	Luke 22:24-30

Preface of Apostles

Louis the Ninth of France was canonized by the Church in 1297. A man of unusual purity of life and manners, he was sincerely committed to his faith and to its moral demands. Courageous and fearless in battle, patient and uncomplaining in adversity, he was an impartial, just, and compassionate sovereign. The one word that summarizes his character is integrity.

Louis' crusading adventures in the Middle East and in North Africa were of little historical consequence. Such ventures were part of the piety of his time. Throughout his life he was diligent in attending divine worship, and constant in his charities, both open and secret. Unusually free of the bigotry of his age, Louis had an intelligent interest in the theological issues of his day. But his primary concern was to put Christian ethics into practice in both his personal and his public life.

Louis was born at Poissy, April 25, 1214, and was crowned King at Rheims on November 29, 1226. His early religious exercises of devotion and asceticism were inspired by his mother, Blanche of Castile. He died August 25, 1270, while on crusade at Tunis, and was buried with his royal peers in the basilica of St. Denis near Paris.

After his canonization, his relics were transferred to the Sainte Chapelle, the lovely Gothic chapel in Paris which he built as a shrine for relics of our Lord's passion. The building is itself a fitting monument to his genuine piety and beautiful character.

Because of his determined effort to live a personal life of Franciscan poverty and self-denial in the midst of worldly power and splendor — he wore a hair shirt under his royal dress — Louis is honored as patron saint of the Third Order of St. Francis.

Louis

King of France, 1270

I   O God, who didst call thy servant Louis of France to an
earthly throne that he might advance thy heavenly kingdom,
and didst give him zeal for thy Church and love for thy
people: Mercifully grant that we who commemorate him this
day may be fruitful in good works, and attain to the glorious
crown of thy saints; through Jesus Christ our Lord, who
liveth and reigneth with thee and the Holy Spirit, one God,
for ever and ever. *Amen.*

II   O God, you called your servant Louis of France to an earthly
throne that he might advance your heavenly kingdom, and
gave him zeal for your Church and love for your people:
Mercifully grant that we who commemorate him this day
may be fruitful in good works, and attain to the glorious
crown of your saints; through Jesus Christ our Lord, who
lives and reigns with you and the Holy Spirit, one God, for
ever and ever. *Amen.*

Psalm	Lessons
21:1-7	Wisdom 3:1-9
or 112:1-9	Luke 12:22-31

Preface of Baptism

Ministry to the deaf in the Episcopal Church begins with Gallaudet. Without his genius and zeal for the spiritual well-being of deaf persons, it is improbable that a history of ministry to the deaf in the Episcopal Church could be written. He has been called "The Apostle to the Deaf."

Gallaudet was born June 3, 1822, in Hartford, the eldest son of Thomas Hopkins Gallaudet, founder of the West Hartford School for the Deaf, whose wife, Sophia, was a deaf-mute.

After graduating from Trinity College, Hartford, Thomas announced his intention of being confirmed and becoming a priest in the Episcopal Church. His father prevailed upon him to postpone a final decision, and to accept a teaching position in the New York Institution for Deaf-mutes. There he met and married Elizabeth Budd, a deaf-mute. Gallaudet was ordained deacon in 1850 and served his diaconate at St. Stephen's Church, where he established a Bible class for deaf persons.

Ordained a priest in 1851, Gallaudet became Assistant at St. Ann's Church, where he conceived a plan for establishing a church that would be a spiritual home for deaf people. This became a reality the following year, with the founding of St. Ann's Church for Deaf-mutes. The congregation was able to purchase a church building in 1859, and it became a center for missionary work to the deaf. As a result of this ministry, mission congregations were established in many cities. Gallaudet died on August 27, 1902.

One fruit of Gallaudet's ministry was HENRY WINTER SYLE who had lost his hearing as the result of scarlet fever. Educated at Trinity; St. John's, Cambridge; and Yale (B.A. and M.A.); Syle was a brilliant student, who persisted in his determination to obtain an education, despite his handicap and fragile health. He was encouraged by Gallaudet to seek Holy Orders, and, having moved to Philadelphia, was supported by Bishop Stevens, against the opposition of many who believed that the impairment of one of the senses was an impediment to ordination. Syle was ordained in 1876, the first deaf person to receive Holy Orders in this Church. In 1888, he built the first Episcopal church constructed especially for deaf persons. He died on January 6, 1890.

Thomas Gallaudet
with Henry Winter Syle

I   O loving God, who willest that everyone should come to
thee and be saved: We bless thy holy Name for thy servants
Thomas Gallaudet and Henry Winter Syle, whose labors
with and for those who are deaf we commemorate today,
and we pray that thou wouldest continually move thy
Church to respond in love to the needs of all people; through
Jesus Christ, who opened the ears of the deaf, and who liveth
and reigneth with thee and the Holy Spirit, one God, now
and for ever. *Amen.*

II   O Loving God, whose will it is that everyone should come
to you and be saved: We bless your holy Name for your
servants Thomas Gallaudet and Henry Winter Syle whose
labors with and for those who are deaf we commemorate
today, and we pray that you will continually move your
Church to respond in love to the needs of all people; through
Jesus Christ, who opened the ears of the deaf, and who lives
and reigns with you and the Holy Spirit, one God, now and
for ever. *Amen.*

Psalm	Lessons
19:1-6	Isaiah 35:3-6a
or 96:1-7	Mark 7:32-37

Preface of Pentecost

Augustine, perhaps the greatest theologian in the history of Western Christianity, was born in 354 at Tagaste in North Africa. In his restless search for truth, he was attracted by Manichaeism and Neoplatonism, and was constantly engaged in an inner struggle with his personal morals. Finally, under the influence of his mother Monnica, Augustine surrendered to the Christian faith in the late summer of 386. He was baptized by Ambrose, Bishop of Milan, on Easter Eve in 387. After returning to North Africa in 391, Augustine found himself unexpectedly chosen by the people of Hippo to be a presbyter. Four years later he was chosen bishop of that city. His spiritual autobiography, *The Confessions of St. Augustine*, written shortly before 400 in the form of an extended prayer, is a classic of Western spirituality.

Augustine wrote countless treatises, letters, and sermons. They have provided a rich source of new and fresh insights into Christian truth.

The Manichaeans had attempted to solve the problem of evil by positing the existence of an independent agency eternally opposed to God. In refutation, Augustine affirmed that all creation is essentially good, having been created by God; and that evil is, properly speaking, the privation of good. A rigorist sect, the Donatists, had split from the Great Church after the persecution of Diocletian in the early fourth century. Against them, Augustine asserted that the Church was "holy," not because its members could be proved holy, but because holiness was the purpose of the Church, to which all its members are called.

Stirred by Alaric the Visigoth's sack of Rome in 410, Augustine wrote his greatest work, *The City of God*. In it he writes: "Two cities have been formed by two loves: the earthly by love of self, even to the contempt of God, the heavenly by the love of God, even to the contempt of self. The earthly city glories in itself, the heavenly city glories in the Lord. . . . In the one, the princes, and the nations it subdues, are ruled by the love of ruling; in the other, the princes and the subjects serve one another in love."

Augustine died on August 28, 430, as the Vandals were besieging his own earthly city of Hippo.

Augustine

Bishop of Hippo, 430

I   O Lord God, who art the light of the minds that know thee, the life of the souls that love thee, and the strength of the hearts that serve thee: Help us, following the example of thy servant Augustine of Hippo, so to know thee that we may truly love thee, and so to love thee that we may fully serve thee, whom to serve is perfect freedom; through Jesus Christ our Lord, who liveth and reigneth with thee and the Holy Spirit, one God, now and for ever. *Amen.*

II   Lord God, the light of the minds that know you, the life of the souls that love you, and the strength of the hearts that serve you: Help us, following the example of your servant Augustine of Hippo, so to know you that we may truly love you, and so to love you that we may fully serve you, whom to serve is perfect freedom; through Jesus Christ our Lord, who lives and reigns with you and the Holy Spirit, one God, now and for ever. *Amen.*

Psalm	Lessons
87	Hebrews 12:22-24,28-29
or 84:7-12	John 14:6-15

Preface of Baptism

The Gospel first came to the northern English in 627, when King Edwin of Northumbria was converted by a mission from Canterbury led by Bishop Paulinus, who established his see at York. Edwin's death in battle in 632 was followed by a severe pagan reaction. A year later, Edwin's exiled nephew Oswald gained the kingdom, and proceeded at once to restore the Christian mission.

During his exile, Oswald had lived at Columba's monastery of Iona, where he had been converted and baptized. Hence he sent to Iona, rather than to Canterbury, for missionaries. The head of the new mission was a gentle monk named Aidan, who centered his work, not at York, but in imitation of his home monastery, on Lindisfarne, an island off the northeast coast of England.

With his fellow monks and the English youths whom he trained, Aidan restored Christianity in Northumbria, King Oswald often serving as his interpreter, and extended the mission through the midlands as far south as London.

Aidan died at the royal town of Bamborough, on August 31, 651. The historian Bede said of him: "He neither sought nor loved anything of this world, but delighted in distributing immediately to the poor whatever was given him by kings or rich men of the world. He traversed both town and country on foot, never on horseback, unless compelled by some urgent necessity. Wherever in his way he saw any, either rich or poor, he invited them, if pagans, to embrace the mystery of the faith; or if they were believers, to strengthen them in their faith and stir them up by words and actions to alms and good works."

Aidan

Bishop of Lindisfarne, 651

I O loving God, who didst call thy servant Aidan from the peace of a cloister to re-establish the Christian mission in northern England, and didst endow him with gentleness, simplicity, and strength: Grant, we beseech thee, that we, following his example, may use what thou hast given us for the relief of human need, and may persevere in commending the saving Gospel of our Redeemer Jesus Christ; who liveth and reigneth with thee and the Holy Spirit, one God, for ever and ever. *Amen.*

II O loving God, you called your servant Aidan from the peace of a cloister to re-establish the Christian mission in northern England, and endowed him with gentleness, simplicity, and strength: Grant that we, following his example, may use what you have given us for the relief of human need, and may persevere in commending the saving Gospel of our Redeemer Jesus Christ; who lives and reigns with you and the Holy Spirit, one God, for ever and ever. *Amen.*

Psalm	Lessons
97:1-2,7-12	1 Corinthians 9:16-23
or 85:8-13	Matthew 19:27-30

Preface of Apostles

"God's warrior" is an epithet by which David Pendleton Oakerhater is known among the Cheyenne Indians of Oklahoma. The title is an apt one, for this apostle of Christ to the Cheyenne was originally a soldier who fought against the United States government with warriors of other tribes in the disputes over Indian land rights. By the late 1860s Oakerhater had distinguished himself for bravery and leadership as an officer in an elite corps of Cheyenne fighters. In 1875, after a year of minor uprisings and threats of major violence, he and twenty-seven other warrior leaders were taken prisoner by the U.S. Army, charged with inciting rebellion, and sent to a disused military prison in Florida.

Under the influence of a concerned Army captain, who sought to educate the prisoners, Oakerhater and his companions learned English, gave art and archery lessons to the area's many visitors, and had their first encounter with the Christian faith. The captain's example, and that of other concerned Christians, from as far away as New York, had their effect on the young warrior. He was moved to answer the call to transform his leadership in war into a lifelong ministry of peace.

With sponsorship from the Diocese of Central New York and financial help from a Mrs. Pendleton of Cincinnati, he and three other prisoners went north to study for the ministry. At his baptism in Syracuse in 1878 he took the name David Pendleton Oakerhater, in honor of his benefactress.

Soon after his ordination to the diaconate in 1881, David returned to Oklahoma. There, he was instrumental in founding and operating schools and missions, through great personal sacrifice and often in the face of apathy from the Church hierarchy and resistance from the government. He continued his ministry of service, education, and pastoral care among his people until his death on August 31, 1931.

Half a century before, the young deacon had told his people: "You all know me. You remember when I led you out to war I went first, and what I told you was true. Now I have been away to the East and I have learned about another captain, the Lord Jesus Christ, and he is my leader. He goes first, and all he tells me is true. I come back to my people to tell you to go with me now in this new road, a war that makes all for peace."

David Pendleton Oakerhater

Deacon and Missionary of the Cheyenne, 1931

I O God of unsearchable wisdom and infinite mercy, thou
didst choose a captive warrior, David Oakerhater, to be thy
servant, and didst send him to be a missionary to his own
people and to execute the office of a deacon among them:
Liberate us, who commemorate him today, from bondage to
self, and empower us for service to thee and to the neighbors
thou hast given us; through Jesus Christ, the captain of our
salvation; who liveth and reigneth with thee and the Holy
Spirit, one God for ever and ever. *Amen.*

II O God of unsearchable wisdom and infinite mercy, you
chose a captive warrior, David Oakerhater, to be your
servant, and sent him to be a missionary to his own people,
and to exercise the office of a deacon among them: Liberate
us, who commemorate him today, from bondage to self, and
empower us for service to you and to the neighbors you have
given us; through Jesus Christ, the captain of our salvation;
who lives and reigns with you and the Holy Spirit, one God,
for ever and ever. *Amen.*

Psalm	Lessons
96:1-7	Isaiah 52:7-10
or 98:1-4	Luke 10:1-9

Preface of Apostles

New Guinea, the second largest island in the world, is still one of the main frontiers of Christian mission, because of its difficult terrain and the cultural diversity of its peoples, who speak some 500 distinct languages. Christian missionaries first began work there in the 1860s and 1870s, with only limited success. The Anglican mission began in 1891, and the first bishop was consecrated in 1898.

During World War II, the suffering of missionaries and of native people was severe. This feast day, observed in the Diocese of New Guinea and in many dioceses of the Church of Australia, marks the witness of eight missionaries and two Papuan martyrs, who were betrayed by non-Christians to the Japanese invaders. But the day also includes remembrance of the faith and devotion of Papuan Christians of all Churches, who risked their own lives to care for the wounded, and to save the lives of many who otherwise would have perished.

The Martyrs of New Guinea

1942

I   Almighty God, we remember before thee this day the blessed
martyrs of New Guinea, who, following the example of their
Savior, laid down their lives for their friends; and we pray
thee that we, who honor their memory, may imitate their
loyalty and faith; through Jesus Christ our Lord, who liveth
and reigneth with thee and the Holy Spirit, one God, for ever
and ever. *Amen.*

II   Almighty God, we remember before you this day the blessed
martyrs of New Guinea, who, following the example of their
Savior, laid down their lives for their friends; and we pray
that we who honor their memory may imitate their loyalty
and faith; through Jesus Christ our Lord, who lives and
reigns with you and the Holy Spirit, one God, for ever and
ever. *Amen.*

Psalm

116:1-8
or   126

Lessons

Revelation 7:13-17
Luke 12:4-12

Preface of Holy Week

Paul Jones was born in 1880 in the rectory of St. Stephen's Church, Wilkes-Barre, Pennsylvania. After graduating from Yale University and the Episcopal Divinity School in Cambridge, Massachusetts, he accepted a call to serve a mission in Logan, Utah. In 1914 Paul Jones was appointed Archdeacon of the Missionary District of Utah and, later that year, was elected its Bishop. Meanwhile, World War I had begun.

As Bishop of Utah, Paul Jones did much to expand the Church's mission stations and to strengthen diocesan institutions. At the same time he spoke openly about his opposition to war.

With the United States entry into the war, the Bishop of Utah's views became increasingly controversial. At a meeting of the Fellowship of Reconciliation in Los Angeles in 1917, Bishop Jones expressed his belief that "war is unchristian," for which he was attacked with banner headlines in the Utah press.

As a result of the speech and the reaction it caused in Utah, a commission of the House of Bishops was appointed to investigate the situation. In their report, the commission concluded that "The underlying contention of the Bishop of Utah seems to be that war is unchristian. With this general statement the Commission cannot agree. . . ." The report went on to recommend that "The Bishop of Utah ought to resign his office," thus rejecting Paul Jones' right to object to war on grounds of faith and conscience.

In the spring of 1918, Bishop Jones, yielding to pressure, resigned as Bishop of Utah. For the next 23 years, until his death on September 4, 1941, he continued a ministry within the Church dedicated to peace and conscience, speaking always with a conviction and gentleness rooted in the Gospel.

In his farewell to the Missionary District of Utah in 1918, Bishop Jones said: "Where I serve the Church is of small importance, so long as I can make my life count in the cause of Christ. . . . Expediency may make necessary the resignation of a Bishop at this time, but no expedience can ever justify the degradation of the ideals of the episcopate which these conclusions seem to involve."

Paul Jones

Bishop and Peace Advocate, 1941

I   Merciful God, who didst send thy beloved Son to preach peace to those who are far off and to those who are near: Raise up in this and every land witnesses, who, after the example of thy servant Paul Jones, will stand firm in proclaiming the Gospel of the Prince of Peace, our Savior Jesus Christ, who liveth and reigneth with thee and the Holy Spirit, one God, now and for ever. *Amen.*

II   Merciful God, you sent your beloved Son to preach peace to those who are far off and to those who are near: Raise up in this and every land witnesses who, after the example of your servant Paul Jones, will stand firm in proclaiming the Gospel of the Prince of Peace, our Savior Jesus Christ, who lives and reigns with you and the Holy Spirit, one God, now and for ever. *Amen.*

Psalm	Lessons
133	Malachi 2:17—3:5
	John 8:31-32

Preface of a Saint (3)

In August, 1878, Yellow Fever invaded the city of Memphis for the third time in ten years. By the month's end the disease had become epidemic and a quarantine was ordered. While 30,000 citizens had fled in terror, 20,000 more remained to face the pestilence. As cases multiplied, death tolls averaged 200 daily. When the worst was over ninety percent of the population had contracted the Fever; more than 5,000 people had died.

In that time of panic and flight, many brave men and women, both lay and cleric, remained at their posts of duty or came as volunteers to assist despite the terrible risk. Notable among these heros were Constance, Superior of the work of the Sisters of St. Mary in Memphis, and her Companions. The Sisters had come to Memphis in 1873, at Bishop Quintard's request, to found a Girls School adjacent to St. Mary's Cathedral. When the 1878 epidemic began, George C. Harris, the Cathedral Dean, and Sister Constance immediately organized relief work among the stricken. Helping were six of Constance's fellow Sisters of St. Mary; Sister Clare from St. Margaret's House, Boston; the Reverend Charles C. Parsons, Rector of Grace and St. Lazarus Church, Memphis; and the Reverend Louis S. Schuyler, assistant at Holy Innocents, Hoboken. The Cathedral group also included three physicians, two of whom were ordained Episcopal priests, the Sisters' two matrons, and several volunteer nurses from New York. They have ever since been known as "The Martyrs of Memphis," as have those of other Communions who ministered in Christ's name during this time of desolation.

The Cathedral buildings were located in the most infected region of Memphis. Here, amid sweltering heat and scenes of indescribable horror, these men and women of God gave relief to the sick, comfort to the dying, and homes to the many orphaned children. Only two of the workers escaped the Fever. Among those who died were Constance, Thecla, Ruth and Frances, the Reverend Charles Parsons and the Reverend Louis Schuyler. The six martyred Sisters and priests are buried at Elmwood Cemetery. The monument marking the joint grave of Fathers Parsons and Schuyler bears the inscription: "Greater Love Hath No Man." The beautiful High Altar in St. Mary's Cathedral, Memphis, is a memorial to the four Sisters.

Constance, Nun, and her Companions

Commonly called "The Martyrs of Memphis," 1878

I   We give thee thanks and praise, O God of compassion, for the heroic witness of Constance and her companions, who, in a time of plague and pestilence, were steadfast in their care for the sick and dying, and loved not their own lives, even unto death: Inspire in us a like love and commitment to those in need, following the example of our Savior Jesus Christ; who with thee and the Holy Spirit liveth and reigneth, one God, now and for ever. *Amen.*

II   We give you thanks and praise, O God of compassion, for the heroic witness of Constance and her companions, who, in a time of plague and pestilence, were steadfast in their care for the sick and dying, and loved not their own lives, even unto death: Inspire in us a like love and commitment to those in need, following the example of our Savior Jesus Christ; who with you and the Holy Spirit lives and reigns, one God, now and for ever. *Amen.*

Psalm	Lessons
116:1-8	2 Corinthians 1:3-5
or 116:10-17	John 12:24-28

Preface of a Saint (I)

Born March 3, 1819, in New York City, Alexander Crummell struggled against racism all his life. As a young man, he was driven out of an academy in New Hampshire, dismissed as a candidate for Holy Orders in New York, and rejected for admittance to General Seminary. Ordained in 1844 as a priest in the Diocese of Massachusetts, he left for England after being excluded from participating in diocesan convention.

After receiving a degree from Cambridge, he went to Liberia as a missionary. The African race, Crummell believed, possessed a "warm, emotional and impulsive energy," which in America had been corrupted by oppression. The Episcopal Church, with its emphasis on rational and moral discipline, was especially fitted for the moral and spiritual regeneration of Afro-Americans. A model Christian republic seemed possible in Liberia. European education and technology, combined with traditional African communal culture, and undergirded by a national Episcopal Church headed by a black bishop, was the vision espoused by Crummell. He traveled extensively in the United States urging blacks to emigrate to Liberia and support the work of the Church there.

On returning to Liberia, he worked to establish a national Episcopal Church. Political opposition and a loss of funding finally forced him to return to the United States. He concentrated his efforts on establishing a strong urban presence of independent black congregations that would be centers of worship, education and social service. When southern bishops proposed that a separate missionary district be created for black congregations, Crummell created a national convocation to fight the proposal. The Union of Black Episcopalians is an outgrowth of that organization.

Crummell's ministry spanned more than half a century and three continents. Everywhere, at all times, he labored to prepare his people and to build institutions that would serve them and provide scope for the exercises of their gifts in leadership and creativity. His faith in God, his perseverance in spite of repeated discouragement, his perceptions that the Church transcended the racism and limited vision of its rulers, and his unfailing belief in the goodness and greatness of black people are the legacy of its Afro-American pioneer.

Alexander Crummell

Priest, Missionary, and Educator, 1898

I   Almighty and everlasting God, we thank thee for thy servant Alexander Crummell, whom thou didst call to preach the Gospel to those who were far off and to those who were near. Raise up, we beseech thee, in this and every land evangelists and heralds of thy kingdom, that thy Church may proclaim the unsearchable riches of our Savior Jesus Christ, who liveth and reigneth with thee and the Holy Spirit, one God, now and for ever. *Amen.*

II   Almighty and everlasting God, we thank you for your servant Alexander Crummell, whom you called to preach the Gospel to those who were far off and to those who were near. Raise up in this and every land evangelists and heralds of your kingdom, that your Church may proclaim the unsearchable riches of our Savior Jesus Christ, who lives and reigns with you and the Holy Spirit, one God, now and for ever. Amen

Psalm	Lessons
19:7-11	Sirach 39:6-11
	Mark 4:1-10, 13-20

Preface of a Saint (2)

John Henry Hobart was one of the leaders who revived the Episcopal Church, following the first two decades of its independent life after the American Revolution, a time that has been described as one of "suspended animation." Born in Philadelphia, September 14, 1775, Hobart was educated at the Universities of Pennsylvania and Princeton, graduating from the latter in 1793. Bishop William White, his longtime friend and adviser, ordained him deacon in 1798 and priest in 1801.

After serving parishes in Pennsylvania, New Jersey, and Long Island, Hobart became assistant minister of Trinity Church, New York City, in 1800. He was consecrated Assistant Bishop of New York on May 29, 1811. Five years later he succeeded Bishop Benjamin Moore, both as diocesan bishop and as rector of Trinity Church. He died at Auburn, New York, September 12, 1830, and was buried beneath the chancel of Trinity Church in New York City.

Within his first four years as bishop, Hobart doubled the number of his clergy and quadrupled the number of missionaries. Before his death, he had planted a church in almost every major town of New York State and had opened missionary work among the Oneida Indians. He was one of the founders of the General Theological Seminary, and the reviver of Geneva, now Hobart, College.

A strong and unbending upholder of Church standards, Hobart established the Bible and Common Prayer Book Society of New York, and was one of the first American Churchmen to produce theological and devotional manuals for the laity. These "tracts," as they were called, and the personal impression he made on the occasion of a visit to Oxford, were an influence on the development of the Tractarian Movement in England. Both friends and foes respected Hobart for his staunch faith, his consuming energy, his personal integrity, and his missionary zeal.

John Henry Hobart

Bishop of New York, 1830

I   Revive thy Church, Lord God of hosts, whensoever it doth fall into complacency and sloth, by raising up devoted leaders, like thy servant John Henry Hobart whom we remember this day; and grant that their faith and vigor of mind may awaken thy people to thy message and their mission; through Jesus Christ our Lord, who liveth and reigneth with thee and the Holy Spirit, one God, for ever and ever. *Amen.*

II   Revive your Church, Lord God of hosts, whenever it falls into complacency and sloth, by raising up devoted leaders, like your servant John Henry Hobart whom we remember today; and grant that their faith and vigor of mind may awaken your people to your message and their mission; through Jesus Christ our Lord, who lives and reigns with you and the Holy Spirit, one God, for ever and ever. *Amen.*

Psalm	Lessons
78:3-7	Jude 20-21,24-25
or 133	John 17:11b-19

Preface of a Saint (1)

Cyprian was a rich, aristocratic, and cultivated rhetorician in North Africa. He was converted to Christianity about 246, and by 248 was chosen Bishop of Carthage. A year later, in the persecution under the Emperor Decius, Cyprian went into hiding. For this he was severely criticized. Nonetheless, he kept in touch with his Church by letter, and directed it with wisdom and compassion. In the controversy over what to do with those who had lapsed during the persecution, Cyprian held that they could be reconciled to the Church after suitable periods of penance, the gravity of the lapse determining the length of the penance. His moderate position was the one that generally prevailed in the Church, over that of the rigorist Novatian, who led a group into schism at Rome and Antioch over this question. In another persecution, under the Emperor Valerian, Cyprian was placed under house arrest in Carthage, and, on September 14, 258, he was beheaded.

Many of Cyprian's writings have been preserved. His Letter No. 63 contains one of the earliest affirmations that the priest, in offering the Eucharist ("the sacrifice"), acts in the place of Christ, imitating his actions.

In his treatise, *On the Lord's Prayer*, he wrote: "We say 'Hallowed be thy Name,' not that we want God to be made holy by our prayers, but because we seek from the Lord that his Name may be made holy in us, . . . so that we who have been made holy in Baptism may persevere in what we have begun to be."

Although there is some question whether his book, *On the Unity of the Catholic Church*, affirms papal primacy, there is no question about the clarity of his statements on the unity of the college of bishops and the sin of schism. "The episcopate is a single whole," he wrote, "in which each bishop's share gives him a right to, and a responsibility for, the whole. So is the Church a single whole, though she spreads far and wide into a multitude of Churches. . . . If you leave the Church of Christ you will not come to Christ's rewards, you will be an alien, an outcast, an enemy. You cannot have God for your Father unless you have the Church for your Mother."

Cyprian

Bishop and Martyr of Carthage, 258

I O Almighty God, who didst give to thy servant Cyprian boldness to confess the Name of our Savior Jesus Christ before the rulers of this world, and courage to die for this faith: Grant that we may always be ready to give a reason for the hope that is in us, and to suffer gladly for the sake of the same our Lord Jesus Christ; who liveth and reigneth with thee and the Holy Spirit, one God, for ever and ever. *Amen.*

II Almighty God, who gave to your servant Cyprian boldness to confess the Name of our Savior Jesus Christ before the rulers of this world, and courage to die for this faith: Grant that we may always be ready to give a reason for the hope that is in us, and to suffer gladly for the sake of our Lord Jesus Christ; who lives and reigns with you and the Holy Spirit, one God, for ever and ever. *Amen.*

Psalm	Lessons
23	1 Peter 5:1-4,10-11
or 116:10-17	John 10:11-16

Preface of a Saint (3)

The historian Eusebius, in his *Life of Constantine*, tells how that emperor ordered the erection of a complex of buildings in Jerusalem "on a scale of imperial magnificence," to set forth as "an object of attraction and veneration to all, the blessed place of our Savior's resurrection." The overall supervision of the work — on the site where the Church of the Holy Sepulchre now stands — was entrusted to Constantine's mother, the empress Helena.

In Jesus' time, the hill of Calvary had stood outside the city; but when the Roman city which succeeded Jerusalem, *Aelia Capitolina*, was built, the hill was buried under tons of fill. It was during the excavations directed by Helena that a relic, believed to be that of the true cross, was discovered.

Constantine's shrine included two principal buildings: a large basilica, used for the Liturgy of the Word, and a circular church, known as "The Resurrection" — its Altar placed on the site of the tomb — which was used for the Liturgy of the Table, and for the singing of the Daily Office.

Toward one side of the courtyard which separated the two buildings, and through which the faithful had to pass on their way from Word to Sacrament, the exposed top of Calvary's hill was visible. It was there that the solemn veneration of the cross took place on Good Friday; and it was there that the congregation gathered daily for a final prayer and dismissal after Vespers.

The dedication of the buildings was completed on September 14, 335, the seventh month of the Roman calendar, a date suggested by the account of the dedication of Solomon's temple in the same city, in the seventh month of the Jewish Calendar, hundreds of years before (2 Chronicles 7:8-10).

Holy Cross Day

I   Almighty God, whose Son our Savior Jesus Christ was lifted high upon the cross that he might draw the whole world unto himself: Mercifully grant that we, who glory in the mystery of our redemption, may have grace to take up our cross and follow him; who liveth and reigneth with thee and the Holy Spirit, one God, in glory everlasting. *Amen.*

II   Almighty God, whose Son our Savior Jesus Christ was lifted high upon the cross that he might draw the whole world to himself: Mercifully grant that we, who glory in the mystery of our redemption, may have grace to take up our cross and follow him; who lives and reigns with you and the Holy Spirit, one God, in glory everlasting. *Amen.*

Psalm	Lessons
98	Isaiah 45:21-25
or 98:1-4	Philippians 2:5-11
	or Galatians 6:14-18
	John 12:31-36a

Preface of Holy Week

The dates of Ninian's life, and the exact extent of his work, are much disputed. The earliest, and possibly the best, account is the brief one in the Venerable Bede's *Ecclesiastical History*.

Ninian was a Romanized Briton, born in the latter half of the fourth century in southern Scotland. He is said to have been educated in Rome and to have received episcopal ordination. But the main influence on his life was Martin of Tours, with whom he spent some time, and from whom he gained his ideals of an episcopal-monastic structure designed for missionary work.

About the time of Martin's death in 397, Ninian established his base at place called Candida Casa ("White House") or Whithorn in Galloway, which he dedicated to Martin. Traces of place names and church dedications suggest that his work covered the Solway Plains and the Lake District of England. Ninian seems also to have converted many of the Picts of northern Scotland, as far north as The Moray Firth.

Ninian, together with Patrick, is one of the links of continuity between the ancient Roman-British Church and the developing Celtic Christianity of Ireland and Scotland.

Ninian

Bishop in Galloway, c. 430

I   O God, who by the preaching of thy blessed servant and bishop Ninian didst cause the light of the Gospel to shine in the land of Britain: Grant, we beseech thee, that, having his life and labors in remembrance, we may show forth our thankfulness by following the example of his zeal and patience; through Jesus Christ our Lord, who liveth and reigneth with thee and the Holy Spirit, one God, for ever and ever. *Amen.*

II   O God, by the preaching of your blessed servant and bishop Ninian you caused the light of the Gospel to shine in the land of Britain: Grant, we pray, that having his life and labors in remembrance we may show our thankfulness by following the example of his zeal and patience; through Jesus Christ our Lord, who lives and reigns with you and the Holy Spirit, one God, for ever and ever. *Amen.*

Psalm	Lessons
97:1-2,7-12	Isaiah 49:1-6
or 96:1-7	Matthew 28:16-20

Preface of Pentecost

Hildegard of Bingen, born in 1098 in the lush Rhineland Valley, was a mystic, poet, composer, dramatist, doctor, scientist. Her parents' tenth child, she was tithed to the Church and raised by the anchoress Jutta in a cottage near the Benedictine monastery of Disibodenberg.

Drawn by the life of silence and prayer, other women joined them, finding the freedom, rare outside women's religious communities, to develop their intellectual gifts. They organized as a convent under the authority of the abbot of Disibodenberg, with Jutta as abbess. When Jutta died, Hildegard, then 38, became abbess. Later she founded independent convents at Bingen (1150) and Eibingen (1165), with the Archbishop of Mainz as her only superior.

From childhood, Hildegard experienced dazzling spiritual visions. At 43, a voice commanded her to tell what she saw. So began an outpouring of extraordinarily original writings illustrated by unusual and wondrous illuminations. These works abound with feminine imagery for God and God's creative activity.

In 1147, Bernard of Clairvaux recommended her first book of visions, *Scivias*, to Pope Eugenius III, leading to papal authentication at the Synod of Trier. Hildegard became famous, eagerly sought for counsel, a correspondent of kings and queens, abbots and abbesses, archbishops and popes.

She carried out four preaching missions in northern Europe, unprecedented activity for a woman. She practiced medicine, focusing on women's needs; published treatises on natural science and philosophy; wrote a liturgical drama, *The Play of the Virtues*, in which personified virtues sing their parts and the devil, condemned to live without music, can only speak. For Hildegard, music was essential to worship. Her liturgical compositions, unusual in structure and tonality, were described by contemporaries as "chant of surpassing sweet melody" and "strange and unheard-of music."

Hildegard lived in a world accustomed to male governance. Yet, within her convents, and to a surprising extent outside them, she exercised a commanding spiritual authority based on confidence in her visions and considerable political astuteness. When she died in 1179 at 81, she left a rich legacy which speaks eloquently across the ages.

Hildegard

Abbess of Bingen and Mystic, 1179

I God of all times and seasons: Give us grace that we, after the example of thy servant Hildegard, may both know and make known the joy and jubilation of being part of thy creation, and show forth thy glory not only with our lips but in our lives; through Jesus Christ our Savior, who liveth and reigneth with thee and the Holy Spirit, one God, for ever and ever. *Amen.*

II God of all times and seasons: Give us grace that we, after the example of your servant Hildegard, may both know and make known the joy and jubilation of being part of your creation, and show forth your glory not only with our lips but in our lives; through Jesus Christ our Savior, who lives and reigns with you and the Holy Spirit, one God, for ever and ever. *Amen.*

Psalm

104:25-34

Lessons

Sirach 43:1-2,6-7,9-12,27-28
John 3:16-21

Preface of the Epiphany

The revival of High Church teachings and practices in the Anglican Communion, known as the Oxford Movement, found its acknowledged leader in Edward Bouverie Pusey. Born near Oxford, August 22, 1800, Pusey spent all his scholarly life in that University as Regius Professor of Hebrew and as Canon of Christ Church. At the end of 1833 he joined Keble and Newman in producing the Tracts for the Times, which gave the Oxford Movement its popular name of Tractarianism.

His most influential activity, however, was his preaching — catholic in content, evangelical in his zeal for souls. But to many of his more influential contemporaries it seemed dangerously innovative. A sermon preached before the University in 1843 on "The Holy Eucharist, a Comfort to the Penitent" was condemned without his being given an opportunity to defend it, and he himself was suspended from preaching for two years — a judgment he bore most patiently. His principles were thus brought before the public, and attention was drawn to the doctrine of the Real Presence of Christ in the Eucharist. From another University sermon, on "The Entire Absolution of the Penitent," may be dated the revival of private confession in the Anglican Communion.

When Newman defected to the Church of Rome in 1845, Pusey's adherence to the Church of England kept many from following, and he defended them in their teachings and practices.

After the death of his wife in 1839, Pusey devoted much of his family fortune to the establishment of churches for the poor, and much of his time and care to the establishment of sisterhoods. In 1845, he established the first Anglican sisterhood since the Reformation. It was at this community's convent, Ascot Priory in Berkshire, that Pusey died on September 16, 1882. His body was brought back to Christ Church and buried in the cathedral nave. Pusey House, a house of studies founded after his death, perpetuates his name at Oxford. His own erudition and integrity gave stability to the Oxford Movement and won many to its principles.

Edward Bouverie Pusey

Priest, 1882

I   Grant unto us, O God, that in all time of our testing we may know thy presence and obey thy will; that, following the example of thy servant Edward Bouverie Pusey, we may with integrity and courage accomplish what thou givest us to do, and endure what thou givest us to bear; through Jesus Christ our Lord, who liveth and reigneth with thee and the Holy Spirit, one God, for ever and ever. *Amen.*

II   Grant, O God, that in all time of our testing we may know your presence and obey your will; that, following the example of your servant Edward Bouverie Pusey, we may with integrity and courage accomplish what you give us to do, and endure what you give us to bear; through Jesus Christ our Lord, who lives and reigns with you and the Holy Spirit, one God, for ever and ever. *Amen.*

Psalm	Lessons
106:1-5	1 Peter 2:19-23
or 84:7-12	Matthew 13:44-52

Preface of a Saint (2)

Theodore was born in 602 in Saint Paul's native city, Tarsus in Asia Minor. He was ordained Archbishop of Canterbury by Pope Vitalian on March 26, 668.

A learned monk of the East, Theodore was residing in Rome when the English Church, decimated by plague, and torn with strife over rival Celtic and Roman customs, was in need of strong leadership. Theodore provided this for a generation, beginning his episcopate at an age when most people are ready to retire.

When Theodore came to England, he established a school at Canterbury that gained a reputation for excellence in all branches of learning, and where many leaders of both the Irish and the English Churches were trained. His effective visitation of all England brought unity to the two strains of tradition among the Anglo-Saxon Christians. For example, he recognized Chad's worthiness and regularized his episcopal ordination.

Theodore gave definitive boundaries to English dioceses, so that their bishops could give better pastoral attention to their people. He presided over synods that brought about reforms, according to established rules of canon law. He also laid the foundations of the parochial organization that still obtains in the English Church.

According to Bede, Theodore was the first archbishop whom all the English obeyed, and possibly to no other leader does English Christianity owe so much. He died in his eighty-eighth year, September 19, 690, and was buried, with Augustine and the other early English archbishops, in the monastic Church of Saints Peter and Paul at Canterbury.

Theodore of Tarsus

Archbishop of Canterbury, 690

I Almighty God, who didst call thy servant Theodore of Tarsus from Rome to the see of Canterbury, and didst give him gifts of grace and wisdom to establish unity where there had been division, and order where there had been chaos: Create in thy Church, we pray thee, by the operation of the Holy Spirit, such godly union and concord that it may proclaim, both by word and example, the Gospel of the Prince of Peace; who liveth and reigneth with thee and the Holy Spirit, one God, for ever and ever. *Amen.*

II Almighty God, you called your servant Theodore of Tarsus from Rome to the see of Canterbury, and gave him gifts of grace and wisdom to establish unity where there had been division, and order where there had been chaos: Create in your Church, by the operation of the Holy Spirit, such godly union and concord that it may proclaim, both by word and example, the Gospel of the Prince of Peace; who lives and reigns with you and the Holy Spirit, one God, for ever and ever. *Amen.*

Psalm	Lessons
34:9-14	2 Timothy 2:1-5,10
or 112:1-9	Matthew 24:42-47

Preface of a Saint (1)

The death of Bishop Patteson and his companions at the hands of Melanesian islanders, whom Patteson had sought to protect from slave-traders, aroused the British government to take serious measures to prevent piratical man-hunting in the South Seas. Their martyrdom was the seed that produced the strong and vigorous Church which flourishes in Melanesia today.

Patteson was born in London, April 1, 1827, of a Devonshire family. He attended Balliol College, Oxford, where he took his degree in 1849. After travel in Europe and a study of languages, at which he was adept, he became a Fellow of Merton College in 1852, and was ordained the following year.

While serving as a curate of Alphington, Devonshire, near his family home, he responded to Bishop G. A. Selwyn's call in 1855 for helpers in New Zealand. He established a school for boys on Norfolk Island to train native Christian workers. It is said that he learned to speak some twenty-three of the languages of the Melanesian people. On February 24, 1861, he was consecrated Bishop of Melanesia.

On a visit to the island of Nakapu, in the Santa Cruz group, Patteson was stabbed five times in the breast, in mistaken retaliation for the brutal outrages committed some time earlier by slave-traders. In the attack, several of Patteson's company were also killed or wounded. Bishop Selwyn later reconciled the natives of Melanesia to the memory of one who came to help and not to hurt.

John Coleridge Patteson

Bishop of Melanesia, and his Companions, Martyrs, 1871

I Almighty God, who didst call thy faithful servants John
Coleridge Patteson and his companions to be witnesses and
martyrs in the islands of Melanesia, and by their labors and
sufferings didst raise up a people for thine own possession:
Pour forth thy Holy Spirit upon thy Church in every land,
that by the service and sacrifice of many, thy holy Name may
be glorified and thy kingdom enlarged; through Jesus Christ
our Lord, who liveth and reigneth with thee and the Holy
Spirit, one God, for ever and ever. *Amen.*

II Almighty God, you called your faithful servant John
Coleridge Patteson and his companions to be witnesses and
martyrs in the islands of Melanesia, and by their labors and
sufferings raised up a people for your own possession: Pour
out your Holy Spirit upon your Church in every land, that
by the service and sacrifice of many, your holy Name may be
glorified and your kingdom enlarged; through Jesus Christ
our Lord, who lives and reigns with you and the Holy Spirit,
one God, for ever and ever. *Amen.*

Psalm

121
or 116:1-8

Lessons

1 Peter 4:12-19
Mark 8:34-38

Preface of Holy Week

Matthew, one of Jesus' disciples, is probably to be identified with Levi, a tax collector ("publican") mentioned by Mark and Luke. In the Gospel according to Matthew, it is said that Matthew was seated in the custom-house when Jesus bade him, "Follow me." When Jesus called him, he at once left everything, followed the Master, and later gave a dinner for him. Mark and Luke also note that Levi was a tax collector. In all three accounts, Jesus is severely criticized for eating at the same table with tax collectors and other disreputable persons.

Tax collectors were viewed as collaborators with the Roman State, extortioners who took money from their own people to further the cause of Rome and to line their own pockets. They were spurned as traitors and outcasts. The Jews so abhorred them that pious Pharisees refused to marry into a family that had a publican as a member. Clearly, Matthew was hardly the type of man that a devout Jew would have had among his closest associates. Yet Jesus noted that it was the publican rather than the proud Pharisee who prayed the acceptable prayer, "Lord, be merciful to me, a sinner." There is frequent favorable reference to publicans in the many sayings of Jesus in the Gospel according to Matthew.

Matthew was called early in Jesus' ministry, but that he wrote the Gospel that bears his name is seriously doubted by scholars. It is, however, generally accepted that his "logia" or "sayings of Jesus" have been included in that Gospel.

It may be that the author of the First Gospel took from Matthew's work some of the numerous parables and comments that make that Gospel so popular a source for homilies and teaching. Through this Gospel, especially, Jesus speaks not only of faith and eternal life, but of duties toward one's neighbors, family, and even enemies.

Tradition has it that Matthew, having converted many persons to Christianity in Judea, traveled to the East; but there is no certain evidence for this. He has been venerated as a martyr, but the time and circumstances of his death are unknown.

Saint Matthew, Apostle and Evangelist

I   We thank thee, heavenly Father, for the witness of thine apostle and evangelist Matthew to the Gospel of thy Son our Savior; and we pray that, after his example, we may with ready wills and hearts obey the calling of our Lord to follow him; through Jesus Christ our Lord, who liveth and reigneth with thee and the Holy Spirit, one God, now and for ever. *Amen.*

II   We thank you, heavenly Father, for the witness of your apostle and evangelist Matthew to the Gospel of your Son our Savior; and we pray that, after his example, we may with ready wills and hearts obey the calling of our Lord to follow him; through Jesus Christ our Lord, who lives and reigns with you and the Holy Spirit, one God, now and for ever. *Amen.*

Psalm	Lessons
119:33-40	Proverbs 3:1-6
	2 Timothy 3:14-17
	Matthew 9:9-13

Preface of Apostles

Born the youngest of fifteen children on December 14, 1775 in Cornish, New Hampshire, Philander Chase attended Dartmouth College, where he prepared to become a Congregationalist minister. While at Dartmouth, he happened upon a copy of the Book of Common Prayer. Next to the Bible, he thought it was the most excellent book he had ever studied, and believed that it was surely inspired by God. At the age of nineteen he was confirmed in the Episcopal Church.

Following graduation from Dartmouth, Chase worked as a schoolteacher in Albany, New York, and read for Holy Orders. Ordained a deacon in 1798, he began mission work on the northern and western frontiers among the pioneers and the Mohawk and Oneida peoples. The first of the many congregations he founded was at Lake George in New York State.

Ordained a priest in 1799, at the age of twenty-three, Chase served as rector of Christ Church, Poughkeepsie, New York, until 1805. He then moved to New Orleans, where he organized the first Protestant congregation in Louisiana. That parish now serves as the cathedral church for the Diocese of Louisiana. In 1810 he returned north to Hartford, Connecticut, where he served for six years as rector of Christ Church, now the cathedral church of the Diocese of Connecticut. In 1817 he accepted a call to be the first rector of St. John's Church in Worthington, Ohio. A year later he was elected the first Bishop of Ohio. He immediately began founding congregations and organizing the diocese. He also established Kenyon College and Bexley Hall Seminary.

In 1831 Chase resigned as Bishop of Ohio and began ministering to Episcopalians and the unchurched in southern Michigan. In 1835 he was elected the first Bishop of Illinois and served in this office until he died on September 20, 1852. During his time in Illinois he founded numerous congregations, together with Jubilee College, which included a seminary. As the senior bishop in the Episcopal Church, he served as the Presiding Bishop from 1843 until his death.

At a meeting of the House of Bishops in 1835, Bishop Doane of New Jersey said of him: "A veteran soldier, a Bishop of the Cross, whom hardships never have discouraged, whom no difficulties seem to daunt."

[Philander Chase]

Bishop of Ohio, and of Illinois, 1852

I   Almighty God, whose Son Jesus Christ is the pioneer and perfecter of our faith: We give thee heartfelt thanks for the pioneering spirit of thy servant Philander Chase, and for his zeal in opening new frontiers for the ministry of thy Church. Grant us grace to minister in Christ's name in every place, led by bold witnesses to the Gospel of the Prince of Peace, even Jesus Christ our Lord, who liveth and reigneth with thee and the Holy Spirit, one God, for ever and ever. *Amen.*

II   Almighty God, whose Son Jesus Christ is the pioneer and perfecter of our faith: We give you heartfelt thanks for the pioneering spirit of your servant Philander Chase, and for his zeal in opening new frontiers for the ministry of your Church. Grant us grace to minister in Christ's name in every place, led by bold witnesses to the Gospel of the Prince of Peace, Jesus Christ our Lord, who lives and reigns with you and the Holy Spirit, one God, for ever and ever. *Amen.*

Psalm	Lessons
108:1-6 or	Isaiah 44:1-6, 8
16:5-11	Luke 9:1-6

Preface of a Saint (1)

To the people of Russia, Sergius is a national hero and their patron saint. He was born at Rostov, about 1314.

Civil war in Russia forced Sergius' family to leave the city and to live by farming at Radonezh near Moscow. At the age of twenty, he and his brother began a life of seclusion in a nearby forest, from which developed the Monastery of the Holy Trinity, a center of revival of Russian Christianity. There Sergius remained for the rest of his life, refusing higher advancement, such as the see of Moscow, in 1378.

Sergius' firm support of Prince Dimitri Donskoi helped to rally the Russians against their Tartar overlords. Dimitri won a decisive victory against them at the Kulikovo Plains in 1380, and laid the foundation of his people's independent national life.

Sergius was simple and gentle in nature, mystical in temperament, and eager to ensure that his monks should serve the needs of their neighbors. He was able to inspire intense devotion to the Orthodox faith. He died in 1392, and pilgrims still visit his shrine at the monastery of Zagorsk, which he founded in 1340. The city contains several splendid cathedrals and is the residence of the Patriarch of Moscow.

The Russian Church observes Sergius' memory on September 25. His name is familiar to Anglicans from the Fellowship of St. Alban and St. Sergius, a society established to promote closer relations between the Anglican and Russian Churches.

Sergius

Abbot of Holy Trinity, Moscow, 1392

I   O God, whose blessed Son became poor that we through his poverty might be rich: Deliver us, we pray thee, from an inordinate love of this world, that inspired by the devotion of thy servant Sergius of Moscow, we may serve thee with singleness of heart, and attain to the riches of the age to come; through the same Jesus Christ our Lord, who liveth and reigneth with thee and the Holy Spirit, one God, now and for ever. *Amen.*

II   O God, whose blessed Son became poor that we through his poverty might be rich: Deliver us from an inordinate love of this world, that we, inspired by the devotion of your servant Sergius of Moscow, may serve you with singleness of heart, and attain to the riches of the age to come; through Jesus Christ our Lord, who lives and reigns with you and the Holy Spirit, one God, for ever and ever. *Amen.*

Psalm	Lessons
34:1-8	Ecclesiasticus 39:1-9
or 33:1-5,20-21	Matthew 13:47-52

Preface of a Saint (2)

Lancelot Andrewes was the favorite preacher of King James the First. He was the author of a great number of eloquent sermons, particularly on the Nativity and the Resurrection. They are "witty," grounded in the Scriptures, and characterized by the kind of massive learning that the King loved. This makes them difficult reading for modern people, but they repay careful study. T. S. Eliot used the opening of one of Andrewes' Epiphany sermons as the inspiration for his poem, "The journey of the Magi:"

> A cold coming we had of it,
> Just the worst time of the year
> For a Journey, and such a long journey:
> The way deep and the weather sharp,
> The very dead of winter.

Andrewes was also a distinguished biblical scholar, proficient in Hebrew and Greek, and was one of the translators of the Authorized (King James) Version of the Bible. He was Dean of Westminster and headmaster of the school there before he became a bishop, and was influential in the education of a number of noted Churchmen of his time, in particular, the poet George Herbert.

Andrewes was a very devout man, and one of his most admired works is his *Preces Privatae* ("Private Devotions"), an anthology from the Scriptures and the ancient liturgies, compiled for his own use. It illustrates his piety and throws light on the sources of his theology. He vigorously defended the catholicity of the Church of England against Roman Catholic critics. He was respected by many as the very model of a bishop at a time when bishops were held in low esteem. As his student, John Hacket, later Bishop of Lichfield, wrote about him: "Indeed he was the most Apostolical and Primitive-like Divine, in my Opinion, that wore a Rochet in his Age; of a most venerable Gravity, and yet most sweet in all Commerce; the most Devout that I ever saw, when he appeared before God; of such a Growth in all kind of Learning that very able Clerks were of a low Stature to him."

Lancelot Andrewes

Bishop of Winchester, 1626

I   O Lord and Father, our King and God, by whose grace the
Church was enriched by the great learning and eloquent
preaching of thy servant Lancelot Andrewes, but even more
by his example of biblical and liturgical prayer: Conform
our lives, like his, we beseech thee, to the image of Christ,
that our hearts may love thee, our minds serve thee, and
our lips proclaim the greatness of thy mercy; through the same
Jesus Christ our Lord, who liveth and reigneth with thee and
the Holy Spirit, one God, now and for ever. *Amen.*

II   Lord and Father, our King and God, by your grace the
Church was enriched by the great learning and eloquent
preaching of your servant Lancelot Andrewes, but even
more by his example of biblical and liturgical prayer:
Conform our lives, like his, to the image of Christ, that our
hearts may love you, our minds serve you, and our lips
proclaim the greatness of your mercy; through Jesus Christ
our Lord, who lives and reigns with you and the Holy Spirit,
one God, now and for ever. *Amen.*

Psalm	Lessons
63:1-8	1 Timothy 2:1-7a
or 34:1-8	Luke 11:1-4

Preface of a Saint (1)

The scriptural word "angel" (Greek: *angelos*) means, literally, a messenger. Messengers from God can be visible or invisible, and may assume human or non-human forms. Christians have always felt themselves to be attended by healthful spirits — swift, powerful, and enlightening. Those beneficent spirits are often depicted in Christian art in human form, with wings to signify their swiftness and spacelessness, with swords to signify their power, and with dazzling raiment to signify their ability to enlighten. Unfortunately, this type of pictorial representation has led many to dismiss the angels as "just another mythical beast, like the unicorn, the griffin, or the sphinx."

Of the many angels spoken of in the Bible, only four are called by name: Michael, Gabriel, Uriel, and Raphael. The Archangel Michael is the powerful agent of God who wards off evil from God's people, and delivers peace to them at the end of this life's mortal struggle. "Michaelmas," as his feast is called in England, has long been one of the popular celebrations of the Christian Year in many parts of the world.

Michael is the patron saint of countless churches, including Mont Saint-Michel, the monastery fortress off the coast of Normandy that figured so prominently in medieval English history, and Coventry Cathedral, England's most famous modern church building, rising from the ashes of the most devastating war of our time.

Saint Michael and All Angels

I   O everlasting God, who hast ordained and constituted the
ministries of angels and men in a wonderful order:
Mercifully grant that, as thy holy angels always serve and
worship thee in heaven, so by thy appointment they may
help and defend us on earth; through Jesus Christ our Lord,
who liveth and reigneth with thee and the Holy Spirit, one
God, for ever and ever. *Amen.*

II   Everlasting God, you have ordained and constituted in a
wonderful order the ministries of angels and mortals:
Mercifully grant that, as your holy angels always serve and
worship you in heaven, so by your appointment they may
help and defend us here on earth; through Jesus Christ our
Lord, who lives and reigns with you and the Holy Spirit, one
God, for ever and ever. *Amen.*

Psalm	Lessons
103	Genesis 28:10-17
or 103:19-22	Revelation 12:7-12
	John 1:47-51

Preface of Trinity Sunday

Jerome was the foremost biblical scholar of the ancient Church. His Latin translation of the Bible from the original Hebrew and Greek texts known as the Vulgate version, along with his commentaries and homilies on the biblical books, have made him a major intellectual force in the Western Church.

Jerome was born in the north Italian town of Stridon about 347, and was converted and baptized during his student days in Rome. On a visit to Trier, he found himself attracted to the monastic life, which he tested in a brief but unhappy experience as a hermit in the desert of Syria. At Antioch in 378, he reluctantly allowed himself to be ordained a presbyter, and there continued his studies in Hebrew and Greek. The following year he was in Constantinople as a student of Gregory of Nazianzus. From 382 to 384 he was secretary to Pope Damasus the First in Rome, and spiritual director of many noble Roman ladies who were becoming interested in the monastic life. It was Damasus who set him to the task of making a new translation of the Bible into Latin — the vulgar tongue, as distinguished from the classical Greek. Hence the name of his translation, the Vulgate.

After the Pope's death, Jerome returned to the East, and established a monastery at Bethlehem, where he lived and worked until his death on September 30, 420. He was buried in a chapel beneath the Church of the Nativity, near the traditional place of our Lord's birth.

Jerome's irascible disposition, pride of learning, and extravagant promotion of asceticism involved him in many bitter controversies over both theological and exegetical questions. Yet he was candid at times in admitting his failings, and was never ambitious for churchly honors. A militant champion of orthodoxy, an indefatigable worker, and a stylist of rare gifts, Jerome was seldom pleasant, but at least he was never dull.

Jerome

Priest, and Monk of Bethlehem, 420

I   O Lord, thou God of truth, thy Word is a lantern to our feet and a light upon our path: We give thee thanks for thy servant Jerome, and those who, following in his steps, have labored to render the Holy Scriptures in the language of the people; and we beseech thee that thy Holy Spirit may overshadow us as we read the written Word, and that Christ, the living Word, may transform us according to thy righteous will; through the same Jesus Christ our Lord, who liveth and reigneth with thee and the same Spirit, one God, now and for ever. *Amen.*

II   O Lord, O God of truth, your Word is a lantern to our feet and a light upon our path: We give you thanks for your servant Jerome, and those who, following in his steps, have labored to render the Holy Scriptures in the language of the people; and we pray that your Holy Spirit will overshadow us as we read the written Word, and that Christ, the living Word, will transform us according to your righteous will; through Jesus Christ our Lord, who lives and reigns with you and the Holy Spirit, one God, now and for ever. *Amen.*

Psalm	Lessons
19:7-11 (12-14)	2 Timothy 3:14-17
or 119:97-104	Luke 24:44-48

Preface of Pentecost

Remigius, also known as Remi, one of the patron saints of France, was born about 438, the son of the Count of Laon. At the age of twenty-two he became Bishop of Rheims.

Noted for his learning and holiness of life, Remigius is chiefly remembered because he converted and baptized King Clovis of the Franks on Christmas Day, 496. This event changed the religious history of Europe. Clovis, by becoming Catholic instead of Arian, as were most of the Germanic people of the time, was able to unite the Gallo-Roman population and their Christian leaders behind his expanding hegemony over the Germanic rulers of the West and to liberate Gaul from Roman domination. His conversion also made possible the cooperation the Franks gave later to Pope Gregory the Great in his evangelistic efforts for the English. No doubt, Clovis' motives in accepting Catholic Christianity were mixed, but there is no doubt of the sincerity of his decision, nor of the important role of Remigius in bringing it to pass. When Clovis was baptized, together with 3,000 of his followers, Remi gave him the well-known charge, "Worship what you have burned, and burn what you have worshiped."

The feast of Remigius is observed at Rheims on January 13, possibly the date of his death. The later date of October 1 is derived from the translation of his relics to a new abbey church by Pope Leo the Ninth in 1049.

Remigius

Bishop of Rheims, c. 530

I   O God, who by the teaching of thy faithful servant and bishop Remigius didst turn the nation of the Franks from vain idolatry to the worship of thee, the true and living God, in the fullness of the catholic faith: Grant that we who glory in the name of Christian may show forth our faith in worthy deeds; through Jesus Christ our Lord, who liveth and reigneth with thee and the Holy Spirit, one God, for ever and ever. *Amen.*

II   O God, by the teaching of your faithful servant and bishop Remigius you turned the nation of the Franks from vain idolatry to the worship of you, the true and living God, in the fullness of the catholic faith: Grant that we who glory in the name of Christian may show forth our faith in worthy deeds; through Jesus Christ our Lord, who lives and reigns with you and the Holy Spirit, one God, for ever and ever. *Amen.*

Psalm	Lessons
135:13-21	1 John 4:1-6
or 103:1-4,13-18	John 14:3-7

Preface of a Saint (1)

Francis, the son of a prosperous merchant of Assisi, was born in 1182. His early youth was spent in harmless revelry and fruitless attempts to win military glory.

Various encounters with beggars and lepers pricked the young man's conscience, and he decided to embrace a life devoted to Lady Poverty. Despite his father's intense opposition, Francis totally renounced all material values, and devoted himself to serve the poor. In 1210 Pope Innocent the Third confirmed the simple Rule for the Order of Friars Minor, a name Francis chose to emphasize his desire to be numbered among the "least" of God's servants.

The order grew rapidly all over Europe. But by 1221 Francis had lost control of it, since his ideal of strict and absolute poverty, both for the individual friars and for the order as a whole, was found to be too difficult to maintain. His last years were spent in much suffering of body and spirit, but his unconquerable joy never failed.

Not long before his death, during a retreat on Mount La Verna, Francis received, on September 14, Holy Cross Day, the marks of the Lord's wounds, the *stigmata*, in his own hands and feet and side. Pope Gregory the Ninth, a former patron of the Franciscans, canonized Francis in 1228, and began the erection of the great basilica in Assisi where Francis is buried.

Of all the saints, Francis is the most popular and admired, but probably the least imitated; few have attained to his total identification with the poverty and suffering of Christ. Francis left few writings; but, of these, his spirit of joyous faith comes through most truly in the "Canticle of the Sun," which he composed at Clare's convent of St. Damian's. The Hymnal version begins:

> Most High, omnipotent, good Lord,
> To thee be ceaseless praise outpoured,
>   And blessing without measure.
> Let creatures all give thanks to thee
> And serve in great humility.

Francis of Assisi

Friar, 1226

I   Most high, omnipotent, good Lord, grant unto thy people grace to renounce gladly the vanities of this world; that, following the way of blessed Francis, we may for love of thee delight in thy whole creation with perfectness of joy; through Jesus Christ our Lord, who liveth and reigneth with thee and the Holy Spirit, one God, for ever and ever. *Amen.*

II   Most high, omnipotent, good Lord, grant your people grace to renounce gladly the vanities of this world; that, following the way of blessed Francis, we may for love of you delight in your whole creation with perfectness of joy; through Jesus Christ our Lord, who lives and reigns with you and the Holy Spirit, one God, for ever and ever. *Amen.*

Psalm	Lessons
148:7-14	Galatians 6:14-18
or 121	Matthew 11:25-30

Preface of a Saint (3)

William Tyndale was born about 1495 at Slymbridge near the Welsh border. He received his B.A. and M.A. degrees at Magdalen College, Oxford, and also spent some time in study at Cambridge. After his ordination, about 1521, he entered the service of Sir John Walsh at Little Sodbury, Gloucestershire, as domestic chaplain and tutor. In 1523 he went to London and obtained a similar position with a rich cloth merchant, Humphrey Monmouth.

Tyndale was determined to translate the Scriptures into English, but, despairing of official support, he left for Germany in 1524. From this point on, his life reads like a cloak-and-dagger story, as King Henry the Eighth, Cardinal Wolsey, and others, sought to destroy his work of translation and put him to death. He was finally betrayed by one whom he had befriended, and in Brussels, on October 6, 1536, he was strangled at the stake, and his body was burned.

William Tyndale was a man of a single passion, to translate the Bible into English; so that, as he said to a prominent Churchman, "If God spare my life, ere many years I will cause a boy that driveth the plough shall know more scripture than thou doest." His accomplished work is his glory. Before his betrayal and death, he had finished and revised his translation of the New Testament, and had completed a translation of the Pentateuch and of Jonah and, though he did not live to see them published, of the historical books from Joshua through 2 Chronicles. His work has been called "a well of English undefiled." Some eighty per cent of his version has survived in the language of later and more familiar versions, such as the Authorized (King James) Version of 1611.

After the fashion of his time, Tyndale could be a bitter controversialist, and his translations sometimes had a polemical purpose. He was a lonely and desperate man, constantly hunted and hounded. In his personal life he was amiable and self-denying. His last words were prophetic: "Lord, open the King of England's eyes."

William Tyndale

Priest, 1536

I Almighty God, who didst plant in the heart of thy servant
William Tyndale a consuming passion to bring the
Scriptures to people in their native tongue, and didst endow
him with the gift of powerful and graceful expression and
with strength to persevere against all obstacles: Reveal to us,
we pray thee, thy saving Word, as we read and study the
Scriptures, and hear them calling us to repentance and life;
through Jesus Christ our Lord, who liveth and reigneth with
thee and the Holy Spirit, one God, for ever and ever. *Amen.*

II Almighty God, you planted in the heart of your servant
William Tyndale a consuming passion to bring the
Scriptures to people in their native tongue, and endowed him
with the gift of powerful and graceful expression and with
strength to persevere against all obstacles: Reveal to us your
saving Word, as we read and study the Scriptures, and hear
them calling us to repentance and life; through Jesus Christ
our Lord, who lives and reigns with you and the Holy Spirit,
one God, for ever and ever. *Amen.*

Psalm	Lessons
1	James 1:21-25
or 15	John 12:44-50

Preface of the Epiphany

Robert Grosseteste, one of the outstanding English bishops of the thirteenth century, rose to preeminence in the Church from humble beginnings in Suffolk. He distinguished himself as a scholar in all branches of study — law, medicine, languages, sciences, and theology.

He was appointed Master of the Oxford School, and first teacher of theology to the Franciscans, when they established a house at Oxford. Grosseteste translated Aristotle's works from the Greek, wrote commentaries on them, and sought to refute the philosopher's views by developing a scientific method based on Augustine's theories. Because of Grosseteste, Oxford began to emphasize the study of the sciences, especially physics, geometry, and mathematics. One notable pupil of Grosseteste was Roger Bacon, a brilliant proponent of the scientific method. Both as teacher and bishop, Grosseteste had a strong influence on John Wycliffe.

In 1235, Grosseteste was consecrated Bishop of Lincoln. He exercised his office with efficiency and conscientiousness, remarking that a bishop's pastoral responsibility was not merely to give instructions but to see that they were carried out. "I am obligated to visit the sheep committed to me with all diligence, as Scripture prescribes," he said.

He traveled regularly to each rural deanery, called together the clergy and laity, preached, confirmed, and dealt with questions of doctrine. "My lord, you are doing something new and exceptional," remarked some of the people during his first visitation. He replied, "Every new thing which implants and promotes and perfects the new man, corrupts and destroys the old. Blessed is the new, and in every way welcome to him who comes to recreate the old man in newness."

Grosseteste actively opposed royal infringements on Church liberties and he did not fear to protest even papal abuses of local prerogatives. He once refused to accept the appointment of the Pope's nephew to a living in his diocese, saying, "As an obedient son, I disobey, I contradict, I rebel . . . my every word and act is not rebellion, but filial honor due by God's blessed command to father and mother."

Robert Grosseteste
Bishop of Lincoln, 1253

I   O God, our heavenly Father, who didst raise up thy faithful servant Robert Grosseteste to be a bishop and pastor in thy Church and to feed thy flock: Give abundantly to all pastors the gifts of thy Holy Spirit, that they may minister in thy household as true servants of Christ and stewards of thy divine mysteries; through the same Jesus Christ our Lord, who liveth and reigneth with thee and the same Spirit, one God, for ever and ever. *Amen.*

II   O God, our heavenly Father, who raised up your faithful servant Robert Grosseteste to be a bishop and pastor in your Church and to feed your flock: Give abundantly to all pastors the gifts of your Holy Spirit, that they may minister in your household as true servants of Christ and stewards of your divine mysteries; through Jesus Christ our Lord, who lives and reigns with you and the Holy Spirit, one God, for ever and ever. *Amen.*

Psalm	Lessons
112:1-9	Acts 20:28-32
or 23	Luke 16:10-15

Preface of a Saint (1)

Philip, who has been traditionally referred to as a Deacon and an Evangelist, was one of seven honest men appointed, some sources say ordained, by the apostles to distribute bread and alms to the widows and the poor in Jerusalem.

After the martyrdom of Stephen, Philip went to Samaria to preach the gospel. In his travels south to Gaza he encountered an Ethiopian eunuch, a servant of the Ethiopian queen, reading the Isaiah text on the Suffering Servant. They traveled together, and in the course of their journey the Ethiopian was converted and baptized by Philip.

Subsequently, Philip traveled as a missionary from Ashdod northwards and settled in Caesarea. It was in Caesarea that he hosted St. Paul. Philip's activities at the end of his life are the subject of speculation, but some sources place him as a bishop at Lydia in Asia Minor. His feast day in the Eastern Church is October 11, and in the West usually June 6. Other provinces of the Anglican Communion also keep his feast on October 11.

Philip, Deacon and Evangelist

I   Holy God, no one is excluded from thy love, and thy truth transformeth the minds of all who seek thee: As thy servant Philip was led to embrace the fullness of thy salvation and to bring the stranger to Baptism, so grant unto us all the grace to be heralds of the Gospel, proclaiming thy love in Jesus Christ our Savior, who liveth and reigneth with thee and the Holy Spirit, one God, now and for ever. *Amen.*

II Holy God, no one is excluded from your love, and your truth transforms the minds of all who seek you: As your servant Philip was led to embrace the fullness of your salvation and to bring the stranger to Baptism, so give us all the grace to be heralds of the Gospel, proclaiming your love in Jesus Christ our Savior, who lives and reigns with you and the Holy Spirit, one God, now and for ever. *Amen.*

Psalm	Lessons
67	Isaiah 53:7-11 *or* Acts 8:26-40
	Matthew 28:18-20

Preface of Apostles and Ordinations

The story of Joseph Schereschewsky is unique in the annals of the Church. He was born on May 6, 1831, of Jewish parents, in the Lithuanian town of Tauroggen. His early education was directed toward the rabbinate, but during graduate studies in Germany, he became interested in Christianity through missionaries of the London Society for Promoting Christianity Amongst the Jews, and through his own reading of a Hebrew translation of the New Testament.

In 1854 Schereschewsky emigrated to America and entered the Western Theological Seminary in Pittsburgh to train for the ministry of the Presbyterian Church. After two years, he decided to become an Episcopalian, and to finish his theological studies at the General Theological Seminary in New York City, from which he graduated in 1859.

After ordination, and in response to Bishop Boone's call for helpers in China, Schereschewsky left for Shanghai. Always facile in languages, he learned to write Chinese during the voyage. From 1862 to 1875 he lived in Peking, and translated the Bible and parts of the Prayer Book into Mandarin. After Bishop Williams was transferred to Japan, Schereschewsky was elected Bishop of Shanghai in 1877, and was consecrated in Grace Church, New York City. He established St. John's University, in Shanghai, and began his translation of the Bible and other works into Wenli. Stricken with paralysis, he resigned his see in 1883.

Schereschewsky was determined to continue his translation work, and after many difficulties in finding support, he was able to return to Shanghai in 1895. Two years later, he moved to Tokyo. There he died on October 15, 1906.

With heroic perseverance Schereschewsky completed his translation of the Bible, typing some 2,000 pages with the middle finger of his partially crippled hand. Four years before his death, he said, "I have sat in this chair for over twenty years. It seemed very hard at first. But God knew best. He kept me for the work for which I am best fitted." He is buried in the Aoyama Cemetery in Tokyo, next to his wife, who supported him constantly during his labors and illness.

Samuel Isaac Joseph Schereschewsky

Bishop of Shanghai, 1906

I   O God, who in thy providence didst call Joseph
Schereschewsky from his home in Eastern Europe to the
ministry of this Church, and didst send him as a missionary
to China, upholding him in his infirmity, that he might
translate the Holy Scriptures into languages of that land:
Lead us, we pray thee, to commit our lives and talents to
thee, in the confidence that when thou givest unto thy
servants any work to do, thou dost also supply the strength
to do it; through Jesus Christ our Lord, who liveth and
reigneth with thee and the Holy Spirit, one God, for ever and
ever. *Amen.*

II   O God, in your providence you called Joseph
Schereschewsky from his home in Eastern Europe to the
ministry of this Church, and sent him as a missionary to
China, upholding him in his infirmity, that he might
translate the Holy Scriptures into languages of that land.
Lead us, we pray, to commit our lives and talents to you, in
the confidence that when you give your servants any work to
do, you also supply the strength to do it; through Jesus
Christ, our Lord, who lives and reigns with you and the
Holy Spirit, one God, for ever and ever. *Amen.*

Psalm	Lessons
84:1-6	2 Corinthians 4:11-18
or 116:10-17	Luke 24:44-48

Preface of Pentecost

Teresa was one of two women declared a "Doctor of the Church" in 1970, primarily because of her two mystical contemplative works, *The Way of Perfection* and *Interior Castle*. She was a close spiritual and personal friend of St. John of the Cross.

Teresa was born near Avila. Even in her childhood, she took much pleasure in the study of saints' lives, and she used to delight in spending times of contemplation, repeating over and over "For ever, for ever, for ever, for ever, they shall see God."

In her autobiography Teresa tells that, following her mother's death, she became quite worldly. To offset this, her father placed her in an Augustinian convent to be educated, but serious illness ended her studies. During convalescence, she determined to enter the religious life; and, though opposed by her father, she became a postulant at a Carmelite convent. Again, illness forced her to return home. After three years, she returned to the convent.

The easygoing life of the "mitigated" Carmelite rule distracted her from her customary prayer life, to which she returned. Taking recourse in two great penitents, Augustine of Hippo and Mary Magdalene, she became increasingly meditative. She began to receive visions—whether from God or the Devil she could not know—and struggled to reject them.

Teresa set out to establish a reformed Carmelite order of the "discalced" religious, who wore sandals or went unshod. Despite many setbacks she traveled for 25 years through Spain. Energetic, practical, efficient, as well as being a mystic and ascetic, she established 17 convents of Reformed Carmelites. Even imprisonment did not deter her.

Despite the demands of her administrative and missionary work, Teresa found time to write the numerous letters that give us rare insights into her personality and concerns. She shows us a practical organizer, a writer of native genius, a warm devoted friend, and, above all, a lover of and the beloved of God.

Her death, following two years of illness, was peaceful. Her last sight was of the Sacrament brought for her comfort; her last words, "O my Lord! Now is the time that we may see each other."

Teresa of Avila

Nun, 1582

I   O God, who by the Holy Spirit didst move Teresa of Avila to manifest to thy Church the way of perfection: Grant us, we beseech thee, to be nourished by her excellent teaching, and enkindle within us a lively and unquenchable longing for true holiness; through Jesus Christ, the joy of loving hearts, who with thee and the same Holy Spirit liveth and reigneth, one God, for ever and ever. *Amen.*

II   O God, by your Holy Spirit you moved Teresa of Avila to manifest to your Church the way of perfection: Grant us, we pray, to be nourished by her excellent teaching, and enkindle within us a keen and unquenchable longing for true holiness; through Jesus Christ, the joy of loving hearts, who with you and the Holy Spirit lives and reigns, one God, for ever and ever. *Amen.*

Psalm	Lessons
42:1-7	Romans 8:22-27
or 139:1-9	Matthew 5:13-16

Preface of Baptism

Thomas Cranmer was the principal figure in the Reformation of the English Church, and was primarily responsible both for the first Book of Common Prayer of 1549 and for its first revision in 1552.

Cranmer was born at Aslockton, Nottinghamshire, on July 2, 1489. At the age of fourteen he entered Jesus College, Cambridge, where by 1514 he had obtained his B.A. and M.A. degrees and a Fellowship. In 1526 he became a Doctor of Divinity, a lecturer in his college, and examiner in the University. During his years at Cambridge, he diligently studied the Bible and the new doctrines emanating from the Reformation in Germany.

A chance meeting with King Henry the Eighth at Waltham Abbey in 1529 led to Cranmer's involvement in the "King's affair" — the annulment of Henry's marriage to Catherine of Aragon. Cranmer prepared the defense of the King's cause and presented it to the universities in England and Germany, and to Rome.

While in Germany, Cranmer became closely associated with the Lutheran reformers, especially with Osiander, whose daughter he married. When Archbishop Warham died, the King obtained papal confirmation of Cranmer's appointment to the See of Canterbury, and he was consecrated on March 30, 1533. Among his earliest acts was to declare the King's marriage null and void. He then validated the King's marriage to Anne Boleyn. Her child, the future Queen Elizabeth the First, was Cranmer's godchild.

Cranmer's sincere belief in the king's supremacy in all matters, civil and religious, was the mainspring of his actions. This explains his many compromises with his reforming ideals; and it finally led to his undoing.

In the reign of Edward the Sixth, Cranmer had a free hand in reforming the worship, doctrine, and practice of the Church. But at Edward's death he unfortunately subscribed to the dying King's will that the succession should go to Lady Jane Grey. For this, and also for his reforming work, he was arrested, deprived, and degraded by Queen Mary the First, daughter of Henry the Eighth by Catherine, and a staunch Roman Catholic.

Cranmer wrote two recantations of his supposedly heretical doctrines during his imprisonment, but at the end he recanted his recantations, and died heroically, saying "forasmuch as my hand offended in writing contrary to my heart, therefore my hand shall first be punished; for if I may come to the fire, it shall first be burned."

And so it happened at Oxford on March 21, 1556.

Nicholas Ridley was born at Willemoteswick, Northumberland, and was educated at Pembroke College, Cambridge, with which he was connected for many years. While there he belonged to a circle of young men deeply attracted to the currents of reform in the Church, and inspired by events on the Continent.

A close friend of Archbishop Cranmer and supporter of his reforming views and interests, Ridley became the Archbishop's chaplain in 1537, and vicar of Herne, Kent, in 1538. He was chosen Master of Pembroke in 1540, and chaplain to King Henry the Eighth and Canon of Canterbury in 1541. Two years later he was acquitted of a charge of heresy.

Early in the reign of Edward the Sixth, Ridley was made Bishop of Rochester and a member of the commission that prepared the first Book of Common Prayer. In 1550 he was transferred to the See of London, where he showed himself a diligent advocate and thorough administrator of the principles of the Reformation. Together with Cranmer and Hugh Latimer, he took part in 1554 in the Oxford disputations against a group of Roman Catholic theologians, and would not recant his Protestant theology. This, together with his opposition to the accession of Queen Mary in 1553, led to his arrest and imprisonment in the Tower of London. From there he was taken to Oxford for his trial, deposition, and death at the stake together with Bishop Hugh Latimer on October 16, 1555.

Hugh Latimer was the outstanding preacher of the Reformation period in England. His pithy and homely sermons against abuses in the Church led to several trials for heresy; but no proof could be established against his orthodoxy. In fact, he had little interest in the refinements of doctrine. His zeal was concentrated on the moral life of Christian clergy and people.

Born of sturdy yeoman stock about 1490 at Thucaston, Leicestershire, Latimer graduated from Clare College, Cambridge, and became a Fellow in 1510. Though he had a conservative bent, he was attracted to the new currents of reform stemming from the Continental Reformation of the 1520s. King Henry the Eighth made him a royal chaplain in 1530, and five years later appointed him to the See of Worcester. In 1539 he resigned his bishopric in opposition to the King's reactionary policies against the progress of the Reformation.

In the reign of Edward the Sixth, Latimer became prominent again as a preacher, but he refused to resume his see. With the accession of Queen Mary in 1553 he was imprisoned, though he might have fled from the country. On October 16, 1555, he was burned at the stake in Oxford with Bishop Nicholas Ridley. His last words to Ridley are famous: "Be of good comfort, Master Ridley, and play the man; we shall this day light such a candle by God's grace in England as (I trust) shall never be put out."

Hugh Latimer and Nicholas Ridley
Bishops, 1555

Thomas Cranmer
Archbishop of Canterbury, 1556

I Keep us, O Lord, constant in faith and zealous in witness, that, like thy servants, Hugh Latimer, Nicholas Ridley, and Thomas Cranmer, we may live in thy fear, die in thy favor, and rest in thy peace; for the sake of Jesus Christ thy Son our Lord, who liveth and reigneth with thee and the Holy Spirit, one God, now and for ever. *Amen.*

II Keep us, O Lord, constant in faith and zealous in witness, that, like your servants, Hugh Latimer, Nicholas Ridley, and Thomas Cranmer, we may live in your fear, die in your favor, and rest in your peace; for the sake of Jesus Christ your Son our Lord, who lives and reigns with you and the Holy Spirit, one God, now and for ever. *Amen.*

Psalm	Lessons
142	1 Corinthians 3:9-14
or 124	John 15:20-16:1

Preface of a Saint (1)

Ignatius of Antioch, martyred in 115, had a profound sense of two ends — his own, and the consummation of history in Jesus Christ. In ecstasy, he saw his impending martyrdom as the fitting conclusion to a long episcopate. He was accounted the second Bishop of Antioch in Syria.

Seven authentic letters which Ignatius wrote to Churches while he journeyed across Asia Minor in the custody of ten soldiers ("my leopards," he called them), give valuable insights into the life of the early Church. Of certain Gnostic teachings that exalted the divinity of Jesus at the expense of his humanity, Ignatius wrote: "Be deaf. . .to any talk that ignores Jesus Christ, of David's lineage, of Mary; who was really born, ate, and drank; was really persecuted under Pontius Pilate; was really crucified and died in the sight of heaven and earth and the underworld. He was really raised from the dead."

In another, he condemned a form of biblicism espoused by some as the method of historical interpretation and the only rule of Church practice. He wrote: "When I heard some people saying, 'If I don't find it in the ancient documents, I don't believe it in the Gospel,' I answered them, 'But it is written there.' They retorted, 'That has got to be proved.' But to my mind it is Jesus Christ who is the ancient documents."

Ignatius maintained that the Church's unity would always spring from that liturgy by which all are initiated into Christ through Baptism. He exhorted: "Try to gather more frequently to celebrate God's Eucharist and to praise him. . . . At these meetings you should heed the bishop and presbytery attentively and break one loaf, which is the medicine of immortality. . . ."

Ignatius regarded the Church as God's holy order in the world. He was, therefore, concerned for the proper ordering of the Church's teaching and worship. He wrote: "Flee from schism as the source of mischief. You should all follow the bishop as Jesus Christ did the Father. Follow, too, the presbytery as you would the apostles; and respect the deacons as you would God's law. . . . Where the bishop is present, there let the congregation gather, just as where Jesus Christ is, there is the Catholic Church."

Ignatius
Bishop of Antioch, and Martyr, c. 115

I   Almighty God, we praise thy Name for thy bishop and
martyr Ignatius of Antioch, who offered himself as grain to
be ground by the teeth of wild beasts that he might present
unto thee the pure bread of sacrifice. Accept, we pray thee,
the willing tribute of our lives, and give us a share in the
pure and spotless offering of thy Son Jesus Christ; who liveth
and reigneth with thee and the Holy Spirit, one God, for ever
and ever. *Amen.*

II   Almighty God, we praise your Name for your bishop and
martyr Ignatius of Antioch, who offered himself as grain to
be ground by the teeth of wild beasts that he might present
to you the pure bread of sacrifice. Accept, we pray, the
willing tribute of our lives and give us a share in the pure
and spotless offering of your Son Jesus Christ; who lives and
reigns with you and the Holy Spirit, one God, for ever and
ever. *Amen.*

Psalm	Lessons
116:1-8	Romans 8:35-39
or 31:1-5	John 12:23-26

Preface of a Saint (3)

Luke was a Gentile, a physician, and one of Paul's fellow missionaries in the early spread of Christianity through the Roman world. He has been identified as the writer of both the Gospel which bears his name, and its sequel, the Acts of the Apostles. He had apparently not known Jesus, but was clearly much inspired by hearing about him from those who had known him.

Luke wrote in Greek, so that Gentiles might learn about the Lord, whose life and deeds so impressed him. In the first chapter of his Gospel, he makes clear that he is offering authentic knowledge about Jesus' birth, ministry, death, and resurrection. The Gospel is not a full biography — none of the Gospels are — but a history of salvation.

Only Luke provides the very familiar stories of the annunciation to Mary, of her visit to Elizabeth, of the child in the manger, the angelic host appearing to shepherds, and the meeting with the aged Simeon. Luke includes in his work six miracles and eighteen parables not recorded in the other Gospels. In Acts he tells about the coming of the Holy Spirit, the struggles of the apostles and their triumphs over persecution, of their preaching of the Good News, and the conversion and baptism of other disciples, who would extend the Church in future years.

Luke was with Paul apparently until the latter's martyrdom in Rome. What happened to Luke after Paul's death is unknown. Early tradition has it that he wrote his Gospel in Greece, and that he died at the age of eighty-four in Boeotia. Gregory of Nazianzus says that Luke was martyred, but this testimony is doubted by most scholars. In the fourth century, the Emperor Constantius ordered the supposed relics of Luke to be removed from Boeotia to Constantinople, where they could be venerated by pilgrims.

Saint Luke the Evangelist

I   Almighty God, who didst inspire thy servant Luke the
physician to set forth in the Gospel the love and healing
power of thy Son: Graciously continue in thy Church the
like love and power to heal, to the praise and glory of thy
Name; through the same thy Son Jesus Christ our Lord, who
liveth and reigneth with thee, in the unity of the Holy Spirit,
one God, now and for ever. *Amen.*

II   Almighty God, who inspired your servant Luke the
physician to set forth in the Gospel the love and healing
power of your Son: Graciously continue in your Church this
love and power to heal, to the praise and glory of your
Name; through Jesus Christ our Lord, who lives and reigns
with you, in the unity of the Holy Spirit, one God, now and
for ever. *Amen.*

Psalm	Lessons
147	Ecclesiasticus 38:1-4, 6-10,12-14
or 147:1-7	2 Timothy 4:5-13
	Luke 4:14-21

Preface of All Saints

Translator of the Scriptures and Prayer Book into Hindi and Persian, Henry Martyn, an English missionary in India, died in Armenia when he was thirty-one years old. Though his life was brief, it was a remarkable one.

Like most English clergymen of the time, he was educated at one of the two ancient universities, Cambridge in his case. He had intended to become a lawyer, but Charles Simeon, the notable Evangelical rector of Holy Trinity, Cambridge, inspired him to go to India as a missionary. After serving as Simeon's curate for a short time, Martyn traveled to Calcutta in 1806 as chaplain of the East India Company.

During his five years in India, Martyn preached the Gospel, organized private schools, and founded churches. In addition to his work as a missionary, Martyn translated the New Testament and the Book of Common Prayer into Hindi, a valuable missionary aid to the young Anglican Church in India. He also began the study of Persian, and translated the New Testament into Persian.

Martyn longed to go to Persia; in 1811, his persistence brought him to Shirmas, to become the first English clergyman in that city. He engaged in theological discussions with learned Muslims and had time to correct his Persian translations. Obviously gifted with a remarkable facility for languages, Martyn hoped eventually to visit Arabia, and to translate the New Testament into Arabic.

While on his way to Constantinople in 1812, however, he died in the city of Tokat. The Armenians of the city recognized his greatness and buried him with the honors usually accorded to one of their own bishops. Very soon afterwards, his life of energetic devotion and remarkable accomplishment became widely known. He is remembered as one of the founders of the modern Christian Church in India and Iran.

Henry Martyn

Priest, and Missionary to India and Persia, 1812

I O God of the nations, who didst give to thy faithful servant
Henry Martyn a brilliant mind, a loving heart, and a gift for
languages, that he might translate the Scriptures and other
holy writings for the peoples of India and Persia: Inspire in
us, we beseech thee, a love like his, eager to commit both life
and talents to thee who gavest them; through Jesus Christ
our Lord, who liveth and reigneth with thee and the Holy
Spirit, one God, for ever and ever. *Amen.*

II O God of the nations, you gave your faithful servant Henry
Martyn a brilliant mind, a loving heart, and a gift for
languages, that he might translate the Scriptures and other
holy writings for the peoples of India and Persia: Inspire in
us a love like his, eager to commit both life and talents to
you who gave them; through Jesus Christ our Lord, who
lives and reigns with you and the Holy Spirit, one God, for
ever and ever. *Amen.*

Psalm	Lessons
98:1-4	Isaiah 49:1-6
or 96:1-7	John 4:22-26

Preface of a Saint (2)

In the Gospel according to Matthew and in the Epistle to the Galatians, the James whom we commemorate today is called the Lord's brother. Other writers, following Mark's tradition, believe him to have been a cousin of Jesus. Certain apocryphal writings speak of him as a son of Joseph's first wife. Whatever his relationship to Jesus — brother, half-brother, or cousin — James was converted after the resurrection. Eventually, he became Bishop of Jerusalem.

In the first letter to the Corinthians (15:7), Paul says that James was favored with a special appearance of the Lord before the ascension. Later, James dealt cordially with Paul at Jerusalem, when the latter came there to meet Peter and the other apostles. During the Council of Jerusalem, when there was disagreement about whether Gentile converts should be circumcised, James summed up the momentous decision with these words: "My judgment is that we should impose no irksome restrictions on those Gentiles who are turning to God" (Acts 15:19).

Eusebius, quoting from an earlier church history by Hegesippus, declares that James was surnamed "the Just." He was holy, abstemious, did not cut his hair nor oil his body, and was continually on his knees in prayer, interceding for his people. "As many as came to believe did so through James," says Hegesippus.

James' success in converting many to Christ greatly perturbed some factions in Jerusalem. According to Hegesippus, they begged him to "restrain the people, for they have gone astray to Jesus, thinking him to be the Messiah . . . we bear you witness that you are just. . . . Persuade the people that they do not go astray . . . we put our trust in you." They then set James on the pinnacle of the temple, bidding him to preach to the multitude and turn them from Jesus. James, however, testified for the Lord. Thereupon, they hurled him from the roof to the pavement, and cudgeled him to death.

Saint James of Jerusalem

Brother of Our Lord Jesus Christ, and Martyr, c. 62

I   Grant, we beseech thee, O God, that after the example of thy
servant James the Just, brother of our Lord, thy Church may
give itself continually to prayer and to the reconciliation of
all who are at variance and enmity; through the same our
Lord Jesus Christ, who liveth and reigneth with thee and the
Holy Spirit, one God, now and for ever. *Amen.*

II   Grant, O God, that, following the example of your servant
James the Just, brother of our Lord, your Church may give
itself continually to prayer and to the reconciliation of all
who are at variance and enmity; through Jesus Christ our
Lord, who lives and reigns with you and the Holy Spirit, one
God, now and for ever. *Amen.*

Psalm	Lessons
I	Acts 15:12-22a
	1 Corinthians 15:1-11
	Matthew 13:54-58

Preface of All Saints

Alfred, alone of all English rulers, has been called "the Great," because of his courage and Christian virtues. Born in 849 at Wantage, Berkshire, the youngest of five sons of King Aethelwulf, Alfred spent his life in a time of "battle, murder, and sudden death" during the Viking invasions and settlement in Britain. He was deeply impressed when, on a visit to Rome at the age of four, he was blessed by Pope Leo the Fourth, and two years later when he witnessed the marriage of Aethelwulf to a young princess of the Frankish court. Following his father's death and the short reigns of his brothers, Alfred became King in 871.

In heroic battles and by stratagems against the Danes, Alfred halted the tide of their invasion, and secured control of the southern, and part of the midland regions, of England for the English. After a decisive victory in 878 at Edington over the Danish leader Guthrum, he persuaded his foe to accept baptism. Alfred died on October 26, 899, and was buried in the old Minster at Winchester.

In his later years, Alfred sought to repair the damage that the Viking invasions had inflicted on culture and learning, especially among the parish clergy. With the help of scholars from Wales and the Continent, he supervised translations into English of important classics of theology and history, including works of Pope Gregory the Great, Augustine of Hippo, and the Venerable Bede. In one of them he commented: "He seemed to me a very foolish man, and very wretched, who will not increase his understanding while he is in the world, and ever wish and long to reach that endless life where all shall be made clear."

Alfred the Great

King of the West Saxons, 899

I O Sovereign Lord, who didst bring thy servant Alfred to a troubled throne that he might establish peace in a ravaged land and revive learning and the arts among the people: Awake in us also, we beseech thee, a keen desire to increase our understanding while we are in this world, and an eager longing to reach that endless life where all will be made clear; through Jesus Christ our Lord, who liveth and reigneth with thee and the Holy Spirit, one God, for ever and ever. *Amen.*

II O Sovereign Lord, you brought your servant Alfred to a troubled throne that he might establish peace in a ravaged land and revive learning and the arts among the people: Awake in us also a keen desire to increase our understanding while we arc in this world, and an eager longing to reach that endless life where all will be made clear; through Jesus Christ our Lord, who lives and reigns with you and the Holy Spirit, one God, for ever and ever. *Amen.*

Psalm	Lessons
21:1-7	Wisdom 6:1-3,9-12,24-25
or 112:1-9	Luke 6:43-49

Preface of Baptism

The only thing the Gospels tell us about Simon is that he was one of the disciples, and that he was called "the Zealot" (*Zelotes*). John mentions Jude in his description of the Last Supper. The Epistle of Jude may be the work of the disciple Jude, who is the man mentioned by John as the brother of James the Greater.

Tradition has consistently associated Simon and Jude as apostles to Persia. Some accounts state that they were martyrs, a tradition generally accepted by the Western Church. The *Monology* of Basil, however, says that Simon died a peaceful death at Edessa. Jude, who was surnamed Thaddeus, has been confused with another Thaddeus, who was also said to have died a quiet death, either in Beirut or Edessa. Whatever the facts, accounts conflict and reliable data are lacking.

There are other scholarly questions about both men. One involves Simon's appellation "Zelotes." Whether in fact he had been a member before his conversion of one of the several factions called "Zealots," or whether this title refers to his zeal for the Jewish law, is not known, but he has consistently been identified by it. For some centuries, and even today, Jude has been regarded in popular devotion as the "patron of desperate or lost causes," but the basis of this tradition is obscure.

The Epistle of Jude concludes with this striking doxology: "Now to him who is able to keep you from falling, and to present you without blemish before the presence of his glory with rejoicing, to the only God our Savior, be glory, majesty, dominion, and authority, through Jesus Christ our Lord, before all time and now and for ever" (Jude 24-25).

Saint Simon and Saint Jude, Apostles

I   O God, we thank thee for the glorious company of the apostles, and especially on this day for Simon and Jude; and we pray that, as they were faithful and zealous in their mission, so we may with ardent devotion make known the love and mercy of our Lord and Savior Jesus Christ; who liveth and reigneth with thee and the Holy Spirit, one God, for ever and ever. *Amen.*

II O God, we thank you for the glorious company of the apostles, and especially on this day for Simon and Jude; and we pray that, as they were faithful and zealous in their mission, so we may with ardent devotion make known the love and mercy of our Lord and Savior Jesus Christ; who lives and reigns with you and the Holy Spirit, one God, for ever and ever. *Amen.*

Psalm	Lessons
119:89-96	Deuteronomy 32:1-4
	Ephesians 2:13-22
	John 15:17-27

Preface of Apostles

James Hannington was born at Hurstpierpoint, Sussex, September 3, 1847, and was educated at Temple School, Brighton. For six years, he assisted his father in the warehouse business. The family became members of the Church of England in 1867, and the following year Hannington entered St. Mary Hall, Oxford, where he obtained his B.A. and M.A. degrees.

Following his ordination at Exeter, Hannington served as a curate in his native town until, in 1882, he offered himself to the Church Missionary Society for its mission in Victoria, Nyanza, Africa. Serious illness soon required his return to England, but he went out again to Africa in 1884 as Bishop of Eastern Equatorial Africa.

Hannington's mission field was the shores of Lake Victoria. On a difficult venture towards Uganda, he and his party were apprehended by emissaries of King Mwanga, who feared this foreign penetration into his territory. After a week of cruel privations and suffering, he and the remaining members of his company were martyred on October 29, 1885.

Hannington's last words were: "Go, tell Mwanga I have purchased the road to Uganda with my blood." Other martyrs of Uganda shared his fate before the Gospel was firmly planted in this heartland of Africa, where today the Church has a vigorous life under an indigenous ministry.

James Hannington

Bishop of Eastern Equatorial Africa, and his Companions, Martyrs, 1885

I   Precious in thy sight, O Lord, is the death of thy saints, whose faithful witness, by thy providence, has its great reward: We give thee thanks for thy martyrs James Hannington and his companions, who purchased with their blood a road into Uganda for the proclamation of the Gospel; and we pray that with them we also may obtain the crown of righteousness which is laid up for all who love the appearing of our Savior Jesus Christ; who liveth and reigneth with thee and the Holy Spirit, one God, for ever and ever. *Amen.*

II   Precious in your sight, O Lord, is the death of your saints, whose faithful witness, by your providence, has its great reward: We give you thanks for your martyrs James Hannington and his companions, who purchased with their blood a road into Uganda for the proclamation of the Gospel; and we pray that with them we also may obtain the crown of righteousness which is laid up for all who love the appearing of our Savior Jesus Christ; who lives and reigns with you and the Holy Spirit, one God, for ever and ever. *Amen.*

Psalm	Lessons
124	1 Peter 3:14-18,22
or 116:1-8	Matthew 10:16-22

Preface of Holy Week

It is believed by many scholars that the commemoration of all the saints on November first originated in Ireland, spread from there to England, and then to the continent of Europe. That it had reached Rome and had been adopted there early in the ninth century is attested by a letter of Pope Gregory the Fourth, who reigned from 828 to 844, to Emperor Louis "the Pious," urging that such a festival be observed throughout the Holy Roman Empire.

However, the desire of Christian people to express the intercommunion of the living and the dead in the Body of Christ by a commemoration of those who, having professed faith in the living Christ in days past, had entered into the nearer presence of their Lord, and especially of those who had crowned their profession with heroic deaths, was far older than the early Middle Ages. Gregory Thaumaturgus (the "Wonder Worker"), writing before the year 270, refers to the observance of a festival of all martyrs, though he does not date it. A hundred years later, Ephrem the Deacon mentions such an observance in Edessa on May 13; and the patriarch John Chrysostom, who died in 407, says that a festival of All Saints was observed on the first Sunday after Pentecost in Constantinople at the time of his episcopate. The contemporary lectionary of the East Syrians set a commemoration of all the saints on Friday in Easter week. On May 13, in the year 610, the Pantheon in Rome — originally a pagan temple dedicated to "all the gods" — was dedicated as the Church of St. Mary and All Martyrs.

All Saints' Day is classed, in the Prayer Book of 1979, as a Principal Feast, taking precedence of any other day or observance. Among the seven so classified, All Saints' Day alone may be observed on the following Sunday, in addition to its observance on its fixed date. It is one of the four days recommended in the Prayer Book (page 312) for the administration of Holy Baptism.

All Saints

I   O Almighty God, who hast knit together thine elect in one communion and fellowship in the mystical body of thy Son Christ our Lord: Grant us grace so to follow thy blessed saints in all virtuous and godly living, that we may come to those ineffable joys which thou hast prepared for those who unfeignedly love thee; through the same Jesus Christ our Lord, who with thee and the Holy Spirit liveth and reigneth, one God, in glory everlasting. *Amen.*

II   Almighty God, you have knit together your elect in one communion and fellowship in the mystical body of your Son Christ our Lord: Give us grace so to follow your blessed saints in all virtuous and godly living, that we may come to those ineffable joys that you have prepared for those who truly love you; through Jesus Christ our Lord, who with you and the Holy Spirit lives and reigns, one God, in glory everlasting. *Amen.*

Psalm	Lessons
149	Ecclesiasticus 44:1-10, 13-14
	Revelation 7:2-4, 9-17
	Matthew 5:1-12
	or
	Ecclesiasticus 2:(1-6) 7-11
	Ephesians 1:(11-14) 15-23
	Luke 6:20-26 (27-36)

Preface of All Saints

In the New Testament, the word "saints" is used to describe the entire membership of the Christian community, and in the Collect for All Saints' Day the word "elect" is used in a similar sense. From very early times, however, the word "saint" came to be applied primarily to persons of heroic sanctity, whose deeds were recalled with gratitude by later generations.

Beginning in the tenth century, it became customary to set aside another day — as a sort of extension of All Saints — on which the Church remembered that vast body of the faithful who, though no less members of the company of the redeemed, are unknown in the wider fellowship of the Church. It was also a day for particular remembrance of family members and friends.

Though the observance of the day was abolished at the Reformation because of abuses connected with Masses for the dead, a renewed understanding of its meaning has led to a widespread acceptance of this commemoration among Anglicans, and to its inclusion as an optional observance in the calendar of the Episcopal Church.

All Faithful Departed

I   O God, the Maker and Redeemer of all believers: Grant to
the faithful departed the unsearchable benefits of the passion
of thy Son; that on the day of his appearing they may be
manifested as thy children; through Jesus Christ our Lord,
who liveth and reigneth with thee and the Holy Spirit, one
God, now and for ever. *Amen.*

II   O God, the Maker and Redeemer of all believers: Grant to
the faithful departed the unsearchable benefits of the passion
of your Son; that on the day of his appearing they may be
manifested as your children; through Jesus Christ our Lord,
who lives and reigns with you and the Holy Spirit, one God,
now and for ever. *Amen.*

Psalm	Lessons
130	Wisdom 3:1-9
or 116:10-17	*or* Isaiah 25:6-9
	1 Thessalonians 4:13-18
	or 1 Corinthians 15:50-58
	John 5:24-27

Preface of the Commemoration of the Dead

In any list of Anglican theologians, Richard Hooker's name would stand high, if not first. He was born in 1553 at Heavitree, near Exeter, and was admitted in 1567 to Corpus Christi College, Oxford, of which he became a Fellow ten years later. After ordination and marriage in 1581, he held a living in Buckinghamshire. In 1586 he became Master of the Temple, in London. Later, he served country parishes in Boscombe, Salisbury, and Bishopsbourne near Canterbury.

A controversy with a noted Puritan led Hooker to prepare a comprehensive defense of the Reformation settlement under Queen Elizabeth the First. This work, his masterpiece, was entitled *Laws of Ecclesiastical Polity*. Its philosophical base is Aristotelian, with a strong emphasis upon natural law eternally planted by God in creation. On this foundation, all positive laws of Church and State are grounded — from Scriptural revelation, ancient tradition, reason, and experience.

Book Five of the *Laws* is a massive defense of the Book of Common Prayer, directed primarily against Puritan detractors. Hooker's arguments are buttressed by enormous patristic learning, but the needs of the contemporary worshiper are paramount, and he draws effectively on his twenty-year experience of using the Book. Hooker's vast learning, and the quality of his style, reveal him to be a man of moderate, patient, and serene character.

Concerning the nature of the Church, Hooker wrote: "The Church is always a visible society of men; not an assembly, but a Society. For although the name of the Church be given unto Christian assemblies, although any multitude of Christian men congregated may be termed by the name of a Church, yet assemblies properly are rather things that belong to a Church. Men are assembled for performance of public actions; which actions being ended, the assembly dissolveth itself and is no longer in being, whereas the Church which was assembled doth no less continue afterwards than before."

Pope Clement the Eighth is reported to have said that Hooker's work "had in it such seeds of eternity that it would abide until the last fire shall consume all learning."

Richard Hooker

Priest, 1600

I   O God of truth and peace, who didst raise up thy servant
Richard Hooker in a day of bitter controversy to defend
with sound reasoning and great charity the catholic and
reformed religion: Grant that we may maintain that middle
way, not as a compromise for the sake of peace, but as a
comprehension for the sake of truth; through Jesus Christ
our Lord, who liveth and reigneth with thee and the Holy
Spirit, one God, for ever and ever. *Amen.*

II   O God of truth and peace, you raised up your servant
Richard Hooker in a day of bitter controversy to defend
with sound reasoning and great charity the catholic and
reformed religion: Grant that we may maintain that middle
way, not as a compromise for the sake of peace, but as a
comprehension for the sake of truth; through Jesus Christ
our Lord, who lives and reigns with you and the Holy Spirit,
one God, for ever and ever. *Amen.*

Psalm	Lessons
37:3-6, 32-33	1 Corinthians 2:6-10,13-16
or 19:7-11 (12-14)	John 17:18-23

Preface of Baptism

William Temple was born October 15, 1881, and baptized three weeks later, on November 6, in Exeter Cathedral. His father, Dr. Frederick Temple, Bishop of Exeter and then of London, became Archbishop of Canterbury when William was fifteen. Growing up at the heart of the Church of England, William's love for it was deep and lifelong.

Endowed with a brilliant mind, Temple took a first-class honors degree in classics and philosophy at Oxford, where he was then elected Fellow of Queen's College. At the age of twenty-nine he became headmaster of Repton School, and then in quick succession rector of St. James's Church, Piccadilly, Bishop of Manchester, and Archbishop of York.

Though he never experienced poverty of any kind, he developed a passion for social justice which shaped his words and his actions. He owed this passion to a profound belief in the Incarnation. He wrote that in Jesus Christ God took flesh and dwelt among us, and as a consequence "the personality of every man and woman is sacred."

In 1917 Temple resigned from St. James's, Piccadilly, to devote his energies to the "Life and Liberty" movement for reform within the Church of England. Two years later an Act of Parliament led to the setting up of the Church Assembly, which for the first time gave the laity a voice in Church matters.

As bishop and later as archbishop, Temple committed himself to seeking "the things which pertain to the Kingdom of God." He understood the Incarnation as giving worth and meaning not only to individuals but to all of life. He therefore took the lead in establishing the Conference on Christian Politics, Economics and Citizenship (COPEC), held 1924. In 1940 he convened the great Malvern Conference to reflect on the social reconstruction that would be needed in Britain once the Second World War was over.

At the same time he was a prolific writer on theological, ecumenical, and social topics, and his two-volume *Readings in St. John's Gospel,* written in the early days of the war, rapidly became a spiritual classic.

In 1942 Temple was appointed Archbishop of Canterbury and reached an even wider audience through his wartime radio addresses and newspaper articles. However, the scope of his responsibilities and the pace he set himself took their toll. On October 26, 1944, he died after only two and a half years at Canterbury.

[William Temple]

Archbishop of Canterbury, 1944

I   O God of light and love, who illumined thy Church through the witness of thy servant William Temple: Inspire us, we pray, by his teaching and example, that we may rejoice with courage, confidence, and faith in the Word made flesh, and may be led to establish that city which has justice for its foundation and love for its law; through Jesus Christ, the light of the world, who liveth and reigneth with thee and the Holy Spirit, one God, now and for ever. *Amen.*

II   O God of light and love, you illumined your Church through the witness of your servant William Temple: Inspire us, we pray, by his teaching and example, that we may rejoice with courage, confidence, and faith in the Word made flesh, and may be led to establish that city which has justice for its foundation and love for its law; through Jesus Christ, the light of the world, who lives and reigns with you and the Holy Spirit, one God, now and for ever. *Amen.*

Psalm	Lessons
119: 97-104	Ephesians 3:7-12
	John 1:9-18

Preface of the Epiphany

We know about Willibrord's life and missionary labors through a notice in the Venerable Bede's *Ecclesiastical History* and a biography by his younger kinsman, Alcuin. He was born in Northumbria about 658, and from the age of seven was brought up and educated at Bishop Wilfrid's monastery at Ripon. For twelve years, 678-690, he studied in Ireland, where he acquired his thirst for missionary work.

In 690, with twelve companions, he set out for Frisia (Holland), a pagan area that was increasingly coming under the domination of the Christian Franks. There Bishop Wilfrid and a few other Englishmen had made short missionary visits, but with little success. With the aid of the Frankish rulers, Willibrord established his base at Utrecht, and in 695 Pope Sergius ordained him a bishop and gave him the name of Clement.

In 698 he founded the monastery of Echternach, near Trier. His work was frequently disturbed by the conflict of the pagan Frisians with the Franks, and for a time he left the area to work among the Danes. For three years, 719-722, he was assisted by Boniface, who at a later time came back to Frisia to strengthen the mission. In a very real sense, Willibrord prepared the way for Boniface's more successful achievements by his relations with the Frankish rulers and the papacy. who thus became joint sponsors of missionary work. He died at Echternach, November 7, 739.

Willibrord
Archbishop of Utrecht, Missionary to Frisia, 739

I O Lord our God, who dost call whom thou willest and send them where thou choosest: We thank thee for sending thy servant Willibrord to be an apostle to the Low Countries, to turn them from the worship of idols to serve thee, the living God; and we entreat thee to preserve us from the temptation to exchange the perfect freedom of thy service for servitude to false gods and to idols of our own devising; through Jesus Christ our Lord, who liveth and reigneth with thee and the Holy Spirit, one God, for ever and ever. *Amen.*

II O Lord our God, you call whom you will and send them where you choose: We thank you for sending your servant Willibrord to be an apostle to the Low Countries, to turn them from the worship of idols to serve you, the living God; and we entreat you to preserve us from the temptation to exchange the perfect freedom of your service for servitude to false gods and to idols of our own devising; through Jesus Christ our Lord, who lives and reigns with you and the Holy Spirit, one God, for ever and ever. *Amen.*

Psalm	Lessons
96: 1-7	Acts 1:1-9
or 98:1-4	Luke 10:1-9

Preface of Apostles

When Leo was born, about the year 400, the Western Roman Empire was almost in shambles. Weakened by barbarian invasions and by a totally inefficient economic and political system, the structure that had been carefully built by Augustus had become a chaos of internal warfare, subversion, and corruption.

The social and political situation notwithstanding, Leo received a good education, and was ordained deacon, with the responsibility of looking after Church possessions, managing the grain dole, and generally administering finances. He won considerable respect for his abilities, and a contemporary of his, Cassian, described him as "the ornament of the Roman Church and the divine ministry."

In 440, Leo was unanimously elected Pope, despite the fact that he was absent at the time on a mission in Gaul. His ability as a preacher shows clearly in the 96 sermons still extant, in which he expounds doctrine, encourages almsgiving, and deals with various heresies, including the Pelagian and the Manichean systems.

In Gaul, Africa, and Spain, Leo's strong hand was felt as he issued orders to limit the powers of one over-presumptuous bishop, confirmed the rights of another bishop over his vicars, and selected candidates for holy orders. Leo's letter to the Council of Chalcedon in 451 dealt so effectively with the doctrine of the human and divine natures of the One Person of Christ that the assembled bishops declared, "Peter has spoken by Leo," and affirmed his definition as orthodox teaching. (See page 864 of the Prayer Book.)

With similar strength of spirit and wisdom, Leo negotiated with Attila when the Huns were about to sack Rome. He persuaded them to withdraw from Italy and to accept an annual tribute. Three years later, Genseric led the Vandals against Rome. Again Leo negotiated. Unable to prevent pillaging by the barbarians, he did dissuade them from burning the city and slaughtering its inhabitants. He worked, thereafter, to repair the damage, to replace the holy vessels in the desecrated churches, and to restore the morale of the Roman people.

Leo the Great

Bishop of Rome, 461

I   O Lord our God, grant that thy Church, following the teaching of thy servant Leo of Rome, may hold fast the great mystery of our redemption, and adore the one Christ, true God and true Man, neither divided from our human nature nor separate from thy divine Being; through the same Jesus Christ our Lord, who liveth and reigneth with thee and the Holy Spirit, one God, now and for ever. *Amen.*

II   O Lord our God, grant that your Church, following the teaching of your servant Leo of Rome, may hold fast the great mystery of our redemption, and adore the one Christ, true God and true Man, neither divided from our human nature nor separate from your divine Being; through Jesus Christ our Lord, who lives and reigns with you and the Holy Spirit, one God, now and for ever. *Amen.*

Psalm	Lessons
77:11-15	2 Timothy 1:6-14
or 23	Matthew 5:13-19

Preface of the Epiphany

Martin, one of the patron saints of France, was born about 330 at Sabaria, the modern Szombathely in Hungary. His early years were spent in Pavia in Italy. After a term of service in the Roman army, he traveled about Europe, and finally settled in Poitiers, whose bishop, Hilary, he had come to admire.

According to an old legend, while Martin was still a catechumen, he was approached by a poor man, who asked for alms in the name of Christ. Martin, drawing his sword, cut off part of his military cloak and gave it to the beggar. On the following night, Jesus appeared to Martin, clothed in half a cloak, and said to him, "Martin, a simple catechumen, covered me with this garment."

Hilary ordained Martin to the presbyterate sometime between 350 and 353, and Martin, inspired by the new monastic movement stemming from Egypt, established a hermitage at nearby Ligugé. To his dismay, he was elected Bishop of Tours in 372. He agreed to serve only if he were allowed to continue his strict, ascetic habit of life. His monastery of Marmoutier, near Tours, had a great influence on the development of Celtic monasticism in Britain, where Ninian, among others, promoted Martin's ascetic and missionary ideals. The oldest church in Canterbury, which antedates the Anglo-Saxon invasions, is dedicated to St. Martin.

Martin was unpopular with many of his episcopal colleagues, both because of his manner of life and because of his strong opposition to their violent repression of heresy. He was a diligent missionary to the pagan folk of the countryside near his hermitage, and was always a staunch defender of the poor and the helpless.

Martin died on November 11, 397. His shrine at Tours became a popular site for pilgrimages, and a secure sanctuary for those seeking protection and justice.

Martin

Bishop of Tours, 397

I   Lord God of hosts, who didst clothe thy servant Martin the
soldier with the spirit of sacrifice, and didst set him as a
bishop in thy Church to be a defender of the catholic faith:
Give us grace to follow in his holy steps, that at the last we
may be found clothed with righteousness in the dwellings of
peace; through Jesus Christ our Lord, who liveth and
reigneth with thee and the Holy Spirit, one God, for ever and
ever. *Amen.*

II   Lord God of hosts, you clothed your servant Martin the
soldier with the spirit of sacrifice, and set him as a bishop in
your Church to be a defender of the catholic faith: Give us
grace to follow in his holy steps, that at the last we may be
found clothed with righteousness in the dwellings of peace;
through Jesus Christ our Lord, who lives and reigns with
you and the Holy Spirit, one God, for ever and ever. *Amen.*

Psalm	Lessons
15	Isaiah 58:6-12
or 34:15 22	Matthew 25:34-40

Preface of a Saint (2)

The historian Thomas Macaulay said about Charles Simeon, "If you knew what his authority and influence were, and how they extended from Cambridge to the most remote corners of England, you would allow that his real sway in the Church was far greater than that of any primate."

Simeon's conversion, in 1779, while still a student, occurred as he was preparing himself to receive Holy Communion, an act required of undergraduates at the University. His first Communion had been a deeply depressing and discouraging experience, because of his use of the popular devotional tract, *The Whole Duty of Man*, which emphasized law and obedience as the means of receiving the Sacrament worthily. When he was again preparing for Communion before Easter, he was given a copy of Bishop Thomas Wilson's *Instructions for the Lord's Supper*. Here was a quite different approach, which recognized that the law could not make one righteous, and that only the sacrifice of Christ, perceived by faith, could enable one to communicate worthily. This time, the experience of Holy Communion was one of peace and exhilaration, a new beginning of a Christian life whose influence is difficult to exaggerate.

Simeon's influence and authority developed slowly, but he soon became the recognized leader of the evangelical movement in the Church of England. He helped to found the Church Missionary Society, and was active in recruiting and supporting missionaries, including Henry Martyn. As a preacher, he ranks high in the history of Anglicanism. His sermons were unfailingly biblical, simple, and passionate.

The influence of Simeon and his friends was thus described by the historian Lecky: "They gradually changed the whole spirit of the English Church. They infused into it a new fire and passion of devotion, kindled a spirit of fervent philanthropy, raised the standard of clerical duty, and completely altered the whole tone and tendency of the preaching of its ministers."

Charles Simeon

Priest, 1836

I O loving God, we know that all things are ordered by thine
unerring wisdom and unbounded love: Grant us in all things
to see thy hand; that, following the example and teaching of
thy servant Charles Simeon, we may walk with Christ in all
simplicity, and serve thee with a quiet and contented mind;
through Jesus Christ our Lord, who liveth and reigneth with
thee and the Holy Spirit, one God, for ever and ever. *Amen.*

II O loving God, we know that all things are ordered by your
unerring wisdom and unbounded love: Grant us in all things
to see your hand; that, following the example and teaching
of your servant Charles Simeon, we may walk with Christ in
all simplicity, and serve you with a quiet and contented
mind; through Jesus Christ our Lord, who lives and reigns
with you and the Holy Spirit, one God, for ever and ever.
Amen.

Psalm	Lessons
145:8-13	Romans 10:8b-17
or 96:1-7	John 21:15-17

Preface of a Saint (1)

Samuel Seabury, the first Bishop of the Episcopal Church, was born in Groton, Connecticut, November 30, 1729. After ordination in England in 1753, he was assigned, as a missionary of the Society for the Propagation of the Gospel, to Christ Church, New Brunswick, New Jersey. In 1757, he became rector of Grace Church, Jamaica, Long Island, and in 1766 rector of St. Peter's, Westchester County. During the American Revolution, he remained loyal to the British crown, and served as a chaplain in the British army.

After the Revolution, a secret meeting of Connecticut clergymen in Woodbury, on March 25, 1783, named Seabury or the Rev. Jeremiah Leaming, whichever would be able or willing, to seek episcopal consecration in England. Leaming declined; Seabury accepted, and sailed for England.

After a year of negotiation, Seabury found it impossible to obtain episcopal orders from the Church of England because, as an American citizen, he could not swear allegiance to the crown. He then turned to the Non-juring bishops of the Episcopal Church in Scotland. On November 14, 1784, in Aberdeen, he was consecrated by the Bishop and the Bishop Coadjutor of Aberdeen and the Bishop of Ross and Caithness, in the presence of a number of the clergy and laity.

On his return home, Seabury was recognized as Bishop of Connecticut in Convocation on August 3, 1785, at Middletown. With Bishop William White, he was active in the organization of the Episcopal Church at the General Convention of 1789. With the support of William Smith of Maryland, William Smith of Rhode Island, William White of Pennsylvania, and Samuel Parker of Boston, Seabury kept his promise, made in a concordat with the Scottish bishops, to persuade the American Church to adopt the Scottish form for the celebration of the Holy Eucharist.

In 1790 Seabury became responsible for episcopal oversight of the churches in Rhode Island; and at the General Convention of 1792 he participated in the first consecration of a bishop on American soil, that of John Claggett of Maryland. Seabury died on February 25, 1796, and is buried beneath St. James' Church, New London.

Consecration of Samuel Seabury
First American Bishop, 1784

I We give thee thanks, O Lord our God, for thy goodness in bestowing upon this Church the gift of the episcopate, which we celebrate in this remembrance of the consecration of Samuel Seabury; and we pray that, joined together in unity with our bishops, and nourished by thy holy Sacraments, we may proclaim the Gospel of redemption with apostolic zeal; through Jesus Christ our Lord, who liveth and reigneth with thee and the Holy Spirit, one God, now and for ever. *Amen.*

II We give you thanks, O Lord our God, for your goodness in bestowing upon this Church the gift of the episcopate, which we celebrate in this remembrance of the consecration of Samuel Seabury; and we pray that, joined together in unity with our bishops, and nourished by your holy Sacraments, we may proclaim the Gospel of redemption with apostolic zeal; through Jesus Christ our Lord, who lives and reigns with you and the Holy Spirit, one God, now and for ever. *Amen.*

Psalm

133
or 33:1-5,20-21

Lessons

Acts 20:28-32
Matthew 9:35-38

Preface of Apostles

Shakespeare made familiar the names of Macbeth and Macduff, Duncan and Malcolm; but it is not always remembered that Malcolm married an English princess, Margaret, about 1070.

With considerable zeal, Margaret sought to change what she considered to be old-fashioned and careless practices among the Scottish clergy. She insisted that the observance of Lent, for example, was to begin on Ash Wednesday, rather than on the following Monday, and that the Mass should be celebrated according to the accepted Roman rite of the Church, and not in barbarous form and language. The Lord's Day was to be a day when, she said, "we apply ourselves only to prayers." She argued vigorously, though not always with success, against the exaggerated sense of unworthiness that made many of the pious Scots unwilling to receive Communion regularly.

Margaret's energies were not limited to reformation of formal Church practices. She encouraged the founding of schools, hospitals, and orphanages, and used her influence with King Malcolm to help her improve the quality of life among the isolated Scottish clans. Together, Margaret and her husband rebuilt the monastery of Iona and founded Dunfermline Abbey, under the direction of Benedictine monks.

In addition to her zeal for Church and people, Margaret was a conscientious wife and the mother of eight children. Malcolm, a strong-willed man, came to trust her judgment even in matters of State. She saw also to the spiritual welfare of her large household, providing servants with opportunity for regular worship and prayer.

Margaret was not as successful as she wished to be in creating greater unity in faith and works between her own native England and the Scots. She was unable, for example, to bring an end to the bloody warfare among the highland clans, and after her death in 1093, there was a brief return to the earlier isolation of Scotland from England. Nevertheless, her work among the people, and her reforms in the Church, made her Scotland's most beloved saint. She died on November 16, and was buried at Dunfermline Abbey.

Margaret

Queen of Scotland, 1093

I   O God, who didst call thy servant Margaret to an earthly throne that she might advance thy heavenly kingdom, and didst give her zeal for thy Church and love for thy people: Mercifully grant that we who commemorate her this day may be fruitful in good works, and attain to the glorious crown of thy saints; through Jesus Christ our Lord, who liveth and reigneth with thee and the Holy Spirit, one God, for ever and ever. *Amen.*

II   O God, you called your servant Margaret to an earthly throne that she might advance your heavenly kingdom, and gave her zeal for your Church and love for-your people: Mercifully grant that we who commemorate her this day may be fruitful in good works, and attain to the glorious crown of your saints; through Jesus Christ our Lord, who lives and reigns with you and the Holy Spirit, one God, for ever and ever. *Amen.*

Psalm	Lessons
146:4-9	Proverbs 31:10 11,20,26,28
or 112:1-9	Matthew 13:44-52

Preface of Baptism

Hugh was born into a noble family at Avalon in Burgundy (France). He became a canon regular at Villard-Benoit near Grenoble. About 1160 he joined the Carthusians, the strictest contemplative order of the Church, at their major house, the Grande Chartreuse, of which he became the procurator. With great reluctance, he accepted the invitation of King Henry the Second to come to England as prior of a new Carthusian foundation at Witham, Somerset. With equal reluctance, Hugh accepted King Henry's appointment to the See of Lincoln in 1186. He died in London, November 16, 1200, and is buried in Lincoln Cathedral, of which he laid the foundation.

As a bishop, Hugh continued to live as much as possible under the strict discipline of his order. His humility and tact, his total lack of self-regard, and his cheerful disposition made it difficult to oppose him in matters of Christian principle. His people loved him for his constant championship of the poor, the oppressed, and outcasts, especially lepers and Jews. He was completely independent of secular influences, and was never afraid to reprove his king for unjust exactions from his people. He firmly refused to raise money for King Richard's foreign wars. Yet Richard said of him, "If all bishops were like my Lord of Lincoln, not a prince among us could lift his head against them."

Hugh

Bishop of Lincoln, 1200

I   O holy God, who didst endow thy servant and bishop Hugh of Lincoln with wise and cheerful boldness, and taught him to commend the discipline of holy life to kings and princes: Grant that we also, rejoicing in the Good News of thy mercy, and fearing nothing but the loss of thee, may be bold to speak the truth in love, in the name of Jesus Christ our Redeemer; who liveth and reigneth with thee and the Holy Spirit, one God, for ever and ever. *Amen.*

II   O holy God, you endowed your servant and bishop Hugh of Lincoln with wise and cheerful boldness, and taught him to commend the discipline of holy life to kings and princes: Grant that we also, rejoicing in the Good News of your mercy, and fearing nothing but the loss of you, may be bold to speak the truth in love, in the name of Jesus Christ our Redeemer; who lives and reigns with you and the Holy Spirit, one God, for ever and ever. *Amen.*

Psalm	Lessons
112:1-9	Titus 2:7-8,11-14
or 15	Matthew 24:42-47

Preface of a Saint (2)

"Hilda's career falls into two equal parts," says the Venerable Bede, "for she spent thirty-three years nobly in secular habit, while she dedicated an equal number of years still more nobly to the Lord, in the monastic life."

Hilda, born in 614, was the grandniece of King Edwin. She was instructed by Paulinus (one of the companions of Augustine of Canterbury) in the doctrines of Christianity in preparation for her baptism at the age of thirteen. She lived, chaste and respected, at the King's court for twenty years, and then decided to enter the monastic life. She had hoped to join the convent of Chelles in Gaul, but Bishop Aidan was so impressed by her holiness of life that he recalled her to her home country, in East Anglia, to live in a small monastic settlement.

One year after her return, Aidan appointed her Abbess of Hartlepool. There, Hilda established the rule of life that she had been taught by Paulinus and Aidan. She became renowned for her wisdom, eagerness for learning, and devotion to God's service.

Some years later, she founded the abbey at Whitby, where both nuns and monks lived in strict obedience to Hilda's rule of justice, devotion, chastity, peace, and charity. Known for her prudence and good sense, Hilda was sought out by kings and other public men for advice and counsel. Those living under her rule devoted so much time to the study of Scripture and to works of righteousness that many were found qualified for ordination. Several of her monks became bishops; at least one pursued further studies in Rome. She encouraged the poet Caedmon, a servant at Whitby, to become a monk and to continue his inspired writing. All who were her subjects or knew her, Bede remarks, called her "mother."

In 663, Whitby was the site of the famous synod convened to decide divisive questions involved in the differing traditions of Celtic Christians and the followers of Roman order. Hilda favored the Celtic position, but when the Roman position prevailed she was obedient to the synod's decision. Hilda died on November 17, 680, surrounded by her monastics, whom, in her last hour, she urged to preserve the gospel of peace.

Hilda

Abbess of Whitby, 680

I   O God of peace, by whose grace the abbess Hilda was endowed with gifts of justice, prudence, and strength to rule as a wise mother over the nuns and monks of her household, and to become a trusted and reconciling friend to leaders of the Church: Give us the grace to recognize and accept the varied gifts thou dost bestow on men and women, that our common life may be enriched and thy gracious will be done; through Jesus Christ our Lord, who liveth and reigneth with thee and the Holy Spirit, one God, now and for ever. *Amen.*

II   O God of peace, by whose grace the abbess Hilda was endowed with gifts of justice, prudence, and strength to rule as a wise mother over the nuns and monks of her household, and to become a trusted and reconciling friend to leaders of the Church: Give us the grace to recognize and accept the varied gifts you bestow on men and women, that our common life may be enriched and your gracious will be done; through Jesus Christ our Lord, who lives and reigns with you and the Holy Spirit, one God, now and for ever. *Amen.*

Psalm	Lessons
122	Ephesians 4:1-6
or 33:1-5,20-21	Matthew 19:27-29

Preface of a Saint (1)

Elizabeth's charity is remembered in numerous hospitals that bear her name throughout the world. She was born in 1207 at Pressburg (now Bratislava), daughter of King Andrew the Second of Hungary, and was married in 1221 to Louis the Fourth, Landgrave of Thuringia, to whom she bore three children. At an early age she showed concern for the poor and the sick, and was thus attracted to the Franciscans who came to the Wartburg in 1223. From them she received spiritual direction. Her husband was sympathetic to her almsgiving and allowed her to use her dowry for this purpose. During a famine and epidemic in 1226, when her husband was in Italy, she sold her jewels and established a hospital where she cared for the sick and the poor. To supply their needs, she opened the royal granaries. After her husband's death in 1227, the opposition of the court to her "extravagances" compelled her to leave the Wartburg with her children.

For some time Elizabeth lived in great distress. She then courageously took the habit of the Franciscans — the first of the Franciscan Tertiaries, or Third Order, in Germany. Finally, arrangements with her family gave her a subsistence, and she spent her remaining years in Marburg, living in self-denial, caring for the sick and needy. She died from exhaustion, November 16, 1231, and was canonized by Pope Gregory the Ninth four years later. With Louis of France she shares the title of patron of the Third Order of St. Francis.

Elizabeth

Princess of Hungary, 1231

I Almighty God, by whose grace thy servant Elizabeth of
Hungary recognized and honored Jesus in the poor of this
world: Grant that we, following her example, may with love
and gladness serve those in any need or trouble, in the name
and for the sake of Jesus Christ; who liveth and reigneth
with thee and the Holy Spirit, one God, for ever and ever.
Amen.

II Almighty God, by your grace your servant Elizabeth of
Hungary recognized and honored Jesus in the poor of this
world: Grant that we, following her example, may with love
and gladness serve those in any need or trouble, in the name
and for the sake of Jesus Christ; who lives and reigns with
you and the Holy Spirit, one God, for ever and ever. *Amen.*

Psalm	Lessons
146:4-9	Tobit 12:6b-9
or 112:1-9	Matthew 25:31-40*
	or Luke 12:32-34

Preface of a Saint (2)

* This passage is also appointed for the following Sunday in Year A.

Edmund ascended the throne of East Anglia at the age of fifteen, one of several monarchs who ruled various parts of England at that period in her history. The principal source of information about the martyrdom of the young king is an account by Dunstan, who became Archbishop of Canterbury ninety years after Edmund's death. Dunstan had heard the story many years before from a man who claimed to have been Edmund's armor bearer.

Edmund had reigned as a Christian king for nearly fifteen years when Danish armies invaded England in 870. Led by two brothers, Hinguar and Hubba, the Danes moved south, burning monasteries and churches, plundering and destroying entire villages, and killing hundreds. Upon reaching East Anglia, the brothers confronted Edmund and offered to share their treasure with him if he would acknowledge their supremacy, forbid all practice of the Christian faith, and become a figurehead ruler. Edmund's bishops advised him to accept the terms and avoid further bloodshed, but the king refused. He declared that he would not forsake Christ by surrendering to pagan rule, nor would he betray his people by consorting with the enemy.

Edmund's small army fought bravely against the Danes, but the king was eventually captured. According to Dunstan's account, Edmund was tortured, beaten, shot through with arrows, and finally beheaded. By tradition, the date of his death is November 20, 870.

The cult of the twenty-nine-year-old martyr grew very rapidly, and his remains were eventually enshrined in a Benedictine monastery in Bedericesworth — now called Bury St. Edmunds. Through the centuries Edmund's shrine became a traditional place of pilgrimage for England's kings, who came to pray at the grave of a man who remained steadfast in the Christian faith and loyal to the integrity of the English people.

Edmund

King of East Anglia, Martyr, 870

I   O God of ineffable mercy, thou didst give grace and fortitude to blessed Edmund the king to triumph over the enemy of his people by nobly dying for thy Name: Bestow on us thy servants, we beseech thee, the shield of faith, wherewith we may withstand the assaults of our ancient enemy; through Jesus Christ our Redeemer, who liveth and reigneth with thee and the Holy Spirit, one God, now and for ever. *Amen.*

II   O God of ineffable mercy, you gave grace and fortitude to blessed Edmund the king to triumph over the enemy of his people by nobly dying for your Name: Bestow on us your servants the shield of faith with which we can withstand the assaults of our ancient enemy; through Jesus Christ our Redeemer, who lives and reigns with you and the Holy Spirit, one God, now and for ever. *Amen.*

Psalm	Lessons
21:1-7	1 Peter 3:14-18
or 126	Matthew 10:16-22

Preface of Baptism

"You must make your choice," C. S. Lewis wrote in Mere Christianity. "Either this man was, and is, the Son of God, or else a madman or something worse. You can shut Him up as a fool, you can spit at Him and kill Him as a demon, or you can fall at His feet and call Him Lord and God."

Lewis did not always believe this. Born in Belfast on November 29, 1898, Lewis was raised as an Anglican but rejected Christianity during his adolescent years. After serving in World War I, he started a long academic career as a scholar in medieval and renaissance literature at both Oxford and Cambridge. He also began an inner journey that led him from atheism to agnosticism to theism and finally to faith in Jesus Christ.

"Really, a young Atheist cannot guard his faith too carefully," he later wrote of his conversion to theism in Surprised by Joy. "Dangers lie in wait for him on every side. . . . Amiable agnostics will talk cheerfully about 'man's search for God'. To me, as I then was, they might as well have talked about the mouse's search for the cat. You must picture me all alone in that room at Magdalen, night after night, feeling, whenever my mind lifted even for a second from my work, the steady, unrelenting approach of Him whom I so earnestly desired not to meet. That which I greatly feared had at last come upon me. In the Trinity Term of 1929 I gave in, and admitted that God was God, and knelt and prayed: perhaps, that night, the most dejected and reluctant convert in all England." Two years later, his conversion was completed: "I know very well when, but hardly how, the final step was taken. I was driven to Whipsnade one sunny morning. When we set out, I did not believe that Jesus Christ is the Son of God, and when we reached the zoo, I did."

Lewis's conversion inaugurated a wonderful outpouring of Christian apologetics in media as varied as popular theology, children's literature, fantasy and science fiction, and correspondence on spiritual matters with friends and strangers alike.

In 1956 Lewis married Joy Davidman, a recent convert to Christianity. Her death four years later led him to a transforming encounter with the Mystery of which he had written so eloquently before. Lewis died at his home in Oxford on November 22, 1963. The inscription on his grave reads: "Men must endure their going hence."

[Clive Staples Lewis]
Apologist and Spiritual Writer, 1963

I   O God of searing truth and surpassing beauty, we give thee thanks
for Clive Staples Lewis, whose sanctified imagination lighteth fires
of faith in young and old alike. Surprise us also with thy joy and
draw us into that new and abundant life which is ours in Christ
Jesus, who liveth and reigneth with thee and the Holy Spirit, one
God, now and for ever. *Amen.*

II   O God of searing truth and surpassing beauty, we give you thanks
for Clive Staples Lewis, whose sanctified imagination lights fires
of faith in young and old alike. Surprise us also with your joy and
draw us into that new and abundant life which is ours in Christ
Jesus, who lives and reigns with you and the Holy Spirit, one
God, now and for ever. *Amen.*

Psalm	Lessons
139:1-9	1 Peter 1:3-9
	John 16:7-15

Preface of a Saint (3)

According to early traditions, Clement was a disciple of the Apostles and the third Bishop of Rome. He is generally regarded as the author of a letter written about the year 96 from the Church in Rome to the Church in Corinth, and known as "First Clement" in the collection of early documents called "The Apostolic Fathers."

The occasion of the letter was the action of a younger group at Corinth who had deposed the elder clergy because of dissatisfaction with their ministrations. The unity of the Church was being jeopardized by a dispute over its ministry. Clement's letter sets forth a hierarchical view of Church authority. It insists that God requires due order in all things, that the deposed clergy must be reinstated, and that the legitimate superiors must be obeyed.

The letter used the terms "bishop" and "presbyter" interchangeably to describe the higher ranks of clergy, but refers to some of them as "rulers" of the Church. It is they who lead its worship and "offer the gifts" of the Eucharist, just as the duly appointed priests of the Old Testament performed the various sacrifices and liturgies in their time.

Many congregations of the early Church read this letter in their worship, and several ancient manuscripts include it in the canonical books of the New Testament, along with a second letter, which is actually an early homily of unknown authorship. The text of First Clement was lost to the western Church in the Middle Ages, and was not rediscovered until 1628.

Clement writes: "The apostles received the Gospel for us from the Lord Jesus Christ; Jesus the Christ was sent from God. Thus Christ is from God and the apostles from Christ. In both instances, the orderly procedure depends on God's will. So thereafter, when the apostles had been given their instructions, and all their doubts had been set at rest by the resurrection of our Lord Jesus Christ, they went forth in the confidence of the Holy Spirit to preach the good news of the coming of God's kingdom. They preached in country and city, and appointed their first converts, after testing them by the Spirit, to be the bishops and deacons of future believers."

Clement

Bishop of Rome, c. 100

I Almighty God, who didst choose thy servant Clement of
Rome to recall the Church in Corinth to obedience and
stability: Grant that thy Church may be grounded and s
ettled in thy truth by the indwelling of the Holy Spirit;
reveal to it what is not yet known; fill up what is lacking;
confirm what hath already been revealed; and keep it
blameless in thy service; through Jesus Christ our Lord, who
liveth and reigneth with thee and the same Spirit, one God,
for ever and ever. *Amen.*

II Almighty God, you chose your servant Clement of Rome to
recall the Church in Corinth to obedience and stability:
Grant that your Church may be grounded and settled in
your truth by the indwelling of the Holy Spirit; reveal to it
what is not yet known; fill up what is lacking; confirm what
has already been revealed; and keep it blameless in your
service; through Jesus Christ our Lord, who lives and reigns
with you and the Holy Spirit, one God, for ever and ever.
Amen.

Psalm	Lessons
78:3-7	2 Timothy 2:1-7
or 85:8-13	Luke 6:37-45

Preface of a Saint (2)

Agricultural festivals are of great antiquity, and common to many religions. Among the Jews, the three pilgrimage feasts, Passover, Pentecost, and Tabernacles, each had agricultural significance. Medieval Christianity also developed a number of such observances, none of which, however, were incorporated into the Prayer Book.

Our own Thanksgiving Day finds its roots in observances begun by colonists in Massachusetts and Virginia, a tradition later taken up and extended to the whole of the new American nation by action of the Continental Congress.

Thanksgiving Day

I   Almighty and gracious Father, we give thee thanks for the
fruits of the earth in their season and for the labors of those
who harvest them. Make us, we beseech thee, faithful
stewards of thy great bounty, for the provision of our
necessities and the relief of all who are in need, to the glory
of thy Name; through Jesus Christ our Lord, who liveth and
reigneth with thee and the Holy Spirit, one God, now and
for ever. *Amen.*

II   Almighty and gracious Father, we give you thanks for the
fruits of the earth in their season and for the labors of those
who harvest them. Make us, we pray, faithful stewards of
your great bounty, for the provision of our necessities and
the relief of all who are in need, to the glory of your Name;
through Jesus Christ our Lord, who lives and reigns with
you and the Holy Spirit, one God, now and for ever. *Amen.*

Psalm	Lessons
65	Deuteronomy 8:1-3,6-10(17-20)
or 65:9-14	James 1:17-18,21-27
	Matthew 6:25-33

Preface of Trinity Sunday

In the Rule for the Order of the Holy Cross, James Huntington wrote: "Holiness is the brightness of divine love, and love is never idle; it must accomplish great things." Commitment to active ministry rooted in the spiritual life was the guiding principle for the founder of the first permanent Episcopal monastic community for men in the United States.

James Otis Sargent Huntington was born in Boston in 1854. After graduation from Harvard, he studied theology at St. Andrew's Divinity School in Syracuse, New York, and was ordained deacon and priest by his father, the first Bishop of Central New York. In 1880 and 1881 he ministered in a working-class congregation at Calvary Mission, Syracuse.

While attending a retreat at St. Clement's Church, Philadelphia, Huntington received a call to the religious life. He considered joining the Society of St. John the Evangelist, which had by that time established a province in the United States, but he resolved to found an indigenous American community.

Huntington and two other priests began their common life at Holy Cross Mission on New York's Lower East Side, ministering with the Sisters of St. John Baptist among poor immigrants. The taxing daily regimen of Eucharist, prayer, and long hours of pastoral work soon forced one priest to leave for reason of health. The other dropped out for lack of a vocation. Huntington went on alone; and on November 25, 1884, his life vow was received by Bishop Potter of New York.

As Huntington continued his work among the immigrants, with emphasis on helping young people, he became increasingly committed to the social witness of the Church. His early involvements in the single-tax movement and the labor union movement were instrumental in the eventual commitment of the Episcopal Church to social ministries.

The Order attracted vocations, and as it grew in the ensuing years the community moved, first to Maryland, and, in 1902, to West Park, New York, where it established the monastery which is its mother house. Huntington served as Superior on several occasions, continuing his energetic round of preaching, teaching and spiritual counsel until his death on June 28, 1935.

James Otis Sargent Huntington

Priest and Monk, 1935

I   O loving God, by thy grace thy servant James Huntington gathered a community dedicated to love and discipline and devotion to the holy Cross of our Savior Jesus Christ: Send thy blessing upon all who proclaim Christ crucified, and move the hearts of many to look unto him and be saved; who with thee and the Holy Spirit liveth and reigneth, one God, for ever and ever. *Amen.*

II   O loving God, by your grace your servant James Huntington gathered a community dedicated to love and discipline and devotion to the holy Cross of our Savior Jesus Christ: Send your blessing on all who proclaim Christ crucified, and move the hearts of many to look upon him and be saved; who with you and the Holy spirit lives and reigns, one God, for ever and ever. *Amen.*

Psalm	Lessons
119:161-168	Galatians 6:14-18
or 34:1-8	John 6:34-38

Preface of a Saint (2)

Within a year of ascending the throne in 1855, the twenty-year-old King Kamehameha IV and his bride, Emma Rooke, embarked on the path of altruism and unassuming humility for which they have been revered by their people. The year before, Honolulu, and especially its native Hawaiians, had been horribly afflicted by smallpox. The people, accustomed to a royalty which ruled with pomp and power, were confronted instead by a king and queen who went about, "with notebook in hand," soliciting from rich and poor the funds to build a hospital. Queen's Hospital, named for Emma, is now the largest civilian hospital in Hawaii.

In 1860, the king and queen petitioned the Bishop of Oxford to send missionaries to establish the Anglican Church in Hawaii. The king's interest came through a boyhood tour of England where he had seen, in the stately beauty of Anglican liturgy, a quality that seemed attuned to the gentle beauty of the Hawaiian spirit. England responded by sending the Rt. Rev. Thomas N. Staley and two priests. They arrived on October 11, 1862, and the king and queen were confirmed a month later, on November 28, 1862. They then began preparations for a cathedral and school, and the king set about to translate the Book of Common Prayer and much of the Hymnal.

Kamehameha's life was marred by the tragic death of his four-year-old son and only child, in 1863. He seemed unable to survive his sadness, although a sermon he preached after his son's death expresses a hope and faith that is eloquent and profound. His own death took place only a year after his son's, in 1864. Emma declined to rule; instead, she committed her life to good works. She was responsible for schools, churches, and efforts on behalf of the poor and sick. She traveled several times to England and the Continent to raise funds, and became a favorite of Queen Victoria's. Archbishop Longley of Canterbury, remarked upon her visit to Lambeth: "I was much struck by the cultivation of her mind. . . But what excited my interest most was her almost saintly piety."

The Cathedral was completed after Emma died. It was named St. Andrew's in memory of the king, who died on that Saint's day. Among the Hawaiian people, Emma is still referred to as "our beloved Queen."

Kamehameha and Emma

King and Queen of Hawaii, 1864, 1885

I O Sovereign God, who raisedst up (King) Kamehameha (IV) and (Queen) Emma to be rulers in Hawaii, and didst inspire and enable them to be diligent in good works for the welfare of their people and the good of thy Church: Receive our thanks for their witness to the Gospel; and grant that we, with them, may attain to the crown of glory that fadeth not away; through Jesus Christ our Savior and Redeemer, who with thee and the Holy Spirit liveth and reigneth, one God, for ever and ever. *Amen.*

II O Sovereign God, who raised up (King) Kamehameha (IV) and (Queen) Emma to be rulers in Hawaii, and inspired and enabled them to be diligent in good works for the welfare of their people and the good of your Church: Receive our thanks for their witness to the Gospel; and grant that we, with them, may attain to the crown of glory that never fades away; through Jesus Christ our Savior and Redeemer, who with you and the Holy Spirit lives and reigns, one God, for ever and ever. *Amen.*

Psalm	Lessons
33:12-22	Acts 17:22-31
or 97:1-2,7-12	Matthew 25:31-40

Preface of Baptism

The Common
of Saints

Concerning the Common of Saints

The festival of a saint is observed in accordance with the rules of precedence set forth in the Calendar of the Church Year, pages 3-6.

At the discretion of the Celebration, and as appropriate, one of the following Commons may be used

a) at the commemoration of a saint listed in the Calendar, in place of the Proper for Lesser Feasts appointed in this book

b) at the patronal festival or commemoration of a saint not listed in the Calendar.

Any of the sets of Lessons assigned to a given Common may be used with any of the Collects.

Common of a Martyr I

I   O Almighty God, who didst give to thy servant N. boldness to confess the Name of our Savior Jesus Christ before the rulers of this world, and courage to die for this faith: Grant that we may always be ready to give a reason for the hope that is in us, and to suffer gladly for the sake of the same our Lord Jesus Christ; who liveth and reigneth with thee and the Holy Spirit, one God, for ever and ever. *Amen.*

II   Almighty God, who gave to your servant N. boldness to confess the Name of our Savior Jesus Christ before the rulers of this world, and courage to die for this faith: Grant that we may always be ready to give a reason for the hope that is in us, and to suffer gladly for the sake of our Lord Jesus Christ; who lives and reigns with you and the Holy Spirit, one God, for ever and ever. *Amen.*

Psalm	Lessons
126	2 Esdras 2:42-48
or 121	1 Peter 3:14-18,22
	Matthew 10:16-22

Preface of a Saint

Common of a Martyr II

I   O Almighty God, by whose grace and power thy holy martyr
N. triumphed over suffering and was faithful even unto
death: Grant us, who now remember *him* with thanksgiving,
to be so faithful in our witness to thee in this world, that we
may receive with *him* the crown of life; through Jesus Christ
our Lord, who liveth and reigneth with thee and the Holy
Spirit, one God, for ever and ever. *Amen.*

II   Almighty God, by whose grace and power your holy martyr
N. triumphed over suffering and was faithful even to death:
Grant us, who now remember *him* in thanksgiving, to be so
faithful in our witness to you in this world, that we may
receive with *him* the crown of life; through Jesus Christ our
Lord, who lives and reigns with you and the Holy Spirit, one
God, for ever and ever. *Amen.*

Psalm	Lessons
116	Ecclesiasticus 51:1-12
or 116:1-8	Revelation 7:13-17
	Luke 12:2-12

Preface of a Saint

Common of a Martyr III

I Almighty and everlasting God, who didst enkindle the flame of thy love in the heart of thy holy martyr *N*.: Grant to us, thy humble servants, a like faith and power of love, that we who rejoice in *her* triumph may profit by *her* example; through Jesus Christ our Lord, who liveth and reigneth with thee and the Holy Spirit, one God, for ever and ever. *Amen.*

II Almighty and everlasting God, who kindled the flame of your love in the heart of your holy martyr *N*.: Grant to us, your humble servants, a like faith and power of love, that we who rejoice in *her* triumph may profit by *her* example; through Jesus Christ our Lord, who lives and reigns with you and the Holy Spirit, one God, for ever and ever. *Amen.*

Psalm	Lessons
124	Jeremiah 15:15-21
or 31:1-5	1 Peter 4:12-19
	Mark 8:34-38

Preface of a Saint

Common of a Missionary I

I   Almighty and everlasting God, we thank thee for thy servant N., whom thou didst call to preach the Gospel to the people of _____ (*or* to the _____ people). Raise up, we beseech thee, in this and every land evangelists and heralds of thy kingdom, that thy Church may proclaim the unsearchable riches of our Savior Jesus Christ; who liveth and reigneth with thee and the Holy Spirit, one God, now and for ever. *Amen.*

II   Almighty and everlasting God, we thank you for your servant N., whom you called to preach the Gospel to the people of _____ (*or* to the _____ people). Raise up in this and every land evangelists and heralds of your kingdom, that your Church may proclaim the unsearchable riches of our Savior Jesus Christ; who lives and reigns with you and the Holy Spirit, one God, now and for ever. *Amen.*

Psalm	Lessons
96	Isaiah 52:7-10
or 96:1-7	Acts 1:1-9
	Luke 10:1-9

Preface of Pentecost

Common of a Missionary II

I   Almighty God, who willest to be glorified in thy saints, and didst raise up thy servant N. to be a light in the world: Shine, we pray thee, in our hearts, that we also in our generation may show forth thy praise, who hast called us out of darkness into thy marvelous light; through Jesus Christ our Lord, who liveth and reigneth with thee and the Holy Spirit, one God, now and for ever. *Amen.*

II Almighty God, whose will it is to be glorified in your saints, and who raised up your servant N. to be a light in the world: Shine, we pray, in our hearts, that we also in our generation may show forth your praise, who called us out of darkness into your marvelous light; through Jesus Christ our Lord, who lives and reigns with you and the Holy Spirit, one God, now and for ever. *Amen.*

Psalm	Lessons
98	Isaiah 49:1-6
or 98:1-4	Acts 17:22-31
	Matthew 28:16-20

Preface of Pentecost

Common of a Pastor I

I O heavenly Father, Shepherd of thy people, we give thee thanks for thy servant N., who was faithful in the care and nurture of thy flock; and we pray that, following his example and the teaching of his holy life, we may by thy grace grow into the stature of the fullness of our Lord and Savior Jesus Christ; who liveth and reigneth with thee and the Holy Spirit, one God, for ever and ever. *Amen.*

II Heavenly Father, Shepherd of your people, we thank you for your servant N., who was faithful in the care and nurture of your flock; and we pray that, following his example and the teaching of his holy life, we may by your grace grow into the stature of the fullness of our Lord and Savior Jesus Christ; who lives and reigns with you and the Holy Spirit, one God, for ever and ever. *Amen.*

Psalm	Lessons
23	Ezekiel 34:11-16
	1 Peter 5:1-4
	John 21:15-17

Preface of a Saint

Common of a Pastor II

I   O God, our heavenly Father, who didst raise up thy faithful servant N. to be a [bishop and] pastor in thy Church and to feed thy flock: Give abundantly to all pastors the gifts of thy Holy Spirit, that they may minister in thy household as true servants of Christ and stewards of thy divine mysteries; through the same Jesus Christ our Lord, who liveth and reigneth with thee and the same Spirit, one God, for ever and ever. *Amen.*

II   O God, our heavenly Father, who raised up your faithful servant N., to be a [bishop and] pastor in your Church and to feed your flock: Give abundantly to all pastors the gifts of your Holy Spirit, that they may minister in your household as true servants of Christ and stewards of your divine mysteries; through Jesus Christ our Lord, who lives and reigns with you and the Holy Spirit, one God, for ever and ever. *Amen.*

Psalm	Lessons
84	Acts 20:17-35
or 84:7-11	Ephesians 3:14-21
	Matthew 24:42-47

Preface of a Saint

Common of a Theologian and Teacher I

I   O God, who by thy Holy Spirit dost give to some the word
of wisdom, to others the word of knowledge, and to others
the word of faith: We praise thy Name for the gifts of grace
manifested in thy servant N., and we pray that thy Church
may never be destitute of such gifts; through Jesus Christ
our Lord, who with thee and the same Spirit liveth and
reigneth, one God, for ever and ever. *Amen.*

II   O God, by your Holy Spirit you give to some the word of
wisdom, to others the word of knowledge, and to others the
word of faith: We praise your Name for the gifts of grace
manifested in your servant N., and we pray that your
Church may never be destitute of such gifts; through Jesus
Christ our Lord, who with you and the Holy Spirit lives and
reigns, one God, for ever and ever. *Amen.*

Psalm	Lessons
119:97-104	Wisdom 7:7-14
	1 Corinthians 2:6-10, 13-16
	John 17:18-23

Preface of a Saint, or of Trinity Sunday

Common of a Theologian and Teacher II

I   O Almighty God, who didst give to thy servant N. special gifts of grace to understand and teach the truth as it is in Christ Jesus: Grant, we beseech thee, that by this teaching we may know thee, the one true God, and Jesus Christ whom thou hast sent; who liveth and reigneth with thee and the Holy Spirit, one God, for ever and ever. *Amen.*

II   Almighty God, you gave to your servant N. special gifts of grace to understand and teach the truth as it is in Christ Jesus: Grant that by this teaching we may know you, the one true God, and Jesus Christ whom you have sent; who lives and reigns with you and the Holy Spirit, one God, for ever and ever. *Amen.*

Psalm	Lessons
119:89-96	Proverbs 3:1-7
	1 Corinthians 3:5-11
	Matthew 13:47-52

Preface of a Saint, or of Trinity Sunday

Common of a Monastic I

I   O God, whose blessed Son became poor that we through his poverty might be rich: Deliver us, we pray thee, from an inordinate love of this world, that, inspired by the devotion of thy servant N., we may serve thee with singleness of heart, and attain to the riches of the age to come; through the same thy Son Jesus Christ our Lord, who liveth and reigneth with thee, in the unity of the Holy Spirit, one God, now and for ever. *Amen.*

II   O God, whose blessed Son became poor that we through his poverty might be rich: Deliver us from an inordinate love of this world, that we, inspired by the devotion of your servant N., may serve you with singleness of heart, and attain to the riches of the age to come; through Jesus Christ our Lord, who lives and reigns with you, in the unity of the Holy Spirit, one God, now and for ever. *Amen.*

Psalm	Lessons
34	Song of Songs 8:6-7
or 34:1-8	Philippians 3:7-15
	Luke 12:33-37
	or Luke 9:57-62

Preface of a Saint

Common of a Monastic II

I   O God, by whose grace thy servant N., enkindled with the fire of thy love, became a burning and a shining light in thy Church: Grant that we also may be aflame with the spirit of love and discipline, and may ever walk before thee as children of light; through Jesus Christ our Lord, who with thee, in the unity of the Holy Spirit, liveth and reigneth, one God, now and for ever. *Amen.*

II   O God, by whose grace your servant N., kindled with the flame of your love, became a burning and a shining light in your Church: Grant that we also may be aflame with the spirit of love and discipline, and walk before you as children of light; through Jesus Christ our Lord, who lives and reigns with you, in the unity of the Holy Spirit, one God, now and for ever. *Amen.*

Psalm	Lessons
133	Acts 2:42-47a
or 119:161-168	2 Corinthians 6:1-10
	Matthew 6:24-33

Preface of a Saint

Common of a Saint I

I   O Almighty God, who hast compassed us about with so great a cloud of witnesses: Grant that we, encouraged by the good example of thy servant *N.*, may persevere in running the race that is set before us, until at length, through thy mercy, we may with *him* attain to thine eternal joy; through Jesus Christ, the author and perfecter of our faith, who liveth and reigneth with thee and the Holy Spirit, one God, for ever and ever. *Amen.*

II   Almighty God, you have surrounded us with a great cloud of witnesses: Grant that we, encouraged by the good example of your servant *N.*, may persevere in running the race that is set before us, until at last we may with *him* attain to your eternal joy; through Jesus Christ, the pioneer and perfecter of our faith, who lives and reigns with you and the Holy Spirit, one God, for ever and ever. *Amen.*

Psalm	Lessons
15	Micah 6:6-8
	Hebrews 12:1-2
	Matthew 25:31-40

Preface of a Saint

Common of a Saint II

I   O God, who hast brought us near to an innumerable
company of angels and to the spirits of just men made
perfect: Grant us during our earthly pilgrimage to abide in
their fellowship, and in our heavenly country to become
partakers of their joy; through Jesus Christ our Lord, who
liveth and reigneth with thee and the Holy Spirit, one God,
now and for ever. *Amen.*

II   O God, you have brought us near to an innumerable
company of angels, and to the spirits of just men made
perfect: Grant us during our earthly pilgrimage to abide in
their fellowship, and in our heavenly country to become
partakers of their joy; through Jesus Christ our Lord, who
lives and reigns with you and the Holy Spirit, one God, now
and for ever. *Amen.*

Psalm	Lessons
34	Wisdom 3:1-9
or 34:15-22	Philippians 4:4-9
	Luke 6:17-23

Preface of a Saint

Common of a Saint III

I   O Almighty God, who by thy Holy Spirit hast made us one
with thy saints in heaven and on earth: Grant that in our
earthly pilgrimage we may ever be supported by this
fellowship of love and prayer, and may know ourselves to be
surrounded by their witness to thy power and mercy. We ask
this for the sake of Jesus Christ, in whom all our
intercessions are acceptable through the Spirit, and who
liveth and reigneth for ever and ever. *Amen.*

II   Almighty God, by your Holy Spirit you have made us one
with your saints in heaven and on earth: Grant that in our
earthly pilgrimage we may always be supported by this
fellowship of love and prayer, and know ourselves to be
surrounded by their witness to your power and mercy. We
ask this for the sake of Jesus Christ, in whom all our
intercessions are acceptable through the Spirit, and who lives
and reigns for ever and ever. *Amen.*

Psalm	Lessons
1	Ecclesiasticus 2:7-11
	1 Corinthians 1:26-31
	Matthew 25:1-13

Preface of a Saint

Guidelines and Procedures for Continuing Alteration of the Calendar in the Episcopal Church—adopted by the 1994 General Convention of the Episcopal Church

I. Introduction

A. The Church is "the communion of Saints," that is, a people made holy through their mutual participation in the mystery of Christ. This communion exists through history, exists now, and endures beyond "the grave and gate of death" into heaven. For "God is not a God of the dead but of the living," and those still on their earthly pilgrimage continue to have fellowship "with those whose work is done." The pilgrim Church and the Church at rest join in watching and praying for that great day when Christ shall come again to change and make perfect our common humanity in the image of Christ's risen glory.

B. The pilgrim Church rejoices to recognize and commemorate those faithful departed who were extraordinary or even heroic servants of God and of God's people for the sake, and after the example, of their Savior Jesus Christ. By this recognition and commemoration, their service endures in the Spirit, as their examples and fellowship continue to nurture the pilgrim Church on its way to God.

II. Guidelines

A. The Church commemorates persons, not abstract qualities. Nevertheless, it does look for certain traits in those whom it chooses specially to commemorate. Among these traits are:

1. *Heroic faith*. This means bearing witness to God in Christ "against the odds." Historically, the greatest exemplars of such faith have been martyrs, who have suffered death for the cause of Christ, and confessors, who have endured imprisonment, torture, or exile for the sake of Christ. Following this precedent, the Episcopal Church in the United States of America has been very specific and has restricted the designation of martyrdom to persons who have chosen to die rather than give up the Christian faith, and has not applied it to persons whose death may have resulted from their heroic faith but who did not consciously choose martyrdom. There are other situations where

choosing and persisting in a Christian manner of life involves confessing Christ "against the odds," even to the point of risking one's life. For this reason the Anglican Communion traditionally has honored monks and nuns like Antony, Benedict, Hilda, Constance and her companions, missionaries like George Augustus Selwyn, and people as diverse as Monnica, Richard of Chichester, and Nicholas Ferrar. More recently the Church has learned to honor social reformers like William Wilberforce and Jonathan Daniels for the same reasons. Heroic faith is, therefore, a quality manifested in many different situations.

2. *Love.* "If I have all faith, so as to remove mountains, but have not love, I am nothing. If I give away all that I have, and if I deliver my body to be burned, but have not love, I gain nothing. . . . So faith, hope, love abide, these three; but the greatest of these is love" (1 Cor. 13:2b-3, 13).

3. *Goodness of life.* People worthy of commemoration will have worked for the good of others. It is important to recognize that the Church looks not only for goodness but also for growth in goodness. A scandalous life prior to conversion does not disqualify one from consideration for the Calendar; rather, the witness of perseverance to the end will confirm holiness of life and the transforming power of Christ.

4. *Joyousness.* As faith is incomplete without love, so does love involve "rejoicing in the Spirit"—whether in the midst of extraordinary trials, or in the midst of the ordinary rounds of daily life. A Christian may not fail in the works of love, but still lack the joy of it—thereby falling short of true Christian sanctity. Such joy, however, is as much a discipline of life as an emotion. It need not lie on the surface of a person's life, but may run deeply and be discerned by others only gradually.

5. *Service to others for Christ's sake.* "There are varieties of gifts. . .and there are varieties of service" (1 Cor. 12:4-5). There is not true holiness without service to others in their needfulness. The Church recognizes that just as human needs are diverse, so also are forms of Christian service—both within the Church and in the world.

6. *Devotion.* People who are worthy of commemoration have shown evidence of seeking God through the means of grace which the Church

recognizes, having "devoted themselves to the apostles' teaching and fellowship, to the breaking of the bread and the prayers" (Acts 2:42). We look both for regularity and for growth in the discipline of prayer and meditation upon God's Word; and we look for this devotion to be manifested not only in a person's private life but also in visible company and communion with his or her fellow Christians.

7. *Recognition by the faithful.* Initiating the commemoration of particular saints is the privilege of those who knew, loved, and discerned the special grace of Christ in a member of their community, and who desire to continue in the communion of prayer with that member now departed. Such instinctive recognition by the faithful begins naturally at the local and regional levels. Evidence of both (a) such commemoration growing locally and (b) such recognition of sanctity spreading beyond the immediate community is essential before the national Church has an obligation to take heed. It may, in fact, decide that the commemoration in question is best left to local observance.

8. *Historical perspective.* In a resolution on the Calendar, the 1958 Lambeth Conference of Bishops stated, "The addition of a new name should normally result from a widespread desire expressed in the region concerned over a reasonable period of time." Generally this has been two generations, or fifty years after death.

B. The qualities or traits just outlined do not exhaust the character of Christian sanctity, nor should they be applied as if each or all of them were legal conditions which a proposed Commemoration must meet before recommendation for observance is granted. These are guidelines to help both the faithful and the official organs of the Church test their own thoughts when proposing, or recommending, a Commemoration. These Guidelines and Procedures are intended to implement Resolution A097a of the 1988 General Convention (Journal, p. 639).

III. Local Calendars and Memorials

Local and regional commemoration normally occurs for many years prior to national recognition.

The Book of Common Prayer (pp. 13, 18, 195, and 246) permits memorials not listed in the Calendar, provides collects and readings for them (the Common of Saints), and recognizes the bishop's authority to set forth devotions for occasions for which no prayer or service has been provided by the Prayer Book. Although the Prayer Book does not require the bishop's permission to use the Common of Saints for memorials not included in the Calendar, it would seem appropriate that the bishop's consent be requested.

While these Guidelines cannot provide procedures for initiating local, diocesan, or regional memorials that would govern all such commemorations, this process is suggested:

A. A parish or diocese establishes a memorial for a specific day, using the above Guidelines to justify the memorial.

B. A collect is appointed from the Common of Saints or composed, perhaps in consultation with the Standing Liturgical Commission, diocesan or parish liturgical commission. Readings and a proper preface may also be appointed if desired. A brief description of the person or group is written, in accord with these Guidelines and Procedures.

C. The parish, diocese, province, or organization proceeds to keep the memorial.

D. Those interested in promoting a wider commemoration begin to share these materials with others, suggesting that they also adopt the memorial. If at some time it is desired to propose a local commemoration for national recognition, documented evidence of the spread and duration of local commemoration is essential to include in the proposal to the Standing Liturgical Commission.

Some commemorations, perhaps many, will remain local, diocesan, or regional in character. This in no way reduces their importance to those who revere and seek to keep alive the memory of beloved and faithful witnesses to Christ.

IV. Procedures For National Recognition

Procedures to amend the Calendar flow naturally from II and III above, as well as earlier documents like Prayer Book Studies IX and XVI (1957 and 1963, respectively). As stated in Resolution A119s of the 1991 General Convention, "all requests for consideration of individuals or groups, to be included in the Calendar of the Church year, shall be submitted to the Standing Liturgical Commission for evaluation and subsequent recommendation to the next General Convention for acceptance or rejection."

A. A proposal to commemorate a person (or group of persons) may be submitted to the Calendar Committee of the Standing Liturgical Commission of the General Convention by three or more Church bodies of recognized organizations within the Episcopal Church—e.g., Diocesan Conventions, Provincial Synods, parishes, seminary faculties, religious communities, ethnic, or women's groups.

Each proposal must include:

a) a detailed rationale for commemoration based on the Guidelines (above) and demonstrating how this person manifests Christ and would enhance the devotional life of the Church;

b) an inspirational 350-word biographical sketch of the person to be commemorated, preferably including some of the person's own words;

c) information concerning the spread and duration of local or international commemoration of this individual or group;

d) suggested collects and readings.

Proposals must be received by the Standing Liturgical Commission Chair no less than 18 months prior to the next General Convention.

B. The chair of the Calendar Committee will communicate with

1. organizations submitting proposed commemorations;

2. the Secretary of the General Convention regarding names and addresses of any groups applying for exhibit space in order to present to Convention delegates a potential addition to the Calendar;

3. the chairs of the Cognate Committees on Prayer Book and Liturgy, in order to facilitate the review of submissions.

C. The Calendar Committee of the Standing Liturgical Commission will arrange for

1. submission of appropriate resolutions to General Convention;

2. publication of same in the *Blue Book*;

3. distribution of pertinent materials to members of the Cognate Committees on Prayer Book and Liturgy, as may be needed;

4. preparation of materials for *Lesser Feasts and Fasts*.

V. Procedures to Remove Commemorations from the Calendar

A Commemoration may be removed from the Calendar by the same procedure by which one is added, namely, the procedure set forth in Article X of the Constitution of the General Convention concerning Alterations and Additions, which requires concurrence by two consecutive Conventions.

Proposed deletions of commemorations must be forwarded to the Chair of the Standing Liturgical Commission no less than 18 months prior to the next General Convention.

A Six-Week Eucharistic Lectionary with Daily Themes and Suggested Collects

(Adapted from Weekday Readings, *a daily lectionary authorized by the 1994 General Convention)*

Concerning the Lectionary

This Lectionary offers thirty-six sets of thematic readings intended for use on the weekdays following the First Sunday after the Epiphany and the Day of Pentecost. These readings may be used in sequence or as a corpus of texts and themes available in whatever order the celebrant and worshiping community wish to use them.

Each Proper includes two brief lessons and a psalm; the psalm reflects the theme of the two lessons. The brevity of the readings invites a brief reflective homily, silence, or the reading of non-biblical meditative material.

The suggested collects, with the page numbers for their traditional and contemporary forms, are from the Book of Common Prayer.

Week One

Monday—The commandment of love
Collect: Proper 9 (179/230) or 7 Epiphany (164/216)
Rom. 13:8–10   Ps. 85:7–13   Luke 6:32–36

Tuesday—The family of God
Collect: 14. For the Unity of the Church (204/255)
Eph. 4:29–32   Ps. 42:1–7   Matt. 12:46–50

Wednesday—The power of prayer
Collect: 6 Epiphany (164/216)
James 5:13–18   Ps. 111:1–10   Luke 11:9–13

Thursday—The commandments of the covenant
Collect: Proper 9 (179/230)
Deut. 6:4–7   Ps. 119:1–6   Matt. 22:34–40

Friday—The promise of the cross
Collect: 6. Of the Holy Cross (201/252)
Rom. 8:35, 37–39   Ps. 23   Mark 8:31–33

Saturday—Sabbath celebration; Creation and Word
Collect: A Collect for Saturdays (56/99) or
    First Sunday after Christmas (161/213)
Gen. 1:31—2:3   Ps. 104:25–32   John 1:1–5, 12–14, 16–18

Week Two

Monday—Christian humility

Collect: Proper 18 (181/233)
1 Pet. 5:5b–7   Ps. 147:5–12   Mark 9:33–37

Tuesday—God's wisdom, an unfolding mystery
Collect: 2. Of the Holy Spirit (200/251)
1 Cor. 2:6–10a   Ps. 49:1–11   Matt. 13:31–33

Wednesday—Dress code for the disciple
Collect: 1 Advent (159/211)
Eph. 6:10–18   Ps. 1   Mark 6:6b–13

Thursday—*The power of our baptism*
Collect: 10. At Baptism (203/254)
1 Pet. 1:3–5; 2:9–10   Ps. 96:1–9   John 9:1, 5–11

Friday—*The role of the servant/disciple*
Collect: A Collect for Fridays (56/ 99)
Isa. 53:11–12   Ps. 66:7–11   Luke 9:18–26

Saturday—*God known in creative power*
Collect: Proper 3 (177/229)
Job 38:1, 4–14, 16–18 Ps. 33:6–11   Mark 4:35–41

Week Three

Monday—*Leaving judgment to God*
Collect: 8 Epiphany (165/216)
James 4:11–12   Ps. 24:1–6   John 12:44–50

Tuesday—*Discipleship seen in justice toward the poor*
Collect: 21. For Social Justice (209/260) or
    22. For Social Service (209/260)
Lev. 19:1–2, 9–14   Ps. 22:22–26   Luke 14:12–14

Wednesday—*Standards for the Church*
Collect: Proper 15 (180/232)
Rom. 12:14–21   Ps. 146   John 15:11–17

Thursday—*Living for the kingdom of God*
Collect: 6 Easter (174/225)
Gal.6:14–16   Ps. 67   Matt. 13:44–46

Friday—*The cost of discipleship*
Collect: A Collect for Fridays (56/ 99)
Jer. 20:7–9   Ps. 13:1–6   Matt. 10:34–39

Saturday—*The significance of the sabbath*
Collect: A Collect for Saturdays (56/ 99)
Exod. 20:8–11   Ps. 145:10–18   Mark 2:23–28

Week Four

Monday—*Enduring trials for the sake of the gospel*
Collect: 6. Of the Holy Cross (202/252)
2 Cor. 11:21b–33   Ps. 55:1–7   Luke 6:20–26

Tuesday—*A foretaste of the kingdom of God*
Collect: Proper 20 (182/234)
Rev. 21:1–4   Ps. 47   Matt. 11:2–6

Wednesday—*The Church sanctified in God's truth*
Collect: Proper 24 (183/235)
Eph. 3:14–19   Ps. 122   John 17:1–8, 17–18

Thursday—*Responding to God's revelation in Christ*
Collect: Proper 17 (181/233)
Rom. 12:1–8   Ps. 34:1–6   John 14:8–14

Friday—*The power of witness*
Collect: Of a Saint 3 (199/250)
Heb. 12:1–4, 12–14   Ps. 27:1–7   Matt. 27:50–51, 54

Saturday—*The sabbath; living as God's new creations*
Collect: A Collect for Saturdays (56/99)
2 Cor. 5:14–21   Ps. 148   Luke 12:22–31

Week Five

Monday—*Gifts of the gospel*
Collect: 4 Lent (167/219)
Eph. 1:15–23   Ps. 98   John 6:35–40, 47–51

Tuesday—*Christ dwelling in us*
Collect: 4. Of the Incarnation (200/252)
Col. 3:16–17   Ps. 132:8–15   John 17:20–26

Wednesday—*Living in faith and confidence*
Collect: Proper 2 (177/228)
Exod. 33:12–17   Ps. 25:3–9   Matt. 10:26–31

Thursday—*God's continuing revelation*
Collect: 2 Of the Holy Spirit (200/251)
Rom. 16:25–27   Ps. 112   John 16:12–15

Friday—*The power of the cross*
Collect: A Collect for Fridays (56/99)
Rom. 3:21–26   Ps. 15   Mark 14:22–25

Saturday—*Sabbath: a time for discernment*
Collect: Proper 10 (179/231)
1 Kings 19:8–13a   Ps. 65:9–14   Mark 1:35–39

Week Six

Monday—*The Christian calling: reflecting God's justice*
Collect: 21 For Social Justice (209/260)
Amos 5:21–24   Ps. 50:7–15   Luke 4:14–21

Tuesday—*A woman's offering*
Collect: Proper 17 (181/233)
1 Sam. 1:9–11   Ps. 33:12–22   Mark 12:38–44

Wednesday—*The Church as window to God's nature*
Collect: Proper 21 (182/234)
Exod. 34:6–7   Ps. 130   Luke 6:37–38

Thursday—*The gift of baptism*
Collect: Collect at the Easter Vigil, following Isa. 55:1–11 (290)
Gal. 3:27–29   Ps. 84:1–8   John 4:13–15

Friday—*Dying in order to be born*
Collect: A Collect for Fridays (56/99)
Gal. 2:19b–20   Ps. 126   John 12: 20–26

Saturday—*Sabbath rest*
Collect: A Collect for Saturdays (56/99)
Heb. 4:9–11   Ps. 29:1–10   Luke 23:50–56

Week of 4 Epiphany

Mon

1	Heb. 11:32–40	Ps. 31:19–24	Mark 5:1–20
2	2 Sam. 15:13–14, 30; 16:5–14	Ps. 3	Mark 5:1–20

Tue

1	Heb. 12:1–4	Ps. 22:22–30	Mark 5:21–43
2	2 Sam. 18:9–14, 24—19:3	Ps. 86:1–6	Mark 5:21–43

Wed

1	Heb. 12:4–7, 11–15	Ps. 103:1–2, 13–18	Mark 6:1–6
2	2 Sam. 24:2, 9–17	Ps. 32:1–8	Mark 6:1–6

Thu

1	Heb. 12:18–24	Ps. 48:1–3, 7–9	Mark 6:7–13
2	1 Kings 2:1–4, 10–12	Ps. 132:10–19	Mark 6:7–13

Fri

1	Heb. 13:1–8	Ps. 27:1–13	Mark 6:14–29
2	Ecclus. 47:2–11	Ps. 18:31–33, 46–50	Mark 6:14–29

Sat

1	Heb. 13:9–17, 20–21	Ps. 23	Mark 6:30–34
2	1 Kings 3:3–14	Ps. 119:9–16	Mark 6:30–34

Week of 5 Epiphany

Mon

1	Gen. 1:1–19	Ps. 104:1–12, 25	Mark 6:53–56
2	1 Kings 8:1–7, 9–13	Ps. 132:6–10	Mark 6:53–56

Tue

1	Gen. 1:20—2:4a	Ps. 8	Mark 7:1–13
2	1 Kings 8:22–23, 27–30	Ps. 84	Mark 7:1–13

Wed

1	Gen. 2:4b–9, 15–17	Ps. 104:25, 28–31	Mark 7:14–23
2	1 Kings 10:1–10	Ps. 37:1–7, 32–33, 41–42	Mark 7:14–23

Thu

1	Gen. 2:18–25	Ps. 128	Mark 7:24–30
2	1 Kings 11:4–13	Ps. 132:11–19	Mark 7:24–30

Fri

1	Gen. 3:1–8	Ps. 32:1–8	Mark 7:31–37
2	1 Kings 11:29–32; 12:19	Ps. 81:8–16	Mark 7:31–37

Sat

1	Gen. 3:9–24	Ps. 90:1–12	Mark 8:1–10
2	1 Kings 12:26–33; 13:33–34	Ps. 106:19–22	Mark 8:1–10

Week of 6 Epiphany (*or* Proper 1)

Mon

1	Gen. 4:1–15, 25	Ps. 50:7–24	Mark 8:11–13
2	James 1:1–11	Ps. 119:65–72	Mark 8:11–13

Tue

1	Gen. 6:5–8; 7:1–5, 10	Ps. 29	Mark 8:14–21
2	James 1:12–18	Ps. 94:12–19	Mark 8:14–21

Wed

1	Gen. 8:6–13, 20–22	Ps. 116:10–17	Mark 8:22–26
2	James 1:19–27	Ps. 15	Mark 8:22–26

Thu

1	Gen. 9:1–13	Ps. 102:15–22	Mark 8:27–33
2	James 2:1–9	Ps. 72:1–4, 13–14	Mark 8:27–33

Fri

1	Gen. 11:1–9	Ps. 33:6–18	Mark 8:34—9:1
2	James 2:14–26	Ps. 112	Mark 8:34—9:1

Sat
1 Heb. 11:1–7   Ps. 145:1–4, 10–13   Mark 9:2–13
2 James 3:1–10   Ps. 12:1–7   Mark 9:2–13

Week of 7 Epiphany (*or* Proper 2)

Mon
1 Ecclus. 1:1–10   Ps. 93   Mark 9:14–29
2 James 3:13–18   Ps. 19:7–14   Mark 9:14–29

Tue
1 Ecclus. 2:1–11   Ps. 112   Mark 9:30–37
2 James 4:1–10   Ps. 51:11–18   Mark 9:30–37

Wed
1 Ecclus. 4:11–19   Ps. 119:161–168   Mark 9:38–41
2 James 4:13–17   Ps. 49:1–9, 16–20   Mark 9:38–41

Thu
1 Ecclus. 5:1–8   Ps. 1   Mark 9:42–50
2 James 5:1–6   Ps. 49:12–19   Mark 9:42–50

Fri
1 Ecclus. 6:5–17   Ps. 119:17–24   Mark 10:1–12
2 James 5:9–12   Ps. 103:1–4, 8–13   Mark 10:1–12

Sat
1 Ecclus. 17:1–15   Ps. 103:1–4, 13–18   Mark 10:13–16
2 James 5:13–20   Ps. 34:1–8   Mark 10:13–16

Week of 8 Epiphany (*or* Proper 3)

Mon
1 Ecclus. 17:24–29   Ps. 32:1–8   Mark 10:17–27
2 1 Pet. 1:3–9   Ps. 111   Mark 10:17–27

Tue
1 Ecclus. 35:1–12   Ps. 50:7–15   Mark 10:28–31
2 1 Pet. 1:10–16   Ps. 98   Mark 10:28–31

Wed

1	Ecclus. 36:1–2, 5–6, 13–17	Ps. 79:8–13	Mark 10:32–45
2	1 Pet. 1:18—2:1	Ps. 147:13–21	Mark 10:32–45

Thu

1	Ecclus. 42:15–25	Ps. 33:1–9	Mark 10:46–52
2	1 Pet. 2:2–5, 9–12	Ps. 100	Mark 10:46–52

Fri

1	Ecclus. 44:1–13	Ps. 149:1–5	Mark 11:11–26
2	1 Pet. 4:7–13	Ps. 96:7–13	Mark 11:11–26

Sat

1	Ecclus. 51:11b–22	Ps. 19:7–14	Mark 11:27–33
2	Jude 1:17–25	Ps. 63 1–8	Mark 11:27–33

Week of Last Epiphany (*or* Proper 4)

Note: The lessons for Wednesday through Saturday of this week are used only for Proper 4. When observing the week of Last Epiphany, the Lenten propers are used beginning on Ash Wednesday.

Mon

1	Tobit 1:1–2; 2:1–8	Ps. 112:1–6	Mark 12:1–12
2	2 Pet. 1:2–7	Ps. 91	Mark 12:1–12

Tue

1	Tobit 2:9–14	Ps. 112:1–2, 7–9	Mark 12:13–17
2	2 Pet. 3:11–18	Ps. 90:1–6, 13–17	Mark 12:13–17

Wed

1	Tobit 3:1–11, 16–17	Ps. 25:1–8	Mark 12:18–27
2	2 Tim. 1:1–12	Ps. 123	Mark 12:18–27

Thu

1	Tobit 6:9–11; 7:1–15	Ps. 128	Mark 12:28–34
2	2 Tim. 2:8–15	Ps. 25:1–12	Mark 12:28–34

Fri

1	Tobit 11:5–15	Ps. 146	Mark 12:35–37
2	2 Tim. 3:10–17	Ps. 119:161–168	Mark 12:35–37

Sat

1	Tobit 12:1, 5–15, 20	Ps. 65:1–4	Mark 12:38–44
2	2 Tim. 4:1–8	Ps. 71:8–17	Mark 12:38–44

The Season after Pentecost

Week of Proper 5

Mon

1	2 Cor. 1:1–7	Ps. 34:1–8	Matt. 5:1–12
2	1 Kings 17:1–6	Ps. 121	Matt. 5:1–12

Tue

1	2 Cor. 1:18–22	Ps. 119:129–136	Matt. 5:13–16
2	1 Kings 17:7–16	Ps. 4	Matt. 5:13–16

Wed

1	2 Cor. 3:4–11	Ps. 99	Matt. 5:17–19
2	1 Kings 18:20–39	Ps. 16:1, 6–11	Matt. 5:17–19

Thu

1	2 Cor. 3:12—4:6	Ps. 85:7–13	Matt. 5:20–26
2	1 Kings 18:41–46	Ps. 65:1, 8–14	Matt. 5:20–26

Fri

1	2 Cor. 4:7–15	Ps. 116:9–17	Matt. 5:27–32
2	1 Kings 19:9–16	Ps. 27:10–18	Matt. 5:27–32

Sat

1	2 Cor. 5:14–21	Ps. 103:1–12	Matt. 5:33–37
2	1 Kings 19:19–21	Ps. 16:1–7	Matt. 5:33–37

Week of Proper 6

Mon

1	2 Cor. 6:1–10	Ps. 98	Matt. 5:38–42
2	1 Kings 21:1–16	Ps. 5:1–6	Matt. 5:38–42

Tue

1	2 Cor. 8:1–9	Ps. 146	Matt. 5:43–48
2	1 Kings 21:17–29	Ps. 51:1–11	Matt. 5:43–48

Wed

1	2 Cor. 9:6–11	Ps. 112:1–9	Matt. 6:1–6, 16–18
2	2 Kings 2:1, 6–14	Ps. 31:19–24	Matt. 6:1–6, 16–18

Thu

1	2 Cor. 11:1–11	Ps. 111	Matt. 6:7–15
2	Ecclus. 48:1–14	Ps. 97	Matt. 6:7–15

Fri

1	2 Cor. 11:18, 21b–30	Ps. 34:1–6	Matt. 6:19–23
2	2 Kings 11:1–4, 9–20	Ps. 132:11–19	Matt. 6:19–23

Sat

1	2 Cor. 12:1–10	Ps. 34:7–14	Matt. 6:24–34
2	2 Chron. 24:17–25	Ps. 89:19–33	Matt. 6:24–34

Week of Proper 7

Mon

1	Gen. 12:1–9	Ps. 33:12–22	Matt. 7:1–5
2	2 Kings 17:5–8, 13–18	Ps. 60	Matt. 7:1–5

Tue

1	Gen. 13:2, 5–18	Ps. 15	Matt. 7:6, 12–14
2	2 Kings 19:9–21, 31–36	Ps. 48	Matt. 7:6, 12–14

Wed

1	Gen. 15:1–12, 17–18	Ps. 47	Matt. 7:15–20
2	2 Kings 22:8–13; 23:1–3	Ps. 119:33–40	Matt. 7:15–20

Thu

1	Gen. 16:1–12, 15–16	Ps. 106:1–5	Matt. 7:21–29
2	2 Kings 24:8–17	Ps. 79	Matt. 7:21–29

Fri

1	Gen. 17:1, 9–10, 15–22	Ps. 128	Matt. 8:1–4
2	2 Kings 25:1–12	Ps. 137:1–6	Matt. 8:1–4

Sat

1	Gen. 18:1–15	C15 or Ps. 123	Matt. 8:5–17
2	Lam. 2:2, 10–14, 18–19	Ps. 74:1–8, 17–20	Matt. 8:5–17

Week of Proper 8

Mon

1	Gen. 18:16–33	Ps. 103:1–10	Matt. 8:18–22
2	Amos 2:6–10, 13–16	Ps. 50:14–24	Matt. 8:18–22

Tue

1	Gen. 19:15–29	Ps. 26	Matt. 8:23–27
2	Amos 3:1–8; 4:11–12	Ps. 5	Matt. 8:23–27

Wed

1	Gen. 21:5, 8–20	Ps. 34:1–8	Matt. 8:28–34
2	Amos 5:14–15, 21–24	Ps. 50:7–15	Matt. 8:28–34

Thu

1	Gen. 22:1–14	Ps. 116:1–8	Matt. 9:1–8
2	Amos 7:10–17	Ps. 19:7–10	Matt. 9:1–8

Fri

1	Gen. 23:1–4, 19; 24:1–8, 62–67	Ps. 78:1–8	Matt. 9:9–13
2	Amos 8:4–6, 9–12	Ps. 119:1–8	Matt. 9:9–13

Sat
1	Gen. 27:1–9, 15–29	Ps. 135:1–6	Matt. 9:14–17
2	Amos 9:11–15	Ps. 85:7–13	Matt. 9:14–17

Week of Proper 9

Mon
1	Gen. 28:10–22	Ps. 91:1–6, 14–16	Matt. 9:18–26
2	Hosea 2:16–23	Ps. 138	Matt. 9:18–26

Tue
1	Gen. 32:22–32	Ps. 17:1–8	Matt. 9:32–38
2	Hosea 8:4–7, 11–13	Ps. 115:1–10	Matt. 9:32–38

Wed
1	Gen. 41:55–57; 42:5–7a, 17–24a	Ps. 33:1–4, 18–22	Matt. 10:1–7
2	Hosea 10:1–3, 7–8, 12	Ps. 105:1–7	Matt. 10:1–7

Thu
1	Gen. 44:18—45:5	Ps. 105:7–21	Matt. 10:7–15
2	Hosea 11:1–9	Ps. 80:1–7	Matt. 10:7–15

Fri
1	Gen. 46:1–7, 28–30	Ps. 37:3–4, 19–20, 28–29, 41–42	Matt. 10:16–23
2	Hosea 14:1–9	Ps. 51:1–12	Matt. 10:16–23

Sat
1	Gen. 49:29–33	Ps. 105:1–7	Matt. 10:24–33
2	Isa. 6:1–8	Ps. 93	Matt. 10:24–33

Week of Proper 10

Mon
1	Exod. 1:8–14, 22	Ps. 124	Matt. 10:34—11:1
2	Isa. 1:10–17	Ps. 50:7–15	Matt. 10:34—11:1

Tue

1	Exod. 2:1–15	Ps. 69:1–2, 31–38	Matt. 11:20–24
2	Isa. 7:1–9	Ps. 48	Matt. 11:20–24

Wed

1	Exod. 3:1–12	Ps. 103:1–7	Matt. 11:25–27
2	Isa. 10:5–7, 13–16	Ps. 94:5–15	Matt. 11:25–27

Thu

1	Exod. 3:13–20	Ps. 105:1–15	Matt. 11:28–30
2	Isa. 26:7–9, 12, 16–19	Ps. 102:12–22	Matt. 11:28–30

Fri

1	Exod. 11:10—12:14	Ps. 116:10–17	Matt. 12:1–8
2	Isa. 38:1–6, 21	Ps. 6	Matt. 12:1–8

Sat

1	Exod. 12:37–42	Ps. 136:1–3, 10–15	Matt. 12:14–21
2	Micah 2:1–5	Ps. 10:1–9, 18–19	Matt. 12:14–21

Week of Proper 11

Mon

1	Exod. 14:5–18	C8 or Ps. 114	Matt. 12:38–42
2	Micah 6:1–8	Ps. 14	Matt. 12:38–42

Tue

1	Exod. 14:21—15:1	C8 or Ps. 114	Matt. 12:46–50
2	Micah 7:14–15, 18–20	Ps. 85:1–7	Matt. 12:46–50

Wed

1	Exod. 16:1–5, 9–15	Ps. 78:18–29	Matt. 13:1–9
2	Jer. 1:1, 4–10	Ps. 71:1–6, 15–17	Matt. 13:1–9

Thu

1	Exod. 19:1–20	C13 or Ps. 24:1–6	Matt. 13:10–17
2	Jer. 2:1–3, 7–13	Ps. 36:5–10	Matt. 13:10–17

Fri

1	Exod. 20:1–17	Ps. 19:7–10	Matt. 13:18–23
2	Jer. 3:14–18	Ps. 121	Matt. 13:18–23

Sat

1	Exod. 24:3–8	Ps. 51:11–16	Matt. 13:24–30
2	Jer. 7:1–11	Ps. 84	Matt. 13:24–30

Week of Proper 12

Mon

1	Exod. 32:15–24, 30–34	Ps. 106:19–23	Matt. 13:31–35
2	Jer. 13:1–11	Ps. 95	Matt. 13:31–35

Tue

1	Exod. 33:7–11; 34:5–10, 27–28	Ps. 103:5–13	Matt. 13:36–43
2	Jer. 14:17–22	Ps. 79:9–13	Matt. 13:36–43

Wed

1	Exod. 34:29–35	Ps. 99	Matt. 13:44–46
2	Jer. 15:10, 15–21	Ps. 59:1–4, 18–20	Matt. 13:44–46

Thu

1	Exod. 40:16–21, 34–38	Ps. 84	Matt. 13:47–53
2	Jer. 18:1–6	Ps. 146:1–5	Matt. 13:47–53

Fri

1	Lev. 23:1–11, 26–38	Ps. 81:1–10	Matt. 13:54–58
2	Jer. 26:1–9	Ps. 70	Matt. 13:54–58

Sat

1	Lev. 25:1, 8–17	Ps. 67	Matt. 14:1–12
2	Jer. 26:11–16, 24	Ps. 140:1–5	Matt. 14:1–12

Week of Proper 13

Mon

1	Num. 11:4–15	Ps. 105:37–45	Matt. 14:22–36
2	Jer. 28:1–17	Ps. 119:89–96	Matt. 14:13–21

Tue

1 Num. 12:1–16   Ps. 51:1–12   Matt. 15:1–2,
                                              10–14
2 Jer. 30:1–2, 12–22   Ps. 102:16–22   Matt. 14:22–36

Wed

1 Num. 13:1–2, 25—14:1, Ps. 106:6–14, 21–23 Matt. 15:21–28
     26–35
2 Jer. 31:1–7   Ps. 121   Matt. 15:21–28

Thu

1 Num. 20:1–13   Ps. 95:1–9   Matt. 16:13–23
2 Jer. 31:31–34   Ps. 51:11–18   Matt. 16:13–23

Fri

1 Deut. 4:32–40   Ps. 105:1–6   Matt. 16:24–28
2 Nahum 1:15; 2:2;   Ps. 124   Matt. 16:24–28
     3:1–3, 6–7

Sat

1 Deut. 6:4–13   Ps. 18:1–2, 48–50   Matt. 17:14–20
2 Hab. 1:12—2:4   Ps. 9:7–12   Matt. 17:14–20

Week of Proper 14

Mon

1 Deut. 10:12–22   Ps. 148   Matt. 17:22–27
2 Ezek. 1:1–5, 24–28   Ps. 148:1–4, 13–14   Matt. 17:22–27

Tue

1 Deut. 31:1–8   Ps. 111   Matt. 18:1–5,
                                              10, 12–14
2 Ezek. 2:8—3:4   Ps. 119:65–72   Matt. 18:1–5,
                                              10, 12–14

Wed

1 Deut. 34:1–12   Ps. 66:1–8   Matt. 18:15–20
2 Ezek. 9:1–7; 10:18–22 Ps. 113   Matt. 18:15–20

Thu

1	Joshua 3:7–17	Ps. 114	Matt. 18:21—19:1
2	Ezek. 12:1–16	Ps. 39:11–15	Matt. 18:21—19:1

Fri

1	Joshua 24:1–13	Ps. 136:1–3, 16–22	Matt. 19:3–12
2	Ezek. 16:1–15, 59–63	C10 or Ps. 11	Matt. 19:3–12

Sat

1	Joshua 24:14–29	Ps. 16:1, 5–11	Matt. 19:13–15
2	Ezek. 18:1–13, 30–32	Ps. 51:11–18	Matt. 19:13–15

Week of Proper 15

Mon

1	Judges 2:11–19	Ps. 51:1–10	Matt. 19:16–22
2	Ezek. 24:15–24	Ps. 79:1–8	Matt. 19:16–22

Tue

1	Judges 5:11–24a	Ps. 85:8–13	Matt. 19:23–30
2	Ezek. 28:1–10	Ps. 60:1–5	Matt. 19:23–30

Wed

1	Judges 9:6–15	Ps. 21:1–6	Matt. 20:1–16a
2	Ezek. 34: 1–11	Ps. 23	Matt. 20:1–16a

Thu

1	Judges 13:1–7	Ps. 139:10–17	Matt. 22:1–14
2	Ezek. 36:22–28	Ps. 51:8–13	Matt. 22:1–14

Fri

1	Ruth 1:1–22	Ps. 146	Matt. 22:34–40
2	Ezek. 37:1–14	Ps. 107:1–8	Matt. 22:34–40

Sat

1	Ruth 2:1–11; 4:13–17	Ps. 128	Matt. 23:1–12
2	Ezek. 43:1–7	Ps. 85:8–13	Matt. 23:1–12

Week of Proper 16

Mon
1	1 Thess. 1:1–10	Ps. 149:1–5	Matt. 23:13–22
2	2 Thess. 1:1–5, 11–12	Ps. 96:1–5	Matt. 23:13–22

Tue
1	1 Thess. 2:1–8	Ps. 139:1–9	Matt. 23:23–26
2	2 Thess. 2:1–17	Ps. 96:7–13	Matt. 23:23–26

Wed
1	1 Thess. 2:9–13	Ps. 126	Matt. 23:27–32
2	2 Thess. 3:6–10, 16–18	Ps. 128	Matt. 23:27–32

Thu
1	1 Thess. 3:6–13	Ps. 90:13–17	Matt. 24:42–51
2	1 Cor. 1:1–9	Ps. 145:1–7	Matt. 24:42–51

Fri
1	1 Thess. 4:1–8	Ps. 97	Matt. 25:1–13
2	1 Cor. 1:17–25	Ps. 33:1–11	Matt. 25:1–13

Sat
1	1 Thess. 4:9–12	Ps. 98	Matt. 25:14–30
2	1 Cor. 1:26–31	Ps. 33:12–22	Matt. 25:14–30

Week of Proper 17

Mon
1	1 Thess. 4:13–18	Ps. 96	Luke 4:16–30
2	1 Cor. 2:1–5	Ps. 119:97–103	Luke 4:16–30

Tue
1	1 Thess. 5:1–11	Ps. 27:1–6, 17–18	Luke 4:31–37
2	1 Cor. 2:10–16	Ps. 145:8–15	Luke 4:31–37

Wed
1	Col. 1:1–8	Ps. 34:9–22	Luke 4:38–44
2	1 Cor. 3:1–9	Ps. 62	Luke 4:38–44

Thu

1	Col. 1:9–14	Ps. 98	Luke 5:1–11
2	1 Cor. 3:18–23	Ps. 24:1–6	Luke 5:1–11

Fri

1	Col. 1:15–20	Ps. 100	Luke 5:33–39
2	1 Cor. 4:1–5	Ps. 37:1–12	Luke 5:33–39

Sat

1	Col. 1:21–23	Ps. 54	Luke 6:1–5
2	1 Cor. 4:6–15	Ps. 145:14–22	Luke 6:1–5

Week of Proper 18

Mon

1	Col. 1:24—2:3	Ps. 62:1–7	Luke 6:6–11
2	1 Cor. 5:1–8	Ps. 5	Luke 6:6–11

Tue

1	Col. 2:6–15	Ps. 145:1–9	Luke 6:12–19
2	1 Cor. 6:1–11	Ps. 149:1–5	Luke 6:12–19

Wed

1	Col. 3:1–11	Ps. 145:10–13	Luke 6:20–26
2	1 Cor. 7:25–31	Ps. 47	Luke 6:20–26

Thu

1	Col. 3:12–17	Ps. 150	Luke 6:27–38
2	1 Cor. 8:1–13	Ps. 139:1–9, 22–23	Luke 6:27–38

Fri

1	1 Tim. 1:1–2, 12–14	Ps. 16	Luke 6:39–42
2	1 Cor. 9:16–27	Ps. 84	Luke 6:39–42

Sat

1	1 Tim. 1:15–17	Ps. 113	Luke 6:43–49
2	1 Cor. 10:14–22	Ps. 116:10–17	Luke 6:43–49

Week of Proper 19

Mon
1 1 Tim. 2:1–8   Ps. 28   Luke 7:1–10
2 1 Cor. 11:17–28, 33   Ps. 40:8–12   Luke 7:1–10

Tue
1 1 Tim. 3:1–13   Ps. 101   Luke 7:11–17
2 1 Cor. 12:12–14, 27–31   Ps. 100   Luke 7:11–17

Wed
1 1 Tim. 3:14–16   Ps. 111:1–6   Luke 7:31–35
2 1 Cor. 12:31—13:13   Ps. 33:1–12, 22   Luke 7:31–35

Thu
1 1 Tim. 4:12–16   Ps. 111:7–10   Luke 7:36–50
2 1 Cor. 15:1–11   Ps. 118:14–29   Luke 7:36–50

Fri
1 1 Tim. 6:1–12   Ps. 49:1–9   Luke 8:1–3
2 1 Cor. 15:12–20   Ps. 17:1–7   Luke 8:1–3

Sat
1 1 Tim. 6:13–16   Ps. 100   Luke 8:4–15
2 1 Cor. 15:35–49   Ps. 30:1–5   Luke 8:4–15

Week of Proper 20

Mon
1 Ezra 1:1–6   Ps. 126   Luke 8:16–18
2 Prov. 3:27–35   Ps. 15   Luke 8:16–18

Tue
1 Ezra 6:1–8, 12–19   Ps. 124   Luke 8:19–21
2 Prov. 21:1–6, 10–13   Ps. 119:1–8   Luke 8:19–21

Wed
1 Ezra 9:5–9   C11 or Ps. 48   Luke 9:1–6
2 Prov. 30:5–9   Ps. 24:1–6   Luke 9:1–6

Thu

1 Haggai 1:1–8	Ps. 149:1–5	Luke 9:7–9
2 Eccles. 1:1–11	Ps. 90:1–6	Luke 9:7–9

Fri

1 Haggai 1:15b—2:9	Ps. 43	Luke 9:18–22
2 Eccles. 3:1–11	Ps. 144:1–4	Luke 9:18–22

Sat

1 Zech. 2:1–11	Ps. 121	Luke 9:43b–45
2 Eccles. 11:9—12:8	Ps. 90:1–2, 12–17	Luke 9:43b–45

Week of Proper 21

Mon

1 Zech. 8:1–8	Ps. 102:11–22	Luke 9:46–50
2 Job 1:6–22	Ps. 17:1–7	Luke 9:46–50

Tue

1 Zech. 8:20–23	Ps. 87	Luke 9:51–56
2 Job 3:1–3, 11–23	Ps. 88:1–8	Luke 9:51–56

Wed

1 Neh. 2:1–8	Ps. 137:1–6	Luke 9:57–62
2 Job 9:1–16	Ps. 88:10–15	Luke 9:57–62

Thu

1 Neh. 8:1–12	Ps. 119:1–8	Luke 10:1–12
2 Job 19:21–27	Ps. 27:10–18	Luke 10:1–12

Fri

1 Baruch 1:15–21	Ps. 79:1–9	Luke 10:13–16
2 Job 38:1, 12–21; 40:1–5	Ps. 139:1–17	Luke 10:13–16

Sat

1 Baruch 4:5–12, 27–29	Ps. 69:34–38	Luke 10:17–24
2 Job 42:1–6, 12–17	Ps. 119:169–176	Luke 10:17–24

Week of Proper 22

Mon
1 Jonah 1:1-17; 2:10 | Ps. 130 | Luke 10:25-37
2 Gal. 1:6-12 | Ps. 111:1-6 | Luke 10:25-37

Tue
1 Jonah 3:1-10 | Ps. 6 | Luke 10:38-42
2 Gal. 1:13-24 | Ps. 139:1-14 | Luke 10:38-42

Wed
1 Jonah 4:1-11 | Ps. 86:1-10 | Luke 11:1-4
2 Gal. 2:1-2, 7-14 | Ps. 117 | Luke 11:1-4

Thu
1 Mal. 3:13—4:2a | Ps. 1 | Luke 11:5-13
2 Gal. 3:1-5 | C16 or Ps. 89:19-29 | Luke 11:5-13

Fri
1 Joel 1:13-15; 2:1-2 | Ps. 9:1-8 | Luke 11:14-26
2 Gal. 3:7-14 | Ps. 111:4-10 | Luke 11:14-26

Sat
1 Joel 3:12-21 | Ps. 97 | Luke 11:27-28
2 Gal. 3:21-29 | Ps. 105:1-7 | Luke 11:27-28

Week of Proper 23

Mon
1 Rom. 1:1-7 | Ps. 98 | Luke 11:29-32
2 Gal. 4:21—5:1 | Ps. 138 | Luke 11:29-32

Tue
1 Rom. 1:16-25 | Ps. 19:1-4 | Luke 11:37-41
2 Gal. 5:1-6 | Ps. 119:41-48 | Luke 11:37-41

Wed
1 Rom. 2:1-11 | Ps. 62:1-9 | Luke 11:42-46
2 Gal. 6:1-10 | Ps. 32 | Luke 11:42-46

Thu
| 1 Rom. 3:21–31 | Ps. 130 | Luke 11:47–54 |
| 2 Eph. 1:1–10 | Ps. 98 | Luke 11:47–54 |

Fri
| 1 Rom. 4:1–8 | Ps. 32 | Luke 12:1–7 |
| 2 Eph. 1:11–14 | Ps. 33:1–12 | Luke 12:1–7 |

Sat
| 1 Rom. 4:13–18 | Ps. 105:5–10, 42–45 | Luke 12:8–12 |
| 2 Eph. 1:15–23 | Ps. 8 | Luke 12:8–12 |

Week of Proper 24

Mon
| 1 Rom. 4:13, 19–25 | C16 or Ps. 89:19–29 | Luke 12:13–21 |
| 2 Eph. 2:1–10 | Ps. 100 | Luke 12:13–21 |

Tue
| 1 Rom. 5:6–21 | Ps. 40:8–11 | Luke 12:35–38 |
| 2 Eph. 2:11–22 | Ps. 85:8–13 | Luke 12:35–38 |

Wed
| 1 Rom. 6:12–18 | Ps. 124 | Luke 12:39–48 |
| 2 Eph. 3:4–12 | C9 or Ps. 113 or Ps. 122 | Luke 12:39–48 |

Thu
| 1 Rom. 6:19–23 | Ps. 1 | Luke 12:49–53 |
| 2 Eph. 3:14–21 | Ps. 33:1–11 | Luke 12:49–53 |

Fri
| 1 Rom. 7:18–25a | Ps. 19:7–14 | Luke 12:54–59 |
| 2 Eph. 4:1–6 | Ps. 24:1–6 | Luke 12:54–59 |

Sat
| 1 Rom. 8:1–11 | Ps. 24:1–6 | Luke 13:1–9 |
| 2 Eph. 4:7–16 | Ps. 122 | Luke 13:1–9 |

Week of Proper 25

Mon

1 Rom. 8:12–17	Ps. 68:1–6, 19–20	Luke 13:10–17
2 Eph. 5:1–8	Ps. 37:27–33	Luke 13:10–17

Tue

1 Rom. 8:18–25	Ps. 126	Luke 13:18–21
2 Eph. 5:21–33	Ps. 128	Luke 13:18–21

Wed

1 Rom. 8:26–30	Ps. 91:9–16	Luke 13:22–30
2 Eph. 6:1–9	Ps. 145:10–19	Luke 13:22–30

Thu

1 Rom. 8:31–39	Ps. 30	Luke 13:31–35
2 Eph. 6:10–20	Ps. 144:1–10	Luke 13:31–35

Fri

1 Rom. 9:1–5	Ps. 147:13–21	Luke 14:1–6
2 Phil. 1:1–11	Ps. 111	Luke 14:1–6

Sat

1 Rom. 11:1–6, 11–12, 25–29	Ps. 94:14–19	Luke 14:1, 7–11
2 Phil. 1:12–26	Ps. 42:1–7	Luke 14:1, 7–11

Week of Proper 26

Mon

1 Rom. 11:29–36	Ps. 16:5–11	Luke 14:12–14
2 Phil. 2:1–4	Ps. 131	Luke 14:12–14

Tue

1 Rom. 12:1–16	Ps. 131	Luke 14:15–24
2 Phil. 2:5–11	Ps. 22:22–28	Luke 14:15–24

Wed

1 Rom. 13:8–10	Ps. 112	Luke 14:25–33
2 Phil. 2:12–18	Ps. 62:6–14	Luke 14:25–33

Thu

1 Rom. 14:7–12	Ps. 27:1–6, 17–18	Luke 15:1–10
2 Phil. 3:3–8a	Ps. 105:1–7	Luke 15:1–10

Fri

1 Rom. 15:14–21	Ps. 98	Luke 16:1–8
2 Phil. 3:17—4:1	Ps. 122	Luke 16:1–8

Sat

1 Rom. 16:3–9, 16, 22–27	Ps. 145:1–7	Luke 16:9–15
2 Phil. 4:10–19	Ps. 112	Luke 16:9–15

Week of Proper 27

Mon

1 Wisdom 1:1–7	Ps. 139:1–9	Luke 17:1–6
2 Titus 1:1–9	Ps. 24:1–6	Luke 17:1–6

Tue

1 Wisdom 2:23—3:9	Ps. 34:15–22	Luke 17:7–10
2 Titus 2:1–14	Ps. 37:1–6, 28–29	Luke 17:7–10

Wed

1 Wisdom 6:1–11	Ps. 2	Luke 17:11–19
2 Titus 3:1–7	Ps. 91:9–16	Luke 17:11–19

Thu

1 Wisdom 7:21—8:1	Ps. 119:89–96	Luke 17:20–25
2 Philemon 1:4–20	Ps. 146	Luke 17:20–25

Fri

1 Wisdom 13:1–9	Ps. 19:1–4	Luke 17:26–37
2 2 John 4–9	Ps. 119:1–8	Luke 17:26–37

Sat

1 Wisdom 18:14–16; 19:6–9	Ps. 105:1–6, 37–45	Luke 18:1–8
2 3 John 5–8	Ps. 112	Luke 18:1–8

Week of Proper 28

Mon

1	1 Macc. 1:1–15, 54–57, 62–64	Ps. 79	Luke 18:35–43
2	Rev. 1:1–4; 2:1–5	Ps. 1	Luke 18:35–43

Tue

1	2 Macc. 6:18–31	Ps. 3	Luke 19:1–10
2	Rev. 3:1–6, 14–22	Ps. 15	Luke 19:1–10

Wed

1	2 Macc. 7:1, 20–31, 39–42	Ps. 17:1–8	Luke 19:11–28
2	Rev. 4:1–11	Ps. 150	Luke 19:11–28

Thu

1	1 Macc. 2:15–29	Ps. 129	Luke 19:41–44
2	Rev. 5:1–10	Ps. 149:1–5	Luke 19:41–44

Fri

1	1 Macc. 4:36–37, 52–59	C9 or Ps. 113 or Ps. 122	Luke 19:45–48
2	Rev. 10:8–11	Ps. 119:65–72	Luke 19:45–48

Sat

1	1 Macc. 6:1–13	Ps. 124	Luke 20:27–40
2	Rev. 11:1–12	Ps. 144:1–10	Luke 20:27–40

Week of the Last Sunday after Pentecost—Proper 29

Mon

1	Dan. 1:1–20	C13 or Ps. 24:1–6	Luke 21:1–4
2	Rev. 14:1–5	Ps. 24:1–6	Luke 21:1–4

Tue

1	Dan. 2:31–45	C12 part I or Ps. 96	Luke 21:5–9
2	Rev. 14:14–20	Ps. 96	Luke 21:5–9

Wed

1	Dan. 5:1–6, 13–28	C12 part I *or* Ps. 98	Luke 21:10–19
2	Rev. 15:1–4	Ps. 98	Luke 21:10–19

Thu

1	Dan. 6:6–27	C12 part I *or* Ps. 99	Luke 21:20–28
2	Rev. 18:1–2, 21—19:3,9	Ps. 100	Luke 21:20–28

Fri

1	Dan. 7:1–14	C12 part II *or* Ps. 97	Luke 21:29–33
2	Rev. 20:1–4, 11—21:4	Ps. 84	Luke 21:29–33

Sat

1	Dan. 7:15–27	C12 part III *or* Ps. 95:1–7	Luke 21:34–36
2	Rev. 22:1–7	Ps. 95:1–7	Luke 21:34–36

Index